RIVERS OF THE SOUTHWEST:
A BOATERS GUIDE TO THE RIVERS OF COLORADO, NEW MEXICO, UTAH AND ARIZONA.

PRUETT **P** PUBLISHING COMPANY
Boulder, Colorado

FLETCHER ANDERSON
AND ANN HOPKINSON

Second Edition
1   2   3   4   5   6   7   8   9

Printed in the United States of America

Library of Congress Cataloging-in-Publication Data

Anderson, Fletcher, 1948-
    Rivers of the Southwest.

    1. Rafting (Sports)—Southwestern States—Guide-books.
2. White-water canoeing—Southwestern States—Guide-
books. 3. Southwestern States—Description and travel—
Guide-books. I. Hopkinson, Ann, 1951-   . II. Title.
GV776.S66A53   1987   917.8   87-2364
ISBN 0-87108-730-8 (pbk.)

ACKNOWLEDGEMENTS

The authors wish to thank the following for information incorporated in this guide: Roger Paris, Walter Kirschbaum, Eric Leeper, Will Perry, Judy Fox, Otis "Doc" Marston, Keith Anderson, Earl Perry, John Wesley Powell, Ben Harding, W. A. Clark, Walt Blackadar, Dave Orlicky, Ron Mason, Grace Anderson, Alexander "Zee" Grant, Bob Waind, Dave Morrissey, Tyson Dines, Doug Wheat, Tom Ruwitch, Filip Sokol, Nat Cooper, Tom and Cathy Stietz, Erik Seidel, Dick Ryman, Bob Feroldi, Bruce Cranmer, Tom and Jane Cooper, Jerry Nyre, Kwagunt Perry, Dugald Bremner, Bob Cornelius, Doug Hahn, Bert Loper, Charlie Moore, Timberline Sports in Salt Lake City, Bino Lowenstein, the Bureau of Land Management, the U.S. Forest Service, the National Park Service, FIBARK Inc., the Rocky Mountain Canoe Association, the Colorado Whitewater Association, and the National Organization for River Sports, and others who will recognize their own contributions where we have failed to credit them.

Deseret Class 5 Water (*Fletcher Anderson*)

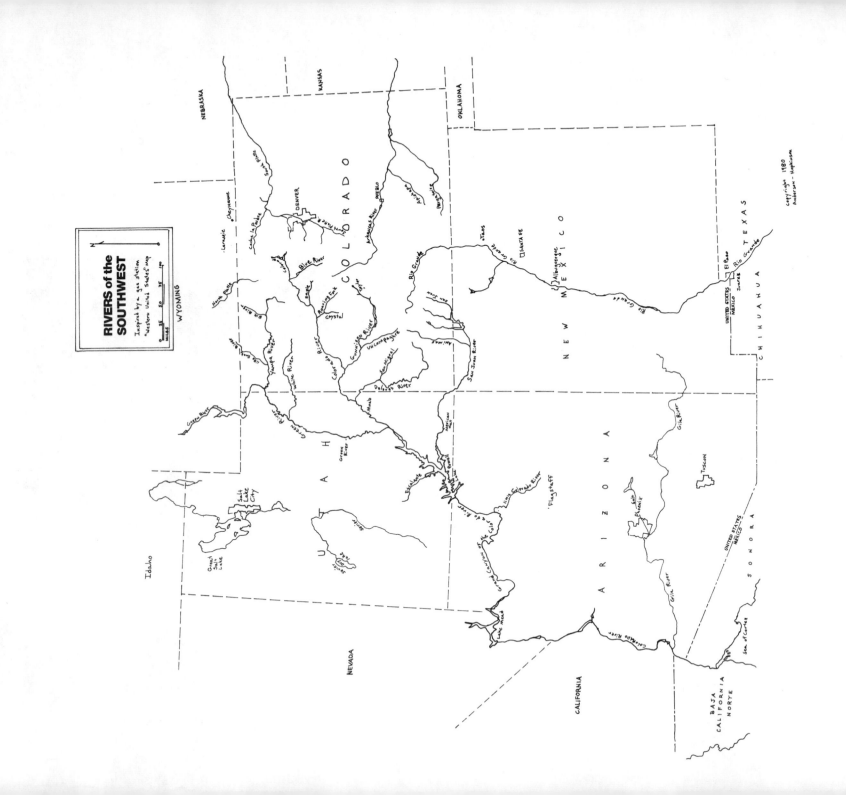

RIVERS of the
SOUTHWEST

Inspired by a gas station
"Western United States" map

0   25   50   75   100
MILES

Preface to the Second Edition

When we sat down with a couple of ballpoint pens and some tattered spiral notebooks a few years back to compile this book, we assumed that there were probably five hundred river runners who might want the information, and we considered publishing this book as a pamphlet for N.O.R.S. It turns out that there are many thousands of you—enough of you (of all of us) so that our combined voices can save most of the region's remaining rivers. We urge you to speak up! One of the easiest ways to do that is by joining the National Organization for River Sports, whose address appears at the back of this book. Their fulltime professional staff has made a substantial difference on many river-related issues in this part of the world. We extend to them our personal thanks.

We assumed when we first wrote this book that in a few years much of it would be rendered out of date by a host of pending dams and water projects. Ronald Reagan, a former actor, had just taken over leadership of the United States government and appointed James Watt to reverse the Interior Department's policy of protecting natural resources. Like some other Reagan appointees, Watt was finally deposed—only to be replaced by another anti-environmental zealot with a lower public profile. Yet, for the most part, the dams have not been built. McPhee dam on the Dolores was already under construction and is now substantially complete. A minor dam now slows the White River near Rangely, Colorado, where a major one was proposed. The various elaborations of the Central Arizona Project are moving slowly. Reagan's extremism has temporarily defeated all the other dams the environmentalists feared by creating an economic climate in which such projects are no longer feasible . . . at least for the next few years.

We hoped when we wrote this book that the courts would force the National Park Service to allow self-guided river runners the same opportunity to visit National Parks which commercial customers enjoy. Reagan's policy has been to turn the management of the parks over to the concessionaires, and your legal right to equal access to National Parks has all but disappeared. In the winter of 1985–86 a federal judge in Denver created a new law, overturning the act which Congress wrote granting the public "free access" to the parks. The Park Service can manage rivers any damn way they want, and what they want is paid concessioner access, not free access in any form. The multimillion-dollar river tour industry has been allowed to virtually homestead the National Parks. Their ownership of the rivers is as secure as a rancher's grazing rights. For people like us hoping to visit these National Park rivers, the short-term outlook is grim. You must wait 15 years for a Grand Canyon river trip permit now. For us, these rivers might as well have been dammed. They no longer exist. James Watt's giveaway of the rivers to the outfitters may be one of the most lasting results of his brief tenure. It will take a major political battle to ever free the rivers. In the meantime, the raft trip industry is in a slump and can't use all the space available to them. Park Service river managers are trying to support the tour industry by requiring more river runners to use outfitter services they neither need nor desire. There are political battles to be fought over western rivers, and our side needs more warriors.

CONTENTS

Cautionary Note

We believe the information in this book is accurate and we hope you find it useful, but river guidebooks have their limits. We can tell you where the rivers are and what to expect, but what you do with that information is strictly up to you. This guidebook can no more assure your safety than a highway road map can make you a safe driver. Without exception, the rivers in this book have better safety records than the adjacent highways, but people *are* getting into trouble on the river in needless ways. River dangers are real and neophyte river runners often don't understand them. Contrary to most people's expectations, most river accidents do not occur on popular difficult mountain river runs; they occur on very easy stretches of small rivers—frequently in or near cities—where people have gone to avoid the perceived dangers of mountain rapids.

Three types of accidents account for 99% of all the river drownings in the region: 1. People drown who have no lifejackets. Unless a river is very flat and small, you really ought to wear a lifejacket. 2. People wrap rafts around bridge pilings. Hitting a rock is usually no major disaster. A bridge piling or other man-made obstruction is a trap. Water rushes past the tall, thin piling without producing the cushion wave which deflects boats away from big, fat rocks. The force of the current wraps the raft around the piling and pins it, and passengers are caught between the raft and the pier or trapped inside the overturned raft. It is wise to regard any man-made object in a river as a severe hazard. 3. People are trapped in the backwash below low head dams. This accident kills more river runners every year in Colorado than all other accident types in the entire history of river running in that state combined! The problem is this: it looks easy to paddle over a five-foot-high or lower dam, and it is. But the water flowing over the dam plunges to the bottom of the river and wells up farther downstream. Then it flows back *upstream* on the surface

back to the dam. A swimmer or any floating object is trapped by the current at the base of the dam. If the dam is of uniform height all the way across the river, your only escape is to dive down and swim out along the bottom under the backwash. Don't be fooled by the numerous two-foot-high irrigation diversion dams which are found on easy runs all over the region. They are far more dangerous than major rapids.

Let us stress something: reading the information in this or any other guidebook does nothing to assure your safety. We cannot tell you how dangerous a rapid is for you to run. Rivers change with high and low water and with the passing of seasons. New rapids form and old ones erode away. We make mistakes. We can't know your river running skills. You are the final authority on questions of river safety. You are there on the bank and you can see the river at the last moment. Don't read the book at that point, don't blindly accept a better boater's opinion; look at the river itself and make your own judgement.

Introduction

The Southwest is generally said to extend from Las Vegas, New Mexico, to Las Vegas, Nevada, and from Durango, Mexico, to Durango, Colorado. For the purposes of whitewater boating, the area must be expanded to include the Rocky Mountains of Colorado, wherein nearly all the region's rivers originate.

Average precipitation in the region is less than 20 inches a year, except in a few of the highest mountain areas of Colorado, and rainfall in parts of Arizona is far less than 10 inches a year. Understandably, a region so acutely devoid of precipitation is also largely devoid of rivers—and in many parts, devoid of roads and human habitation as well.

Nevertheless, perhaps no other region on earth offers such an astounding variety of whitewater. Paddlers from all parts of Europe and North America make veritable pilgrimages to the Southwest, and for obvious reasons. No less than 52 peaks in the state of Colorado stand over 14,000 feet high. From the snowfields on their flanks are born uncounted crystal-clear streams of violent activity and unchecked continuous steep drops which rival the finest streams of the Alps. These in turn collect to form the beginnings of the region's exceptional major rivers in large intermountain valleys.

To the east, these rivers disgorge themselves abruptly onto the edge of the Great Plains, across which they ooze their way eastward through cottonwood groves and sandbars to join the Mississippi. South of the mountains, the rivers quickly join to become the Rio Grande, which cuts through its own deep canyon in northern New Mexico before moderating its descent and gliding past centuries-old Indian pueblos and sunbelt retirement communities toward the Gulf of Mexico.

All rivers west of the divide are part of the Colorado River drainage.

After leaving the snow-covered mountains, they move across the threshold of the desert in deep, narrow canyons, which in time link up to form a canyon whose essence is beyond verbal description: The Grand Canyon of the Colorado River.

The Colorado River is perhaps the most overexploited of rivers in a nation which sets records for river exploitation. The river is so overdammed that its waters no longer flow to the sea. By international treaty, a specified token minimum flow of water must be delivered to the Mexican border. This water arrives in heavily salinated form through a pipe.

Nevertheless, numerous economically and environmentally dubious projects are in store for the river basin in the future. The last gasp of life of the Colorado River is thus the Grand Canyon itself. The Grand Canyon is so overwhelming that after running it, one sometimes forgets that other rivers exist.

About This Book

This is a guidebook for whitewater kayakers, rafters, and canoeists. It seeks to be a source to which people who are actually interested in running these rivers can turn for accurate and reliable information. Because of the large number of rivers covered, it does not contain a mile-by-mile or rapid-by-rapid description of each river, nor does it contain a checklist of riverside attractions for bored raft passengers. It does contain the maps, water flow information, and general descriptions we feel are necessary to determine which rivers you wish to visit, and to boat them safely. Where more detailed guides exist, the reader is directed to them. Many rivers listed in this guide cannot be legally run without federal government permits, so permit application information is included.

THE WHITEWATER RATING SCALE

Whitewater is rated universally on a difficulty scale of I–VI with specified rating criteria. As used in this book, those criteria are as follows:

The International Whitewater Rating System

Class I: Still or moving water with few (if any) riffles or obstructions.

Class II: Small rapids with waves up to 3 feet high and obvious clear channels not requiring scouting.

Class III: Powerful rapids with waves up to 5 feet high. Some maneuvering required to avoid obstacles. (Generally speaking, Class III is the upper limit for commercial rafting, except in very large, wide-open rivers, and Class III is the upper limit for open canoes except in very rare circumstances.)

Class IV: Long, difficult rapids requiring intricate maneuvering in turbulent water. Scouting often necessary. Rescue difficult.

Class V: Extremely difficult, extremely violent rapids, requiring difficult and precise maneuvering to avoid numerous serious obstacles. Rescue difficult at best and impossible at worst. The Class V designation is reserved for those rapids which only a tiny minority of paddlers can run safely (or at all).

Class VI: The most extreme whitewater. This classification is generally synonymous with unrunnable. (In Europe, it is common practice to downgrade a rapid from Class VI to Class V if someone succeeds in running it.)

This system would be more useful if there were more general agreement on exactly how such admittedly subjective judgements should be made. Unfortunately, boaters from various regions of the world use the scale quite differently.

As a group, paddlers from the U.S. Eastern Seaboard are not particularly impressed by what most western paddlers think are difficult, intricate maneuvers. On the other hand, they sometimes seem to regard any wave capable of splashing their spraycovers as being at least 5 feet high. Further, those paddlers from the two regions who like to brag about themselves, do so in different ways. The eastern paddlers may say "The run was Class V, but I had no problem." Westerners, by contrast, will rate even the most difficult rapids as "really just a Class III," hoping to impress people with their self-confidence.

Many rivers in Wyoming, Utah, New Mexico, Kansas, and Missouri have been assigned official ranking by paddlers who often tend to overrate difficulty. Thus, a paddler fresh from, say, the "Class IV" rapids of Alpine Canyon of the Snake River, near Jackson, Wyoming, will encounter similar difficulty in the "Class II" waters of South Canyon Rapids of the Colorado near Glenwood Springs.

Paddlers from Europe and California will find that paddlers in Colorado and some other areas of the Southwest (including the authors of this book), use the rating scale about the same way they do, but never exactly. Inevitably, some rapids we rate Class III will turn out to be harder than some we rate Class IV. There is no final word on any rapid's rating. *High water levels can make all rivers in this guide as much as a full degree more difficult. Beware of high water.*

In order to confuse the issue further, two other whitewater scales are used in the area covered in this book.

The Fibark Scale

This scale is seen most often in the program of the Salida, Colorado, Fibark boat races—the oldest kayak slalom and wildwater races in the Western Hemisphere. It predates the arrival to Colorado of the International Scale. It is essentially the same as the I–VI International Scale but with a I–VII range. Thus, the increases in difficulty ratings of rapids theoretically occur somewhat sooner than on the I–VI scale. (Grab your pocket calculator!) In practice, however, the scales are interchangeable—perhaps because the Salida boaters occasionally contemplate running the odd Class VI rapid and need the additional Class VII designation for the stuff even they leave alone.

Class I water *(Ann Hopkinson)*   Class II water *(Fletcher Anderson)*

Class III water *(Fletcher Anderson)*   Class IV water *(Fletcher Anderson)*   Class V water *(Ann Hopkinson)*

The Deseret Scale (These rapids are rated X!)

The Deseret Empire is comprised of all of the state of Utah and the adjacent areas of Arizona, Idaho, and Wyoming. This region is somewhat distinguished from the rest of the United States by the political and religious views of its inhabitants. Many people in the Deseret Empire believe that American Indians descended from the lost tribes of Israel. Many expect that bad times are coming, so they store a year's supply of food in their basements. Many don't drink coffee, and huge families are frequent. Also, many believe the Flood of Noah occurred in about 1,000 B.C. The rates of alcoholism, drug abuse, and violent crime in these areas are whole orders of magnitude lower than the rest of the nation. All of this helps explain why they developed their own whitewater rating scale. The Deseret Scale rates rapids from 1 to 10. From a purely mathematical standpoint, there should be a direct correlation between a rapid's Deseret rating and the double of its International rating (i.e., Deseret Class 8 should be International Class IV). However, it is difficult to apply the criteria of the International method to wide-open, unobstructed rapids with 10-foot-high waves. Are they giant Class II, or are they unobstructed Class V? Remember, too, that the Deseret Scale is used mainly by commercial rafters with motor-powered rigs over 30 feet long. Such a rig could never make the maneuvers normally accepted as the criteria for Class IV. For river runners encountering the Deseret Scale, the best thing to do is assume that it is being applied to a wide-open rapid whose average wave height equals the number on the scale in feet. A Class 10 rapid in the Grand Canyon really does have 10-foot waves.

We cannot resist adding at this point that one's first view of a Class 10 rapid is frequently sufficient to cause one to believe in not only the Deseret Scale, but also in storage of food, angels bearing golden tablets, and certainly the Noah Flood!

BOAT RECOMMENDATIONS

This would seem to be a fairly straightforward sort of thing, but it isn't:

Kayaks

Kayaks can run any sort of whitewater, but not all kayakers can. When a run is recommended for kayaks, study the difficulty rating and description and determine if you can make the run or not. A novice kayaker should stay in water of Class II difficulty or less. Intermediates should limit themselves to Class III. Kayakers good enough to run Class V water safely do not need our advice on how to do it!

Many runs listed in this guide were paddled extensively in the 1950s in foldboats. However, very few people today paddle water over Class II in a foldboat. Before the coming of fiberglass, many excellent foldboats were built specifically for whitewater. Modern foldboats are for cruising lakes. Stick with rigid boats for whitewater, and use only genuine whitewater kayaks for anything over Class II.

Canoes

A decked whitewater canoe looks just like a kayak and can do anything a kayak does. A standard bathtub-shaped family cruiser open canoe with no extra floatation and funny little seats riveted to the gunnels belongs in Class I water or on a lake. In between lie a whole range of crafts paddled by boaters of widely differing abilities. "Expert" open canoeist might mean a Red Cross canoe safety

Deseret Class 10 water (*Bart Henderson*)

A foldboat (*Fletcher Anderson*)

instructor in an aluminum bathtub powered with skinny little hardware-store paddles; it might mean marathon racers whose bent paddles and rippling muscles propel their slender wooden shell fast enough to tow water-skiers; or it might mean a whitewater paddler kneeling in the center of a short canoe nearly filled with extra floatation. As far as whitewater goes, the latter is an expert and the former might be only intermediates. When our recommendations mention open canoes, we mean canoes specifically outfitted for whitewater with extra floatation and bracing for a kneeling paddler — and we assume some degree of whitewater expertise on the part of the paddler. Sitting paddlers in ordinary open canoes should only occasionally attempt Class II water. On the other hand, Rocky Mountain open canoe champions like Jerry Nyre and Bob Feroldi can and do run rivers more difficult than those we recommend. Open canoeists from the eastern U.S. often find western rapids are much longer than back home, and the waves are bigger. Swamping is far more likely.

Rafts

When we say rafts, we *always* mean multichambered specialized whitewater rafts either paddled or rowed by skilled boatmen with oar frames. We *never* mean discount store single chamber suicide rigs (even though Alan Cranmer has twice run the Grand Canyon in a 4-foot-long vinyl "Tiger II").

In general, no raft belongs on a mountain river rated Class IV or above. It can certainly be done, but in an accident a swimmer could easily be trapped under the raft or caught between the raft and a rock. On a wide open desert river, rafts can attempt anything — though they don't always make it.

Legal Problems

Is it legal to boat in this region? We think "yes," but we could be wrong. Two of the groups that seem to be saying "no" are the Federal Government and the State of Colorado. The issues are summarized below:

Boaters vs. Colorado Landowners

With only a very few exceptions, relations between boaters and private landowners in the region have been friendly. It is clearly in everyone's best interest to keep things that way, and the obvious way to do so is by respecting the rights of the riverbank landowners and not abusing their property. Unfortunately, some river users (mostly fishermen and tubers perhaps — but in at least a few cases, rafters and kayakers) have behaved rather badly in this respect. Litter is almost entirely absent from many of the wilderness canyons of the Southwest, but parts of many rivers near roads are veritable dumps. Huge fire rings of blackened stone, full of half-burned garbage, can be found on many popular runs. Fences have been cut to facilitate the passage of large rafts, and school buses used to carry raft customers have been parked on private land, without permission, in ways that block access roads. Understandably, some landowners have become upset.

One such individual was a rancher named Con Ritschard of Kremmling, Colorado. On July 3, 1976, a tuber named David Emmert and four others attempted to tube and fish the Colorado River through Ritschard's land. Ritschard leases fishing rights on his land. Emmert had previously rented a cabin from Ritschard and fished on Ritschard's ranch; later, however, the two had had several arguments and Emmert had been warned to stay off the ranch. After yet another argument, Ritschard called the sheriff and had the Emmert party arrested for trespassing.

Ritschard maintained that he owned the land and thus the right to pass over it, except in airplanes. Since he owned the riverbank and the land over which the river flows, he also owned the right to run the river or to fish in it.

Emmert maintained that all moving water in Colorado is owned by the state until it is appropriated (in a ditch or pipe) for a specific use. Thus, as a member of the public he could use the river like any other public thoroughfare. Eventually, the State Supreme Court ruled in favor of rancher Ritschard.

The ruling does not apply to navigable waterways—but which waterways are legally navigable? Under the "Daniel Ball" rule, navigable rivers are only those so defined when a state enters the Union. Nobody declared *any* rivers in Colorado navigable under that rule. Another possible definition is that rivers used for interstate commerce are legally navigable. This would seem to include rivers used by commercial rafters and by kayak schools. Still another view is that rivers with a history of navigation are navigable. (All significant runs in the Southwest were made at least 20 years ago. Even most of the obscure Class IV and V runs were first done in the early 1960s.) Finally, there is the view which we as boaters like the best: any river in which publicly owned water flows which is de facto navigable is de jure navigable.

Fortunately, there have been only a very few isolated confrontations since the Emmert ruling. Partly, this may be due to the troubles landowners would have in getting convictions. The river must be fenced and posted. The fence might well require a Corps of Engineer's permit, since the *water* is public property and is tributary to certified navigable waterways. The fence could not be a concealed lethal device or boobytrap and, finally, the courts would have to reconsider the whole question of navigability.

This is our advice: Don't get involved in a riverside argument with a landowner. He is undoubtedly a friend of the local sheriff. He may have a gun, and he may have a very poor understanding of law. He will certainly tell all his neighbors about his troubles with boaters. It goes without saying that your put-in and take-out must be on public lands.

Boaters vs. Colorado Sheriffs

Law enforcement officers in Colorado and *apparently* in Utah, Arizona, and New Mexico have the right to close rivers to boating for safety reasons. Following a rash of bad publicity for boaters in

1980 involving the Emmert case and a series of television kayak thrill shows, the Colorado sheriffs began doing just that. First to be closed was the Yampa, on which one of the television shows was filmed. Rivers were soon closed in several other counties as well. (Most of these safety closures involved Class II water, popular with innertubers.) Steve Boyd, a respected Colorado kayaker, was arrested for paddling the Eagle River in 1980 while it was under closure. Boyd won his case, the court ruling that

1. there was no criminal intent,

2. the method of notification of closure by the sheriff was inadequate,

3. the law was unconstitutionally vague in that it provided insufficient criteria for judging river safety, and

4. the law appeared to contain an exemption for kayaks, which are specialized whitewater craft that are used to seek out water not safely navigable by any other means.

At present, Boyd's ruling does *not* have effect statewide, even though it concerns a state law (and no comparable ruling exists for Utah, New Mexico, or Arizona). It is speculated that specialized whitewater craft will be exempted from future closures—as is currently the case near Glenwood Springs on the Colorado River and near Steamboat Springs on the Yampa River. Alternately, some form of waiver system may be employed—in effect, the issuing of boating licenses—as is currently the practice for the Cache la Poudre River near Fort Collins, Colorado.

John Brown of the Colorado Whitewater Association has met with sheriffs and search and rescue groups over the past few years and explained kayak safety to them; and in general boaters and law enforcement officers are on good terms. The lawmen aren't against boating—just against drowning—and they welcomed Brown's information. There have been only two kayaking deaths in Colorado in the period from 1965 to 1980, but many tubers and fishermen have drowned.

Boaters vs. the Federal Government

No one doubts that it is legal to run the various canyons of the Colorado River drainage which fall under the jurisdiction of the

Bureau of Land Management (BLM) and the National Park Service (NPS). From a practical standpoint, however, it is sometimes almost impossible to obtain a permit to do so. River management policy on those rivers places a high priority on creating a favorable business climate for river tour operations. Thus, no new companies are allowed to compete with established operators, and the bulk of river access is automatically granted each year to a handful of local tour businesses. The public tries for the leftover launch dates in a confusing series of lotteries, waiting lists, and mail-in contests, held in winter, before the season. Every year, many thousands of people do not get permits and must, therefore, sign up for commercial tours in order to gain access to their own national parks. There has been considerable agitation over the past years about adopting a system which would issue all river trip permits to members of the public, letting them decide afterward whether they would go on a commercial tour, arrange their own self-guided trip, or select some intermediate option such as bringing their own boat but hiring a local guide.

River tour operators clear literally millions of dollars a year, thanks in part to their present near-monopoly on river use. They have been extremely effective in lobbying to maintain fixed-allotment schemes. The authors of this guide brought the problem before the Federal Courts with a test case in 1980. The court dismissed the case because the arrest was invalid. In 1985 the court apparently rewrote the law, giving the Park Service power to do whatever it wants.

Perhaps the most unpopular management plan of all was that in effect in the Grand Canyon from 1972 until 1980. Under that plan, over 97 percent of the people who ran the river were on commercial trips, less than 3 percent noncommercial. Over 90 percent of the noncommercial applicants were turned away. In 1980, a new plan was put into effect which would increase both commercial and noncommercial use, and result in about an 80 percent/20 percent commercial/noncommercial split. Noncommercial trips would be on a first-come, first-served basis, with a waiting list. Also, motorized rafts were to be phased out by 1985. By mid-summer, the noncommercial waiting list was over seven years long and still growing, even though its length may have kept many people from applying. It is now over 15 years long.

Regrettably, Congress enacted legislation overruling the Park Service and allowing the return of motors to the rivers, plus additional increases in outfitter allotments. The Park Service promises to do all it can to regain control, but their powers vis-à-vis the tour companies are limited.

Relations between the tour operators and noncommercial river runners are sometimes strained for these reasons. It is important, however, for paddlers to remember that the individual boatmen and rangers they meet on the river have little or nothing to do with all the behind-the-scenes wheeling and dealing that actually creates the worst aspects of the permit systems. Express your outrage to the park administrators and your congressman, but try to get along with the people you actually meet on the river.

The Park Service Act of 1916 allows the Park Service to allow park use to concessioners, but goes on to stipulate that "no natural wonders, curiosities, or objects of interest shall be leased, rented, or granted to anyone on such terms as to interfere with free access to them by the public" (16 USC 3). However, the day when that law will be applied to rivers is yet to come.

BOATING-RELATED ENVIRONMENTAL IMPACT

River running in general, and kayaking in particular, has the potential of being the lowest impact outdoor pursuit of all. "Take only photographs, leave only footprints" says Smokey the Bear (or Ranger Rick, Woodsy Owl, or some other talking animal with a green hat). At any rate, in a kayak you don't even leave footprints.

Unfortunately, the maximum potential for low impact is not always realized. But it *should* be because all the campsites on all the rivers in this guide will probably be used by someone else shortly after your visit. Many popular spots in the national parks are used every night, all season long.

Some of the guides on commercial raft trips are the cleanest of the clean campers on the rivers, and whatever inclination their customers may have to run amok is quickly curtailed by their unending vigilance.

There are also some commercial practices which add unnecessarily to environmental impact. Chief among these is the desire to run trips filled to the maximum group size allowed by law. The principal form of human impact in most desert canyons is trampling of the ground and vegetation at campsites. Four people can camp quite comfortably in a space as little as two spread-out ponchos of ground or less, but a group of 30 or more in search of individual privacy can spread out over a couple of acres. Once spread out, they are beyond the supervision of the guide and free to drop cigarette butts or pop tops if they so desire. That sort of casual litter is hard to police because the people who drop it do not notice it themselves.

One day on the Colorado River we overtook a single party of 250 customers, 27 guides, and 5 or 6 raft groupies all pulled over on a beach for lunch and a few dozen cases of beer. "Only once in a life-time" read some of their tee shirts, "is one so lucky as to unite with earth, wind, and moving water . . ." What they should have said, perhaps, is "back to nature with a vengeance."

Most of the trashing out of the canyons, so certain commercial operators would have us believe, is done by noncommercial boaters. The reason, they maintain, is that on any given river, three-fourths of the private boaters have never been there before and may never come back again. (Indeed, the permit system almost guarantees that such will be the case.) These first-time visitors don't understand the local environmental requirements, the argument claims, and just assume the canyon is in its pristine state because it can easily absorb the sort of impact they personally are about to create. Just to make

sure that nobody using this guide will maintain such an attitude, the next paragraphs are going to harangue you about *proper environmental behavior.*

Cleanliness is next to Godliness. The peculiar environmental nature of the region, its extremely limited number of rivers, the limited availability of campsites, and the very large numbers of people using them, all combine to require environmental measures which may seem excessive to visitors from other parts of the world. These measures are required by law on nearly all federally managed rivers in the region. The regulations are neither arbitrary nor excessive, assuming that as many people will continue using these rivers as do now. On the contrary, they were developed as a result of a lengthy period of trial and error and environmental monitoring, and there is evidence of continued environmental degradation in some areas, which indicates that in some respects the rules are not strong enough. Nearly everyone on the river adheres religiously to these rules, and most of the garbage you encounter is left by a tiny minority of the visitors.

A campfire—nine years ago this kind of fire was acceptable, but this is no longer so (see text) (*Fletcher Anderson*)

Here are the Rules:

1. *Haul out all your trash.* It may be acceptable to burn and bury trash in dense rain forests, but it is absolutely unacceptable here. *Anything* you carried in with you can be carried out as well. Trash deteriorates slowly in this region. One thousand years ago, the Pueblo Indians left Mesa Verde in Southwestern Colorado. Today, their old homes still remain. So do their trash dumps!

2. *Use only biodegradable soap.* If the river is big and muddy, you can use it in the main stream. If not, don't pour it out within about 50 feet of the river or campsite. Dirty or greasy dishwater poured in the sand brings flies and yellow jackets in abundance for the next campers. Under no circumstances should any soap be used in a side stream, particularly at its juncture with the main river where rare and endangered fish species usually congregate. Strain your dishwater in a screen. Put the stuff that is left on the screen in your garbage, to be carried out.

3. *Build NO campfires.* This is a rule for some canyons. Blackened fire rings are unattractive at best. Driftwood

supplies in desert canyons downstream from dams are limited.

4. *Observe the following procedures, when fires are permitted.* Never, ever, build a fire ring of stones. Instead, build your fire on a metal fire pan. When the fire is out, put the ashes in your garbage and carry them out with you. Failing that, dump the ashes in midstream in the river (dumping them in an eddy leaves a bathtub ring on the beach). Obviously, don't attack trees, either alive or dead, for firewood. Pick up driftwood instead.

5. *Leave the canyon in better condition than you found it.* Do not build raft launching ramps, tent platforms, benches around the kitchen, docks, raft mooring stakes, fire rings, trenches, ditches, rock jetties to help float your raft nearer the beach, etc. Leave the canyon looking as though no one else had ever been there before. If someone else was less considerate than you, undo their damage. Dig up their raft mooring stake and throw it in the river. Dismantle their rock jetty. Tear down their lean-to and spread its parts. (Of course, if permanent camping facilities exist, use them in preference to disturbing other areas.)

6. *Carry out human waste.* What a cute name the regulatory agencies use! Encountering the same material in the wilds, one might be more inclined to describe it with some other terminology. For those who still haven't figured it out, human waste is not good old American red-necks, white trash, or blue varicose veins on the nose. Human waste is feces. Human waste in campsites in some areas actually poses a health hazard. In an arid environment like the Southwest, it deteriorates slowly. Archaeologists know what prehistoric Mesa Verde Indians ate — they know because they have studied their 2,000-year-old feces under the microscope!

In the past, it was considered appropriate to bury human feces in a pit 2 feet deep, with a healthy dose of chemicals. Then it was discovered that the bacteria count in the sand on some beaches had reached dangerous levels. In the Grand Canyon, where campsites are limited, one frequently could unearth a previous party's burial in the course of digging a new pit. (How unpleasant!) Now the idea is to keep all feces at least 200 feet from the river, off-river camps, and attraction sites. The only practical way for a raft party to achieve this is to carry out all feces in waterproof ammunition cans. This is actually easier than digging latrine holes and is required by regulation for the Grand and Cataract canyons.

Kayakers can do the same. A kayakers-only trip of four individuals we know ran the Grand Canyon in 1979; they carried out all their feces in screw-top plastic pickle jars. Fletcher Anderson, on a solo run in 1978, used duct-taped zip-lock bags — a less satisfactory system. Both of these trips left behind no feces at all — as opposed to raft parties who do not set up porta-potties at lunchtime. Kayakers have another option: the problem is not feces in the canyons per se, rather it is feces near camps and off-river attractions. A kayaker can stop away from any potential camp and hike and bury his waste 200 feet from the river at that point.

Toilet paper never gets left behind! Take it out with your trash. Don't urinate in camp either. Do it well away from camp, or directly into the river, where thousands of cubic feet of water per second will immediately dissipate it.

7. *Do not make obtrusive loud noises or use mechanical devices.* Most of the people on the river are there, at least

Kayakers drift the flats in Marble Canyon (*Ann Hopkinson*)

in part, to escape from the noise and pollution of the cities. If you are there for other reasons, you still have a certain moral obligation not to preempt everyone else's wilderness experience with your own behavior. An outboard motor may be a good idea for crossing, say, Lake Powell or Lake Mead, at the end of your trip, but it certainly has no place in the canyons above.

The put-in for a river trip is a congregating point for people about to engage in "silent sports," who don't need to hear the screaming generator sometimes used to inflate your raft. It doesn't take that long to use a hand pump.

In camp, there may be others nearby intent on hearing the "sounds of time and the river flowing"—subtle sounds that are easily drowned out by portable tape decks and endless revelling.

8. *Limit your group size.* Whatever impact you have will be multiplied many times over by traveling and camping in an excessively large party. In fact, a group of 30 people does much more than twice the damage done by a group of 15. A campsite more than twice as large will be trampled because everyone will be trying to camp at its perimeter. Noise will more than double as everyone competes to be heard. Trails will clog on hikes, and new trails will be formed, until there are numerous trails all having the same origin and destination. The amount of trash accidentally left behind in the confusion will certainly more than double as well. Finally, any sort of personal communion with the wilderness will be lost in what often amounts to a traveling suburban cocktail party.

We suggest that if you have more than 15 people in your group, you should divide up and camp and travel as two separate parties. (Check local regulations to see if it is permissible.)

Finally, don't look on all these rules as a hassle. Thanks to these practices, the condition of many of the rivers in this guide is much better today than it was 10 years ago—but it still isn't what it could be. Your help in restoring the rivers justifies the privilege you enjoy in running them. Variations of these rules are in effect on all the federally managed rivers listed in this guide. Check with the appropriate regulatory agencies for the rivers you run.

The human bridge, Elves Chasm *(Will Perry)*

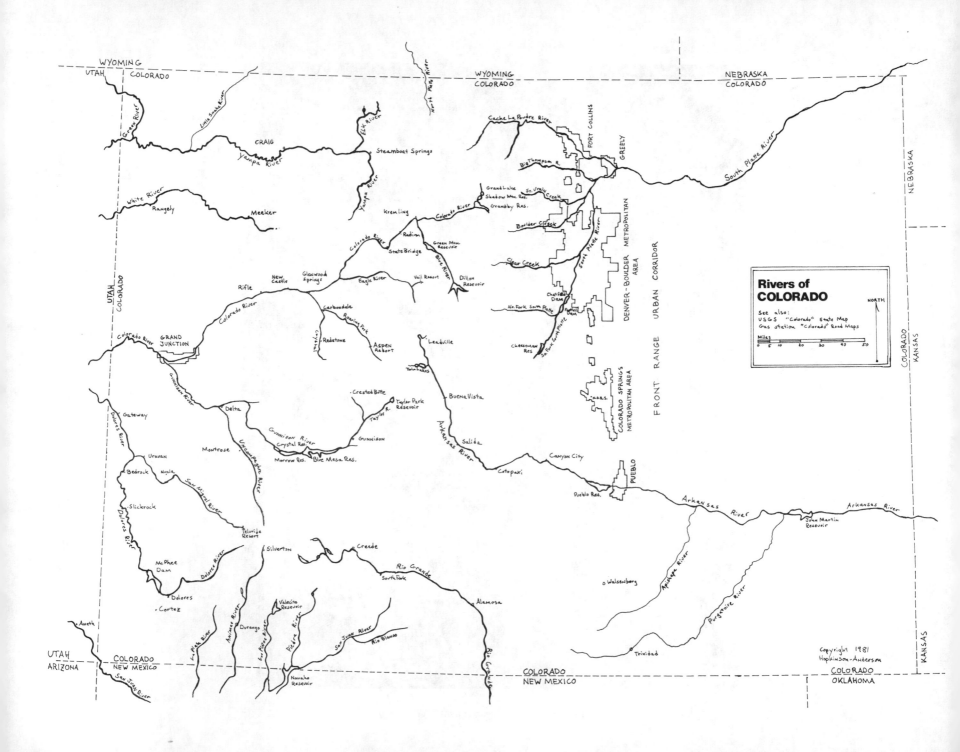

WYOMING
UTAH   COLORADO

WYOMING
COLORADO

NEBRASKA
COLORADO

Green River

Little Snake River

CRAIG

Elk River

Yampa River

Steamboat Springs

North Platte River

Cache La Poudre River

FORT COLLINS

GREELY

South Platte River

NEBRASKA

White River

Rangely

Meeker

Yampa River

Kremling

Colorado River

Grand Lake
Shadow Mtn. Res.
Granby Res.

St. Vrain Creek

Big Thompson R.

Boulder Creek

Clear Creek

South Platte River

DENVER - BOULDER
METROPOLITAN
AREA

Radium

Green Mtn.
Reservoir

State Bridge

Blue River

Colorado River

New Castle

Glenwood Springs

Eagle River

Vail Resort

Dillon
Reservoir

Rifle

Colorado River

Carbondale

Roaring Fork

Chatfield
Dam

No. Fork South Platte

**Rivers of
COLORADO**

NORTH

See also:
USGS "Colorado" State Map
Gas station "Colorado" Road Maps

Miles
0 5 10   20   30   40   50

FRONT RANGE URBAN CORRIDOR

Colorado River

GRAND
JUNCTION

Crystal River

Redstone

ASPEN
Resort

Leadville

Cheesman
Res.

So. Fork South Platte

Gunnison River

Gateway

Delta

Crested Butte

Taylor Park
Reservoir

Taylor R.

Twin Lakes

Buena Vista

COLORADO
SPRINGS
METROPOLITAN
AREA

Dolores River

Uncompahgre River

Montrose

Gunnison River
Crystal Res.

Gunnison

Arkansas River

Salida

Uravan

Bedrock

Nucla

San Miguel River

Morrow Res.   Blue Mesa Res.

Canyon City

Cotopaxi

PUEBLO

Slickrock

Dolores River

Telluride
Resort

Silverton

Creede

Pueblo Res.

Arkansas   River

Arkansas River

John Martin
Reservoir

McPhee
Dam

Dolores River

Rio Grande

South Fork

Alamosa

o Walsenburg

Apishapa River

Dolores

Cortez

o Aneth

La Plata River

Animas River

Los Pinos River

Durango

Valecito
Reservoir

Piedra River

San Juan River

Rio Blanco

Purgatoire River

o Trinidad

Copyright 1981
Hopkinson-Anderson

KANSAS

COLORADO

KANSAS

UTAH
ARIZONA

COLORADO
NEW MEXICO

Navaho
Reservoir

Rio Grande

COLORADO
NEW MEXICO

COLORADO
OKLAHOMA

San Juan River

Chapter I

Rivers of the Eastern Slope

Arkansas River
Central and Eastern Colorado

How can one write anything authoritative about the Arkansas River? Every boater in the West has been there many times and knows at least some portion of the river intimately—undoubtedly more intimately than it will be described here. Boaters from other regions will have heard more than their share of Arkansas stories and may struggle in vain to correlate them with this guide. Nevertheless:

General Description

Somewhere in the cirque basin on the west flank of 14,148-foot Mt. Democrat, the rivulets of melting snow have joined together into a torrent large enough to warrant a name, and that name is the Arkansas River.

It will emerge abruptly from the mountains at Canon City, Colorado, 8,850 vertical feet and 125 horizontal miles later. In that space, it will have undergone several schizophrenic changes of personality, increased its flow one hundred times over, left behind its ancestral channel to carve its way through the northern end of the Wet Mountain range, acquired the flow of waters destined by nature for the Colorado River, and lost some of its own natural flows under the divide by man-made tunnel to the South Platte River.

Arkansas River: Leadville, Colorado to Balltown, Colorado (Jct. of Colo. 82 and U.S. 24)

Roughly 15 Miles, Class I, II; drops 26' per mile. Suitable for kayaks.

A sparkling little trout stream trickles across the broad floor of a 9,000-foot-high glaciated valley between the 14,000-foot Sawatch Mountains to the west and the 13,800-foot Mosquito Range to the east. The river, at times, is augmented by the diverted headwaters of the Eagle and Frying Pan rivers. This could be an excellent place for beginning boaters to get out on the water, but it is more commonly waded by fly fishermen. The highest mountain on your right is 14,433-foot Mt. Elbert.

Arkansas River: Balltown to 1 mile below Granite, Colorado (Balltown is the roadside bar at the Jct. of U.S. 24 and Colo. 82)

4 Miles, Class II; drops 30' per mile. Suitable for kayaks.

At Balltown the volume of the river at least triples when it is joined by the flows of Lake Creek and the diverted flows of the (normally

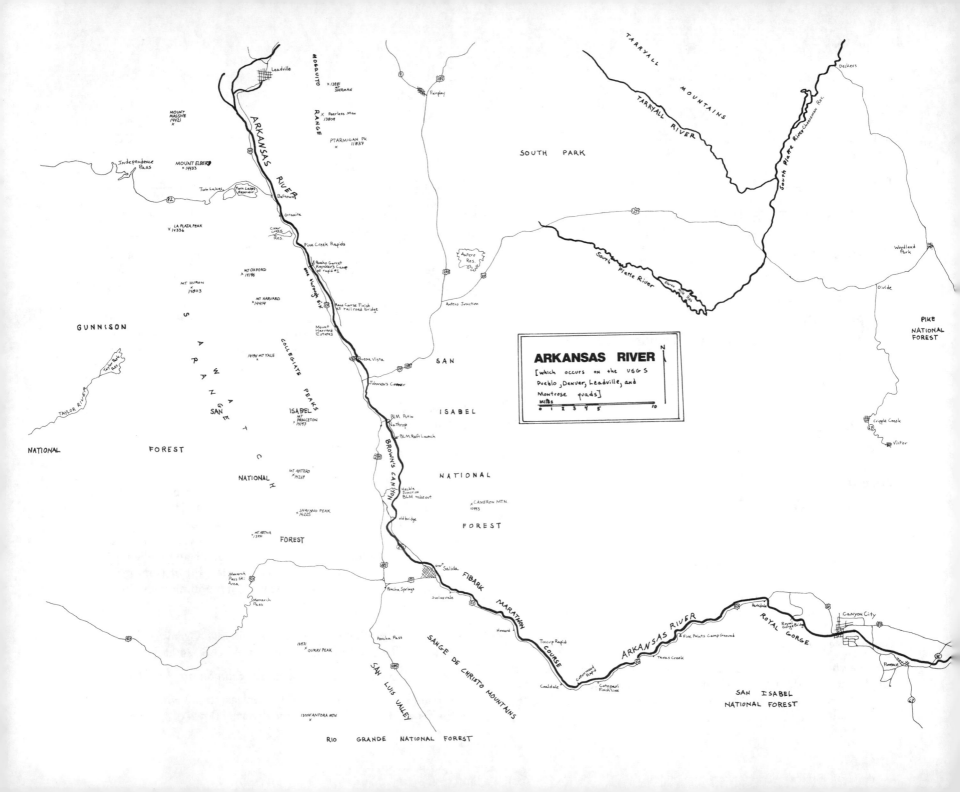

west-flowing) Roaring Fork River. Now, the innocent little trout stream that trickles through Leadville carries the melted snows of 14,000-foot mountain peaks and the diverted flows of three major tributaries of the Colorado River (diverted through tunnels under the Continental Divide).

Depending on the machinations of the Denver Water Board, the river here can be a flood or a trickle as water is held, released or diverted from Twin Lakes Reservoir on Lake Creek. Though it is only Class II, it is Class II with a vengeance and headed for more serious rapids at a very high speed. Granite, Colorado, has a Mexican restaurant heavily patronized by kayakers.

ARKANSAS RIVER: Below Granite and subsequent 2 miles of river (Pine Creek Rapids)

Circa ¼ Mile (rapids proper), Class V; drops over 60' in the rapid. Suitable for kayaks.

The mild and unassuming Arkansas slips away from U.S. 24 into a little inner gorge in the valley floor. There all hell breaks loose! The higher the water levels, the worse it gets—and it is rarely run when the 1 through 6 gauge (in the next section) exceeds 5 feet.

Pine Creek Rapids is regarded as a right of passage by a certain subculture of Colorado hair boaters. "A man ain't a man (or a woman a woman) until he/she's run Pine Creek" they declare from behind their mirror sunglasses. By this definition, there are only about two women kayakers in Colorado. This attitude has lured several macho men of dubious technical paddling skill into Pine Creek Rapids, and their predictable failures have given them some impressive-looking scars and still more impressive war stories, "I had only a tenth of a second to roll up. . . . My life flashed before my eyes . . . and then, I saw GOD! . . . etc."

Two rafters attempted to run Pine Creek in 1975. One of them dove out of the raft above the rapid and reached shore. Kayakers Tom Ruwitch and Fil Sokol were able to drag the lifeless body of the other rafter from the river at great risk to themselves, but their hour-long attempt to revive him with CPR was unsuccessful. The message here is that for most people, Class V rapids should be left alone.

Several people claim to be the first to have run Pine Creek Rapids; however, most of these claims are for dates in the 1970s. Walter Kirschbaum ran the rapid solo in 1957. Most of the hero boaters

of the 1960s also made the run. "I love to do endos here" say the hair boaters—but they mean accidental back endos when they fail to penetrate some of the deeper holes.

In August, the water is low enough for the rapid to be termed Class IV+. Run it then and tell your stories next spring.

There are about two miles of Class II/III water between here and rapid #1—the start of the next section. All of this rapid is visible from a dirt road on the left bank.

ARKANSAS RIVER: Boater's campground to Mt. Harvard Estates Bridge (1 through 6 on the Arkansas)

6 Miles, Class IV; drops 66' per mile. Suitable for kayaks.

The camping area is located 10.3 miles upstream from Buena Vista, Colorado, on the far side of the river from U.S. Highway 24, just across two parallel one-lane bridges. On any given summer day, some of the cars parked here will have license plates from New Hampshire, West Virginia, Idaho, North Carolina, Oregon, California, Texas, and even Alaska and Canada.

This next stretch of water is, for many, the Mecca of Colorado whitewater. This is the site of numerous national championships, North America's Cup Races, and the annual Colorado Cup. Is this run really better than anything in all the other states mentioned? Probably not. Nevertheless, the same cars make the same 4,000-mile round-trip drive year after year to get here.

The camping area is on private land, and we camp here thanks to the courtesy of the landowner. For the most part, kayakers leave very clean campsites, but this is one area where they are sometimes less diligent. *You have no right to camp here!* This is private land. *Do not* drive your car all over the landscape. *Do not* build a big campfire against the side of a rock and leave a black scar. *Do not* pitch your tent in the fragile little stand of green grass and aspen upstream. *Do not* leave behind pop tops from your cans and old scraps of duct tape. We are all guests here and should behave accordingly. If for no other reason, don't do anything ugly because if you do, the local boaters will all be mad at you.

After struggling through this long-winded irrelevant introduction, you deserve to know what the river is like. Without resorting to adjectives like "stupendous" or "magnificent," it can only be said that the next 6 miles are, for western boaters, the very definition of Class IV. There is a tendency to equate "popular run" with "intermediate run." That is not the case here—this is definitely an *expert* run. Although the rapids are not continuous, they are long and (at low water) complex. At high water they are big and powerful, and many a visiting national caliber wildwater racer returns home without his boat. For the recreational paddler, there are numerous holes in which to demonstrate various airborne acrobatic talents.

The rapids were named in 1963 when several Colorado paddlers were searching for a site at which to hold the 1964 National Slalom Championships. No hair-raising names suggested themselves, so people began referring to them as #1, #2, etc. Not everyone counts the same way, so we also have a #4½ and a #5½. Also, the first rapids is #2 because #1 is the rapid in the camping area which ends at the bridge.

There is a gauge bolted to the right-hand bridge abutment of the lower of the two bridges at the campground. Three feet on the gauge means about 1,200 cfs. Six feet means about 3,500 cfs—about the crest in a normal runoff year. In the last week of May in 1980, Cully Erdman reported that when he extended his leg, knee-deep into the water, he could touch the top of the gauge post with his toe—a flow

One through Six stretch, C-1 "in the soup" (*Fletcher Anderson*)

of around 9,000 cfs! In the droughts of 1977 and 1981, the flow crested around 1 foot.

At 3 feet on the gauge, there are some intricate (for a wildwater boat) maneuvers to be made, but the overall push of the water is not overwhelming. Below that level, the maneuvers become progressively more complex as more and more rocks are exposed, until at 1 foot (in August) the whole run is a tight little rock garden. Above 3 feet, the force of the water increases steadily and the rocks are replaced with various sorts of hydraulic features which are increasingly difficult to avoid at high levels. At levels above 6 feet, the run is a mini-Grand Canyon and most of the eddies are to be found among the lower branches of riverside trees.

Some expert rafters have made the run successfully at about 3 feet on the gauge—but true expertise in rafting is less common than most rafters care to admit—and most raft runs of this stretch end with broken oars or a pierced raft. There is better rafting water downstream.

The normal take-out for this run is at the railroad bridge 6 miles below the put-in. A dirt road roughly parallels the entire stretch on the left bank. A further mile of paddling gets you to the Mt. Harvard Estates development on the left side of the river, on the main highway. Midway through the run is a bridge leading to the Otero Pumping Station (which takes Arkansas water to the South Platte). The highway is a few hundred yards from this bridge.

ARKANSAS RIVER: Mt. Harvard Estates to Nathrop, Colorado

14 Miles, Class I, II; drops 51' per mile. Suitable for kayaks.

Mt. Harvard Estates are 5 or 6 miles north of Buena Vista, Colorado, on U.S. 24. Nathrop is 8 miles south. Although U.S. Highway 24 (and 285) runs down the river valley, it is not always close to the river itself. The river sometimes flows in an inner gorge cut into the broad valley bottom. Aside from the put-in and the take-out, there is access at Johnson's Corner, midway through the run, from the spur of U.S. 24/285 which heads east toward South Park, and the last 4 miles of the run are close to the road.

The river flow here is unobstructed, so the steep gradient and large flows express themselves as mile after mile of amorphous fast-moving choppy waves.

This is not a popular run—perhaps because of the poor access and the really excellent runs nearby.

ARKANSAS RIVER: Nathrop to highway bridge 6 miles above Salida (Brown's Canyon)

10 Miles, Class III+; drops 30' per mile. Suitable for kayaks and rafts.

The gradient has lessened from that of the previous Class II run, and you might expect that the river would become still easier. You would be mistaken, for the river has to cut its way through a mass of crumbly granite in a very narrow canyon shared with the Denver and Rio Grande Railroad. The river's flow can be as much as half again larger than at 1 through 6 because of snow runoff from the Collegiate Range (the nearby Mounts Oxford 14,196 feet, Harvard 14,414 feet, Yale 14,196 feet, Princeton 14,197 feet, and Antero 14,269 feet—named in honor of Antero Junior College no doubt).

In marked contrast to its continuous gradient nature above, the river here becomes distinctly pool/drop. It is possible to paddle a kayak to within a few feet of the lip of most of the drops and look over to find a route. The rapids themselves are steep chutes with waves occasionally as much as 6 feet high (at least at peak runoff—more like 2 feet high by late summer). The rapids require very little in the way of maneuvering, but a very dependable brace is called for, particularly in high water. A thriving commercial raft industry exists here and at times groups of 10 or 15 rafts of screaming tourists will come through literally bumper-to-bumper. For that reason, the run is less popular now with kayakers than it was 10 or 15 years ago (the commercial rafting boom hit here in about 1977). The rafting boom is hitting the places the kayakers fled to, and the view now seems to be that if you must have crowding, you might as well be crowded in the best water around—and for a competent intermediate paddler, that means Brown's Canyon. The kayaks are returning. You do not find wilderness in Brown's Canyon, but you do find outstanding whitewater.

The normal put-in for kayakers is at the new BLM launch site across the river from Nathrop. Most rafters prefer to drive 3 miles downstream on a poor quality dirt road, on the left bank, to avoid the slow water that precedes the rapids.

The normal take-out for kayakers is at a little bridge just off the main highway within sight of the very high bridge of Colorado 291. Most rafters prefer to drive a 3-mile bumpy dirt road down to "Heckla Junction," thus cutting off the last 2½ miles of river and avoiding the last major rapid: "Siedel's Suck Hole." This rapid consists of one large and deep hole which extends nearly all the way across the river. Rafts are often turned over back upstream, though kayaks either go by on the right, penetrate the hole, or roll up after being back endoed. Erich Siedel was an East German wildwater champion who escaped to the West on a training run through the Baltic Sea and moved to Salida in 1952. He first ran "Siedel's Suck Hole" at full flood that year and his flimsy racing foldboat folded up in the midst of an accidental back endo, leaving him paddling a floppy bag of broken sticks.

ARKANSAS RIVER: Brown's Canyon take-out to Salida

6.5 Miles, Class I; drops about 15' per mile. Suitable for kayaks, rafts, and canoes.

The riverbed is wider, the flow is slow. Almost no one boats here, as the next section is so widely known—and there is a dangerous weir in this section!

ARKANSAS RIVER: Salida to Cotopaxi

26 Miles, Class I, II, III+; drops 23' per mile. Suitable for kayaks, rafts, and possible for canoes.

This is the course of the annual Salida-Cotopaxi Whitewater Marathon, the oldest whitewater kayak race in the Western Hemisphere. The wildwater was first held in 1948, the slalom in 1955. Since its inception, the race has drawn top European paddlers to this country, many of whom eventually moved here and passed on their paddling knowledge to the local boaters. As of 1981, only seven people in history have ever finished the race in under two hours. Negotiating the large waves in many of the rapids is unusually tiring. Cottonwood Rapid, Class III+, is particularly difficult for a paddler who has just come 22 miles at full speed. As with Pine Creek, there is a local subculture based on the theory that "a man ain't a man (or a woman a woman) until he/she has raced Salida"—and the entry field of the marathon is typically composed of only a small, but elite group of "real" men and women. The men's record is 1 hour, 55 minutes, 27.9 seconds, held by Michael Stroebel of Munich, West Germany. The women's record of 2 hours, 7 minutes, 5.7 seconds, held by Ann Hopkinson of Glenwood Springs, Colorado, was dropped to 2 hours, 4 minutes, 56 seconds by world champion Karen Wahl of Stuttgart, West Germany in 1985.

There is often a semipermanent slalom course set in the town of Salida. The building next to the river on F Street is the headquarters of the Fibark Whitewater Club. The adjacent building is the Palace Cafe, wherein western racers attempt to disorient the digestive systems of visiting eastern competitors with Mexican food.

Numerous Class II, II+ rapids occur throughout the course. The hardest rapid is probably "Bear Creek," Class III+ (at high water, II at low) about 3 miles below Salida. Someone has painted "Jesus Saves" on the rock face just upstream. Pray in the large eddy on the right. Beyond Howard, Colorado (10 miles from Salida), there is a great deal of flat water and relatively few rapids. Just beyond Coaldale, the river makes a 90° left turn and carves its way into the end of the Wet Mountain ridge. Here lies "Cottonwood Rapid"—a short steep Class III, IV chute of large breaking waves (Class II–III at low water).

Access to almost any point on the river is easy via U.S. Highway 50.

(*Above and right*) wildwater paddlers in race through rapids One through Six at 1980 U.S. Wildwater National Championships (*Jack Burkholder*)

ARKANSAS RIVER: Cotopaxi to Parkdale, Colorado

19 Miles, Class II, III; drops 40' per mile. Suitable for kayaks and rafts.

Numerous Class II and III rapids come in quick succession throughout this section, making it popular with kayakers and rafters alike. About 3 miles below the town of Texas Creek is 5 Points Campground. The annual April lower Arkansas Wildwater Race starts there and goes for 5 miles to the usual slalom site. Again, access to the entire stretch is easy via U.S. 50, but beware of an unfriendly landowner in Parkdale with a German shepherd dog and a 12-gauge shotgun! This gentleman would like to charge for access to the Royal Gorge, just below his land, and has sold exclusive rights to a rafting company. Take-out *above* his land, and do not try to pet his dog!

ARKANSAS RIVER: Parkdale to Canon City (the Royal Gorge)

8 Miles, Class IV; drops 50' per mile. Suitable for kayaks, possible for some rafts.

By now, so much has happened on the Arkansas that one would think that it must be over. Not yet! The best part of all starts here! Somehow the river must get through a 1,500-foot-high ridge directly in its path. It does so by carving the vertical-walled, 1,500-foot-deep Royal Gorge. This black-walled gorge is far deeper than it is wide. The already narrow path of the river is further constricted by the railroad—which at one point is nailed to the wall and hangs out over the water. In earlier days, big business was not hampered by the bureaucratic red tape of which it complains of today. *Two* railroads wanted to build through the Royal Gorge. They hired track crews and began construction, but space at the bottom of the gorge is extremely limited. The question of rightful claim to the best ground was settled by hired machine gunners. Occasionally, sappers from one railroad would dynamite the tracks of the other. Several workers died of gunshot wounds. Eventually, one railroad bought out the other. One still may encounter bits of twisted railroad rail in the rapids—reminders of the good old days to which the sagebrush rebellion will return us.

The rapids are pool/drop, but the drops are long and the pools are short and steep. At high water the tail waves of one rapid extend into the throat of the next. At *very* low water the rapids are only Class III.

In the dead center of this lonely gorge is an aerial tramway, an inclined railroad, a curio stand and ice-cream shop, and the world's highest suspension bridge (which leads to nowhere).

Parachutists love to dive from this bridge. Kayakers flock to the ice-cream stand. The tourists regard everyone as equally crazy.

There is a take-out 2 miles above Canon City proper, reached via "Tunnel Drive," which leaves Highway 50 near the city limits. It is just as easy to paddle on down to the edge of town.

The gorge was first paddled in 1948 by two foldboaters. Many people run it today. Nevertheless, it is emphatically no place for beginners. Although the rapids require only rudimentary maneuvering, they feature powerful hydraulics which would surely upset a novice boater. Commercial rafting operations have moved into the gorge in the last few years, but they are relatively small-scale, and extremely friendly.

ARKANSAS RIVER: Canon City to Pueblo Reservoir

29 Miles (depending on reservoir levels), Class I; drops 15' per mile. Suitable for kayaks, rafts, and canoes. (This run is detailed in Earl Perry's Rivers of Colorado.*)*

Rivers of the Great Plains are distinctly different from those of the mountains. The Class IV Arkansas suddenly becomes a gentle meandering strip of cottonwood-lined moisture in the dry rolling hills of the short grass prairie. The narrow strip of riverbank is a critical habitat for all the prairie wildlife, as well as for domestic livestock. The river is not absolutely flat, rather its flow is broken by many pleasant little ripples.

The main road is close to the river from Canon City to the Portland Cement Plant. Secondary roads from U.S. 50 reach the river at 4, 6, and 10 miles below the Portland plant. Livesey, on Colorado 96, west of Pueblo, is 16 miles below Portland, and has easy river access. The take-out at Pueblo Reservoir marina may require 2 or 3 miles of lake paddling.

Jerry Wedekin breaks the ice above the Royal Gorge, February 1981. *(NORS)*

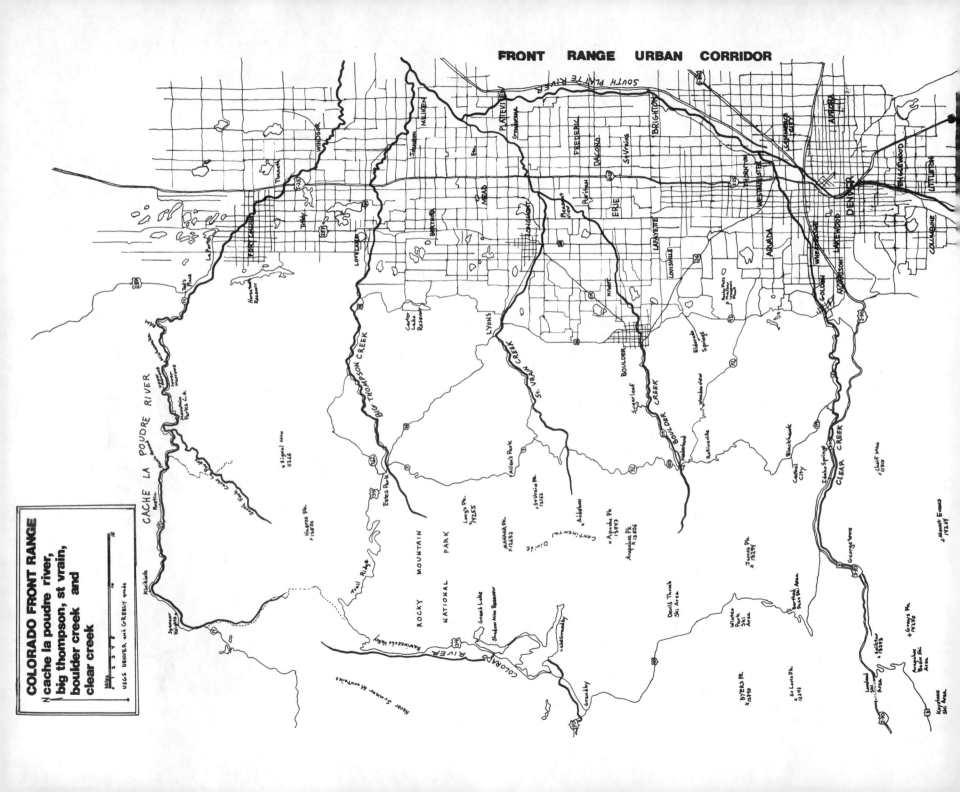

FRONT RANGE URBAN CORRIDOR

COLORADO FRONT RANGE
cache la poudre river,
big thompson, st vrain,
boulder creek and
clear creek

USGS DENVER and GREELEY grads

ARKANSAS RIVER: Below Pueblo Reservoir

2,000 Miles, Class I; not much drop. Suitable for kayaks, canoes; sandbars interfere with rafts.

At this point, the river is only 4,900 feet above sea level. New Orleans, Louisiana, is 2,000 miles away. Thus, it takes a careful look to tell which way is downhill. Numerous irrigation diversions rapidly reduce the size of the river, but several small tributaries keep it just big enough to paddle. In 1979, there was a 1,200-mile canoe race along the Arkansas in central Kansas and Oklahoma, to New Orleans on the Mississippi — a run which includes many reservoirs.

CACHE LA POUDRE RIVER

General Description

The Cache la Poudre River was named (probably in 1798) by the legendary fur trader Ceran de St. Vrain when he cached a supply of gun powder there before returning down the Platte River with his furs to spend the winter in Independence, Missouri.

Kayakers discovered the Poudre in the 1950s. It quickly became one of the most popular boating rivers in the West — certainly the most popular river in the Colorado Front Range. It is famous nationwide, thanks in part to the annual whitewater races which draw competitors from across the United States, Canada, and Europe.

Less widely known is the fact that the canyon is seriously threatened with three major dams and a series of power plants and conduits which would completely end all boating on the river.

These reservoirs would be particularly useless for anything except storing water. Their sides would be extremely steep and their water levels would annually fluctuate over 100 feet in elevation — making access difficult and fish breeding impossible. The parts of the river not buried by the reservoirs would be dry because the water would be diverted in culverts to generate electrical power. Local construction interests are lobbying strongly in favor of the $1,300,000,000 federally funded pork barrel project. Other, cheaper, local alternatives exist.

Hunters, fishermen, conservationists, kayakers, and local residents successfully lobbied for Wild and Scenic river protection. The Cache la Poudre is the only Wild and Scenic river in Colorado. Boating the Poudre requires a liability waiver obtained in person at the sheriff's office in Fort Collins.

CACHE LA POUDRE RIVER: Headwaters to Spencer Heights

18 Miles, drops average 100'+ per mile. Suitable for kayaks? Class?

There appears to be just enough water to boat at least some of this stretch, but we are not aware of anyone having done so. A poor road from Fall River Pass in Rocky Mountain National Park follows the river to where both join Colorado Highway 14. Poudre Falls, a waterfall about 15' high, is close to the road and is sometimes run for the camera.

CACHE LA POUDRE RIVER: Spencer Heights to Idylwild

8 Miles, Class II (some III+); drops 50' per mile. Suitable for kayaks.

Just above Spencer Heights an underground culvert from the headwaters of the Laramie River brings additional water into the Poudre. For the next 6 miles, the water is fast moving, but unobstructed. Two or three miles above Idylwild, the channel narrows to produce a mile or so of Class III–III+ water. Low branches from riverside trees swamp the water's surface.

CACHE LA POUDRE RIVER: Idylwild to picnic ground 3.5 miles below Rustic

8 Miles, Class II, III+; drops 75' per mile. Suitable for kayaks.

This stretch is sometimes known as the Rustic Run. The very fast, but very shallow (even in May–June runoff) Cache la Poudre ranges widely across the bottom of its U-shaped valley. The river is not always right next to Colorado 14, and that makes this the only "wild" section of the Poudre. The rapids tend to be long, choppy little things with numerous possible routes.

The canyon narrows noticeably at the end of the run.

CACHE LA POUDRE RIVER: Picnic ground 3.5 miles below Rustic to Mountain Park Campground

5½ Miles, Class II, III, IV; drops 90' per mile. Suitable for kayaks.

This is the course of the annual Cache la Poudre Wildwater Race. The finish line is at the upper end of Mountain Park Campground.

Half a mile below the put-in is a highway bridge over the river on which someone has painted "Grandpa's Bridge." There is much easy Class IV water in the next mile as the canyon narrows down. A mile below "Grandpa's Bridge" is the Pinagree Park road bridge. A narrow little inner gorge of Class IV water about ½ mile in length follows this bridge.

Two miles below the Pinagree Park Bridge is a little private one-lane bridge leading to some summer homes. Right under this bridge is a 7-foot drop-off into a ¼ mile long Class IV rapid. The annual Cache la Poudre Slalom is set somewhere in this rapid.

Mountain Park Campground is at the end of the rapid. The bridge from the highway to the campground is another ½ mile or so downstream.

CACHE LA POUDRE RIVER: Mountain Park Campground to Narrows Campground

3 Miles, Class II, III; drops 65' per mile. Suitable for kayaks.

This 3-mile stretch is in a mildly wider, flatter canyon than above. The drop is continuous. Even at high water, the rapids are shallow and choppy.

This was the old wildwater course paddled in the 1960s. The slalom of that era was set in the Class III rapid in Narrows Campground.

Although there is about ½ mile of Class II+-III water below the campground, everyone takes out here because below lies upper Narrows Rapid.

CACHE LA POUDRE RIVER: Upper Narrows Rapid

½ Mile, Class VI; drops (estimated) 450' per mile. (Don't do it!)

This obvious Class VI rapid is always to be avoided, although portions of it were run in October 1967 by Fletcher Anderson and by Doug Hahn in October 1977.

At these very low (circa 100 cfs) levels the rapid is a staircase of narrow waterfalls around big boulders. The dangers of pinning, broaching, wedging, and impacting on rocks are high. Anderson's run did so much damage to his boat that he built a new one rather than repair the old—once his left forearm and right ankle healed.

At high water (2,000 cfs), the rapid is a roaring, pulsing cascade of foam. Inner-tubers attempting this rapid over the years have (predictably) died. The entire river is now closed to inner-tubing. Bill Clayton and Bob Waind hung a slalom gate in this rapid prior to the 1968 Poudre Races, scaring the hell out of visiting European racers who spotted it as they drove up the road.

CACHE LA POUDRE RIVER: Upper Narrows Rapid to one-lane highway bridge

1 Mile, Class IV; drops (estimated) 110' per mile. Suitable for kayaks.

This is the so-called "Middle Narrows Run." The river is very narrow and numerous large boulders have fallen into it, producing many Class IV drops. Many people make this run, portage the lower narrows, and continue down the next run.

CACHE LA POUDRE RIVER: Narrows one-lane bridge to bottom of rapid

0.2 Miles, Class V; drops (estimated) 200' per mile. Suitable (but not recommended) for kayaks.

This boulder-choked Class V rapid is easily portaged along the highway, but it has been run at most water levels. There is a distinct possibility of pinning at low water, and of hydraulic entrapment followed by rock bashing at high water. Some of the moves are more difficult than they look, and careful scouting is mandatory.

CACHE LA POUDRE RIVER: Lower Narrows to Mishawaka Bar

4 Miles, Class II, III, IV; drops 45' per mile. Suitable for kayaks.

This is the upper half of the Mishawaka Run. Here, at high water, one finds a classic Rocky Mountain run—big water in a small river. There are many forest service campgrounds in the first couple of miles. Thereafter, the road impinges considerably on the riverbed and the Class III and IV water begins. These are all relatively short drops, easily scouted from the road on the way up. Endo spots abound.

The Mishawaka Bar has a dining room on stilts over part of the river. Drink beer and watch your friends on the river through the big picture windows. If only they had a nice Class IV rapid here!

CACHE LA POUDRE RIVER: Mishawaka Bar to diversion dam

7.7 Miles, Class II, III, III + ; drops circa 50' per mile. Suitable for kayaks.

This run is variously known as the "Lower Mishawaka," "Poudre Park," and "Bridges" run. Most of the kayaking on the river takes place on this run.

Three miles above the dam is Poudre Falls, a difficult, steep, narrow Class III + –IV rapid which can be scouted from the highway. The rest of the run has no difficult rapids. Play spots abound in the Class III water. Paddlers must constantly be aware of the many poorly placed bridge pilings on the many rickety private bridges leading to summer houses across the river. Less obvious, but equally dangerous, are the *stumps of old bridge pilings* which sometimes lurk just below the water's surface. These hazards make it foolish to raft here.

The dam is a cement irrigation and domestic water diversion structure about 7-feet high. Rock fill on the downstream side eliminates a possible keeper wave, but the result is that the current slams down onto a cement pad and then ricochetes across jagged rocks. The dam has been run without serious injury, both by novices who missed the take-out and by the experts who went over the lip trying to rescue them. Nevertheless, we suggest you don't try to run it.

CACHE LA POUDRE RIVER: Diversion dam to first irrigation diversions

4 Miles, Class II; drops 45' per mile. Suitable for kayaks and some rafts.

Despite the lack of difficult rapids, the water is still fast moving here—making the run an exciting one for novice paddlers. The first mile of the run is away from the highway and should be avoided by beginners because of artificial weirs. This is the only section of the Poudre suitable for rafting.

CACHE LA POUDRE RIVER: Irrigation diversions near "Ted's place" to confluence with South Platte in Greeley, Colorado

36 Miles, Class I; drops 17' per mile. Not recommended.

We can't really recommend boating this stretch of river. About a dozen irrigation diversions remove the majority of the river's water. That, combined with the reduced drop, make the run safe for inner-tubers. Broken bottles make it dangerous for bare feet. All in all, the irrigation ditches are a better bet than the river. Nevertheless, the run is popular with some open canoeists. A better choice would be to run the South Platte from the confluence down (put-in at the take-out for this run—see South Platte section of this guide).

CACHE LA POUDRE RIVER: South Fork

7 Miles, Class IV; drops 171' per mile. Suitable for kayaks.

Ben Harding developed an interest in this apparently unboatable tributary of the Poudre when it was included in the Wild and Scenic Rivers Study area. He reports that in spring runoff of a good year there is just enough water to float a kayak. The two worst rapids are beaver dams. One must duck under overhanging willow branches while going over the lip.

A road leaving Colorado 14, 5 miles below Rustic, leads into the put-in. The river may not be much for kayaking, but it offers superb fly fishing for native trout and a roadless environment.

BIG EMPTY SPACE #1
Eastern Colorado

(An Interlude)

A quick glance at the map is all it takes to see that fairly large portions of the region don't have any rivers in them. Even those rivers represented are somewhat imaginary—a result of the map maker's aversion to a blank sheet of paper. Faint blue lines on the paper turn out to be, in reality, sandy arroyos.

Rivers on the eastern slope of the Rocky Mountains are transporting the maximum amount of water when they hit the edge of the Great Plains. Thereafter, they rapidly lose water which seeps into the water table and various underground aquifers bound for the Midwest. This loss of water was a natural process even before modern irrigation diversion, and on more than one occasion, mountain men attempting to float their furs down the South Platte by bull boat in the 1830s were left high and dry by the unpredictable river. Now, the flows are dam controlled and more dependable, and Colorado River water has been diverted into the South Platte drainage.

No less an individual than John Wesley Powell noted more than a hundred years ago that the Great Plains could never all be brought under cultivation: the total rainfall in the area, including the eastern slope of the Rockies, being insufficient to irrigate more than a small portion of the lands. Modern farmers are unwittingly proving him correct as their massive deep-well irrigation projects rapidly lower the water table in all their aquifers—an environmental sin for which their children or grandchildren will ultimately pay the price.

All of this suggests a region not particularly suited to boating. Actually, the plains sections of the South Platte and Arkansas *are* boatable all the way to the Mississippi and there are two other intriguing possibilities:

In the falls and summers of 1968 through 1973, the authors of this book were engaged in archaeological research in Southeastern Colorado. Some of this work was along the mountain front on the Apishapa and Purgatoire rivers near Trinidad, Colorado. The Purgatoire and the slightly smaller Apishapa are both more than big enough there to float a kayak or canoe. Both rivers meander out into the rolling hills of the short grass prairie and emerge 80 miles away on the Arkansas near La Junta, Colorado, still carrying an adequate flow. No roads follow these rivers, and no ranch houses line their banks. The land is much as it was when man first visited. What mysteries lie hidden within the dark shadows of the Apishapa Canyon? The world awaits the report of some later-day John Wesley Powell...

UPPER SOUTH PLATTE RIVER

General Description

The South Platte is Denver's river, in the sense that it is the only river in town, in the sense that it provides a variety of priceless recreational experiences for Denver residents, and in the sense that

the Denver Water Board owns its water and has plans to cover most of the upper river with reservoirs and put nearly all the water into pipes.[1]

While it is primarily a river of the plains, the headwaters of the river actually lie high in the mountains (higher today than in the past, for the headwaters of the Colorado River now feed the little South Platte through a variety of intermountain diversion tunnels). Mountain rivers are almost entirely fed by snowmelt. Rivers of the foothills and plains are fed by arbitrary and capricious rainfall, and dam-controlled rivers flow in curious unpredictable bursts of water whose schedules defy any sort of human logic. Thus, little can be said of the South Platte's flows except that year after year, it always seems to be there. Rarely will more than 500 cfs be found in any portion of the river, except during a rain-induced flash flood—but if the natural flow ever drops below about 200 cfs, it will be augmented by dam releases. The river in the mountains is thus boatable (and inner-tubeable) April through August. It is boatable year round in and below Denver—save when January and February cold spells freeze it over.

Headwaters of the South Platte: The headwaters are too small to float a boat in, but in case you felt curious: at a mean elevation of about 9,500 feet near Fairplay in the very heart of the Rocky Mountains, lies a 750 square mile piece of strangely flat, short grass prairie drained by dozens of little creeks. Here, the game that summers in the nearly 14,000-foot mountains bands together to last out the long winter, feeding on a seemingly inexhaustable supply of natural hay. Here, came the Indians to feed on the plentiful game and bask in the comparatively tolerable winter climate, in preference to chasing scattered groups of animals over the blizzard-swept high plains. Here, following the advice of the Indians, came the mountain men in search of beaver. They called the area the Bayou Salad—a reference to the saltlike evaporate deposits found near some water holes. Gold ore lay in the gravels of the Bayou Salad, and in the past century huge dredging machines began to dig it up and wash the gravel (one of these dredges still sits landlocked just south of Fairplay).

The game and the Indians, the beaver and the mountain men, and the gold and the miners are gone now—but the vast expanses of grassland remain. Today, the area is called South Park and scat-

[1]The Foothills treatment plant and Two Forks Dam Project.

tered herds of cattle stretch across it as far as the eye can see. Are the cattle and the ranchers also but a passing moment of history? No doubt the earlier residents of South Park looked as permanent in their day as today's residents do now.

The myriad of little streams, which are the headwaters of the Platte, are collected in a myriad of reservoirs, their flows regulated and parceled out (so it is said) for the betterment of mankind. By Cheesman Reservoir, near Deckers, enough water has accumulated to produce a boatable river.

THE SOUTH PLATTE RIVER: Cheesman Dam to South Platte, Colorado

16 Miles, Class I, II, III; drops 60' per mile, then 25' per mile. Suitable for kayaks, small rafts, and canoes.

Colorado Route 67, going west from Sedalia, Colorado, will take you over the top of the Rampart Range and down into the Platte Canyon on a gravel road. Deckers will be upstream, and Cheesman Dam is above Deckers. "South Platte," Colorado, is the confluence of the north and south forks of the river at the entrance of Waterton Canyon.

The Class III rapids on this run are all located in the 5-mile stretch from the dam to Deckers where the river drops over 50 feet per mile. The dirt road from Deckers up to the dam has detoured away from the river for the first 2½ miles of this run in order to arrive at the top of the dam. The put-in is a hassle.

The remaining 11 miles from Deckers to the confluence drops only 25 feet per mile, with more or less continuous gradient—not a very awesome drop for a less than 500 cfs river. Many unthreatening Class II rapids are to be found, particularly in the second half of the run.

Most beginning boaters in the Denver and Colorado Springs area make a few trips to this part of the South Platte to get their first taste of moving water. On a summer weekend, they will share the river with literally thousands of fishermen, inner-tubers, sun bathers, beer drinkers, trail bikers, and sightseers.

The proposed Two Forks Dam would cover this entire stretch with the largest body of stagnant water in Colorado. The Denver Water Board wants to condemn the homes of the people who live here and build the dam to store diverted Colorado River water. (They own the rights to more water than they can store and divert at present.) The city of Denver (for whom the water board works) has enough water, but the water board diverts more water than Denver needs and sells it to the suburbs. They "need" more water in order to encourage the rampant growth of still more suburbs. Indeed, they have already sold too much water and Denver residents have their domestic water rationed in the summer months as a result.

NORTH FORK OF THE SOUTH PLATTE RIVER: Bailey to Foxton

Approximately 15 Miles, Class II, III, some IV; drops 80' per mile. Suitable for kayaks.

Ha, ha we pulled a fast one on you: this is the *other* fork of the South Platte (see the map and all will be obvious). Bailey is on U.S. 285, 28 miles west of Denver. A dirt and paved road leaves U.S. 285 at Conifer and drops 8 miles to the river at Foxton.

It is possible to boat the 10 miles of river above Bailey as well—the higher you go, the steeper the gradient until you reach about 150 feet per mile between Grant and Webster. The Roberts Tunnel brings water from Dillon Reservoir on the Blue River, under the divide to the South Platte near Grant—assuring more than adequate flows, although the manipulations of the Denver Water Board play havoc with predicting them. You can expect between 250 and 500 cfs throughout most of the summer—but not always.

Below Bailey, the river leaves behind the traffic and strip development of U.S. 285 and enters a quiet little V-shaped canyon. Crumbly granite boulders have tumbled into the river producing many little rapids, a few of which are intricate enough to be Class IV difficulty when the flow is excessively high. Most are easy II, III —despite the 80 foot per mile drop. Except for a few short sections, this entire run is directly adjacent to the dirt road from Bailey to Foxton.

THE SOUTH PLATTE RIVER: Foxton to "South Platte," Colorado

4½ Miles, Class II, III; drops 80' per mile. Suitable for kayaks.

Except for the last mile or so, the river is still dropping pretty fast, but the boulders which make the rapids above Foxton so interesting are less prevalent. All of this run and much of the preceding one would be buried under Two Forks Dam, as would the little towns you pass.

A dirt road is adjacent to almost the entire run.

THE SOUTH PLATTE RIVER: "South Platte" to Chatfield Reservoir (Waterton Canyon)

9 Miles, Class III, IV, V; drops 70' per mile. Suitable for kayaks (here is where the Deckers section joins the Foxton section).

The combined flows of the two forks of the South Platte should be expected to produce flows of at least 1,000 cfs at peak runoff (May–June), but they usually don't because if a lot of water is being released into one fork, the other will be shut down. Thus, we are talking about a bigger, but still rather small river. Flows over 2,000 cfs in Waterton Canyon are rare. A very narrow, deep canyon is the home of one of the remaining herds of mountain sheep. Boulders falling into the river have created numerous constricted little rapids. Be on the lookout for a tiny cement dam which is normally portaged, and a house-sized boulder in midstream which is passed by a very narrow channel on the left. The Foothills Dam, a component of the Two forks Project, is under construction in mid-canyon and will soon destroy much of the area. Beware of construction debris near and below the dam site. Some maps indicate a dirt road in the canyon, but this road is not open to automobiles. You must shuttle all the way around. As with most Class IV and V water in the region, this canyon, too, was first paddled by the legendary Walter Kirschbaum—in 1959.

So ends the mountain part of the South Platte. Roads west of the lake make it unnecessary to paddle across Cheesman Reservoir.

A CANCER ON THE PLAINS

The Front Range Urban Corridor

(An Interlude)

When Ann Hopkinson goes to work, she looks for cancer. And when she crosses the Front Range and looks out over the plains at the sprawling gray mass of the Front Range Urban Corridor, she has a sense of déjà vu. The view through the microscope and the view from Lookout Mountain are remarkably similar, for they are both cancer.

"What do you mean I have Cancer?"[2] said Richard Nixon to John Dean. What is cancer? Why does it grow?

Back in the 1940s Denver was just another of dozens of viable small cities spread across the Great Plains. Agricultural products flowed in, the cities processed them and shipped them away in modified form to other parts of the world. Manufactured goods came into being in the cities and were distributed out into the country. The whole mechanism was fed by sun and water and its noxious by-products were on a scale that the earth and air could reassimilate. The whole process was kept under control by the forces of nature, the self-regulatory process of supply and demand, and the inspired intervention of government regulation. The cities of the plains were, in a word, healthy organs of the great body of the civilized earth. True enough, all had not gone steadily in the past: Colorado was and is littered with the remnants of the boom and bust cycles of exploiting nonrenewable resources. Entire towns had lived and suddenly died when the supply of gold, silver, coal, and so on was suddenly exhausted. The dust bowl drought and depression were a disease from which earth and civilization were still recovering. In the long view, however, the steady husbandry of renewable resources was a healthy long-lasting way of life on the plains.

Yet mysteriously in the 1950s, the healthy organ that was Denver began to run amok. Something was making Denver grow at a rate faster than was healthy. Denver lay at the foot of the Rocky Mountains on the very edge of the plains. Thus, it prospered not only from the traditional plains sources of beef and agriculture, but also from the suddenly resurgent life of the mountains (timber, tourism, and minerals), and from being a trans-shipment point between the two.

Alas, Denver lay at a site economically, but not ecologically, suited for massive growth. Among other things, Denver lies in a geographic basin. Particularly in winter, dense air is trapped by a rise of land east of the city. Smoke, dust, and noxious gases accumulate in the depression of the South Platte Valley. Denver lies in a region of very limited (less than 17 inches per year) rainfall and sits astride no major river. It is a locale where a city of 300,000 might do well, but one where a city of over 2,000,000 must be cause for great concern.

Thus, when Denver exceeded its environmentally dictated maximum size in the 1950s, it should have been recognized as a cancer—a collection of misguided cells, bent upon uncontrolled and rapid growth. Now, like a tumor, it grows ever more rapidly, sucking nutrients from the healthy neighboring organs, much to the detriment of the rest of the body. When once it was a functional organ

---

[2]Undoubtedly a misquote, following Dean's Watergate "cancer on the presidency" speech.

in the integrated whole, now it is in effect a sort of self-created parasite.

It gets worse: tumors vesicularize, that is to say, they cause the development of new blood vessels which bring the tumor a massive blood supply diverted from the rest of the body—all to feed and cleanse its runaway growth. Water, says every politician from the governor on down, is the lifeblood of the West. (People who say that generally intend to do something horrible to the West's naturally flowing "lifeblood.") Western Colorado water flows east through pipes to feed the rampant growth on the Front Range. The Denver Water Board sells more and more water to developers who spread the suburbs wider and wider over the arid plain. Western Colorado dries up, and little pieces of it begin to die.

A tumor becomes necrotic when the inner center of its mass of misguided cells begin to die off. Anyone visiting the Denver inner city can scarcely argue (save for rhetorical purposes) that the city has not become necrotic. What else are those miles of broken down buildings inhabited by broken down humanity? What, indeed, are those miles of empty lots where bulldozers have leveled those same buildings and displaced their inhabitants if not the dead core of the city? And what are the incredibly high rates of violent crime and poverty, if not more signs of the same decaying process?

Typical view of urban South Platte River *(Fletcher Anderson)*

The poisonous by-products of the tumor's growth find their way into the bloodstream and do further damage—analyze the water of the South Platte and see that this is so. Analyze the air over Denver on a windless winter day, when air pollution can be worse than that of Los Angeles.

Finally, in its worst phase, the tumor becomes metastatic. Little balls of cells break off of the main tumor and drift through the lymphatic system to other sites in the body. There, they lodge and form the beginnings of new tumors. Is Interstate 25 the lymphatic system of Colorado, and are the other rampantly growing cities in the Front Range Urban Corridor invasive sites of cancerous Denver tissue? Or are they independent tumors in and of themselves? A human body, when its cancer has become metastatic, is well on its way toward death.

Colorado has metastatic cancer and no one knows how to cure it—not everyone wants to.

LOWER SOUTH PLATTE
The Urban South Platte

General Description

When it hits the plains at Chatfield Reservoir, the South Platte has dropped down to a 5,400-foot elevation. New Orleans is around 1,500 miles away. Thus, the drop for the remainder of the entire river is only about 3½ feet per mile—not the stuff of which whitewater is made. In its natural state, the river would have already begun losing water at this point. Chatfield Dam withdraws both irrigation and Denver area domestic water, adding to the river's natural diminution. The riverbanks seem to be the best area to locate junk yards, feed lots, interstate highways, oil refineries, railroad yards, and other equally attractive scenic wonders. Finally, the treated sewage of the metro Denver area empties directly into the river, as do all the municipal storm drains. The result is not a river at all, but rather just a component of the municipal sewer system—and the riverbed has been treated accordingly by generations of engineers who cemented over its banks and filled its channel with impassable hydraulic dissipation structures.

Nevertheless, over 90 percent of the kayakers in the Southwest live in the Denver area. Here was moving water close to their homes and some of them began paddling it. They publicized their

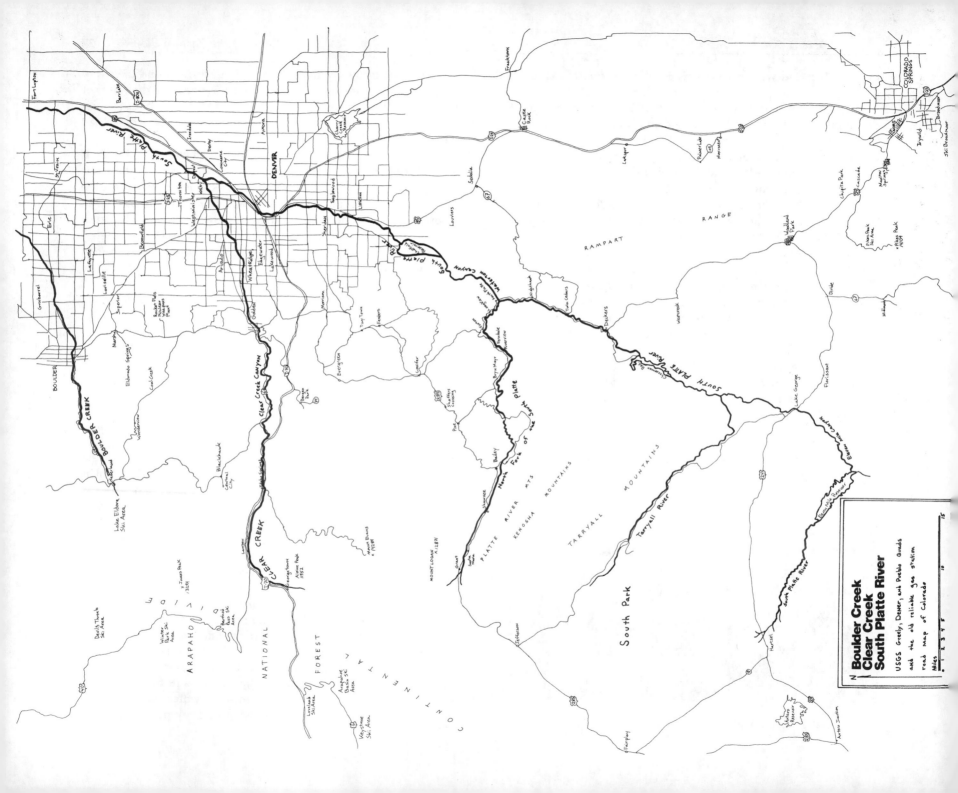

little urban river with an annual race called "The Sewer Slalom," and they lobbied with anyone who would listen to them for bikeways and green grass while they organized weekend river trash cleanup parties. The idea caught on, and today a well-funded South Platte Greenway Board is converting the entire river corridor into a city park. The South Platte is still something of a sewer, but it is also the focal point of the park. Denver architect Ron Mason served the Greenway in the capacity of river adviser for many years. More recently, U.S. Wildwater Team Member Gary Lacy, then of Wright-McLaughlin Water Engineers, went to work on the middle reaches of the parkway. Tom Steitz, a canoeist, has worked with the Corps of Engineers on the Littleton segment.

So the South Platte in Denver is well on its way toward becoming a pleasant and boatable (if evil smelling) piece of river.

The season for this river is year round, although in a bitter cold January or February, paddling will be limited to the area adjacent to the Public Service Company's Zuni Power Plant where cooling water from the steam turbines melts the ice.

Snowmelt-related spring flows (May, June) can be in the 1,200–3,500 cfs range—but Chatfield Dam reduces them to varying degrees. Except for the months of May and June, flows of 20 to 500 cfs are

typical and continue long after runoff as water is released to serve irrigators many miles downstream. After a big summer thunderstorm, inky black water will rush down the city storm drains and the flow can jump to over 4,000 cfs (!) for periods of a day or longer. Rain floods in 1969 and 1973 crested at 18,000 cfs, turning the rapids near the railroad yards into a veritable lava falls (Chatfield Dam promises that flows over 5,000 cfs will never occur again). "Head for high ground" warned local TV weatherman Bowman in June 1965 —and he was right: a rain flood of over 110,000 cfs roared through Denver, taking with it junk yards, buildings, bridges, and all else in its path. The waters receded and the kayakers put-in, much to the consternation of law officers and civil defense workers. Today, a hard-core of Denver office workers have their kayaks ready. When the rain floods hit, they call in sick and head for the river.

We recommend the following runs:

SOUTH PLATTE RIVER: Chatfield Dam to Hampden Avenue

Roughly 10 Miles, Class I, II (with artificial waterfall hazards); drops 11' per mile. Recommended for kayaks, rafts, and whitewater canoes.

This is the section of the river which the Corps of Engineers will improve. The suburb of Littleton has begun work on the largest of the parks which will line the river. The first stretch of river is vaguely (very vaguely) natural, but channelization begins in earnest at Columbine Golf Course, only 4½ miles into the run. From here on down, the run is less desirable. At least three unrunnable artificial dams block the river. Hampden Avenue is the end of the Corps of Engineers' area.

SOUTH PLATTE RIVER: Hampden Avenue to 8th Street Park

6.5 Miles, Class I, II; drops 12' per mile. Recommended for kayaks, rafts, and whitewater canoes.

At present, we cannot recommend running this section, but work is planned which will make it much more desirable. The river is closely paralleled by South Santa Fe Drive, Interstate 25, and the railroad. It is frequently banked by riprap and cement, and it has at least four artificial dam hazards which have not yet been improved. The worst of these was the Denver Wood Products Dam—a 7-foot sheer drop into an absolutely symmetrical keeper wave full of trap-

Lone wildwater paddler trains in evening after work. He has successfully negotiated the inflatable dam below Zuni Power Plant (*Fletcher Anderson*)

ped floating debris. There is a take-out on the right at a break in the cement retaining wall about 150 feet above the drop. A very high boat chute now bypasses the dam.

Yet as workers fixed that dam, the Corps of Engineers built the worst drowning machine on the river at Union Avenue. A six-foot-high structure with a gently sloping downstream face, the Union Avenue Dam looked runnable. In fact, a powerful backwash below the dam trapped anyone tricked into paddling over it. Two people died in the first summer and several others had close calls. That dam is also now being rendered safer for boating at a cost of $150,000. Civil engineer and N.O.R.S. president Gary Lacy argued vehemently before the dam was built that it would kill people, and that it could be built in a safer configuration for less money. Now he is designing the safety improvements.

SOUTH PLATTE RIVER: 8th Street Park to below 20th Street

3 Miles, Class II; drops 11' per mile. Recommended for kayaks, rafts, and whitewater canoes.

This is the section of river by which the bike paths, etc., are nearest

Artificial kayak chute made with an inflatable dam, below Zuni Power Plant (*Fletcher Anderson*)

completion. This is also the course of the annual "Uptown Downriver" races which mass start in the flat water near the footbridge in 8th Street Park. Though the flow at the footbridge may be marginal, the city of Lakewood Municipal Sewer outfall will increase it 100 yards downstream. The water is flat here because the Zuni Power Plant (½ mile downstream on Zuni Street) stops it with an inflatable fabric dam. A remarkable cement trough sits atop the fabridam on the left side, put there specifically so that boaters could run the dam! It works great, even for tippy wildwater boats and open canoes—but your stern will always smash at the bottom on the cement.

One and a half miles below the fabridam is Confluence Park where Cherry Creek joins the Platte. Cherry Creek, too, is becoming a parkway with bike paths, etc. A permanent slalom course was installed in 1977 over the Confluence Park cement boat bypass chute, but by 1985 boaters had to admit that they could not keep pace with the vandalism which plagued the facility. They removed the remaining debris and intend to rebuild at another site much farther upstream in another sort of neighborhood. You can take the neighborhood out of the river, but you can't take the river out of the neighborhood.

Local juvenile delinquents frequent the area and vandalize the slalom if no better target presents itself. Several of them once pushed a Safeway Savemobile shopping cart off one of the bridges, in an attempt to murder Gary Lacy and Fletcher Anderson. They missed. Usually, they throw rocks and beer cans full of sand or they urinate off the bridges. About a dozen boaters a year have their cars broken into at Confluence Park parking lot. Don't leave anything valuable in your car. The park is changing the nature of the neighborhood— but the change is not complete. The presence of large numbers of kayakers at Confluence Park seems to drive the delinquents away.

The bikeway ends at a landing dock below 20th Street, three excellent artificial rapids later.

URBAN SOUTH PLATTE RIVER: Below 20th Street

Many miles, Class I; drops 5' (?) per mile. Not recommended.

At present, don't bother. The sewer outflows and drainage from the Commerce City Oil Refineries make the water very unpleasant.

SOUTH PLATTE RIVER: Below Denver

Circa 180 Miles to the Nebraska line, Class I; drops 5' per mile. Recommended for kayaks, canoes—sandbars impede rafts.

The farther you get from Denver, the more chance the sewage has to dissipate. By Greeley, the flows of Clear Creek, Boulder Creek, St. Vrain, Big Thompson, and the Cache la Poudre rivers have joined the South Platte. Earl Perry, in *Rivers of Colorado*, describes a very pleasant flatwater run on the 100-mile stretch below Greeley.

Flows above the Cache la Poudre confluence are on the order of 400–3,500 cfs—often larger in winter than in summer due to dam-controlled irrigation releases. July through October flows can be marginal, but that is the season of rain floods, which can occasionally exceed 10,000 cfs and frequently add circa 2,000 cfs. The Cache la Poudre usualy adds at least half again the existing flows of the Platte. Many irrigation diversions remove the same amount. The river flows quietly beneath the cottonwood trees between fields of irrigated farmland.

The South Platte Narrows Dam, near Fort Morgan, is one of those remarkable irrigation projects which would bury more irrigated farmland than it would create. Jimmy Carter vetoed the bill to fund the dam in 1977. The dam's supporters have high hopes for Ronald Reagan, despite his claims of fiscal conservatism.

Though it is beyond the scope of this guide, there is outstanding flatwater canoeing along the Platte all through the state of Nebraska.

CLEAR CREEK

General Description

It is only a small river, but there are those who love it. Were it not for its proximity to the Front Range Urban Corridor, this river would probably have gone undiscovered. Indeed, generations of kayakers drove by it on U.S. 6 without thinking to stop and paddle.

Perhaps the first kayaking on Clear Creek was in the late 1950s when a few whitewater pioneers ran the stretch from Dumont to Idaho Springs. It was, in their view, small, difficult, and unrewarding —and they did not return.

After some abortive attempts in 1972 and 1973, the river was independently rediscovered in 1974 by Bill Clark, Ben Harding, and others from Boulder, Colorado, and by former English World Team Member, Ian Harvey, with former U.S. World Team Member, Fletcher Anderson; both parties paddling the canyon from Interstate 70 to Golden, Colorado. Were these the actual first runs of this section, or had someone else rediscovered the river as well? Word spread quickly and by 1978, Clear Creek Canyon could be considered one of the "standard" whitewater runs of Colorado. Motorists occasionally run off the road and drown, as do many tubers, giving the river a "killer" reputation. For a rafter, or for a novice kayaker, it could indeed be a killer. Expert kayakers have repeatedly demonstrated their ability to run Clear Creek safely, but they wisely exercise unusual caution when they do so. The Jefferson County, Colorado, sheriff closed all rivers in his county permanently to boating for safety reasons. Half of Clear Creek Canyon is thus closed. Kayakers ignore the closure and the sheriff is, as of this writing, issuing warnings, not citations.

CLEAR CREEK CANYON: I-70 to Golden, Colorado

13 Miles, Class III, IV, V, V+; drops 115' per mile. Recommended for kayaks.

The flow of this stream rarely, if ever, exceeds 1,000 cfs and is more often less than 500 cfs, even during a typical May–June high water season. The canyon is a steep V-shaped hole over 1,000 feet deep through the hard igneous and metamorphic rocks of the Pike's Peak and Idaho Springs formations. The construction of U.S. 6 and the earlier construction of a now defunct narrow gauge railroad have added many sharp boulders to the already boulder-choked creek bed. The result is a continuous, on-going rapid nearly 13 miles long. The boulders choking the rapid are frequently closely spaced and many chutes are only just wide enough to accommodate a kayak. These chutes are sometimes less than a boat's length above other smaller chutes, and they never seem to line up. To make things more complicated, a few of the little chutes have five-foot or so drop-offs into counter waves that go over your head. All good clean fun for an expert paddler, but an intermediate could easily not get lined up in time for one of these narrow slots. The results would be an instantly pinned or wrapped boat, possibly with the boater trapped inside. If you have the necessary threshold level of ability to make the run safely, you may join the little group of paddlers, some of whom regard this river as the ultimate whitewater experience in Colorado.

The Class III sections of the run are in the areas where U.S. 6 goes through tunnels and the river canyon loops off away from the road. The Class V and V+ sections are in the intermediate vicinity of highway bridges and tunnel entrances. It is thus advisable to stop and scout near all bridges, as the drops are frequently blind and the routes not obvious. Although all the drops have been run, one or another is portaged on most trips as their relative difficulties vary with water levels. At lower water, the river has less push, so the run is generally safer and easier, despite the increased number of rocks.

U.S. 6 provides easy access to the entire run and it is easy to scout the most difficult passages. A careful scouting and a realistic appraisal of your ability is imperative before attempting this run.

BOULDER CREEK

General Description

If you liked Clear Creek, you'll love Boulder Creek—for it is smaller, more constricted, and steeper. Many of the expert kayakers in Colorado live in the northern Denver suburb of Boulder, into which this creek flows. Were it not for that, it never would have been boated. Perhaps if Bill Clark's house were not located above the run and Ben Harding's below, even they would not have paddled here. Once they ran, many of their devotees followed. Surely Clark and Harding encourage others to make this run, because then they can sell more boat repair materials!

BOULDER CREEK: Sugarloaf Road to city limits

3 Miles, rocky Class IV, V; drops 200' per mile. Recommended for kayaks.

A tiny (always less than 500 cfs—typically less than 200 cfs—frequently run at less than 100 cfs) creek descends at incredibly high speed over sharp jagged rocks through a channel artificially narrowed by a defunct narrow gauge railroad bed and a modern two-lane highway. Eddies are few, and at times the river is less than one boat-length wide. The standard paddling technique was clearly inspired by watching the movements of the ball in a pinball machine.

BOULDER CREEK: in town

3 Miles, Class II; drops 20' per mile.

Within the Boulder city limits, Gary Lacy is directing an ambitious project which will make Boulder Creek the South Platte Greenway of Boulder—a park running the length of the city. The river improvements are substantially complete and a small Class II run reaches from Eben Fine Park to 28th Street.

BIG THOMPSON RIVER

General Description

If Boulder Creek is getting to be old stuff for you, you can follow Clark's and Harding's example and press on to the Big Thompson!

BIG THOMPSON RIVER: Estes Park to Loveland outskirts

15 Miles, Class ? (small, hard); drops 145' per mile. Recommended only for kayaks.

Only rarely is there enough water in the Big Thompson to float a kayak (during the Big Thompson Flood of 1977, several houses were washed away; otherwise, expect less than 100 cfs). When there is enough, Clark and Harding may be observed careening off the jagged boulders down the little riverbed like kayak bobsledders run amok.

SOUTH ST. VRAIN CREEK

General Description

If you liked—etc., you'll love St. Vrain Creek. Maybe one year in five, Clark and Harding find enough water to bang down the 260-foot-per-mile grade toward Lyons, Colorado. Oh Gawd, could they really be telling the truth? They claim 1978 was the last good year—and the first year they tried this and other marginal creeks of the Front Range. Quite a few other rivers will have to be dammed before many boaters head here.

(*Opposite*) Buena Vista nightlife scene: 2 Colorado Wildwater paddlers after the race (*Jack Burkholder*)

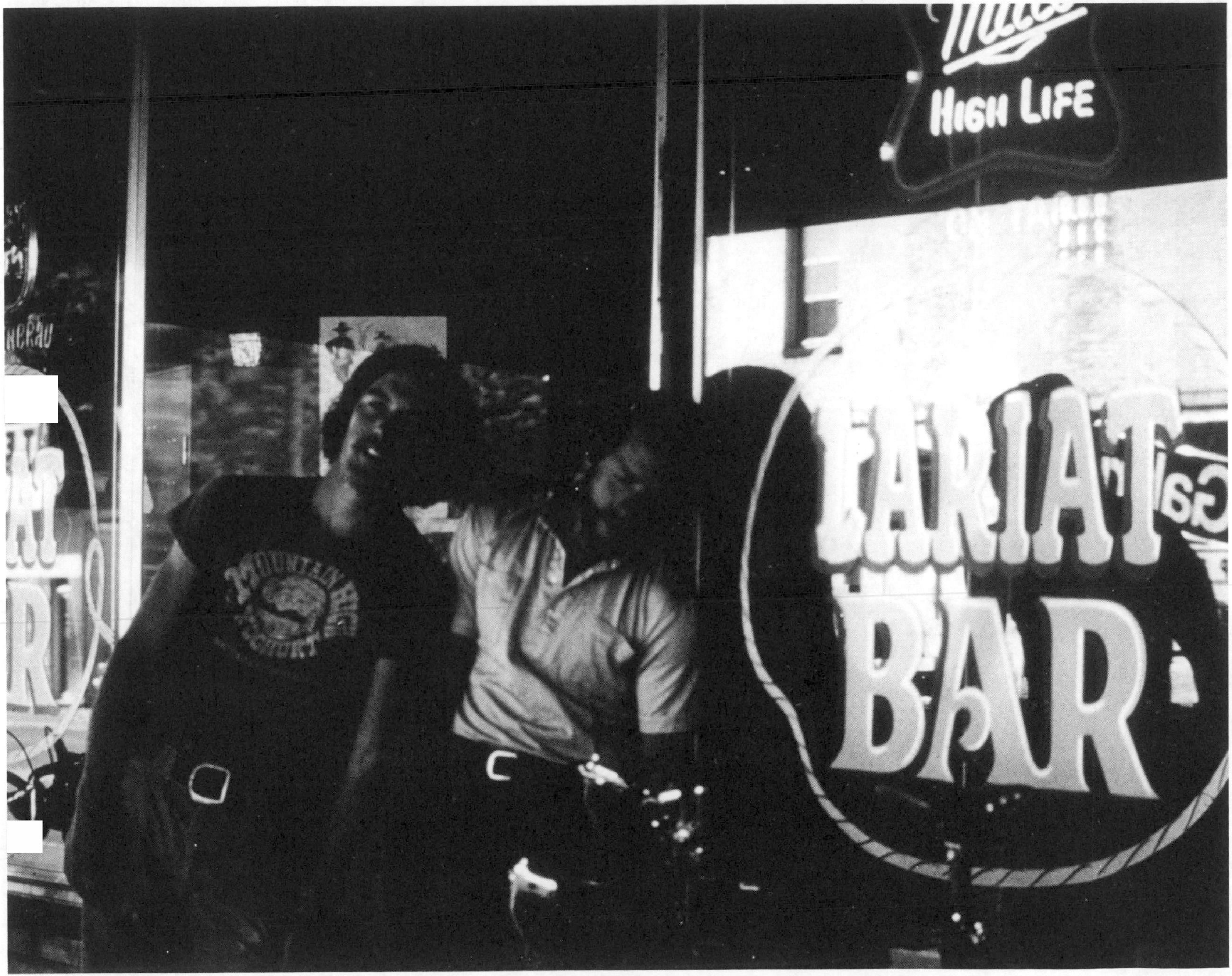
HIGH LIFE
LARIAT
BAR

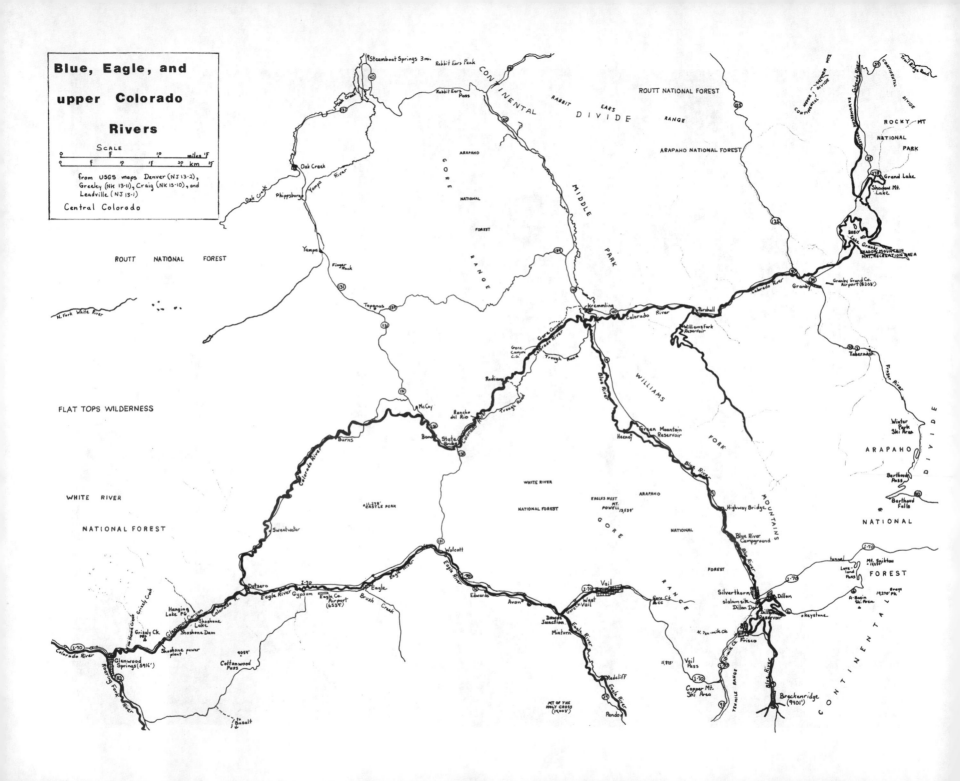

Blue, Eagle, and upper Colorado Rivers

Scale

from USGS maps Denver (NJ 13-2),
Greeley (NK 13-11), Craig (NK 13-10), and
Leadville (NJ 13-1)
Central Colorado

Chapter II

Upper Colorado River and Major Tributaries

Blue River

Eagle River

Byers Canyon

Middle Park

Gore Canyon

Easy Stretches of Upper Colorado River

Blue River

General Description

Two large portions of the Blue River have been transformed into two large reservoirs: Lake Dillon and Green Mt. Reservoir. In addition to restricting the river's natural runoff, Lake Dillon buries two river runs (on the Blue River and Ten Mile Creek) which were popular with foldboaters in the 1950s. One lively stretch remains, however, to give the "young ones" a taste of what it must have been like back in the days when rivers flowed free, when Colorado towns were real towns instead of gigantic complexes of second homes.

However, the Blue's season is very short—the first two weeks in July—due to the fact that much of the water gets shipped under the mountains to Denver. In exceptionally wet years the season is longer. In 1981, there was *no* season. It depends on when and for how long the water overflows the dam. But we had best begin at the beginning and start at the top.

The headwaters of the Blue River lie on and about Hoosier Pass above Breckenridge. The Blue between here and Dillon Reservoir is quite small and not normally run. Much of it has been deformed and defoliated by gold dredging.

BLUE RIVER: Lake Dillon Dam to Blue River Campground

9 Miles, Class I, II (uppermost first 100 yds. is Class III at high water); drops 22' per mile. Suitable for kayaks.

Below Dillon Dam, within feet of the outlet tunnel, a short artificial rapid was made in the fall of 1980 by the bulldozing of numerous large boulders. A permanent slalom course is in the works to be constructed here by summer 1981. This is very close and convenient to I-70 (exit at Silverthorne, Dillon). The course area is very short, Class II and III, depending on water level.

Thereafter, an 8-mile stretch of choppy, shallow Class I and II water is closely paralleled by Rt. 9, heading northwest out of Silverthorne and providing continuous access.

This is a clear mountain trout stream, a fairly even streambed dotted with riverine pebbles. Much of it is bordered by brush and trees and is quite scenic, but newly constructed low bridges must be portaged throughout the run.

BLUE RIVER: Blue River Campground to the next highway bridge

3 Miles, Class III+; drops 66' per mile. Suitable for kayaks.

At Blue River Campground the "lively little stretch" which was referred to earlier, begins. This is the section run in the annual Blue River Wildwater Race. The road travels above and away from the river for much of this windy stretch. There is one rapid, which can be sort of scouted from the road at its highest point. The rapid occurs where the Blue River enters a minicanyon. It has a blind approach from around a sharp bend and a bit of maneuvering is required.

This is a snappy little run at high water, with little or no chance of recovery if one swims (the swim is not likely to be deadly—just long and cold). There are no eddies and lots of overhanging trees and bushes. The water is ice cold. Many a brand new kayak was lost here in July 1979, an unusually high runoff year, when several intermediate-level boaters remembered this as a run they had handled adequately the year before at lower water.

The take-out is at the first highway bridge beyond Blue River Campground, about 3 miles down.

BLUE RIVER: Highway Bridge to Green Mt. Reservoir

9 Miles, Class I, II; drops 44' per mile. Suitable for kayaks, possible (but not recommended) for rafts and canoes.

From the bridge down to Green Mt. Reservoir, one encounters shallow chop. It is similar to the 8-mile stretch between Silverthorne and the campground, although slightly more remote, with slightly bigger waves. The access is not continuous. There are a couple more bridges before the reservoir on secondary roads.

BLUE RIVER: Green Mt. Reservoir to Kremmling (confluence with Colorado River)

13 Miles, Class III; drops almost 100' per mile first 4 miles, then 5' per mile. Suitable for kayaks, lower section suitable for rafts and canoes.

Blue River (at outlet from Lake Dillon Dam), slalom course in the artificial rapid (*Jack Burkholder*)

Below Green Mt. Dam the Blue River enters a small and picturesque canyon with Class III water. This is a 4-mile stretch without access by road or trail, and highly recommended for advanced intermediate paddlers.

As the canyon opens up, the road crosses the river from which point onwards it gears down to Class I and II water. The river flows through sparsely populated, sweeping ranchland, with the Gore Range and Williams Fork Mountains visible in the distance. The road roughly follows the river all the way to Kremmling, but not closely enough to provide continuous access.

EAGLE RIVER

Central Colorado

General Description

Maps: USGS "Leadville" Quad 1:250,000
White River National Forest Travel Map, U.S. Dept.
  of Agric.
Colorado Service Station Road Map

The Eagle River is a steeply-dropping, narrow river. Originating at an elevation of 10,300 feet on Tennessee Pass near Leadville, Colorado, it drops to an elevation of only 6,200 feet at its juncture with the Colorado River, some 60 miles downstream. In so doing, it passes through a variety of ecologic zones and a curious array of scenery. Yet much of that scenery is lost to paddlers—in part because much of the river is in a deep narrow gorge, and in part because its rapids demand constant action by the paddler. The river changes dramatically in character in various sections which range all the way from Class I to Class IV.

EAGLE RIVER: Camp Hale to Minturn

12 Miles, 1,400 vertical feet (117' per mile) continuous Class IV, V with some VI. Suitable for kayaks.

Camp Hale is the large meadow 5 miles below the summit of Tennessee Pass. This is the site of the camp in which the ski troops of the 10th Mountaineering Division of the U.S. Army trained in World War II. Many of these skiers returned after the war and were the pioneers of that sport in Colorado. It is worth noting that some of them were also the first to introduce the kayak here as well; one of those individuals being Keith Anderson—father of one of the authors of this book.

This section of river has never been run in its entirety and could thus be described as the last significant first run in Colorado. Minturn kayaker, Lloyd Yandle, made repeated forays into the bottom end of the gorge in the 1970s but was always stopped by logjams. Someone will eventually make it, and for that reason it is included here.

The Eagle River flows slowly through the Camp Hale Meadow, having a flow of far, far less than 1,000 cfs at even the peak of its spring runoff. At the end of the meadow, it leaves Highway 24 and drops quickly into a dark and narrow gorge, in which it forms an almost continuous rapid extending all the way to Minturn, save for a brief respite in the vicinity of the town of Redcliff. The worst part of this run is probably the 4 miles below Redcliff where the gradient and flow both increase. The river has not been run primarily because everyone scouting it encounters numerous logjams which could prove fatal to anyone paddling near them. The first run of this stretch, if it occurs, will have to follow a spring flood, which is unusually proficient at clearing out these logs.

EAGLE RIVER: Minturn to Dowd Junction, Colorado

2 Miles, Class I and II. Suitable for kayaks.

Dowd Junction is the point at which Gore Creek and Interstate 70 join the Eagle River. This 2-mile stretch is Class II water, flowing through the railroad yards. Don't be tricked into running it, because you are just above the infamous Dowd Junction Chute.

EAGLE RIVER: The Dowd Junction Chute

½ Mile, Class IV, V; drops 250' per mile. Suitable for kayaks.

The Dowd Junction Chute is the rapids formed by the pinching off of the river channel between the railroad embankment on the right and the Minturn exit cloverleaf of I-70 on the left. In early spring and late summer, this is a nice Class IV rapid, but in May and June, with 2,000 cfs or more of water, it is a serious Class V. Numerous boats have been lost here, and a couple of inner-tubers have lost their lives. The rapid becomes a series of bank-to-bank holes, some of which are keepers, many of which produce accidental back endos. The rapid is about ¼ mile long, and a swim usually uses up the whole ¼ mile because the current is too fast for a swimmer to grab bushes on the shore or even stand up in the less than 2-foot-deep water near the bank. People who swim this rapid at high water often need a few stiches in their legs, and sometimes have broken bones. The nearest medical services are in Vail, 5 miles east on Interstate 70. It is imperative that a swimmer in this rapid get out of the water as soon as possible because a logjam usually develops on the lefthand abutment of the railroad bridge a couple of hundred yards below the rapid. Lost paddles can usually be recovered in this jam.

EAGLE RIVER: Below Dowd Junction to Avon, Colorado

5 Miles, Class III, IV; drops 60' per miles. Suitable for kayaks.

The river has left the aspen and coniferous forests of the higher mountains and is in a region of piñon-juniper woodland and sagebrush flats. Cottonwood and occasional boxelder trees line the river bottom. Although this is the very heart of the Vail strip development, the wall-to-wall condominiums are mostly out of sight from the river. Interstate 70 is in the valley, but away from the river. The old highway is still in use as a frontage road and provides access to the entire river from here to Gypsum, Colorado.

This run is extremely popular with Vail paddlers, particularly when the Dowd Junction Chute is unrunnable, but they are few in number and the river is never crowded.

EAGLE RIVER: Avon to 2 miles below Edwards

6 Miles of meandering rocky Class I, II, with easy access via the frontage road, drops less than 40' per mile. Suitable for kayaks, possible in small rafts, and some canoes.

Edwards is, at present anyway, the western end of the Vail strip development. In these sprawling trailer parks, dwell the people who work in the domestic service and restaurant industries serving the hotel and condominium dwellers at the eastern end of the strip, as far as 20 miles away. Is Vail what Pablo Solari had in mind when he conceived of the linear city?

EAGLE RIVER: Edwards to 5 miles above Eagle

15 Miles, Class II, some III. Suitable for kayaks.

Here the valley narrows and the drop increases slightly, producing several Class II and possible III rock garden rapids in the first 7-mile stretch.

EAGLE RIVER: 5 miles above Eagle to confluence with the Colorado River

20 Miles, meandering Class I, some II; drops less than 20' per mile. Suitable for kayaks, small rafts, and canoes.

The valley widens out dramatically to form broad open fields. Drop is only about 20 feet per mile, and because of that, the river meanders widely in some places. This is a pleasant stretch of river but is almost never boated—perhaps because it is so near some more dramatic stretches of the Colorado River. Flows from the Eagle River seldom exceed 3,000 cfs, but the high water season is generally long—typically mid-May to mid-July.

GORE CREEK: Gerald E. Ford golf course to Dowd Junction

4 Miles, Class III, IV; drops 90' per mile. Suitable for kayaks.

Gore Creek is the tributary of the Eagle River which flows through the upper half of the "Vail Strip." Gerald E. Ford was an obscure conservative congressman from the Midwest who became America's only unelected president in the mid-1970s. Ford rented condominiums on the Vail strip, and one of the local golf courses is named after him. This is a popular 5-mile evening run for Vail residents. Although it drops a whopping 90 feet per mile in the lower half of the run, it is mostly Class III with some IV, because flows seldom exceed 300 cfs. Beware of logs and a couple of barbwire fences. Also, scout before running to determine if a huge strainer—a deer fence—still blocks the river near the end of the run, just past the West Vail exit.

BYERS CANYON

COLORADO RIVER: 3 miles below Granby to 2 miles below Hot Sulfur Springs

8½ Miles, Class IV; drops 25' per miles. Suitable for kayaks.

(The authors have not made this run and base this description on secondhand information.)

Byers Canyon is probably the highest whitewater in the Colorado River, save for a mile or so at the Lake Granby outlet.

An already narrow canyon is further narrowed by the construction of the Denver and Rio Grande Western Railroad and U.S. Highway 40. The blasting associated with the construction of these two arteries filled the river with boulders having unusually fresh, sharp, jagged edges. Thus, although the rapids are not particularly difficult, the wear and tear on boats (and swimmer's shins) is unusually high. Although U.S. Highway 40 closely parallels the river, access is *not* easy except at the beginning and end of the run. Access at other points involves climbing long, steep, jagged, unstable talus slopes.

Flows in Byers Canyon might reach 5,000 cfs in May and June and drop to around 300 cfs in September or October (much of the Colorado's water comes in from the Middle Park drainage around Kremmling). At high flows, the river is characterized by holes and waves; at low flows, by boulder gardens linked by little chutes.

Byers Canyon is an enjoyable, but not a popular run—perhaps because of its sharp rocks, its access, or its relative remoteness from the interstate highways. It has long been predicted that when crowding on the Cache la Poudre and in Glenwood Canyon make those runs less desirable, boaters will move to Byers Canyon. As of this writing, that move has still not taken place, but it seems more imminent now than ever. In the meantime, here is perhaps the only neglected whitewater run in the Central Rockies.

MIDDLE PARK

KREMMLING AREA: In Middle Park

The Colorado here flows peacefully through private ranchland. However, you as a floater, are highly unlikely to do the same. A great deal of hostility exists toward boaters in this area, so don't try paddling around here unless you have *specific* permission from the landowner(s).

Instead, as you drive by in your car, admiring the scenic ranchland, you can regard the area as a historical landmark, for it was in the area east of Kremmling that the suit was spawned which resulted in a Colorado Supreme Court case and the 1979 Emmert Decision (see Introduction).

GORE CANYON

General Description

Lord Gore was an English aristocrat who toured the West on a hunting expedition in the previous century. One of his camps was west of the modern town of Kremmling in the mountains which now bear his name.

The 11,000-foot Gore Range Mountains lie directly in the path of the Colorado River, and it does not go around them or exit into the North Platte via North Park. Instead, it cuts directly through the range without the least hint of a turn through a very narrow V-shaped gap, 3,000-feet deep, called Gore Canyon. The river meanders widely over the flats in Middle Park near Kremmling, because the Gore Range has dammed it up. Gore Canyon is the spillway.

Whitewater boaters have always known Gore Canyon was there, but only in the past decade have very many of them boated it. The reason is simple enough: Gore Canyon is the most difficult paddleable whitewater in the Colorado River. Although the canyon run is only 4 miles long, it drops 400 feet in elevation. Two hundred feet of that drop occurs in the third mile of the run alone.

In an era when railroad travel was still the normal way to get around, many of us would stare from the windows of the Denver Zephyr into the shady depths of the canyon and marvel at terrifyingly constricted little rapids far below us, and wonder about the scale. Was this canyon actually runnable? One man who did not wonder about such things was Walter Kirschbaum. It was his goal to paddle all the whitewater stretches of the Colorado River and its major tributaries. By 1962, only Gore Canyon and the upper Roaring Fork remained. Gore Canyon, he knew from scouting, would prove to be the most demanding run of all. Accordingly, he built a special boat strictly for that run. Taking as his starting point the high volume slalom design he had used for Cross Mountain Canyon, he constructed a boat with double the normal amount of fiberglass in the hull. Thus equipped, he anxiously awaited the low water of late fall that he knew was necessary for a successful attempt. By late October, the time had come.

Four years earlier, Kirschbaum had been the world's slalom champion. Then he had given up racing and applied himself to the exploration of wilderness rivers. Perhaps in 1962 no one else in the world was equally qualified to make the run—certainly no one else

in Colorado was—and in 1962 Gore Canyon represented the outer limits of possibility in whitewater boating. Kirschbaum would have to make the run alone.

In retrospect, it seems impossible that he could have done it all in his tiny canvas-decked boat—yet if you knew the man and had seen him paddle under pressure, you know how he could have succeeded. Three miles into the canyon is a treacherous little passage through a Class V+ rapid with a 90° right turn leading into a 7-foot waterfall. Kirschbaum's boat hit bottom hard, smashing its bow. He stuffed the end of the boat full of tangled root of driftwood to keep its shape and taped his paddling jacket over the nose to keep out the water. Now he could not afford any more bow hits in the 2 miles of whitewater which remained—and somehow, he made the rest of the run clean. He camped on a little beach near the town of Radium, silently expressing his genuinely religious feelings for the river and its canyons.

Roger Paris duplicated Kirschbaum's solo run in 1969. It was 3 years later before the next boaters attempted Gore Canyon. In October of 1972, Bill Clark, Tom Ruwitch, Ron Mason, and Filip Sokol entered the narrow canyon in the first of the recently developed vacuum-bagged S-glass epoxy kayaks. Here at least were boats strong enough to withstand the stress of such a run. To make a short account of an epic adventure, they actually found the experience enjoyable—but they made five portages.

If they made it, we certainly can, reasoned Fletcher Anderson and Lloyd Yandle in 1973—but Anderson and Yandle had not heard the details of the preceding party's run and they approached the canyon in July, when 10,000 cfs of water were cascading down the same gorge which everyone else had run in October at less than 700 cfs. With them was Ann Hopkinson, who had at that point been paddling less than one year. Here were all the makings of a disaster. Scarcely a mile into the canyon, it was obvious to all that this was a far more difficult undertaking than anyone had realized.

Below a sharp drop, both men were flipped over backwards and rolled up. Hopkinson, above, saw this and headed for another chute on the right side. Then occurred the most horrifying series of events in all their lives. There was no right-hand chute. In the boil, below a rock the size of a house, appeared Ann's paddle and one tennis shoe. An agonizing minute later, her gashed and deformed boat followed—but still no Ann. A sickening feeling tore at their guts, as though they were dying with her. Clearly, the force of the current which mangled her boat had pinned her under the rock. She was wedged tight in the pounding current and darkness where no one could reach her, unable to break free. In the ensuing seconds all three of their lives drained away.

And then, miraculously, she broke the surface of the water far below the rock, woozy and lifeless, her face a mask of blood. She clung to the bow of Anderson's boat, which was ready and waiting for her rescue, and he ferried her frightened body to shore. A piece of one of her teeth was gone. A hole in her cheek cut clear through into the inside of her mouth.

Clearly, Ann could not continue. With a decision notable to this day, both for its lack of gallantry and lack of sound judgement, Anderson and Yandle decided to complete the run. Ann Hopkinson headed for Kremmling to get her face sewn up and her broken teeth repaired.

Below, waited a thundering gorge of whitewater that few kayakers have ever seen. Extensive scouting would reveal only the most marginally possible routes through the rapids. Both boaters attempted to stay together in vague compliance with normal safety practices, but rescue would have been impossible anyway. Anderson turned over backward at least five times before he lost count. Yandle, in the lead, tumbled over and over in ways he could not describe. Yet, for both, it was one of those instances when you discover hidden abilities you did not know existed and perhaps could not call upon again. Somehow they always rolled up, somehow they missed the worst obstacles, and somehow their braces always managed to drag them out of the pounding holes—and well they did, for otherwise this tale could not be told. They made two short portages. They intended a third but missed the eddy.

Finally, in deepening shadows of evening, they emerged from the last of the rapids. An hour later, they were paddling shattered, sinking boats with their last reserves of strength, toward the flickering light of a campfire in the gloomy darkness.

And by the fire was Ann Hopkinson, wondering if they had died, like she had so nearly done, in the dark shadows of Gore Canyon. Ah, foolhardy youth forever lost—for in the canyon they had all three aged many years. Never again would the lure of the unknown and the unrunnable exert such a pull on their souls.

Gore Canyon has never again been attempted at high water, but a new generation will surely someday expand their own outer limits of boating to meet still greater challenges.

COLORADO RIVER: Gore Canyon entrance to Gore Canyon Campground

6 Miles (the last 1½ are flat), Class IV, V, VI; drops 100–200' per mile. Recommended for kayaks.

This very short, steep run at low water is not the horror that one would encounter there in June. By late August—certainly by September or October—the flows are near or below 1,000 cfs. At that point, the run is a very enjoyable one for *expert* boaters and growing numbers of them attempt it. Certainly no one else should attempt it at any water level, for a swim in such a river would be exceedingly dangerous.

The steep drop has already been alluded to. Very large boulders have fallen from the cliffs and choke the river. Apparently, any rock smaller than a Volkswagon gets swept away during high water, so the low water river is a series of narrow chutes between the remaining larger rocks. Abrupt blind drops of 5 feet or greater height are common, and considerable scouting is necessary. At high water, the entire canyon is an amorphous violent mass of changing whitewater. Huge, but almost invisible holes are everywhere. The run has been made without portage *only twice* since Kirschbaum's 1962 run; by the late Walt Blackadar in 1976, and by "Macho" Matt Gaines in 1981. The portages, though short, are made over a jumble of talus and can be time-consuming. Thus, though the run is short in miles, it generally takes a very long day to complete. Plan accordingly. One of the Idaho hero hair boaters recently claimed to have run the canyon with only one portage. It later developed that his single giant portage encompassed several separate little portages the locals make.

Ill-informed rafters have twice attempted this run. Both attempts failed dramatically in the first mile. As always, we repeat our assertion that a raft should not run a Class IV or better mountain river.

Access: A dirt road leaving U.S. 40 just west of Kremmling, goes directly to the put-in. The road to State Bridge leaves Colorado 9 2 miles south of Kremmling. The Gore Canyon Campground is reached on the first side road heading toward the river, about 9 miles from Colorado 9.

EASY STRETCHES OF UPPER COLORADO RIVER
(includes Radium, State Bridge, Rodeo Rapid)

62 Miles, Class I, II; drops 17' per mile.

Access: Lower Gore Campground, Radium Bridge, Rancho del Rio Bridge, State Bridge, from McCoy to confluence (of Colorado River and Eagle River) nearly continuous access, Dotsero to Shoshone Dam—along I-70.

This entire stretch of the Colorado River from below Gore Canyon to the Shoshone Hydroelectric Diversion Dam in Glenwood Canyon (just below Hanging Lake parking lot on I-70) is Class I–II, and can provide pleasant one-half day, one day, or overnight trips if you do not object to stretches of very flat water. Deer, eagles, and herons are not uncommon.

Lower Gore Campground is reached from the Trough Road (which runs from Rt. 9, 2 miles south of Kremmling to State Bridge, where it joins Rt. 131). This is a winding, dirt and gravel road part of the way, high above the famed hair run Gore Canyon. The road has some incredible open exposure and views to the valley bottom (one of the views includes that of a car which rolled off the edge and presently lies about 1,500 below, giving the viewers a better sense of perspective). The lower Gore Campground road is the first dirt road heading down toward the river (north) after the Colorado River emerges from the very narrow Gore Canyon (which can be seen from the Trough Road).

There are a few Class II rapids and several very flat stretches between here and Radium. The scenery is peaceful green ranchland, a few cliffs flank the river; the road is never seen.

The run has become a popular commercial trip since the rafting boom hit in 1973.

When you pass below a small wooden bridge (the first so far), you are in and almost by Radium, another access point.

A stretch of flat, nearly motionless water ensues, with very green, grassy banks, occasional cattle, and some rolling hills. These first 2 miles are called "the Red Gorge of the Colorado," presumably commemorating the iron in the soil, the native Americans of bygone times, or Communist agitators of the 1960s. The river narrows at one point, with an ominous-looking cliff on the left which helps to create a full-on Class II rapid. Several Class II rapids are to be found throughout this stretch, although on the whole, the current moves fairly slowly.

Rancho del Rio is on river left, just above a bridge 3 miles upstream from State Bridge. It is here that the road rejoins the river, but in most parts it is high above the river and therefore not obtrusive. This area is heavily populated with deer in winter and early spring. Piney Creek, ¼ mile upstream from State Bridge, runs in from the left (south-southeast) and provides a nice place to hike, as well as good fishing (sometimes). This stretch of the Colorado is still Class II but has more rocks, waves, and maneuvering than the upper stretches. It is an excellent run for beginner kayakers because it provides eddies, waves, and good rescue possibilities. However, many an open aluminum canoe, manned by people new to the sport, has been wrapped and ruined in this innocuous little stretch. More than 30 commercial raft companies run day trips from Rancho del Rio Bridge and above to State Bridge, Bond, or McCoy. These runs are all boatable throughout the summer, most years, but they are pretty flat by mid-August.

Below Bond, the road almost continuously follows the river, as does the railroad. However, it is a secondary dirt road with little traffic. In high water, there are numerous little drops with delightful waves, but by very late summer it becomes more of a rock garden than a river. Rodeo Rapids, Class III, just below Burns, was formed by a 1980 landslide. It has very sharp rocks. It is easy to scout from the road. The boating and scenery on this stretch are equal to that in the State Bridge area, but it is a longer drive from Steamboat Springs and Vail, so commerical rafting is less prevalent.

At Dotsero, I-70 becomes part of the immediate scenery. The river takes on more of a bottomland quality; its banks and bed are comprised entirely of mud and clay, the water is almost dead calm. Five miles below Dotsero, the river enters Glenwood Canyon.

In the canyon section, before the Shoshone Reservoir, two easy Class II rapids will be found—named Upper Paiute Falls and Lower Paiute Falls. At certain water levels (very low) they have nifty, very smooth surfing waves.

And finally, before we get to the Shoshone Dam, you can't find a much more scenic spot for flatwater paddling than the lake in Glenwood Canyon. The effectuation of plans to build a four-lane interstate through the canyon will undoubtedly detract severely from that experience.

The lake is narrow and has a bit of current, so it is not unbearable drudgery to row down its length for even the slowest of rafts.

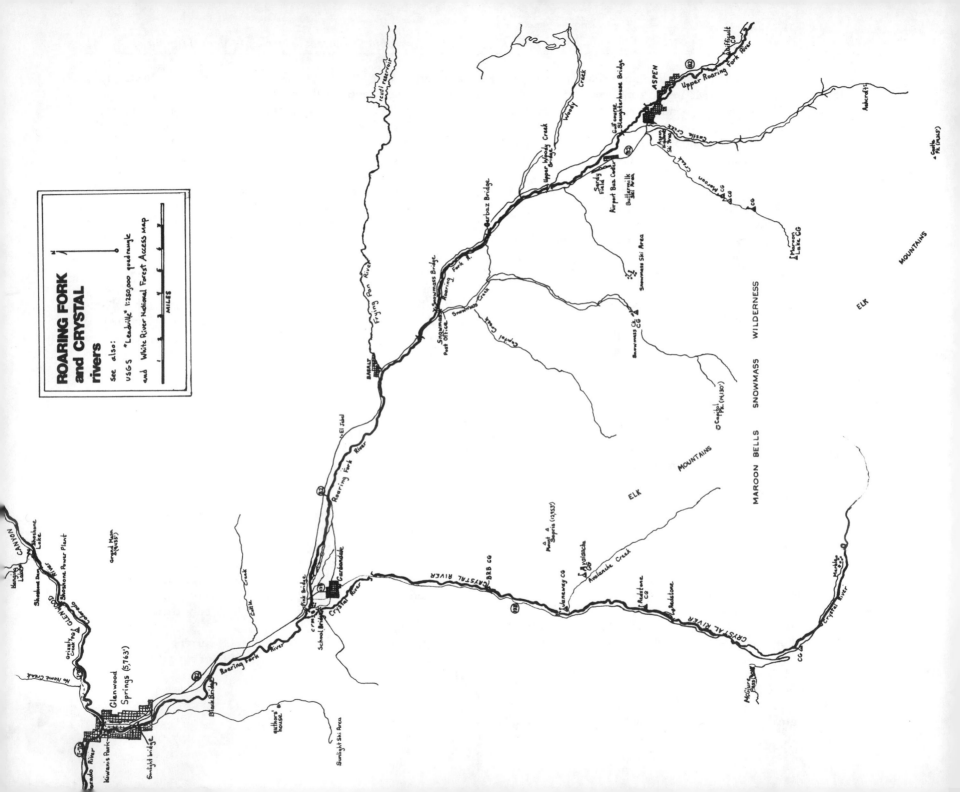

ROARING FORK
and CRYSTAL
rivers

See also:

USGS "Leadville" 1:250,000 quadrangle
and White River National Forest Access Map

MILES

CANYON

Hanging Lake
Shoshone Dam
Shoshone Lake
Shoshone Power Plant

Grizzly No. 2 Creek
GLENWOOD Creek
Colorado

No Name Creek

Colorado River

Kiwani's Park

Glenwood Springs (5,763')

Sunlight bridge

Grand Man 2 (9,455')

Cattle Creek

author's house

Sunlight Ski Area

Roaring Fork River

Black Bridge

School Bridge

Pink Bridge

Carbondale

Roaring Fork River

El field

Frying Pan River

reudi reservoir

BASALT

Snowmass Bridge

Snowmass Post Office

Snowmass Creek

Roaring Fork R.

Garbuz Bridge

Upper Woody Creek Bridge

Woody Creek

Sandy Field

Airport Bus Center

Golf course Slaughterhouse Bridge

ASPEN

Upper Roaring Fork River

Difficult CG

Castle Creek

Aspen Ski Area

Buttermilk Ski Area

Snowmass Ski Area

CG
CG
CG

Maroon CG

Castle Pk (14,265')

Ashcroft

Maroon Lake CG

ELK MOUNTAINS

Snowmass CG CG

Crystal Creek

Capitol Pk (14,130')

MAROON BELLS SNOWMASS WILDERNESS

ELK MOUNTAINS

ELK MOUNTAINS

Mount Sopris (12,953')

Avalanche Creek

Avalanche CG

CRYSTAL RIVER

BRB CG

Janeway CG

Redstone CG

Redstone

CRYSTAL RIVER

CG

Crystal River

CG

McClure Pass (8,755')

Chapter III

Middle Colorado River and Major Tributaries

Roaring Fork River
Fryingpan River
Glenwood Canyon
Upper Grand Valley
Ruby and Horsethief Canyons
Westwater Canyon
Professor Valley
Taylor River
Gunnison River
Uncompahgre River
Dolores River

Roaring Fork River

General Description

Maps: USGS "Leadville" 1:250,000 Topo
      White River National Forest Visitor's Map
      Colorado Service Station Road Map

The Roaring Fork River is a heavily kayaked and rafted river. The heavy use it receives testifies both to its outstanding quality and its proximity to the Aspen resort community.

Originating on 12,000-foot Independence Pass, it drops 6,300 feet in 60 miles to join the Colorado River in Glenwood Springs. Water flows in the town of Aspen range from a maximum of around 2,000 cfs in May or June, to unboatable lows by the end of August. By the time the river reaches Glenwood Springs, it can sometimes transport 6,000 cfs or more and would be boatable year round were it not sometimes subject to freezing over in the winter.

Despite its location, near the very heart of the Rocky Mountains, the lower end of the Roaring Fork Valley is fairly low in elevation and experiences fairly mild weather, making it a popular early season kayaking area.

Land of the Lotus Eaters

The resort community of Aspen is a tourist attraction of considerable interest to visiting boaters.

Nineteen eighty statistics reveal that Aspen leads the rest of Colorado in several ways:

It has the highest sales of fur coats and Vuarnet Mirror sunglasses.

It has the highest per capita rates of cocaine and heroin use.

It has the third highest "driving under influence" rate.

It has the highest per capita sales of Hollowform Kayaks, but so few expert kayakers that it is easier to list their names than count them. A new kayak is more chic than a Gucci handbag, but actually paddling it is not mellow.

It has over 100,000 beds—but fewer than 2,000 year-round residents.

Is it the westernmost suburb of New York or the easternmost suburb of Los Angeles? Either way, it is an island of chic in the tacky old Colorado mountains.

The rest of the region pronounces "Aspen" as "has-been" or "ass-pain" and refers to its residents as "Aspen holes."

The "Aspen holes" refer to the rest of the world as "down valley" and call its residents "dirt bags."

The "Aspen holes" have the last word: Aspen has the region's highest per capita income *and* lowest employment rate (lots of trust funds!).

Decadence: a way of life.

The Aspen kayakers are a peculiar group, but friendly and outgoing (the best ones anyway). Go paddling with them, visit Aspen, and see how the other half lives!

ROARING FORK RIVER: Aspen Slaughterhouse Bridge to upper Woody Creek Bridge

6 Miles, 80' per mile drop; long stretches of nearly continuous constricted Class IV with some V at high water; one 6' waterfall; locally known as "Slaughterhouse Run." Suitable for kayaks.

Slaughterhouse Bridge is located at the west end of the town of Aspen proper, just below Castle Creek. A foot trail follows the old railroad grade along the upper part of the run. Study the rapids in

Roaring Fork River, Slaughterhouse Run provides an enjoyable afternoon for Brian Fitzpatrick (*Jack Burkholder*)

the first mile or two to determine whether or not to attempt the run. Should you decide to paddle, keep an eye out for the waterfall about a mile from the put-in. The falls can be run on the extreme river left but are scouted or portaged from the right. The falls were first run in 1964 by Walter Kirschbaum and Fletcher Anderson. The waterfall tends to break boats and so is usually portaged. The rapids are not absolutely continuous on this run but are close enough together so that a reliable Eskimo roll is essential for a safe run. The entire run is too constricted, and some of the maneuvers are far too intricate for rafts.

Halfway through the run is an abandoned railroad bridge. This is the site of the Snowmass Slalom Race. A short trail leads from here to the Aspen Airport business center. If you had trouble above, you can carry out here instead of paddling the remaining 3 miles, which are a little more difficult.

ROARING FORK RIVER: Upper Woody Creek Bridge to lower Woody Creek (Gerbaz) Bridge

4 Miles, Class II, III; dropping about 50' per mile. Suitable for kayaks. (Only Class II to III very shallow, choppy water because it is largely unobstructed.)

Despite its Class III rating, novices should avoid this stretch of river because the flow is extremely fast and the banks are overhung with brush.

ROARING FORK RIVER: Lower Woody Creek (Gerbaz) Bridge to Basalt, Colorado

Locally known as "Woody Creek Run"—8 Miles, Class II, III; drops 33' per mile. Suitable for kayaks and rafts.

After a couple of miles of fast, shallow, choppy Class II water, the river enters Woody Creek Canyon. Here are found a series of Class III rapids with big, well-formed waves which attract both commercial rafters and endo-happy kayakers. The longest of these is called "Toothache." This is the course of the annual Woody Creek Wildwater Race, which finishes at the Snowmass Bridge, a run of 6 miles. One and a half miles further on, Highway 82 crosses the river. Two more excellent play spots occur in between. From there it is two more miles, and two more short rapids with excellent surfing waves, to Basalt.

Fred Davies runs Slaughterhouse Falls, Roaring Fork River (*Jack Burkholder*)

ROARING FORK RIVER: Basalt to Carbondale, Colorado

11 Miles, Class I, II; drops circa 40' per mile. Suitable for kayaks and rafts.

Extremely fast-moving, gravel-bottomed, braided stream channels with a great deal of brush overhanging the banks. This run is of little interest to most boaters because of the more attractive stretches of river adjacent to it.

ROARING FORK RIVER: Carbondale to Black Bridge

Locally known as "Pink to Black" (after the bridge's colors) or "Whitehouse Run" (after a house now painted brown). 6 Miles, Class I, II; drops about 30' per mile. Suitable for kayaks and rafts; possible for some canoes.

The Colorado Rocky Mountain School, where world-champion paddler Roger Paris taught kayaking for 10 years, is located just west of Carbondale proper on the grounds between the Crystal and Roaring Fork rivers. The best put-ins are on the secondary roads which go past the school to bridges on either river. The Roaring Fork Bridge is preferable at low water. The rapids on this stretch are fairly harmless, and provide an excellent first whitewater run

for beginning boaters. The Colorado Rocky Mountain School, the Roger Paris Kayak School, and the Aspen Kayak School all use this run, as do several commercial raft companies from the Aspen area; however, the current is swift and there is little crowding. Looking upstream, the isolated and usually snow-covered peak you see is 12,953-foot Mount Sopris—perhaps the most beautiful peak in Colorado, especially as viewed from the river.

The Black Bridge (the first bridge you come to) is the take-out. This bridge is also called "the steel bridge" and is reached from the old highway—check your odometer on the shuttle and it will be easy to find.

ROARING FORK RIVER: Black Bridge to Glenwood Springs

Locally known as "Cemetery Run"—5½ Miles, Class I, II, III— (III for high water); drops about 50' per mile. Suitable for kayaks and rafts.

The first three miles of this run are more of the same conditions encountered in the preceding run. Then comes a series of wide-open, unobstructed Class II (and Class III at high water) drops with big rolling waves (at least at high water). The last of these is "Cemetery" rapids, about 300 yards long, practically within the town of Glenwood Springs. It was named after the cemetery on the bluff to the right. This run first gained popularity when foldboaters began paddling it in the early 1950s. It is still popular today, and understandably so. The easiest take-out is at Kiwanis Park in Glenwood, well below the second of the high bridges, on the left bank.

Slaughterhouse Falls on Roaring Fork River. Brian Fitzpatrick takes the "hair" route by running it on the right side (*Jack Burkholder*)

FRYINGPAN RIVER

This extremely attractive mountain river acquired a massive dam in 1966 which cut out most of the paddleable water. Now, over twenty years later, a small hydroelectric generator is finally being installed at the outlet and people are still wondering what to do with all the water they impound. Two river runs remain, above and below Ruedi Reservoir. The reservoir itself is Aspen's answer to Maui—a mecca for yachtsmen, windsurfers, and the odd flatwater kayaker.

UPPER FRYINGPAN RIVER: (above Ruedi Reservoir)

4.5 Miles, Class V except at very low water; drops 110' per mile. Kayaks only.

Four and a half miles above the reservoir is a small concrete dam right next to the road from which you can put in. Except in the month of June there is rarely enough water to float a boat. At flows over about 500 cfs it is wise for most people to stay away. Beware of log jams and numerous unmarked lethal barbed wire fences. Other than that, this is an outstanding run for very expert kayakers who favor very tiny steep-dropping rivers. Because this is a very continuous gradient, severe whitewater run, it is necessary to scout extensively on the drive up the river to the put in.

Crystal River slalom below the CRMS bridge. Roger Paris paddles to victory in 1968 slalom (*Nat Fleck*)

LOWER FRYINGPAN RIVER: (below Ruedi Reservoir)

Dam outlet to Taylor Creek.
7 Miles, some extremely fast-moving Class II-III, some flatwater; drops 50' per mile. Kayakable, but not recommended.

This stretch of water is very popular with fly fishermen, and landowners have put up many barbed wire fences across the river to keep them out. Kayakers encounter too many of these fences to make for an enjoyable run.

LOWER FRYINGPAN RIVER: Taylor Creek to Basalt, Colorado

5 Miles, Class IV; drops 80' per mile. Suitable for kayaks.

When, indeed if, you can boat this stretch of river depends entirely on the amount of water being released by Reudi Reservoir dam. Normally June and July will provide the minimum 150 cfs or so needed to paddle this very narrow river . . . but some summers it may never be runnable at all. The last half of the run is more demanding than the first, featuring a couple of quite steep drops with sharp ledges and holes.

Throughout this run, keep your eyes open for logs which can wedge all the way across the narrower parts of the river, and for possible single-strand barbed wire fences installed the previous fall and not yet washed out.

It is worth gambling on the possibility of a good run here, since, if the water level is too low, many other runs on nearby rivers will still be fine. Conversely, paddlers headed for the Roaring Fork might consider a brief side trip to look over the Fryingpan.

CRYSTAL RIVER
Central Colorado

General Description

The Crystal River is a tributary of the Roaring Fork, which is in turn a tributary of the Colorado. We have no complete flow data from this river, but it is roughly half that of the Roaring Fork. The boatable stretch is also half as long as the Roaring Fork. All in all, it is a diminutive little brother of the Roaring Fork seemingly not worth the extra mileage to drive up there. Yet local kayakers' eyes light up at the very mention of the river. Nice as it is, runs of the Roaring Fork can eventually get to be just another afternoon on the river by mid-summer. The Crystal is somehow always something special. Why? Perhaps because the quiet Crystal River Canyon is such a refreshing escape from the mirror-sunglasses-jive of the Aspen resorts. Mass-produced commercial rafting never finds its way here, nor do any but more experienced kayakers. There is a solitary feeling to boating this river, even in large groups. Opportunities to perform endos, pirouettes, and hot dog maneuvers are limited to perhaps two spots on the entire river. Even dramatic eddy turns are seldom witnessed by anyone else in your group, since most of the eddies can barely accommodate one kayak at a time. Nevertheless, even some of the most flagrant kayak exhibitionists love this river. The canyon is one of those deep, narrow gashes in the earth, so beloved by western paddlers, wherein light flickers indirectly down to the river off the faces of tree-speckled sandstone cliffs. Throughout most of its length, the river drops at a rate of better than 70 feet per mile through a channel, seemingly intended for a river half the size of the one which occupies it.

The water can be ice cold with above-timberline snowfields less than three miles away, and it is (of course) crystal clear, except in spring floods.

CRYSTAL RIVER: Marble to Redstone, Colorado

5 Miles, Class IV (?); drops 70–80' per mile. Suitable for kayaks.

This is known locally as the "Marble Run" and is the highest practical run on the river. The run begins calmly enough at the bridge in Marble. From there it passes through a beautiful 5-mile canyon full of Class IV water long before emptying into a large alpine meadow at the Marble turnoff. One and a half miles later, it forces its way into a narrow defile and begins descending continuously at a rate of 70–80 feet per mile. Yahoo! There is scarcely room enough for the two-lane paved road, with less than one lane's width left for the river. There are occasional holes and rocks to avoid, but generally the whole river is one long chute of standing waves. Though running this ongoing 4-mile-long rapid might only require Class III boating ability, stopping in any of its almost imaginary eddies is more of a Class IV proposition and stop you must! Half a mile into the canyon the river passes under the road through a culvert, and crosses back under through a second culvert a mile beyond that. Needless

Typical view of the Crystal River, Avalanche Run. The marble blocks in the background are a common sight; they were rejects from the quarry upstream which were dumped off trains to stabilize the railroad bed. (*Will Perry*)

to say, one should inspect these culverts and compare the available airspace with the dimensions of one's boat and body. Two miles more, and the run is over.

Throughout this run one should check for fallen trees which can easily wedge bank-to-bank.

CRYSTAL RIVER: Redstone to Avalanche Creek Bridge

3½ Miles, Class V; drops about 70' per mile. Suitable for kayaks.

Do not put-in at the Redstone Bridge, because scarcely 2 miles farther on at the end of the flatwater is an almost certainly unrunnable Class VI rapid which drops about 80 feet in 100 yards. Put-in below there, to run another 3 miles of essentially continuous Class V water.

There are two national forest campgrounds up Avalanche Creek, on the edge of the Snowmass Wilderness Area. On the left side of the river, about 100 yards away, is the present home and office of the Roger Paris Kayak School. Roger Paris is twice world, and three times U.S. National Slalom Champion and former U.S. National Team Coach. He also instructed the authors of this book in kayaking, and later employed Anderson as an instructor.

CRYSTAL RIVER: Avalanche Creek to BRB Resort

5–6 Miles, Class III, IV; drops 50–60' per mile. Suitable for kayaks.

This is the course of the annual Crystal River Wildwater Race. The first couple of miles are very choppy, fast-moving, shallow Class II water. Then the riverbed alternately narrows and widens to form a number of fast chutes with high peaked waves in them. The largest of these is called "the Big One," about 2½ miles from Avalanche Creek. As the water level drops, holes, and finally rocks appear in these chutes. Many of these rocks are rejected slabs of marble from the Yule quarry above the town of Marble which the railroad used for erosion control. It sometimes happens that one of these peaked waves will toss the bow of a long wildwater boat over onto the bank, causing it to lose the race. At high water, eddies are small, the current swift; therefore, swims and rescues can be prolonged. Thus, boaters for whom Class III water is difficult should exercise caution at high water. (High water begins abruptly around the middle or end of May—it ends equally abruptly when the last of the snowcover is no longer visible on Mount Sopris and on peaks near McClure Pass.)

CRYSTAL RIVER: BRB Resort to confluence

Total distance about 6 Miles, Class I, II. Suitable for kayaks.

Below BRB the river exits the canyon and its gradient lessens considerably. The river is no longer near the highway, though it passes under several bridges on secondary roads which serve the ranches through which it flows. Rafts and open canoes might have difficulty with snags on these bridges and should avoid this run. There is a reasonable take-out at the highway bridge just above Carbondale and a better one at the Colorado Rocky Mountain School Bridge west of Carbondale, two miles farther downstream. Below this bridge is the slalom course of the annual Crystal River Slalom. The confluence with the Roaring Fork is a little less than a mile away.

There is a movement to dam the Crystal River which is currently held up for lack of an ideal dam site and a reasonable use for the water. Aspen is a potential customer for any electricity generated, and it seems that oil shale developers 80 miles downstream would be glad to use up every drop of water in the entire area. Thus, there are fears that the dam project could be revived.

GLENWOOD CANYON

Introduction

General Description

Here is what would have been perhaps the ultimate wilderness canyon in the state of Colorado—would have been, except for a railroad line and a highway.

Access into the Roaring Fork and Grand valleys from the east, in the early days, was not easy. The original road left the Colorado River near Gypsum, crossed a low, flat divide (Cottonwood Pass), and entered the Roaring Fork Valley via Cattle Creek, between Glenwood Springs and Carbondale. Snow usually closed the road for much of the winter. The discovery of gold along the upper Roaring Fork created a demand for a railroad. The old road was not a particularly choice location for one, being too steep and too remote. Instead, a line was pushed west from Leadville under a 12,000-foot divide via the Carleton Tunnel into the Frying Pan River Valley. The railroad line then entered the Roaring Fork Valley at Basalt—but the climb to the Carleton Tunnel required extra engines and massive snowplowing.

At that time, there appeared on the scene an engineer the likes of whom we shall not see again: Robert Brewster Stanton. In the early 1870s, the silver of Silverplume, Colorado, could not be hauled downhill to the railroad at Georgetown (then Colorado's largest city) without great difficulty. Stanton extended the lines of the railroad up to Silverplume by means of the marvelous Georgetown Loop—in its day, an unprecedented engineering feat, now a tourist railroad.

Everyone realized that the Grand River (now called Colorado) provided a less steep access into Roaring Fork Valley than the Carleton Tunnel route, but they also realized that the engineering costs of putting a railroad through Glenwood Canyon would be in excess of any possible gain. Stanton, the visionary, realized that once such a line existed, it could become the principal east-west route through the middle of the nation, and would therefore pay for itself whatever the cost.

For Stanton, the principal consideration of such a route was that it be able to carry an immense amount of freight and passengers. Accordingly, he built a 6-foot-wide roadbed to carry two narrow steel rails. The size of Stanton's project may seem inadequately small by modern standards (the highway department wants a 100-foot-wide roadbed), but his railroad line is still in use over 100 years later and is still the principal freight line through the mountains. In the 1940s, the president of the railroad was riding in the cab of a locomotive through the canyon. If only everyone could have such a splendid view, he thought. Thus was born the glass-topped vista-dome railroad car.

Visionary engineers of a later era were called upon to produce a major interstate highway to fill the same function that Stanton had in mind for the railroad. Hills are the biggest problem for a railroad, but curves are the problem for interstates. Thus, the interstate should pass over the flat, low divide of Cottonwood Pass—6 miles south of the canyon, and no engineering challenge at all. For modern highway planners, however, the principal considerations are that they spend a great deal of money and create employment. Thus, an army of contractors is engaged in an engineering feat beside which the Great Wall of China is but a backyard fence. At a cost of $350,000,000 they will be able to shorten the driving time from New York to Los Angeles by almost two minutes. Meanwhile, traffic is being delayed half an hour per trip during the ten-year construction period. The faster speeds on the finished highway will make up the time lost during construction a mere 150 years—after the year 2139, every two minutes will be pure time saved. Isn't progress wonderful! All we lose in the process is the view that inspired the vista-dome train and the most popular kayaking river in Colorado.

Stanton sought to build the railroad west to California, and in 1889 and 1890 he ran the Grand Canyon of the Colorado River in suicidally inadequate boats to survey the route (building over the basin and range area of Utah and Nevada would have been prohibitively expensive). Thank God his railroad was not built, or today the Grand Canyon, too, would be threatened by interstate—a consequence Stanton could never have foreseen.

On July 1, 1938, Harold Franz, the first known whitewater kayaker in Colorado, paddled his boat in two days from Glenwood Springs to Grand Junction. He ran his shuttle on Stanton's railroad. Today, massive environmental destruction is in store for the area (which is rich in oil shale). In 1981 the machinery arrived not over the interstate, but rather on Stanton's railroad. A year later, the boom was over and the machinery was hauled away—again over Stanton's railroad.

MIDDLE COLORADO RIVER: Shoshone Dam to Shoshone Power Plant (in Glenwood Canyon)

2 Miles, Class II, VI; drops 150' per mile (not runnable).

The Colorado River enters a pipe at the Shoshone Dam and returns to the river 2 miles later through the turbines of the Shoshone Hydroelectric Plant. This diversion can take only about 2,000 cfs maximum flow, so at high water (May, June) an astounding 20,000 cfs of water still goes down the main channel. Most of the drop in this section occurs in two major rapids. This severe drop occurs at points where the railroad on the left and the highway on the right severely constrict the river and fill its bed with sharp, angular boulders. The result is two thundering Class VI rapids. The upper of these is a narrow chute which, at its center, drops at a 45° angle for about 20 yards into a mass of spray. People viewing this rapid sometimes speculate that a hero kayaker of the future will someday run it. In the very early 1960s, a group of five Aspen architects attempted the rapid in a large rubber raft. The raft shredded in a couple of seconds. Four of the architects died, the fifth being recovered a mile downstream in poor condition.

There is a movie made by Bob Waind in 1962, which appears to depict former National Champion Ron Bohlander running this rapid

Sandy Campbell on Shoshone Run of Colorado River. Scree banks on both sides were formed by construction of railroad and highway beds. Medium-low water level (*Will Perry*)

in a kayak. The movie was made in the following manner: Bohlander is filmed by Waind paddling around above the rapids warming up and looking scared. In the next shot, a clothing store mannequin, dressed as Bohlander, has been taped into the boat and has an old paddle screwed to its hands. The mannequin disappears into the foam, rolls and cartwheels through the rapids, and finally part of the boat is seen floating out of the bottom of the rapid. For the final shot, Waind and Bohlander have recovered the remains of the boat. The next shot commences with the boat upside down at the point where the preceding shot ended. Bohlander rolls up with his life jacket askew, his paddle shattered, his boat demolished, etc., gasping for breath. The resulting film certainly *looks* like Bohlander running the rapid. The movie was shown to boaters in California at the next season's National Championship. After expressing initial shock, the California paddlers told us that they themselves routinely paddle water like that. We have been waiting for one of them to come show us how for the last 20 years!

The second Class VI drop in this section is less severe and was first paddled in 1976 by Billy Ward and Brent Brown. They selected a water level low enough so that Brent would throw his paddle out ahead of himself and then slide along the rocks pushing with his hands until he caught up with it. In 1984 Culley Erdman and Kevin Padden ran this distinctly lethal looking drop at moderate water levels and repeated the run at record high water levels of 24,000 cfs. A few others ran it at medium level. In 1985 construction of the highway moved the entire river channel a good distance to the south, rendering the rapid much more channelized and easier to run—but also making the runout below the rapid more dangerous.

MIDDLE COLORADO RIVER: Shoshone Power Plant to Grizzly Creek (Glenwood Canyon—Shoshone Run)

2 Miles, Class III, IV; drops circa 50' per mile. Suitable for kayaks, possible for rafts at low water.

This is the course of the annual Cool Down Wildwater Race. The slalom is usually in the second or fourth rapid. This is probably the most popular 2 miles of whitewater in the state of Colorado. Six outstanding Class III/IV rapids occur in quick succession at the bottom of Colorado's finest limestone canyon on its mightiest river.

June flows of over 22,000 cfs produce huge rolling waves and deep bursting holes. By September, flows of only 1,200 cfs result in rock gardens and pool/drop rapids of only Class III difficulty. Thus, one short stretch gives us both big water, intricate little rock dodging, and everything in between. Every water level is different, but all are marvelous. Once the most popular kayaking and second most popular rafting river in Colorado, this run sees little use now and will not until the highway construction ends (projected completion date is 1993). The eastbound lanes of the new interstate highway encroach severely on the river channel throughout this entire section, straightening out the river somewhat. It thus becomes more raftable, but rescues become more difficult with no more right side eddies and sharp jagged rock along that bank. The aesthetics of the twelve-mile-long concrete wall are a matter of personal opinion. As of this writing, the bike path has been completely flooded two years in a row. Where there was once parking for hundreds of cars near the put-in, there is now no parking at all. Conservationists find themselves in the unusual position of fighting *for* a parking lot here.

Rafts are barred from this run at levels over 3,000 cfs—above which they often overturn and spill passengers for miles. Expert open canoeists generally avoid the river here at over 3,000 cfs as well. Kayakers of intermediate ability should be aware that the increase in difficulty from Class III to Class IV occurs at about that level. It is safe to put-in just above the last rapid, "Superstition," at any level, as there is an easy rescue below it. Flows are posted on the door of the power plant at the put-in. The run is not accessible or scoutable throughout its entire length. The interstate obliterated the parking, the scouting, and the access. Driving time through the canyon could be as much as two minutes faster.

MIDDLE COLORADO RIVER: Grizzly Creek to Glenwood Springs (lower Glenwood Canyon)

5 Miles, Class II; drops 20' per mile. Suitable for kayaks, rafts, and canoes at low water.

Grizzly Creek had gas stations, private homes, and commercial rafting operations. In 1981 the highway department bulldozed it all away. Some rafters do not hesitate to launch trips of 200 or more people at a time from this spot. What the hell, the canyon already has a railroad and a highway. Let the big trips go by, or paddle ahead and peace and quiet will return because the river leaves the highway for half of this section. This was the most popular day trip in the state for 1950s foldboaters, for here is the deepest and most beautiful portion of the canyon. In late afternoon and early morning the sunlight filters down indirectly to the river and the walls are lit with a soft, diffuse haze.

It is easier to take-out on the left side of the river in Glenwood Springs away from the highway. It will become still easier to take-out when Two Rivers Park is completed on the right bank in Glenwood.

MIDDLE COLORADO RIVER: Glenwood Springs to New Castle

11½ Miles, Class I, II; drops under 20' per mile. Suitable for rafts, kayaks; canoes at low water.

The Colorado State Canoe and Kayak Marathon Championships go from Grizzly Creek to New Castle. So do most of the commercial rafting operations. There are many Class II rapids connected by flatwater, one of which is somewhat bigger than all the others: South Canyon Rapids, under the South Canyon Bridge, 5 miles from Glenwood Springs, is a straightforward unobstructed run about 50 yards long; however, at full runoff (12,000 cfs) it can have waves nearly 5 feet high. These appear to be much larger to a neophyte boater, and many tip-overs result. In the summer of 1980, the new bridge was completed just downstream from the old bridge, and no less than seven commercial rafts wrapped around the righthand bridge abutment. Many more bounced off it. Invariably, these were rafts rowed by big strong men. Rafts rowed by petite young things and out of control paddle rafts had no trouble. This would suggest that the repeated disasters were caused by some action of the boatmen, not the river. Nevertheless, rafters should be aware of the potential danger of this man-made obstruction during high water.

This is a particularly nice run during the off-season when everything else is too low to paddle. In both spring and fall, the river is frequented by large numbers of migratory waterfowl.

The valley bottom is shared by the river, the railroad, and the highway—but the valley bottom below Canyon Creek is wide and the river is removed from the road.

Access points are at the I-70 New Castle "rest stop," South Canyon, West Glenwood, and Glenwood Springs exits.

UPPER GRAND VALLEY

MIDDLE COLORADO RIVER: New Castle to DeBeque, Colorado (the upper Grand Valley)

Circa 40 Miles, Class I; drops 15' per mile. Suitable for kayaks, rafts, and canoes.

This river was the Grand River until 1922 when the government changed the name; their logic being that the Rio Colorado of the West (or Colorado River) should have a source—and why not in the state of Colorado? Thus, the river that originates in Grand Lake near Granby and flows past Grand Mesa, Grand Hogback, and Grand Junction, through the upper and lower Grand valleys and the Grand Canyon is now the Colorado River. The mainstream of what becomes the Rio Colorado of the West starts in Wyoming and is therefore called the "Green." Now, only *one* major tributary of the *entire* river is still free-flowing. Perhaps, therefore, the whole river should be renamed "Yampa."

The 47-mile portion of this run below the town of Rifle is described in detail in Earl Perry's *Rivers of Colorado.*

This area is part of the National Sacrifice Area for Energy Development, so eventually the oil shale-laden beautiful cliffs forming the north wall of the valley may be despoiled—as may the many little towns along the way and the lives of the people who live there. For now though, the river alternately meanders through or splits its channel around the cottonwoods and willows as it flows peacefully down the valley, removed from the roar of the highway. The river is particularly beautiful in early spring when the trees leaf out and in late fall when the leaves turn.

Access is to be found at New Castle, by Silt, by the Rifle exit from I-70, by the I-70 bridge 4 miles below Rifle, by Rulison, at the bridge near DeBeque, and at many other points.

MIDDLE COLORADO RIVER: DeBeque to Palisades exit of I-70 (DeBeque Canyon)

16 Miles, Class I (with 2 portages); drops 17–18' per mile. Suitable for kayaks, rafts, and canoes.

The river enters a distinct canyon 3 or 4 miles below DeBeque. There are no rapids, but many pleasing little riffles around island stands of willow and tamarisk. Almost no one paddles here—the

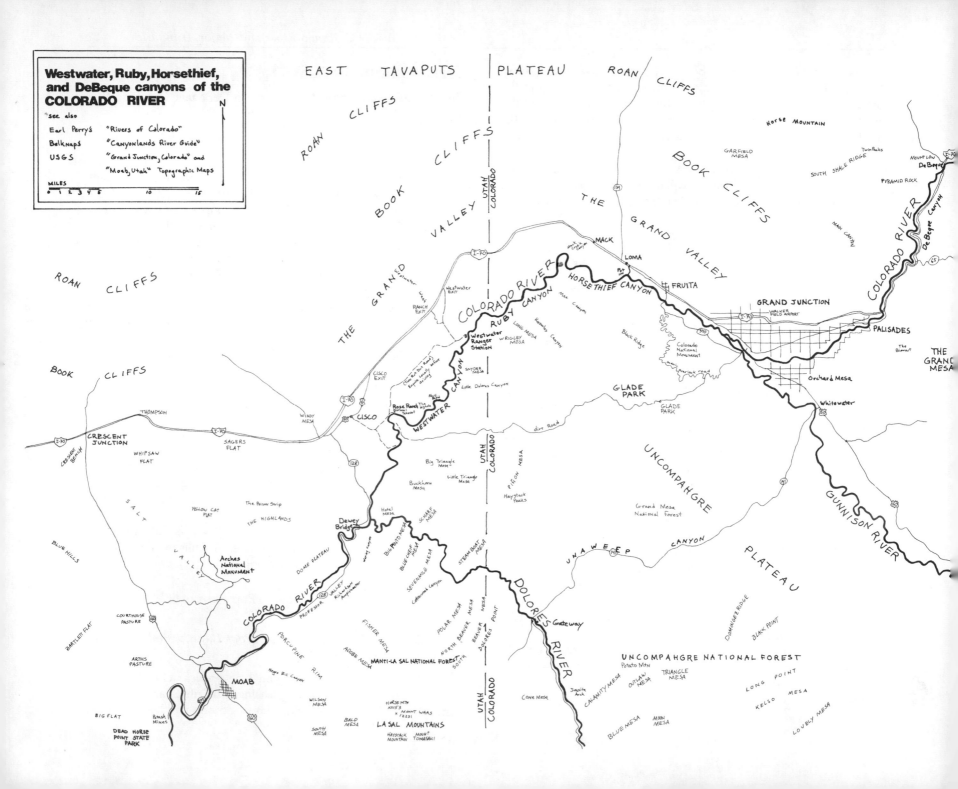

Westwater, Ruby, Horsethief, and DeBeque canyons of the COLORADO RIVER

see also

Earl Perry's	"Rivers of Colorado"
Belknaps	"Canyonlands River Guide"
USGS	"Grand Junction, Colorado" and
	"Moab, Utah" Topographic Maps

N

MILES
0 1 2 3 4 5   10   15

EAST TAVAPUTS PLATEAU

ROAN CLIFFS

ROAN CLIFFS

BOOK CLIFFS

BOOK CLIFFS

ROAN CLIFFS

BOOK CLIFFS

THE GRAND VALLEY

GRAND VALLEY

Horse Mountain

GARFIELD MESA

Twin Peaks

SOUTH SHALE RIDGE

Mountain

MOUNTAIN LION

DeBeque

PYRAMID ROCK

MAIN CANYON

COLORADO RIVER

DeBeque Canyon

65

UTAH COLORADO

I-70

MACK

LOMA

Pot Hole

FRUITA

Westwater Exit

Westwater Ranger Station

RUBY CANYON

HORSETHIEF CANYON

Mee Canyon

LONG MESA

Kamallo Canyon

WRIGLEY MESA

Black Ridge

GRAND JUNCTION

WALKER FIELD AIRPORT

PALISADES

THE GRAND MESA

THE Blowout

RANCH EXIT

Westwater Exit

SNYDER MESA

Little Dolores Canyon

Colorado National Monument

Orchard Mesa

CISCO EXIT

(Close East Dirt Road) Exercise bends with driving

Rose Ranch

WESTWATER CANYON

GLADE PARK

GLADE PARK

Overlook road

I-70

WINDY MESA

CISCO

dirt Road

Whitewater

50

ROAN CLIFFS

BOOK CLIFFS

THOMPSON

I-70

CRESCENT JUNCTION

CRESCENT BEACH

SAGERS FLAT

WHIPSAW FLAT

128

Big Triangle Mesa

Little Triangle Mesa

UNCOMPAHGRE

PIÑON MESA

PLATEAU

91

GUNNISON RIVER

The Poison Strip

YELLOW CAT FLAT

THE HIGHLANDS

Buckhorn Mesa

Haystack Peaks

Grand Mesa National Forest

BLUE HILLS

SALT VALLEY

Arches National Monument

Dome Plateau

Dewey Bridge

Hotel Mesa

S. HARE MESA

STEAMBOAT MESA

UNAWEEP CANYON

141

DOMINGUEZ RIDGE

BLACK POINT

COLORADO RIVER

128

Professor Valley

Richardson Amphitheater

BIG PINTO NECK

BLUE CHIEF MESA

SEVENMILE MESA

Cottonwood Canyon

POLAR MESA

NORTH BEAVER MESA

DOLORES POINT

DOLORES RIVER

Gateway

UNCOMPAHGRE NATIONAL FOREST

COURTHOUSE PASTURE

PORCUPINE RIM

FISHER MESA

SOUTH BEAVER MESA

Potato Mtn

CALAMITY MESA

OUTLAW MESA

TRIANGLE MESA

LONG POINT

KELSO MESA

LOVELY MESA

BARTLETT FLAT

ARTHS PASTURE

Negro Bill Canyon

ADOBE MESA

MANTI-LA SAL NATIONAL FOREST

Juanita Arch

Cone Mesa

BLUE MESA

MOON MESA

MOAB

191

WILSON MESA

HORSE MTN X1153   MOUNT WAAS 12331

LA SAL MOUNTAINS

BIG FLAT

Potash Mines

DEAD HORSE POINT STATE PARK

128

SOUTH MESA

BALD MESA

HAYSTACK MOUNTAIN

MOUNT TOMASAKI

UTAH COLORADO

locals are more interested in the area below Grand Junction and the out-of-towners are in a hurry to get somewhere else. Too bad, because the water is warm and the scenery pleasant. The canyon itself is a miniature precursor of the great sandstone canyons through which the river will pass downstream. You must portage two large irrigation diversion dams visible from the highway near the end of the run.

MIDDLE COLORADO RIVER: Palisades exit I-70 to Loma exit I-70 (the lower Grand Valley)

33 Miles, Class I; drops circa 12' per mile. Suitable for kayaks, rafts, and canoes.

Contrary to out-of-date maps, metropolitan Grand Junction covers this entire area — but it doesn't intrude heavily on the river. Massive irrigation diversions feed miles upon miles of fruit orchards. The irrigation canals themselves are popular boating areas. The slow-flowing river gains the waters of the Gunnison halfway through the town. Access is everywhere.

RUBY AND HORSETHIEF CANYONS

MIDDLE COLORADO RIVER: Loma to Westwater BLM Ranger Station (Ruby and Horsethief canyons)

26.7 Miles (2 days +), Class I, II; drops 9' per mile. Suitable for kayaks, rafts, and canoes.

The beauties of this run are many: it can be run almost year-round (March through December, generally); it abounds with wildfowl and deer (especially in late fall); it is easily accessible, yet rarely crowded; it can be legally run on the spur of the moment (i.e., a boating permit is not required); warm, sunny weather is the norm, the climate is semiarid. Sandstone cliffs, occasional cottonwood groves, side canyons, aesthetically exposed mudbars, floating pumpkins, and sunshine are a few of the distractions you can expect to encounter.

Many campsites exist throughout the run. It is not uncommon to make a leisurely four- or five-day trip on this stretch. An excellent and popular campsite aptly named Black Rocks can be found on river left at mile 17.4. Smoothed and polished black metamorphic rocks sculpted into potholes and flutes form the rapid as well as the beach of clean and abundant white sand. At low water, several levels of

diving platforms are available on the black cliffs, with a convenient return passageway up through the weathered rocks. Hide out up here and jump on your friends' boats as they pull into camp.

A detailed mile-by-mile account of these canyons can be found in Earl Perry's *Rivers of Colorado*. This stretch was also written up in a magazine article by Vern Huser.

Access: Put-in less than a mile from the Loma exit off I-70. Go to the south side of the highway, follow the road heading east for ¼ mile or less, at which point it heads sharply downhill to a beach, put-in area, and pleasant campsite.

Take-out: The take-out is at Westwater Ranger Station, which can be reached by either of two Westwater area exits off I-70. Just follow the dirt roads from either exit. One Y-junction will be encountered (where the roads from the two exits meet), keep heading downhill (turn left if you are coming from the east, bear right if you are ap-

Colorado River, Ruby and Horsethief Canyons in fall (*Fletcher Anderson*)

proaching from the west — see map). Be prepared for mosquitoes if you arrive after sunset!

WESTWATER CANYON

MIDDLE COLORADO RIVER: Westwater Ranger Station to Rose Ranch (Westwater Canyon)

17.5 Miles, Class III, IV; drops 11.4' per mile (20.8' per mile in rapids). Suitable for kayaks and rafts.

The BLM administers Westwater Canyon and issues permits by the lottery method on a monthly basis; that is, applications received in a given month will be for launches in the following month. Ten days following the close of the filing period, unfilled dates can be reserved on a first-come, first-served basis. To apply for a permit, write Bureau of Land Management, Grand Resource Area Office, P.O. Box M, Moab, Utah 84532, phone (801) 259-6111 ext. 211 (the BLM sends maps with campsites and rapids, etc., with application forms).

Westwater is described by the Belknaps in *Canyonlands River Guide.*

Westwater Canyon is a good one-day or overnight desert river trip which imparts a feeling of having left the world of automobiles and industrialization far behind. It is one of the best and most fun runs in the region. It is very popular, especially in the late summer and fall. At this time, all the other good short runs are too low, but Westwater is at its best at low levels. It is run a lot commercially, as well as publicly. The heavy use is the only drawback, but up to now the canyon has remained relatively clean.

The most common form of wildlife seen in the area is the upper lip of the flannel-mouthed sucker, combing the eddies for morsels. Also seen are great blue herons, mule deer, an occasional egret, Canadian geese, various ducks, and (rarely) bighorn sheep.

The trip begins with 3 miles of open, flat water with a good view of the approaching sandstone cliffs which mark the beginning of the canyon. On entering the canyon, a few riffles and an increase in drop are apparent. At mile 5 or 6 the river cuts through a dark-walled inner gorge formed of resistant pre-Cambrian gneiss. The seven or eight major rapids (all pool/drop) occur in the 3½-mile

stretch of the inner gorge. The most famous of these is Skull Rapid, which can be recognized by a large striated cliff on the right as the river begins a bend to the left. Skull has a huge hole at the bottom and a catchall swirling eddy, called The Room of Doom, below the hole to the right. Many an animal (not to mention all the other flotsam including boats and boaters) has been caught in The Room. The rapid was at one point named Dead Sheep Rapid after a flock of dead sheep seen bobbing in the eddy. In following years a lone skull wedged in a crack in the rocks, giving the rapid its current name.

Kayakers tend to congregate in the rapid below Skull, where likely endo spots occur at low water levels.

The final stage of the trip is 5 miles of slow-moving, flat water. It is a beautiful stretch, especially at the end of the day when the light is at a low angle and the air is cool.

The inner canyon is extremely narrow and the character and difficulty of the river varies drastically according to water levels. At 25,000 cfs and above, you are boating up with all those huge cottonwoods that were jammed in rocks 30 feet above your head when you came the previous autumn. Newly arrived floating cottonwoods, gigantic and complete with all their branches, are not only a spectacular, but a dangerous aspect of boating the canyon at full flood (30,000 cfs, late June, usually). Following a gyrating 60-foot tree into the gorge is an experience long remembered. There are no distinct rapids at this level, nor do any eddies exist. The inner gorge fills in like a narrow staircase being flooded with a firehose. Seething, swirling, and surging whirlpools replace the rapids; they form and reform, can submerge a kayaker to his or her armpits, and can flip rafts as well as kayaks. Rescue is difficult to impossible due to the lack of eddies, the steep cliff walls, and the 2–3 feet of surge.

The 17.5-mile run takes about an hour and one-half at this level and is not advised except for kayakers with good rolls. It is worth seeing once just to ogle at the immense power of the water and to rip through there riding high 20 or 30 feet above where people will be camping and negotiating rocky rapids a month hence.

When the water drops to 15,000 cfs and lower, the rapids reappear and it is an exciting level for rafting. The well-known hole at the bottom of Skull Rapid becomes large and deep. Westwater remains an excellent raft run until it is so low that the rafts cannot negotiate the rocks of Skull Rapid. This occurs at around 1,200 cfs, higher for large rafts. It sometimes drops this low by mid-August but sometimes stays higher through October.

Kayakers, of course, can run Westwater at any level, but it is most interesting and fun at the very lowest levels. At 3,000 cfs and under, it is chock-full of surfing waves and endo holes, the water is warm and the rocks are hot and a kayaker can spend all day trying to beat the same endo wave to death.

Camping: Few campsites are available. There are five, according to the BLM, but everyone always camps at Little Dolores Beach as their first choice. This is at the beginning of the rapids, at mile 7. In general, the only drinking water available is the Colorado River, which has recently passed through Grand Junction and miles of irrigation ditches — and must be boiled.

Access: The put-in is at Westwater Ranger Station and access is described in the Ruby to Horsethief description immediately prior to this section. No fresh drinking water is available, so bring your own and bring a lot, because you are in the desert. The take-out is just below Rose Ranch, also on BLM land. Take the Cisco, Utah, exit from I-70, head west until you enter town. Turn left before you pass the gas station and head south on a graded gravel and dust road. At the fork, turn left and park near the yellow portable toilets.

Shuttles can be arranged with other boaters at Westwater put-in on weekends. The caretaker at Rose Ranch will sometimes do them for $20 or so, but he can be hard to find. The shuttle is about 30 miles each way, half on good dirt roads, half on interstate. There is a shortcut shuttle on unmaintained dirt roads, which parallels the railroad some of the way.

A lot of beginner kayakers have run Westwater and survived, but they invariably swim nearly the entire length of the rapids section and come out looking like beaten dogs. There are rocks and holes where a person could get hurt, so a moderate to expert degree of skill is advisable.

MIDDLE COLORADO RIVER: Rose Ranch to Dewey Bridge

16 Miles, Class I; drops 3' per mile. Suitable for kayaks, rafts, and canoes. (In Belknap's Canyonlands River Guide*)*

This section is flat, wide, slow-flowing and open. It is rarely boated. Word is that there are some tasty catfish lurking down there in those murky waters, but you've got to have the right bait.

The Dolores River empties into the Colorado River about 1½ miles above the long, enclosed, (barely) one-laned, white Dewey Bridge.

Colorado River, Westwater Canyon. A view from left rim, looking upstream (*NORS*)

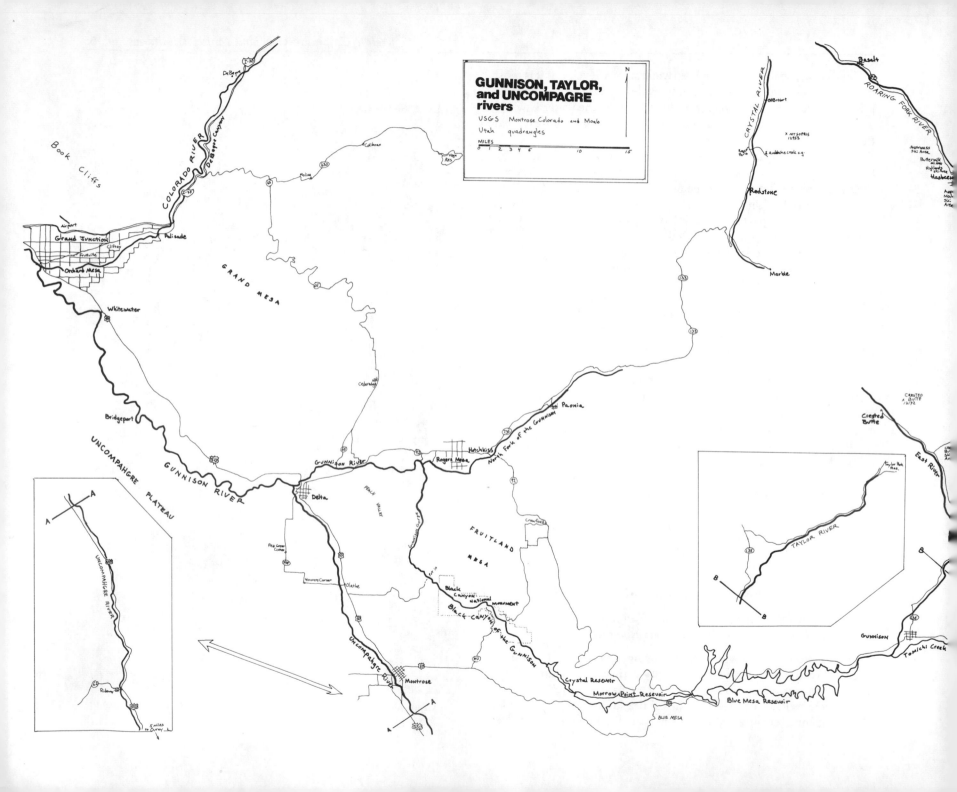

GUNNISON, TAYLOR, and UNCOMPAGRE rivers

USGS Montrose Colorado and Moab
Utah quadrangles

MILES
0 1 2 3 4 6   10   15

N

Book Cliffs

COLORADO RIVER

DeBeque Canyon

DeBeque

I-70

Collbran

Molina

Vega Res.

Grand Junction

Airport

Clifton

Fruitvale

Palisade

Orchard Mesa

Whitewater

GRAND MESA

Bridgeport

UNCOMPAHGRE PLATEAU

GUNNISON RIVER

Delta

PEACH VALLEY

Pea Green Corner

Mowers Corner

Olathe

Cedaredge

Paonia

North Fork of the Gunnison

Hotchkiss

Rogers Mesa

Crawford

FRUITLAND MESA

Gunnison Curve

Black Canyon National Monument

Black Canyon of the Gunnison

Crystal Resevoir

Morrow Point Resevoir

Blue Mesa Resevoir

BLUE MESA

Uncompahgre River

Montrose

CRYSTAL RIVER

DR Resort

X MT SOPRIS 12353

Redstone

Marble

Basalt

ROARING FORK RIVER

Snowmass Ski Area

Butteringe

Highlands Ski Area

Hasbeen

Aspen Mtn. Ski Area

133

133

CRESTED BUTTE 12172

Crested Butte

East River

Taylor Park Res.

TAYLOR RIVER

136

Gunnison

Tomichi Creek

A — A

UNCOMPAHGRE RIVER

Ridgway

5 miles to Ouray

A

A

B

B

PROFESSOR VALLEY

MIDDLE COLORADO RIVER: Dewey Bridge to Moab, Utah (Professor Valley)

30 Miles, Class I, II; drops 5.2' per mile. Continuous access. Suitable for rafts, kayaks, and canoes. (In Belknap's Canyonlands River Guide*)*

This is a beautiful area of red sandstone towers and cliffs, interspersed with a few green ranches in the river and creek bottoms. Fisher Towers, a famous climbing area, is close by. Excellent opportunities for beginner boaters await here, what with continuous access, enough waves and safe open rapids to make it interesting, great scenery, and invariably warm, sunny weather. A lot of nice beaches and campsites can be found. Nonboaters picnic and camp by the river here on weekends, but it is not overcrowded. Commercial raft companies operate on the stretch just above Moab, but not on a massive scale. The BLM is threatening to require permits for this run.

"Canyonlands at Night" is an upstream jet boat ride and light show which departs nightly from Moab.

MIDDLE COLORADO RIVER: Moab to Potash

15 Miles, Class I; drops—negligible. Continuous access. Suitable even for rubber duckies.

The river is green and glassy with towering red sandstone formations reflected from its surface. Some Indian petroglyphs and cliff dwellings are visible from the road 3 and 4 miles from the junction of the Potash road and Rt. 163.

(The lower Colorado River description begins on page 90.)

TAYLOR RIVER

TAYLOR RIVER: Taylor Park Reservoir to Almont, Colorado

18 Miles, Class II, III; drops 66' per mile. Suitable for kayaks.

This extremely small river might be better termed a creek, although it is one of the major tributaries of the Gunnison River. It is also the closest good whitewater to the city of Gunnison and the resort community of Crested Butte. It has become a popular run for boaters living in the area, and a slalom training course is often left set for the duration of the summer. The river is too small and the water too shallow for rafts (except for the teeny weeny hardware-store variety). The kayak season begins when the snow starts melting; it ends in early August. A road parallels the entire run, providing easy scouting and nearly continuous access.

The river contains numerous very shallow rapids. Waves are very small, but some of these rocky little rapids require tight and accurate maneuvering.

Driftwood snags and occasional barbed wire fences sometimes block the river. The current is slow enough so that these usually do not amount to serious safety hazards.

The narrow canyon cuts through a dense coniferous forest at a mean altitude of 9,000 feet. Temperatures in the shady river canyon are usually a little cooler than in the wide valley below, and early morning temperatures can be very cold even in mid-summer.

GUNNISON RIVER

General Description

This river may once have been the finest whitewater river in Colorado. Unfortunately, more than half its length is now inundated by three major dams and a fourth dam is being proposed to eliminate the best remaining whitewater. Wild and Scenic River protection has been proposed for that same stretch (which includes the remainder of the Black Canyon of the Gunnison). Most whitewater boaters in the Southwest live in the Front Range Urban Corridor, east of the Colorado Rockies. The drive from there to the Gunnison River passes many excellent whitewater runs, and it is understandable that boaters choose those runs in preference to the much longer drive to the Gunnison. Although it has been known to boaters for many years, the river has only just begun to gain popularity. This is unfortunate, for it means that when more dams are proposed, few voices are raised in opposition—and there are few rivers more worth saving than this one.

TAYLOR GUNNISON RIVER: Almost to Blue Mesa Reservoir

15 Miles (more or less), Class I; drops 13' per mile. Suitable for kayaks, possible for canoes and rafts.

There is some dispute locally as to whether the first 12 miles of this run through the city of Gunnison are the highest part of the Gunnison River or the lowest part of the Taylor. Does the Gunnison begin at the junction of the Taylor and East rivers or does it begin where those combined flows are joined by Tomichi Creek? Our innate love of controversy prevents us from offering an opinion.

Whichever river it is, it is flat and slow-moving across the bottom of the Gunnison or Taylor (choose one) Valley.

There is easy access at several points above Gunnison on secondary roads leaving Colorado Highway 135, and below Gunnison on various roads leaving U.S. 50—but the river is not continuously bordered by road.

The run is a popular one with Gunnison-based open canoeists and rafters who vary their choice of access points, according to the length of time they wish to spend on the river.

Barbed wire fences may be encountered anywhere on this run, particularly after the end of June when the water is dropping.

GUNNISON RIVER: Blue Mesa, Morrow, and Crystal reservoirs

32 Miles, total drop 800'.

Morrow Point and Crystal reservoirs are narrow, fjord-like lakes where only small, hand-carried craft are permitted (or practical). The put-ins are at the bases of steep trails. As reservoirs go, these two are relatively remote and scenic and can provide a rewarding flatwater paddle. Morrow Point reputedly has large tour boats that give free tours to the public.

Totally destroyed by these three dams are the upper three-fifths of the fabled Black Canyon of the Gunnison. Walter Kirschbaum, the first to paddle the canyon, regarded it as one of the classic great runs in North America. His first run (in 1961 or 1962) was solo through the entire Black Canyon. In later years, prior to the filling of Crystal Reservoir, the Cimarron to East Portal stretch was enjoyed by thousands.

Kirschbaum and the upper Black Canyon are both dead now. We can only imagine what led him to think so highly of this lost canyon while we work to save the lower portions of the same river.

GUNNISON RIVER: Crystal Dam outlet to Chucker Trail (through Black Canyon of the Gunnison National Monument)

16 Miles, Class III, IV, V (many mandatory portages); drops 75' per mile. Suitable for kayaks.

Here is a truly remarkable run, both for its fantastic canyon and the extreme physical hardship involved. The Black Canyon of the Gunnison, at its deepest, is a full 2,000 feet deep and only just barely 2,000 feet rim to rim. There are, in places, vertical walls of black basalt laced with white gneiss which stand fully 1,800 feet high. It appears, from the viewpoint of a paddler at the canyon's bottom, that the walls actually close in at the rim, nearly forming some sort of slit-shaped cavern.

The second (and perhaps the only other) run of the Black Canyon through the monument was made by Ron Mason, Filip Sokol, Bill Clark, and Tom Ruwitch in August 1975. Our information on the run is derived from that source.

The run from Crystal Dam to east portal of the Gunnison water diversion tunnel (a distance of about 1½ miles) is smooth Class I.

Below the diversion dam, one encounters short stretches where the drop begins to exceed 100 feet per mile. Within the next 5 miles or so are seven Class V rapids and seven additional boulder-choked drops with passages too narrow to accommodate a boat. These mandatory portages consumed a great deal of time, so that the party camped shortly thereafter above SOB gully.

The second day began with a mandatory portage over a mile long. This section of river is made continuously unnavigable by rock filters and high waterfalls which crash directly onto talus piles. The drop for this 1 mile is 320 feet. At one point, it was necessary to lower the boats by rope while descending a rock chimney. Rudimentary technical rock-climbing skills are necessary for this portage.

Mason et al. ran the river at a flow of 325 cfs, which they believe is the best level.

All in all, it can be argued that this is a river to be run, as George Herbert Leigh-Mallory might have phrased it, "because it is there." The best way to visit the bottom of the Black Canyon is by hiking down the side canyons or by technical rock climbing—and it is certainly worth the climb.

Even hiking has its perils: On a sunny day in 1968, a group of college students hiked to the canyon bottom. They undressed and swam in the tiny (less than 250 cfs) river and stretched out to sun themselves on a rock ledge on the other side. At that point, the capricious engineers at the dam saw fit to release an estimated 2,000 cfs of water. All night the students huddled, cold, hungry and naked, on a little rock ledge from which they could neither swim across nor climb to the rim. The following afternoon, the waters receded enough for them to risk the swim and escape from the canyon. Surely this is what constitutes a true "wilderness experience."

GUNNISON RIVER: Chucker Trail to North Fork confluence (the Gunnison Gorge)

13.5 Miles, Class III, IV; drops 38' per mile. Suitable for kayaks and rafts.

When we first wrote of this beautiful and then undiscovered canyon there was no commercial use of this river, but we let the cat out of the bag. Now there are 17 outfitters running the canyon and proposals to limit non-commercial use to keep the river free for the outfitters are in the works. Permits may soon be necessary, and would be obtained from:
Bureau of Land Management
Uncompahgre Resource Area
2505 South Townsend Avenue
Montrose, Colorado 81401
303-249-2244

Drive north on U.S. 50, 9 miles out of Montrose, Colorado, to Falcon Drive. Go east about 4 miles on Falcon Drive to where it becomes Peach Valley Road. Peach Valley Road meanders south and east for about 10 miles to a BLM-improved picnic grounds at the Chucker Trailhead. It is a nearly 1-mile hike down to the river. This hike seems to keep the river fairly uncrowded. A fair number of kayakers make the hike and a few raft outfitters horse-pack in rafts and customers. Many of the raft companies are primarily fly-fishing guide services.

A secondary road leaves Colorado 92 in the Rogers Mesa area and reaches the riverbank at the confluence and take-out.

After the hike, you find yourself deep within a less extreme version of the incredible Black Canyon. Soon, you pass on into a wider sandstone canyon. Here is the wintering ground of hundreds of thousands of migratory waterfowl. A home of Peregrine falcons and river otters (perhaps the only such in Colorado) and of mountain sheep, a magnificent trout fishery, and—thanks to the steep canyon walls—a true wilderness river corridor undisturbed by the hand of man. Here, in short, is the sort of canyon you thought only existed in your dreams.

The high water flows usually exceed 1,000 cfs, but rarely exceed 2,500. Below about 600 cfs, most of the rapids are Class II/III. Above

that level, at least four of the rapids are Class IV and at least a dozen of them are good solid Class III. Kayakers have no trouble scouting them from the river as they approach, but rafts would do well to pull over to find the route through some of the blind ones. High water is typically May and June, and August flows are in the 300–400 cfs range; however, the dams upstream can play havoc with normal flow patterns, particularly with regard to chopping off spring highs.

Although this is an easy day's run, it is not difficult to find excuses for camping in such a remarkable canyon.

The Wild and Scenic River: You can send your support to: Bureau of Land Management, P.O. Box 1269, Montrose, Colorado 81401.

Approaching the rim, you cross broad expanses of rolling piñon–juniper forest and sagebrush-covered hills. Suddenly, at your feet, is a breathtaking view of the deep black-walled river gorge. In it is some of the nation's finest and least visited boating.

The canyon is the home of bighorn sheep, Colorado river otters, Peregrine falcons, and bald eagles—all dwindling or endangered species. It is also home to elk, deer, ducks, and other game animals.

Clearly, this is exactly what the Wild and Scenic Rivers Act is all about, but there is considerable resistance to protecting the river because of *the proposed dam.* Everybody else gets a big useless pork barrel Bureau of Reclamation project in their area, argue local entrepreneurs, when do we get ours? Unfortunately, there is no good site for one in the Montrose–Delta area. All they could come up with is an economic boondoggle which would destroy the remaining Gunnison River.

Jimmy Carter axed the Bureau's plans to dam the river, along with a selection of the other economically unproductive water projects. There is now reason to fear that the old Fruitland Mesa project will be reborn. The Reagan administration wants to cut "wasteful" government spending—but does not consider pork barrel dams "wasteful."

Economically, the dam could never pay for itself, but the Federal Government could pay for the dam. The dam is a sort of welfare payment for western Colorado contractors. The city of Delta and town of Paonia want the temporary jobs the dam will bring. The local congressmen, too, are totally against wasteful government spending—except in their districts. The Bureau of Reclamation has cooked up a dubious economic study which purports to show—through exaggerated benefits and unrealistically low costs—that the nation would eventually break even on the cost of the dam. Break even, that is, except for the loss of the Gunnison River.

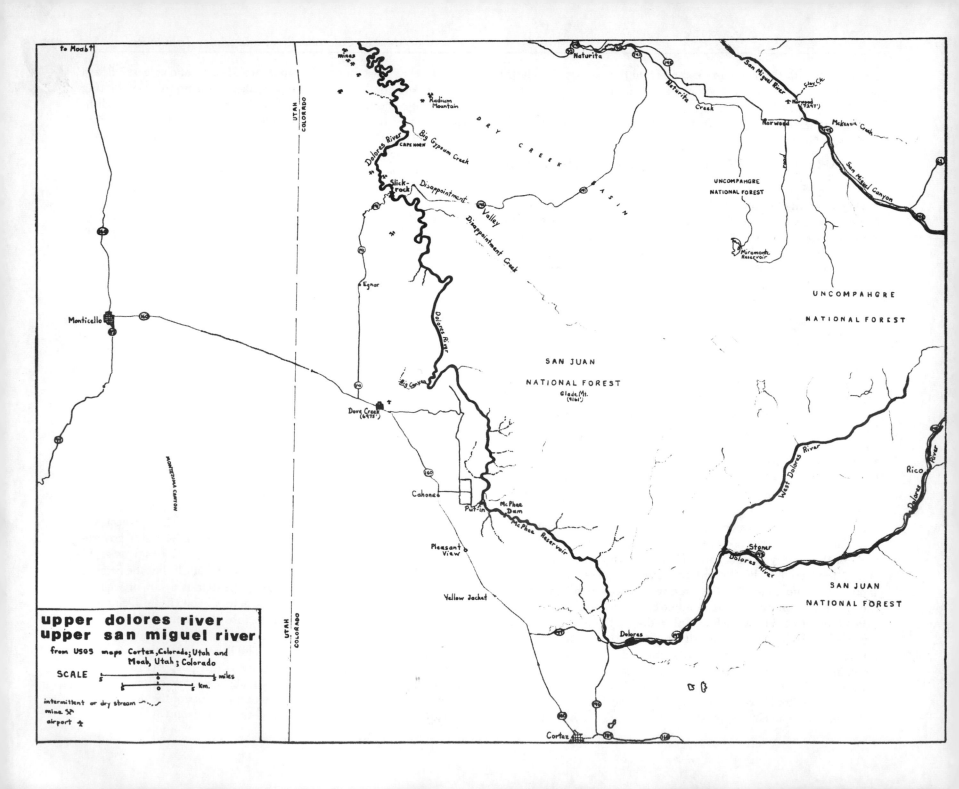

upper dolores river
upper san miguel river

from USGS maps Cortez, Colorado; Utah and
Moab, Utah; Colorado

SCALE

intermittent or dry stream
mine
airport

GUNNISON RIVER: Rogers Mesa to Delta

18 Miles, Class I; drops 15' per mile. Suitable for rafts, kayaks, and canoes. Irrigation dams!

Rogers Mesa is 18 miles upstream from Delta. The water is flat and there is much evidence of human habitation along the bank. Irrigation dams pose a serious threat if not watched for. Several novices have drowned here.

GUNNISON RIVER: Delta to Whitewater (love that name!)

Circa 30 Miles, Class I (some II–?); drops 6½' per mile. Suitable for kayaks, rafts, and canoes.

The railroad, but not U.S. Highway 50, parallels the river through (surprise!) an 800-foot-deep canyon along the edge of the tree-covered Uncompahgre Plateau. The water is flat and easy to paddle, but the scenery is splendid. The canyon is not wilderness — in addition to the railroad, there are a few isolated ranches.

Secondary roads leave U.S. 50, headed for the river, at distances of 8, 10, 13, and 17 miles from Delta, making possible a variety of trips of different lengths. The last 12 miles of canyon above Whitewater are said to be the best. This is a secret run of the open canoeists.

Whitewater, Colorado, despite its romantic name, is a rather ordinary farming community on U.S. 50 just beyond the fringes of the Grand Junction suburbs. West of here is the remarkable Unaweep Canyon, once a channel of the ancestral Colorado River, now the channel of Colorado Highway 141.

GUNNISON RIVER: Whitewater to confluence

10 Miles, Class I; drops circa 5' per mile. Suitable for kayaks, rafts, and canoes.

After another 5 miles of canyon, shared with the railroad, the river loses water into a variety of irrigation canals in the Grand Junction suburbs, and eventually finds its way to the Colorado River.

UNCOMPAHGRE RIVER

UNCOMPAHGRE RIVER: Ouray, Colorado to Ridgeway

10 Miles, Class II, III, III+; drops 100' per mile. Not very suitable even for kayaks. Irrigation dams!

An extremely fast-moving, very tiny Uncompahgre River leaves the "little Switzerland of America" in the San Juan Mountains, and flows down a deep U-shaped glacial valley toward Ridgeway. Beware of logs, fences, and irrigation dams in the first 5 miles where the drop *exceeds* 120 feet per mile. Thereafter, the valley floor is broad and the drop is more like 40 feet per mile.

The river is continuous gradient and good eddies are few. Tree limb snags are common where the river splits into braided channels over a myriad of gravel bars. There is nearly continuous access from U.S. 550 for the first 5 miles below Ouray. There are secondary roads every couple of miles thereafter.

UNCOMPAHGRE RIVER: Ridgeway to Delta

Circa 45 Miles, Class I, II, II+; drops 44' per mile. Suitable for kayaks.

The extremely tiny (less than 200 cfs) river keeps gaining tributaries and losing drop as it goes along, until it is a rather flat 400 cfs or so at Montrose.

There is some nice whitewater in the 12 miles below Ridgeway, and more or less ready access from U.S. 550. Thereafter, irrigation ditches can remove a substantial amount of the river's water and the steep drop is gone. Various unnamed secondary roads (and U.S. 550) hit the river everywhere that gaps in the willows will allow them to.

The confluence with the Gunnison River is a few hundred yards from the Delta sewage lagoons.

DOLORES RIVER

UPPER DOLORES: Above Rico

Class IV, V, VI. Semisuitable for kayaks.

The diehard small stream boater can put-in on the Dolores as high as he/she likes, as in spring there is sufficient water for boating and the road up Lizard Head Pass, Route 145, roughly follows the stream.

As you would expect, the river becomes more and more difficult the higher one ascends. Tight, rocky, nasty drops abound. A few sections have been run, but this stretch has interested very few boaters up to now.

DOLORES RIVER: Rico to Stoner

20 Miles, Class II, III; drops 60' per mile. Suitable for kayaks.

As with the previous stretch, this is not normally run. The river frequently disappears from the road, making car-scouting impossible. Weirs and fences must be contended with, as they are numerous along this stretch.

UPPER DOLORES: Stoner to McPhee dam

32 Miles, Class I (with continuous small, choppy waters); drops 31' per mile. Suitable for kayaks.

This stretch is (still) a mountain stream with clear, cold water and a fairly uniform riverbed. It passes through hilly green ranchland, and the scenery is truly pleasant. Eddies are few. There is a small dam below the town of Dolores which must be portaged. At its highest level, the reservoir backs up water over nearly all this run.

DOLORES RIVER: Damsite (or near Cahone) to Slickrock

47 River Miles (or 44 depending on put-in) (2–3-day trip), Class II+, III and one Class IV rapid (easily portaged). Shuttle one way 33 miles. Suitable for kayaks and rafts. Season: Mid-April to late May. Administered by: BLM, Montrose District Office, Highway 550 South, P.O. Box 1269, Montrose, Colorado 81401, phone (303) 249-7791.

This section of the Dolores is one of the most popular and beautiful. The river enters a wild and deep canyon which combines red sandstone cliffs with coniferous forest. It retains the character of a mountain stream, rocky and clear when low. Wildlife is abundant; black bears are occasionally seen, as are elk, deer, beaver, mountain lion, and pine martens.

Because of its beauty and remoteness, the Dolores, for 105 miles below McPhee Dam, has been proposed for inclusion in the Wild and Scenic River system. Unfortunately, there has been no action on this in the last few years, despite recommendations by the appropriate government agencies for inclusion. Opposition comes from those interested in mining nearby uranium and those interested in building another dam.

While on the subject of opposition, a word about McPhee Dam. This is one of the famed seven Colorado River water projects, but it is one which survived. The construction costs of this dam (financed with federal money) are far in excess of the predicted benefits which will be derived from it. The cost to benefit ratio is 0.7. In other words, it would have cost the taxpayers less to directly subsidize the beneficiaries with cold hard cash. The dam will benefit approximately 100 people in the area, most of whom plan to change from being pinto bean growers (dry farmers) to being fruit growers (irrigators). The town of Dove Creek is presently the "Pinto Bean Capital of the World," but it won't be for long, so you should be sure to see it. Who knows where the new Pinto Bean Capital of the World will crop up?

In addition to the purely economical side of this issue, the fact that all of the water of the Colorado River has already been allocated fails to sway the dam's proponents. While we form new orchards in Dove Creek, Colorado, the fruit growers of California, who have been using Colorado River water for decades, will find that they have less of it and that it is of poorer quality, thereby making the well-established California orchards less suitable for agricultural output — yet it is the Congress of the nation which was responsible for the dam.

Still more dams like this one are constantly being proposed and funded, drawing on Colorado River water which is presently 100 percent allocated. So join your favorite conservation organization, write your congressmen and senators, and help save the rivers!

The Dolores River is unusual in that a permit is not required to run it, yet. It is run commercially and is popular with privates. Parts of it are bordered by private land, among these the put-in near Cahone and the take-out at Slickrock.

The season is variable, but normally begins during the first week of April and extends through May. During dry snow years, the season is short and dependent on weather — the last two weeks in May are the normal peak period. It is best to check with the BLM for flow information (address, etc., with heading for this section). During good snow years, with a hot spell of weather, this river can really flood and becomes a Class IV run. There are times when *everyone* portages the famed (Class IV) Snaggletooth Rapid which, incidentally, underwent a change in 1980 due to rocks having shifted.

The weather can be very cold; snow is not uncommon in May and June, nor are mosquitoes, so be sure to be prepared for both. By June, unbearably hot and buggy conditions are the norm. Timing is the key on this river.

Snaggletooth is located about 3 miles below the pumphouse (on

Deer Creek (*Bart Henderson*).

Olo Canyon (*Fletcher Anderson*).

The river near Saddle Canyon (*Fletcher Anderson*).

The canyon above Elves Chasm (*Fletcher Anderson*).

Blue River at outlet from Lake Dillon Dam: slalom course in the artificial rapids (*Jack Burkholzer*).

Deer Creek Falls (*Fletcher Anderson*).

Colorado River, Ruby and Horsethief canyons in the fall (*Fletcher Anderson*).

Sandbar near Saddle Canyon (*Fletcher Anderson*).

left). There is a stretch of trail on river left for scouting and portaging. Below Snaggletooth there is a 3-mile stretch of numerous Class II and III rapids. The river flattens out and slows down 6–8 miles above Slick Rock. In the deep part of the canyon just above the pumphouse, there is an Indian ruin with pictographs.

Access: The main put-in is at the McPhee Damsite, to which a road leads from Rt. 160, just northwest of the town of Pleasant View. There is also a put-in near Cahone. Both entail driving about 6 miles down dirt roads into the canyon. The Cahone put-in is on private land. Please be aware that you are a guest on private property, i.e., keep it clean and respect any signs.

The take-out is at the bridge in Slickrock. There is a fee of $1.50 per day for parking at the take-out. This should be paid to the landowner who can be found in the Slickrock Cafe and Post Office. It is especially important to be courteous and amenable to the wishes of the landowner here because in the past boaters have been rude and refused to pay her small fee. She has threatened to deny access to all boaters. Understandably, she has tired of people behaving as if it were their right to trespass, park, litter, etc., on her land.

DOLORES RIVER: Slickrock to Bedrock

58 River Miles, Class II; drops 10' per mile. Suitable for kayaks, rafts, and canoes. Shuttle one way 60 miles, paved roads. Season: Mid-April through late May.

This stretch of the Dolores enters more desertlike country and continues through a scenic sandstone canyon. It is an easy run and can be slow going at low water. It is suitable for open canoes, whereas the Cahone to Slick Rock run is not recommended for open boats.

Many advise not to come here in June unless it is unusually cold. The bugs and heat can be really terrible, a fact to which many will attest in much stronger language. Others have had great trips in June, so take your choice.

DOLORES RIVER: Bedrock to confluence with San Miguel (Paradox Valley)

8 Miles, Class II, III; drops 13' per mile. Suitable for kayaks, rafts, and possible in canoes.

A dirt road parallels the river here and access is nearly continuous.

The river enters the Paradox Valley, so called because the river flows (NE) at a 90° angle to the valley (which runs NW to SE).

When crossing the Paradox Valley near the town of Bedrock, there is a beautiful sweeping view of the La Sal Mountains and the Paradox Valley. Here one finds a pocket of Colorado that is reminiscent of the character of the entire state as it was 15 years ago. This valley shows little or no change caused by the great influx of recreationists and energy developers which have had such a marked impact on the better known parts of Colorado. This is a pleasant and scenic run, with quite a few little rapids. The last third of this section is a really pretty little canyon, as the river nears the confluence with the San Miguel. James Watt advocated using the valley as a uranium spent fuel dump.

The water here is incredibly salty. The river flows through salt domes, remnants of shallow seas, which are scattered about this region.

DOLORES RIVER: Confluence with San Miguel to Gateway

35 Miles, Class II; drops 8' per mile.

This section (as are those above) is administered by the BLM, Montrose, Colorado (see Damsite to Slickrock section).

Dolores River, just above confluence with San Miguel (*Ann Hopkinson*)

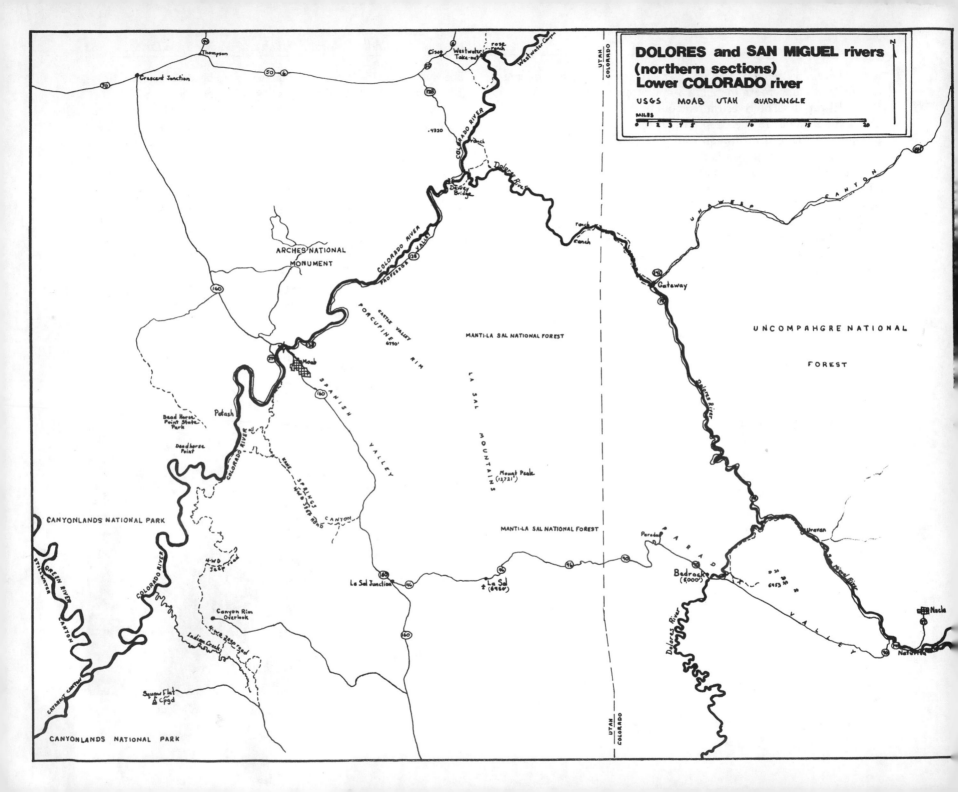

DOLORES and SAN MIGUEL rivers
(northern sections)
Lower COLORADO river

USGS MOAB UTAH QUADRANGLE

The road is hundreds of feet above the river at the confluence and for about 5 miles below it. The canyon is deep, red, and spectacular.

A deteriorating hanging flume (of wood) still hangs above the river, clinging to the side of the canyon wall. It once brought water from the San Miguel River to the Lone Tree Placer. It was built in the 1890s to carry water to the arid, gold-bearing sands of the placer. Workmen were lowered in cradles from a shelf 400 feet above the river or were suspended from a cantilever frame beyond the end of the completed platform. It was never finished due to the gold panic of 1893 and was only operated on a limited basis. The placer produced next to no gold so that the whole operation was finally abandoned.

The San Miguel River causes a doubling of the size of the Dolores at their juncture. Flows are totally dependent on snow and spring weather, as they are throughout this region. Crests of 3,000–7,000 cfs are usual, but they reach as high as 17,000 cfs in big years when rain floods augment snowmelt crests. The boating season is still April and May (same as the runs farther upstream), in wet years April through July.

A water level gauge can be read from the northwestern end of the Highway 141 bridge in Gateway. Its scale ranges from 0 to 7, roughly equivalent to 200 cfs and 9,000 cfs, respectively. Adequate water for rafts is 1.5 and above, preferably 2.5. Open canoes, except for experts, should stay below 3 unless they portage (Perry, *Rivers of Colorado*—1978).

The rapids were all formed by flash-flooding side canyons which deposited debris into the main river. Most of them tail out at the end, as is typical with this breed of rapid. The first rapid, Wingate, is at mile 2.5 and has a sharply undercut cliff at bottom right. Four more Class II and above rapids are encountered before arrival in Gateway.

Good drinking water, the only available on the trip, can be obtained about 6 miles below the confluence, 15 feet below the road and 50 feet downstream from the "Spring Water" sign. Due to the large amount of uranium mining in this region, it is strongly advised that you not succumb to the temptation of taking sips of river water.

When the Chinle formation, a more erodible rock, appears at mile 16, both camps and rapids become more frequent.

Access: The road (Highway 141) parallels the river but is cut into the side of the canyon, high above the river. There is no parking at the confluence of the Dolores and the San Miguel. You must either put-in at Bedrock or be dropped-off at the confluence. The take-out is 100 yards above the Gateway Bridge on the right, on Highway Department property.

For a mile-by-mile detailed description of this run, we recommend Earl Perry's *Rivers of Colorado.*

DOLORES RIVER: Gateway to confluence with the Colorado River (Dewey Bridge)

30 Miles, Class II, III; drops 18' per mile. Suitable for kayaks and rafts. Season: Mid-May through mid-June. Permit required from: BLM, Grand Resource Area, P.O. Box M, Moab, Utah 84532, phone (801) 259-6111 ext. 200.

This section is similar to the ones above: with some Class II and III rapids, sandstone formations and mesas flanking the river. It is a Wild and Scenic Study river, as are the upstream sections of both the Dolores and the Colorado.

The shuttle is incredibly long (140 miles) for the length of the river traveled. However, a dirt road goes upstream from the Dewey Bridge for about 3 miles. On both banks at Gateway, dirt roads travel downstream for about 8 miles. Both lead to ranches.

At the Utah–Colorado border, a complicated Class III rapid (aptly called Stateline) could cause some trouble for rafts or inattentive kayakers.

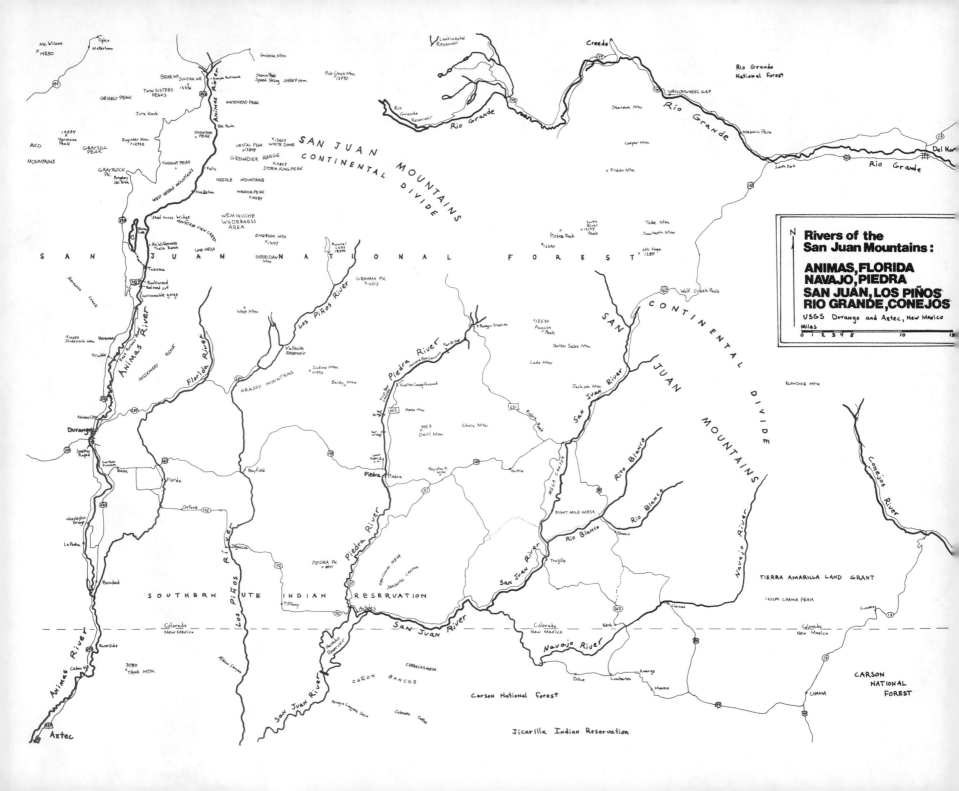

Rivers of the San Juan Mountains:

ANIMAS, FLORIDA NAVAJO, PIEDRA SAN JUAN, LOS PIÑOS RIO GRANDE, CONEJOS

USGS Durango and Aztec, New Mexico

Miles

0 1 2 3 4 5   10   15

LOWER COLORADO RIVER AND MAJOR TRIBUTARIES

THE SAN JUAN MOUNTAINS
Introduction

General Description

The 14,000-foot San Juan Mountains fit neatly into the southwestern corner of the state of Colorado, above the surrounding 4–5,000-foot plateau. These are distinctly unreal looking mountains —the sort of extreme spires and overhanging crags a small child might draw. On these jagged spires are deposited the region's heaviest snowfalls, and from them roar down the region's most awesome and devastating avalanches.

The Needle Mountains section of the San Juans is protected by the Weminuchee Wilderness Area. Most of the rest of the range is in the San Juan National Forest.

The combination of steep mountains and heavy snowpack produce numerous spectacular rivers, all but a few of which are well beyond the abilities of the average boater. Not all of these rivers are listed in this guide. Indeed, not all of them have been run. It is probable that the unlisted rivers are miniature versions of those described. Access is a problem for all rivers except those described.

Will Perry on the Rio de los Piños, San Juan Mountains. (All rivers of the San Juans look much like this—big boulders, steep drop, constricted routes.) *(Judy Fox)*

PIEDRA RIVER: Piedra Road Bridge to Hunter Campground (2nd Box Canyon)

20 Miles, Class III, IV; drops 60' per mile. Suitable for kayaks.

Piedra Road Bridge is accessible via a dirt road which heads north from U.S. 160, 2 miles west of Pagosa Springs. Hunter Campground is 10 miles north of Piedra. First Fork Road vaguely parallels the river but is not close enough for continuous access.

There is a gauge at Highway 160 near the town of Piedra. The flow for 2nd Box Canyon is roughly half that indicated on the gauge. Peak flows of circa 1,000 cfs can be anticipated in May. In April and earlier, and in July or later, this stretch is often unrunnably low. It has occasionally been successfully rafted, but more often rafting attempts end in disaster.

Drop is fairly uniform and Class II and III rapids come in quick succession. Dense forest lines the banks and fallen trees in the river are common.

Second Box Canyon proper begins about 6 miles below the put-in and continues for about a mile. At full flood, a great deal of water can push through this little rock garden—perhaps producing a Class IV rapid.

Hunter Campground is 2 miles below the end of 2nd Box Canyon.

PIEDRA RIVER: Hunter Campground to Piedra (1st Box Canyon —Why is 1st Box below 2nd? Do they count backward here?)

10 Miles, Class III, IV; circa drops 50' per mile, but drop exceeds 100' per mile in 1st Box Canyon proper. Suitable for kayaks.

First, a word of warning: portaging in the 1st Box Canyon can require mountaineering skills on a par with the boating skills required to run the river—climbing out might be still more difficult. At very high flood stages (over 2,500 cfs on the gauge at Piedra), this rapid approaches or reaches a Class V and should be avoided by nearly all paddlers. We believe *no* rafter should *ever* try Class V water, and very, very few belong in Class IV. Rafting attempts to run this river usually fail, and the nature of the climb-out could turn one of these raft adventures into a disaster.

And now, a word of encouragement: if you *are* a paddler of Class IV ability, this is a spectacular little river of fascinating, complex rapids and a unique sort of mountain forest scenery. The tranquil canyon is in beautiful harmony with the rampaging little river.

This is the very definition of a wild and scenic river and has been recommended for study as such. Timber interests feel otherwise.

First Box Canyon occurs about a mile below the put-in, and if you have any doubts, walk down and scout it. The 100 foot per mile drop produces the run's worst rapids in the ensuing circa 1 mile long canyon. Most people should avoid this area at flows over 2,000 cfs.

Below Box Canyon is another mile or two of less difficult (but still Class IV, except at low water), boulder field rapids. Thereafter, the run is mostly, but not entirely, Class II. There is a packhorse bridge about 4½ miles above Piedra, and another 3 miles above. Piedra Campground, on the right bank a mile above U.S. 160, is the best take-out.

PIEDRA RIVER: Piedra to confluence with the San Juan under Navajo Reservoir

10–15 Miles, Class I; drops 20' per mile. Suitable for kayaks, possibly for small rafts and canoes.

The Piedra changes dramatically to become a meandering stream lined with cottonwood groves as it flows among the tree-covered mesas of the Southern Ute Indian Reservation.

Colorado 151 joins the river about 4 miles below the town of Piedra and provides numerous access points all the way to the reservoir.

NAVAJO RIVER: Chroma to confluence

23 Miles, Class I; 20' per mile drop. Usually not boatable.

Navajo River rest in peace. This was once a seldom visited little canyon in the remote reaches of the Jicarilla Apache Reservation. Since 1970, nearly all its water has gone through the Azotea Tunnel into the Chama River (described elsewhere in this guide).

In a very wet year, it might still be possible to make the run. It used to flow beside old homesteads in a tight little sandstone canyon, shared with the old abandoned narrow gauge railroad grade.

ANIMAS RIVER: Silverton to Rockwood, Colorado

28 Miles, Class IV, some V; drops 80' per mile. Suitable for kayaks.

Here is yet another of the "classic" runs of the West—big, powerful whitewater in a narrow constricted canyon flowing through a fantastic high mountain wilderness area. It has been called one of the five best river runs in the world—but only for those possessing genuine whitewater expertise.

This canyon has been attempted by rafters on more than one occasion. All of these attempts have resulted in lost rafts, and a few have resulted in death. "Absolutely unrunnable" claims one Durango raft guide. "A killer river, pure and simple" says another. Yet, expert kayakers, since Ron Mason in 1966, have known otherwise and run the river frequently and quite safely. Even most expert paddlers should probably leave this stretch alone at levels much above 2,000 cfs (typically May through early July). At less than 1,000 cfs (typically late August through September), determined paddlers of low-expert ability might make the run with comparitive safety. There is a gauging station in Durango.

This run has been done in one day, but is normally a two, or even three day run because of the scouting required. The put-in is at 9,230-foot elevation, so an April or May run could easily be snowed out. Warm weather in those months could dramatically change the flow overnight. Better, therefore, to catch the river on the way down in late summer or fall.

Put-in at Silverton, Colorado—don't be misled by the size of the river, as it will double in about ¼ mile and nearly double again within the next 5 miles thereafter.

If these first rapids prove to be too difficult, take-out now because far more powerful rapids will be found below. A foot bridge at Elk Park (5 miles into the canyon) is on a trail up to U.S. 550. If you have *any* doubts, do not hesitate to use this 2 mile, 2,600 vertical foot trail or walk back upstream. Alternately you can *sometimes* get a boat on the narrow gauge tourist train in an emergency (but don't count on it).

Nine miles into the canyon, the serious whitewater begins. One of the earliest rapids is a definite Class V (portagable, thank God, at high water) with huge powerful holes. There follows 6 or 7 miles of thoroughly enjoyable ongoing Class III, IV water to the Needleton Railroad stop and backpacker's bridge. Be aware of a runnable circa 10-foot-high waterfall in the midst of this section which will occur at the end of one of the Class IV sections. Scout extensively until you are certain you have passed it. Another Class IV rapid begins only about 60 feet beyond the falls. Roll up fast!

(All of this can be portaged along the railroad tracks.)

Two miles below the Needleton Bridge is an abandoned steel bridge. The next half mile stretch requires considerable scouting.

Below Cascade Creek (roughly 17 miles into the run) the river—and the waves—become larger, but the drop is less continuous and the channel less boulder strewn. There are several III and IV rapids with intervening stretches of easier water.

The hydroelectric plant at Tacoma is a prominent landmark. Water from Electra Lake (above and out of sight on the right) descends through large visible pipes to the plant and pours into the river from a culvert. Electra Lake was so named in 1906 when a dam to feed the electric plant increased its size.

The usual take-out is at the high steel bridge one mile below the plant. Walk two miles along the narrow gauge railroad tracks through the cut to Rockwood. Durango kayaker, Milt Wiley (Crazy Milt Wiley and his beautiful daughter: a legend of the west—but that's another story), has built a bicycle-powered device which runs along the railroad tracks and carries four people and their kayaks. The railroad would like to catch him, but he's too quick for them.

For the more daring, the next mile below the bridge is a 100 foot per mile vertical-walled little slot of heavy boulder-filled Class IV and V rapids. A second take-out lies at the end of this stretch two miles below the bridge on the right. You must climb up a steep little forested gully to the railroad cut high above.

It is potentially fatal to miss this take-out, for the next mile and a half of river is unrunnable Class VI in an extremely narrow boulder and log-choked chute dropping 250 feet to the mile. Suicidal inner-tubers have attempted this mile and a half gorge with predictable results. Some of the bodies have yet to be recovered.

ANIMAS RIVER: East Animas Road Bridge to Durango

14 road, 25 river miles, Class I; drops 5' per mile. Suitable for kayaks, rafts, and canoes.

This run is detailed in Earl Perry's *Rivers of Colorado*. East Animas road runs up the valley on the east side, U.S. 550 on the west. The bridge is 14 miles from town.

The river meanders across (and sometimes floods) a mile-wide floodplain of glacial debris. Despite the occasional old auto body erosion control schemes, this is a beautiful run offering spectacular scenery, a plethora of bird life, and tranquil relaxed floating. Open canoeists from the Durango area often paddle here, particularly when the high water closes the runs below Durango.

There is a put-in/take-out at the Trimble Lane Bridge, 6 road miles (11 river) above Durango, another at the Animas City Bridge on the outskirts of town, and several within the city limits.

ANIMAS RIVER: Durango to Bondad

16 Miles, Class II, II+; drops 20–25' per mile. Suitable for kayaks, rafts, possible for canoes.

Beginning in a high walled canyon, this run reaches on out into the flatlands to the south.

Smelter Rapids—Class III with big holes at high water—lies, appropriately enough, opposite the old smelter. It can be avoided by putting in from the La Posta Road ½ mile below the rapid. Go 4 miles south on 5th Avenue (La Posta Road) from U.S. 160.

Numerous Class II riffles occur throughout most of the run, and it is here that Durango area kayakers acquire the skills which they later employ on more mountainous runs. Here, too, is the run most favored by rafters and open canoeists—except at flood stages when waves grow large enough to easily swamp open canoes.

A particular hazard on this run, especially on the lower reaches,

Judy Fox on the San Juan River—warm water, no lifejacket, no rocks
(Fletcher Anderson)

are derelict irrigation diversion weirs. Some of these were built of concrete, wood, and old railroad rails and now the ends of the rails stick out into the current. Approach all these structures with caution lest you be swept into them before you determine where the rails are.

Take-out is at the Bondad Bridge on U.S. 550.

Up to 400 cfs of the Animas may soon be diverted into the La Plata River for irrigation. At high water, the effect would be negligible, but at low water it could mean an end to paddling.

ANIMAS RIVER: Bondad to confluence

Circa 30 Miles, Class I; drops 12' per mile. Suitable for kayaks, canoes, and small rafts.

The river hits the flats and begins meandering along among the cottonwoods roughly parallel to U.S. 550 on to Aztec, New Mexico, Farmington, and the confluence with the San Juan. To the best of our knowledge, little boating takes place on this stretch—but presumably more residents of Aztec and Farmington will take up paddling and this will be their backyard run.

SAN JUAN RIVER: East Fork confluence on U.S. 160 to Pagosa Springs

9 Miles, Class IV; drops 66' per mile. Suitable for kayaks.

The east fork comes in from the east (!) about 9 miles above Pagosa Springs. A narrow, sometimes tree-lined little stream closely follows U.S. 160 and offers (when runnable) many small constricted Class IV rapids.

SAN JUAN RIVER: Pagosa Springs to Trujillo (Mesa Canyon Run)

16 Miles, Class II (II+ at highwater); drops 31' per mile. Suitable for kayaks, probably possible for small rafts and some canoes.

Boating within the city limits takes you past everyone's trash piles before moving on by the sewage disposal lagoon, etc.

The rest of the run is a seldom visited and infrequently run little canyon on Southern Ute Indian and San Juan National Forest land. South facing slopes are piñon-juniper woodlands and north slopes are ponderosa forest. One can see occasional evidence of previous habitation and (rarely) modern Ute Indians. This is their land, and they could close the canyon to boating if boaters behave badly. This is a secret run of expert open canoeists and local kayakers.

The biggest rapid is a recirculating hole at the end of a long Class II stretch near the mouth of Squaw Canyon, perhaps seven miles into the run.

A solor rafter in search of somewhere to unload the gear of the fifteen kayakers he is traveling with on the San Juan River *(Fletcher Anderson)*

Ten miles downstream from Pagosa Springs is the bed of the Rio Blanco—once a Class II run—the water of which now goes through a pipe to the Chama.

A secondary road leads south from Pagosa Springs and parallels the last 5 miles of river to Trujillo. Another secondary road goes west from U.S. 84 along the Rio Blanco to the confluence, but dead ends at the river on the left bank.

San Juan River: Trujillo to Navajo Reservoir

27 Miles, Class II, (followed by flat Class I); drops 20' per mile. Suitable for canoes and kayaks.

A dirt road from the reservoir to Trujillo parallels the river and provides easy access at numerous points. There are a few Class II rapids in the early part of the run, however, this is mostly flat water with a few little riffles. As with some other easy runs in the region, there is no population center in the immediate vicinity and boaters must pass by other similar runs to get here. Thus, very few people paddle this stretch. In exchange for a little longer drive over a fair amount of dirt road, you end up with a river all to yourself. This is not true wilderness and you will see a few little ranches tucked in among the cottonwoods, but that style of agriculture is, for

many of us, a reassuring sight in these days of corporate agrobiz and water diversion projects.

San Juan River: Navajo Reservoir to Farmington

Approximately 40 Miles, Class I; drops approximately 14' per mile. Suitable for kayaks, canoes, small rafts.

The San Juan frequently leaves behind a great deal of water in Navajo Reservoir, making this stretch only marginally boatable. When it is flowing, the river moves through a constantly shifting maze of sandbars toward Farmington. There is a lot of irrigated farmland here and substantially more population than above the reservoir.

San Juan River: Farmington, New Mexico to Bluff, Utah

100 Miles, Class I; drops 8' per mile. Suitable for rafts, kayaks, and canoes.

The river in the immediate vicinity of Farmington receives the combined flows of the Animas and the La Plata rivers, turns a thick muddy brown, and heads off across the desert. Just beyond Farmington, the river enters the Navajo Indian Reservation and irrigated farming is replaced by dry sagebrush followed by desert. The Navajos don't get much of the water from Navajo Reservoir— apparently the glory of having it named "Navajo" was considered a sufficient benefit by the bureaucrats who conceived of the project.

The warm sluggish water oozes its incredible sediment load through braided stream channels, sandbars, and tamarisk covered islands of its own making; however, at high water (May and June) there can be over 10,000 cfs of thick muddy water which shifts the islands and sandbars around at a startling rate. This is the season of the fabled sand waves: the sandy bottom of the river channel will be shifted by the fast current and the resulting irregularity will produce a wave. In a matter of only a few seconds, the wave will shift more bottom sand and a whole series of big symmetrical waves will appear where there was only flat water before. For a minute or two the waves will persist and migrate in stately uniformity up or downstream from their point of origin. Then the sand will be leveled again and the waves will dissipate as rapidly as they appeared. These waves are, typically, at least three feet high (higher than eye level for a seated kayaker), but occasionally grow to heights of

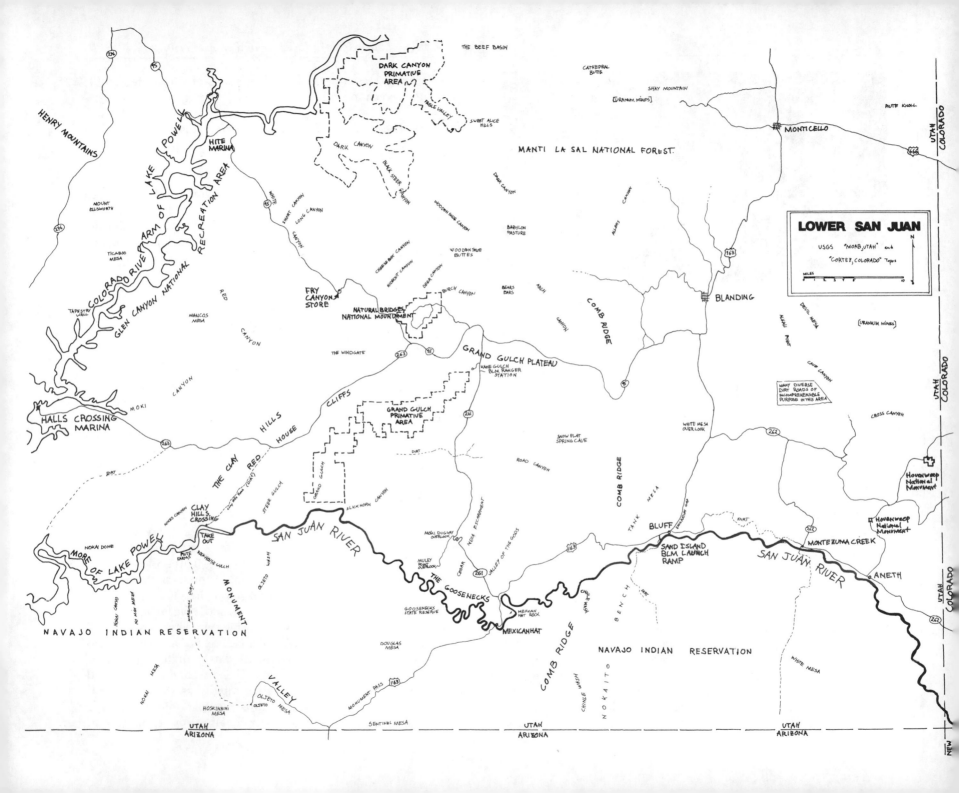

seven or eight feet! For someone unaware of the process, the entire phenomenon can be somewhat threatening—but the waves are absolutely harmless and are considered the best kayak surfing to be found on any river in the world.

What a remarkable phenomenon—why is this piece of river not very popular? Well, on either side of the river are endless sagebrush flats occasionally interrupted by rumbling oil and gas wells connected by grimy dirt roads and pipelines. Their effect is to change the character of the land from isolation to desolation. Below Bluff, Utah, the same river will do its stuff in the midst of a beautiful wilderness sandstone canyon lined with Indian ruins. *That* stretch of the river now sees fairly heavy use and those who prefer the inanimate rumblings of the oil fields to the screams and shrieks of the tourists might be more inclined to boat up here. Interestingly enough, wildlife is scared off by tourists, but not by oil wells (though there is some obvious habitat destruction).

There is access to the river at Farmington; at Shiprock, New Mexico, 30 miles downstream; at the U.S. 160 crossing about 25 miles further on; at Aneth, Utah (spoken as though with a lisp), another 20 miles below there; and roughly 25 miles below Aneth at Bluff, Utah. The best take-out near Bluff is at Sand Island recreation site, a few miles west of town. No permits are required for this run, almost no people are encountered except at the access points, and the result is one of the few remaining desert rivers that can be run on the spur of the moment. The others require a permit which must be obtained many months in advance. Run wild! Go naked! Eat, drink, and be merry, for tomorrow you may be in Utah!

LOWER SAN JUAN RIVER

84 Miles (good 3–5 day trip), Class I, II; drops 8' per mile. Suitable for kayaks, rafts, and canoes.

Access: Bluff, Mexican Hat, Clay Hills Crossing (on Lake Powell).

This most popular portion of the San Juan River is located on the Navajo Indian Reservation, an intriguing culture area to visit. The Navajos are statistically the best off of all the native American tribes. They have the most land and the largest population. They are also the only people able to coax any subsistence out of that dry land and able to raise sheep where others are not. However, they are almost too good at raising sheep and overgrazing has become a problem.

The San Juan is a true desert river, with flows ranging from around 15,000 muddy cfs at runoff (early June, generally), to a trickle of precious clear green water in late summer and fall. A typical year will provide a high water period just under 10,000 cfs from mid-May to mid-July. The season varies greatly year to year, depending on weather. It is usually good throughout June and a week or two into July. It is runnable much earlier (in April). The water gets soupy warm after the hot weather sets in, making the San Juan a great river for swimming, Eskimo rolling, mudfights, waterfights, kids, dogs, beginners, etc. It can be cold and rainy if you go too early in the season. Summer arrives with a vengeance when it arrives, but sometimes it comes surprisingly late. It is best to check on flows and weather before you go (river flow information: USGS in Moab, or Bureau of Reclamation, Salt Lake City, or BLM Moab District, Monticello, Utah).

Camping: Good campsites are plentiful. No clean drinking water is available (raw sewage is emptied into the river at Bluff and Mexican Hat). One must either carry water or settle and boil (for 20 minutes) the river water (leaf of prickly pear will settle out the silt when placed in the boiling water).

It is best to bring your entire drinking water supply with you and not to impose on the Indians for water. Many of their wells have water but are unsafe for drinking. The reservation does not have an abundant water supply.

LOWER SAN JUAN RIVER: Bluff to Mexican Hat, Utah

30 Miles (1–2 day trip), Class I, II; drops 8' per mile. Suitable for kayaks, rafts, and canoes.

Logistical Information: The San Juan is administered by the BLM (Moab District, San Juan Resource Area, P.O. Box 7, Monticello, UT. 84535, phone (801) 587-2201). Permits are required and are limited to one private launch per day. Applications should not be submitted more than 60 days in advance.

This stretch is run commercially; and it is normal to see other private parties on the river, as well.

The put-in is at Sand Island Campground, reached via a short road which leaves Highway 163 a mile or so west of Bluff, and heads south to the river. Sand Island Campground has shade, outhouses, and parking spaces—but no water.

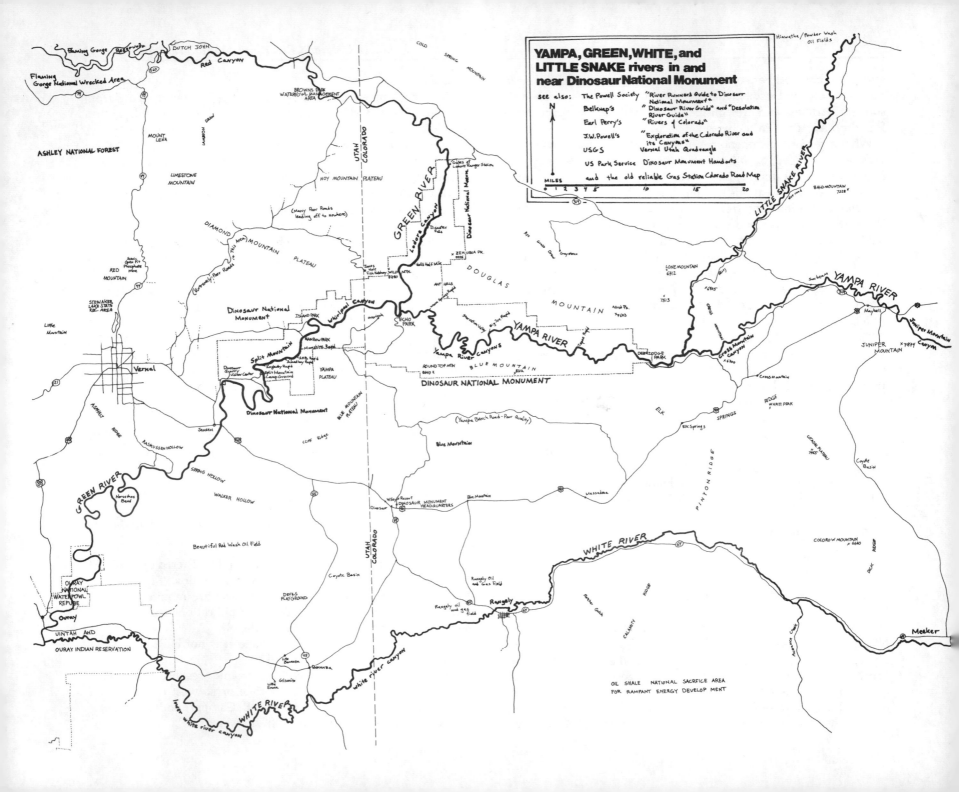

YAMPA, GREEN, WHITE, and LITTLE SNAKE rivers in and near Dinosaur National Monument

see also:

The Powell Society	"River Runners Guide to Dinosaur National Monument"	
Belknap's	"Dinosaur River Guide" and "Desolation River Guide"	
Earl Perry's	"Rivers of Colorado"	
J.W. Powell's	"Exploration of the Colorado River and its Canyons"	
USGS	Vernal Utah Quadrangle	
US Park Service	Dinosaur Monument Handouts	

and the old reliable Gas Station Colorado Road Map

N

MILES
0 1 2 3 4 5   10   15   20

Hiawatha / Powder Wash Oil Fields

COLD SPRING MOUNTAIN

Flaming Gorge Reservoir

DUTCH JOHN

Red Canyon

Flaming Gorge National Wrecked Area

BROWNS PARK WATERFOWL MANAGEMENT AREA

MOUNT LENA

HORNY DRAW

ASHLEY NATIONAL FOREST

LIMESTONE MOUNTAIN

HOY MOUNTAIN PLATEAU

UTAH / COLORADO

GREEN RIVER

Gates Lodore Ranger Station

Dinosaur National Monument

LITTLE SNAKE RIVER

BALD MOUNTAIN 7228

Lodore Canyon

Disaster Falls

(Many Poor Roads leading off to nowhere)

DIAMOND MOUNTAIN PLATEAU

RED MOUNTAIN

Scenic Open Pit Phosphate Mine

(Formerly Poor Roads in This Area)

ZENOBIA PK. 9006

Hells Half Mile

DOUGLAS

Mrs. Grass Creek / Greystone

LONE MOUNTAIN 6112

STEINAKER LAKE STATE REC AREA

Little Mountain

Dinosaur National Monument

Jones Hole Fish Hatchery

WILD MTN 8390

ANT HILLS

MOUNTAIN

Zenobia Pk. 7693

6705

7513

Sunbeam

YAMPA RIVER

Maybell

ISLAND PARK

Whirlpool Canyon

overlook

ECHO PARK

Warm Springs Valley

Big Joe Rapid

YAMPA RIVER

JUNIPER MOUNTAIN 7874

JUNIPER MOUNTAIN

Juniper Canyon

Vernal

RAINBOW PARK

Mitchell Rapid

Yampa River Canyons

DEERLODGE PARK

CROSS MOUNTAIN CANYON

CROSS MOUNTAIN 6700

SPLIT MOUNTAIN

Tepee Rapid

ROUND TOP MTN 6610

BLUE MOUNTAIN

Cross Mountain

Dinosaur Quarry Visitor Center

Split Mountain Campground

YAMPA PLATEAU

DINOSAUR NATIONAL MONUMENT

ELK

SPRINGS

RIDGE

WANTI PEAK

ASPHALT RIDGE

Dinosaur National Monument

BLUE MOUNTAIN PLATEAU

(Yampa Bench Road - Poor Quality)

Elk Springs

COLOROW PLATEAU 7155

Coyote Basin

RASMUSSEN HOLLOW

Jensen

CLIFF RIDGE

Blue Mountain

SPRING HOLLOW

GREEN RIVER

Horseshoe Bend

WALKER HOLLOW

Wigolo Resort

DINOSAUR MONUMENT HEADQUARTERS

Blue Mountain

Massadona

PINYON RIDGE

COLOROW MOUNTAIN x 6640

Coyote Basin

Dinosaur

WHITE RIVER

67

PICK RIDGE

Beautiful Red Wash Oil Field

UTAH / COLORADO

Rangely Oil and Gas Field

Parker Gulch

OURAY NATIONAL WATERFOWL REFUGE

DEVILS PLAYGROUND

Coyote Basin

Rangely oil and gas field

Rangely

67

CALAMITY RIDGE

Piceance Creek

Ouray

UINTAH AND OURAY INDIAN RESERVATION

45

Little Bonanza

Bonanza

Little Emma

Gilsonite

white river canyon

OIL SHALE NATIONAL SACRIFICE AREA FOR RAMPANT ENERGY DEVELOPMENT

Meeker

lower white river canyon

WHITE RIVER

Mexican Hat can be used as a take-out (or put-in, or cold beer stop), depending on your available time. It has a cafe, bar, and small store (with ice cream and cold beer).

River Description: Boating the San Juan is an ideal way to see the desert and Canyonlands topography. Pueblo cliff dwellings and granaries abound in this stretch. The Indian dwellings are all "undeveloped" by any government agency, thus allowing people the pleasure of finding and examining them on their own. The Federal Antiquities Act does forbid the collection of any Indian artifacts. Be sure to walk up Chinle Wash—the large side canyon on river left 10 miles below Bluff. It has ruins on both sides, some quite high up. The canyon in the second half of the run is caused by the river cutting through the Mexican Hat Anticline, of which there is a superb view on the main highway adjacent to the Mexican Hat (a sandstone formation 4 miles east of the town of the same name).

Waterwise, sand waves are the big attraction of this stretch. The shifting sand of the riverbed creates waves which appear and disappear magically before your very eyes. They are more apparent at high water and are great for surfing in a kayak or canoe.

LOWER SAN JUAN RIVER: Mexican Hat to Clay Hills Crossing (on Lake Powell)

54 Miles (2–4 days), Class I, II; drops 8' per mile. Suitable for kayaks, rafts, and canoes. Season: April–July. Your permit from the Monticello BLM office covers this stretch as well.

Below Mexican Hat the river enters the Goosenecks, a series of spectacularly entrenched meanders. The water is flat and the canyon is deep and convoluted. It is interesting to climb up to the top of some of the inner canyon walls which have been whittled to a thin divider between meanders of the river. Another worthwhile side trip, before putting in, is to go to the Goosenecks Lookout Point, reached by following the signs from Utah 261, 3 miles north of Mexican Hat.

The river straightens out somewhat after 10 miles as the crow flies, 20+ miles as the river flows. Slickhorn Canyon, when it has water in it, is the stuff of which Eliot Porter photographs are made. Grand Gulch, a short distance lower down, is well-known for its Pueblo Indian ruins, but they are located 9 miles and more from the river. The Grand Gulch Primitive Area was closed to visitors in January 1981, because it was getting trashed out from overuse.

Kayakers on the San Juan River *(Fletcher Anderson)*

There is only one rapid with an obstacle in the entire lower San Juan River. This is below Grand Gulch and is called "Rock Dead Center." The rapid is easily seen on approach. At high water it becomes a set of waves. Some of the waves throughout the lower stretch of the San Juan are fairly large at high water—up to 6 feet at the mouth of Grand Gulch. It is the best and safest river in the Southwest for a beginning boater; being warm, safe, scenic, semiremote, providing access to a lot of good hikes, while having waves and eddies for learning skills.

Take-out: Nine miles of dirt road lead to the take-out from Utah 263. This road is clay and impassable after heavy rain or snow. The take-out consists of a dirt parking lot (no water). The shuttle takes about four hours from Mexican Hat.

YAMPA RIVER

General Description

At one time, the melting snows of the west slope of the Rocky Mountains cascaded down toward the Colorado River, through a myriad of free-flowing wild rivers. Those days are gone and now there remains *only one* free-flowing major branch of the Colorado River system. The notion of one last river remaining wild and free is a thorn in the side of those who have the dams for dams' sake mentality. Just one more dam and they will have the whole thing under control. The West will be tamed! The way will be open for development and progress! We'll sell the water and power to the synfuel folks! Good-bye cowboys and outdoorsmen, hello energy trash and organized crime!

Let's bring northwestern Colorado more of the cultural benefits of boomtowns like Rock Springs, Wyoming! Yessirree, we'll have it all: dangerous drugs, teenage prostitutes, gun fights in the streets, alcoholism, Mafia labor organizers, the whole shebang! Just one more dam is all that stands between us and progress. Is it any wonder that with such inestimable benefits to mankind at stake, the dammers are willing to bend the environmental rules just a little bit? The ends must surely justify the means.

Opposing the dams is a poorly funded and loosely organized group, composed of commercial rafters, the National Organization for River Sports, the Colorado Whitewater Association, the American Wilderness Alliance, the Sierra Club, and other environmentalists. Said Ronnie Reagan's secretary of the interior, James Watt, "These people are committed to destroying what I want to achieve, and that means destroying me."[3] If you want to help destroy what he wants to achieve by sparing the last free-flowing tributary of the Colorado River, send a donation to the above-named organizations. As might be expected, the best dam sites were the first ones to be used. There are strong environmental arguments against the Yampa River dams. Repent your synfuels ways!

The river itself: Its source lies among the 12,000-foot peaks west of the town of (what else) Yampa. The normally boated portion begins—with a pause near the town of Steamboat Springs. Yampa is a Ute Indian name for a wild tuberous plant which still grows in the valley and was a welcome addition to the Utes' otherwise nearly all-meat diet. The word "Yampa" could also be translated as "big medicine" or "powerful magic." The broad, grassy meadows of the valley are ideally suited to grazing cattle and have been used for that purpose for over 100 years. Energy development near Craig and tourism near Steamboat Springs have changed the economic picture of the valley considerably, so that the cowboys you see there now are usually all hat and no cattle. Quite a few ranchers are still hang-

[3]Quoted in the March 30, 1981 issue of *Time* magazine.

ing on and they tend to regard river runners as just another part of the assault of strip miners, reservoirs, and condominiums that threaten to drive them off their land. These ranchers deserve our support if for no other reason than that cattle grazing is the least environmentally harmful known use of the land in the valley. We urge you to sympathize with the ranchers' position and to respect their property rights.

The river flows west beyond the better ranchlands into western Colorado sage country through a series of sandstone canyons. The canyons by Juniper Springs and Cross Mountain are proposed dam sites. The final canyon is in Dinosaur National Monument and is the first half of a multi-day run on the Yampa and Green rivers. An extremely biased permit allocation plan in effect for this canyon is currently being challenged in the courts by the authors of this guide.

YAMPA RIVER: Colorado Highway 131 bridge to Steamboat Springs

8 Miles, Class I, II; drops 4' per mile (?). Suitable for kayaks and canoes; not recommended for rafts.

It is quite possible to boat a 15-mile or so section of the Yampa, upstream from this stretch, but it is rarely, if ever, done.

Highway 131 is parallel to, but remote from, the river. Dirt secondary roads can shorten this run to 6, 5, or 3 miles duration. It is imperative that everyone using *any* put-ins on the upper Yampa be extremely cautious about trespassing on private land. Stay on the road right-of-ways and do not harass the ranchers. A list of approved put-in sites for the entire valley can be obtained at Steamboat sports stores.

There is often not enough water in the river to float a boat except in the months of April, May, June, and July.

The river is always glassy smooth and never very deep, as it meanders through the hay meadows above Steamboat Springs. The banks are protected against erosion naturally by willow and artificially by an unusual collection of old automobile bodies. The river's edge is a critical component of the overall wildlife habitat, particularly for birds. "Look! Isn't that a belted kingfisher (*Megaceryle alcyon*) perched on that 1949 Hudson (V8 Hornet 4-door)?"

This section of river was subject to "safety" closures to boating in 1979. Colorado Whitewater Association president and N.O.R.S.

Steamboat Rock in Echo Park *(Fletcher Anderson)*

representative, Gary Lacy, met with the sheriff's department and the closure no longer applies to whitewater boats.

The only real hazard on this run is a railroad bridge about 5 miles above Steamboat Springs, which crosses the river at a decidedly acute angle. It would be extremely difficult to get a raft between the closely spaced, sharply angled abutments at high water.

The last 3 miles of this run are the site of an annual flatwater mass-start wildwater race.

The river in the city limits of Steamboat Springs is being made into a park and has acquired some Class II manmade rapids. This stretch is referred to locally as "Chan's half mile," Chan being the kayaker/bulldozer operator who pushed the rocks around to form the rapids.

A permanent slalom course is set on the right-hand channel of the river in the park at the upstream edge of town, across from the municipal hot springs swimming pool. The prime motivators behind this project were Gary Lacy and Peter Looram.

There are several possible take-outs in town, the best being at City Park, near the public library at the western edge of town proper. This is the wildwater finish as well.

YAMPA RIVER: Steamboat Springs to Craig, Colorado

42 Miles, Class I; drops 7' per mile (?). Suitable for kayaks, rafts, and canoes.

Throughout this run the river is a flat Class I, but at high water (typically the end of May to mid-June) a flow of nearly 10,000 cfs pushes strongly into overhanging brush on the outer sides of the curves. The river can be run (if you really want to) from the end of March to November. Low flows are around 100–200 cfs.

The valley near Steamboat Springs is full of wide-open, deep, grassy meadows at the foot of the mountains and is well on its way toward being overrun by tourist condominiums. Craig was a cattle ranching community of the scrub sagebrush country in the throes of being converted to an energy boomtown.

Strip mines or condominiums, the end result for cattle ranchers is displacement. A few of them have developed a not at all unreasonable case of xenophobia and do not like strangers on their land. Act accordingly.

There are access points in Steamboat Springs, at Milner (mile 10), at U.S. 40 bridge (mile 17), at the dirt road north of Hayden (mile 22), U.S. 40 bridge (mile 26), and in the city of Craig (mile 42). Other access points involve crossing private land and should be avoided.

YAMPA RIVER: Craig to Juniper Springs, Colorado

53 Miles, Class I; drops 4' per mile. Suitable for kayaks, rafts, and canoes.

Earl Perry provides a detailed description of this run in *Rivers of Colorado*. The authors of this guide have not made the run and derive their information from that source, and from personal communications with Perry and with Ben Harding. The run can be made about 8 miles shorter by putting-in from Colorado 13, south of Craig.

Here is to be found one of those rare opportunities for a neophyte boater to make a beautiful overnight run on an unthreatening river, with no permit hassles. The trip is a popular one but is not yet crowded.

The river departs from the vicinity of U.S. 40 at Craig. After crossing 15 miles of open, flat country below Craig, the river enters a steep-walled, 4-mile-long canyon. Twenty-two miles into the run is the start of a second canyon which is 20 miles in length. Perry recommends several campsites in this stretch. An ugly gash of a railroad cut extends 2 miles into the top of this canyon and carries coal to the electrical plant near Craig. The remaining 18 miles are in essentially pristine condition.

Two factors could dramatically change the nature of this run: first, although no commercial floating takes place here, a multi-million dollar rafting operation has existed for many years in Dinosaur Monument, 30 miles below the take-out. In the unlikely event that they were able to attract more customers than their other operations could accommodate, or that their use allotments in Dinosaur Monument were reduced, the commercial rafters would probably expand their operations into Juniper Canyon. Depending on the scope of their expansion, the river could become dramatically more crowded in only one or two seasons. Such crowding would certainly be the lesser of two evils, for it would help block the Juniper Springs Dam.

The second factor that could change this run is that dam. The proposed site for the dam is 2 miles below the take-out for this run. Nearly the entire run would be inundated by the proposed reservoir. The Juniper Springs Dam is a component of the Cross Mountain-Juniper Project and is discussed together with that dam after the description of the Cross Mountain run.

Ann Hopkinson and Eric Leeper in the Yampa Canyons *(Fletcher Anderson)*

YAMPA RIVER: Juniper Springs to U.S. 40 bridge, 3 miles east of Maybell (Juniper Canyon)

Circa 5 river miles, Class I, II, III; drops circa 25' per mile. Suitable for kayaks and rafts.

The river carves a 1,500-foot-deep, V-shaped slot through Juniper Mountain. Many Class II rapids are in this short little gorge. Exploratory blasting at the dam site, 2 miles into the run, has converted a Class II rapid into a probable Class III (particularly at high water). The portage is said to be difficult, but not impossible. This short, but very attractive, little run is far from any boating centers and is seldom run—Class II paddlers prefer to end their run above because of the one Class III rapid, while Class IV and V paddlers usually run nearby Cross Mountain Canyon instead.

YAMPA RIVER: U.S. 40 near Maybell to entrance to Cross Mountain Canyon

17 linear miles (but river meanders considerably), Class I; drops 4' per mile. Suitable for kayaks, rafts, and canoes.

Several ranches line the banks of the once again glassy calm Yampa River. The put-in is on U.S. 40 at the bridge 3 miles east of Maybell. There is access at a bridge on Colorado 318, 6 miles from Maybell and 10 miles into the run. This collection of ranch buildings is sometimes called Sunbeam, Colorado. Ten miles west of Maybell, a dirt road heads 4 miles north into the river bottomland, turns west for another 4 miles, and reaches the river near the entrance to Cross Mountain. To the best of our knowledge, this section is rarely run—boaters interested in this kind of water going to the nearby Juniper Springs run upstream instead. The various proposed versions of the Cross Mountain Dam would inundate various portions of this area—probably at least to Sunbeam or beyond.

The Cross Mountain-Juniper Project: You have just passed through the area which would be flooded. This project would essentially destroy most of the river between Craig and Cross Mountain, and in the process, *would cover and eliminate nearly all the irrigated farmland in the immediate vicinity.* The dams are favored by the Colorado River Conservation District (CRCD)—an agency which is supposed to provide water *for* irrigation. Their goal is, of course, to build dams—but to justify themselves, they must some-

Ann Hopkinson and Eric Leeper in the Yampa Canyons *(Fletcher Anderson)*

how use the water they impound for farming. Thus, the water would be shipped as far away as Jensen and Ouray, Utah. Critics of the project argue that the result would probably be a net *loss* of irrigated land, so why not just keep the irrigated farms that already exist along the riverbottom? The answer is energy development. The dams would have hydroelectric plants which would generate 78 megawatts of peaking power. The nearby Craig coal-burning plant produces 894 megawatts, and the Hayden coalburner produces 500 megawatts. There is a new plant projected for the Craig area of about 1,000 megawatt capacity. The total megawatt output of the Craig vicinity is far in advance of the region's projected needs, but the electricity generated there can be sent over power lines to other regions of the country, far, far from northwestern Colorado. No one doubts that there would be customers from the electricity generated.

Now suppose that there were some holdup which interfered with the completion of the 100+ mile long agricultural water delivery systems. Well, the Rangely oil field is only 42 miles away, and there is talk of forcing a little more oil out of that field with a peripheral flood: pump water (or better yet, super-heated steam) into wells on the periphery of the field and force residual oil out of wells in the center. There is not enough local water in Rangely. The un-

completed pipe from Cross Mountain would lead right by there. No sense letting all that water go to waste, argue dam proponents. For that matter, the oil shale lands lie between Rangely and Grand Junction—still closer than the potential agricultural users. Oil shale development might well use up all the water available in the West. Some estimates say that every barrel of shale oil will require five barrels of water in the production process. The electricity from the dam could be used to pump and heat the water. The money earned could help pay for more dams!

This sort of reasoning outrages those who want to protect the land—the Colorado River Conservation District is "cheating," claim environmentalists. Who cares—we'll move in, we'll all make a little money, and then we'll all go home, say the developers—the CRCD is exercising a little creative planning to help end our dependence on foreign oil.

You are just about to enter the canyons that the project would dry up.

YAMPA RIVER: Cross Mountain Canyon

2½ Miles, Class IV, V; drops circa 150' per mile. Suitable for kayaks.

Millions of daytime television viewers have seen this canyon portrayed as THE MOST DIFFICULT!! THE MOST DANGEROUS!! whitewater in North America. They sat on the edge of their seats as THE WORLD'S GREATEST!! kayakers tried and failed to run THE WORST!! rapid for THE FIRST!! time. Their hearts were in their throats as the helicopter carried one of the kayakers to the emergency room in Craig. Was he STILL ALIVE?? Those kayakers sure are crazy sons of bitches—time to pop another can and switch channels to catch the ball game.

Television obviously loves to hype things up with an excess of superlatives. Hundreds of less than "WORLD CLASS!!" paddlers run Cross Mountain Gorge every year—without resorting to helicopter rescue.

At very high water (over 10,000 cfs in early June), the first major rapid is a hole all the way across the river, which is usually portaged. The rest of the run is good solid big Class IV–IV+ water. By September or October, a very small (circa 250–500 cfs) river flows through a series of abrupt pool/drop rapids. Several boaters of only intermediate ability have successfully run the canyon at these levels (with experts standing by to rescue them if needed, of course).

Once again, we must repeat our warning that rubber rafts do not belong in Class IV water. Expert commercial boatmen from the Vernal, Utah, area have attempted to raft this little canyon at high, low, and intermediate water levels. They flipped their rafts and lost or damaged most of their gear on every attempt. The canyon could possibly be rafted, but it probably shouldn't be.

In 1979 David Yeamans and others set out in a raft to "debunk the Cross Mountain myth." This they did, running the river with style, grace, and aplomb (and of course adrenaline). These were the years when he lived on adrenaline, bandages, and beer. Now with a growing family he also explores the thrills of Class I and II water as well. Rafters of his caliber *can* raft many of the "unraftable" rivers of the West. Generally, like Yeamans himself, they kayak them instead. A raft can become a very dangerous object to anyone who falls out of it on such a run, running over them and grinding them against rocks. It is danger, not difficulty, which dissuades rafters from attempting the most difficult runs. Rafters have died here . . .

The take-out for this run is in Deer Lodge Park. The road to the National Monument boat launching ramp passes close to the end of the canyon. Dirt roads leave U.S. Highway 40 about 10 and 15 miles west of Maybell, head north to the river bottom, and turn west to the canyon. It is standard practice to drop your boat at the put-in, drive to the take-out, and walk back on the south side of the river scouting the canyon. This canyon was first run at high water without portage by Walter Kirschbaum in 1963. Kirschbaum was the world's champion and "world class" by anyone's standards. An earlier run by Utah paddlers was more portage than paddling.

YAMPA RIVER: Deer Lodge Park to Echo Park (Yampa River Canyon or Bear Canyon). In Dinosaur National Monument

46 Miles, Class II, II+/III; drops 11' per mile. Suitable for kayaks and rafts.

A very detailed map of this run is found in Westwater Books/ Belknap Guide's *Dinosaur River Guide.* We strongly recommend purchasing it. Campsites are assigned and easily located with the help of the Belknap Guide. Earl Perry does *not* discuss this run in *Rivers of Colorado,* but he was the Dinosaur National Monument river ranger.

The combination of a big river, low gradient, an indescribably

Dinosaur National Monument, home of the Brontosaurus Burger (*Fletcher Anderson*)

beautiful canyon, and easy open rapids has led to heavy demand from boaters. The combination of a river outfitting industry with multimillion-dollar annual revenues and some easily influenced drafters of the river management plan has had predictable results: the outfitters essentially *own* the river now. In 1980, the authors of this guide applied for a permit to run the river and were assigned number 950 on the waiting list. *All* the outfitters still had hundreds of available trips open, and the Park Service told us to hire an outfitter or forget running the river. We ran anyway in order to drag the Park Service and their plan into court. The case was dismissed because the arrest was invalid. The plan remained unchallenged.

In 1985 Stuart Bray, Mary Conwell, Eric Leeper and others tried the same thing on the Green River in the same park. A large band of rangers staked out the river for a week, caught most of the party, and arrested those who escaped at the take-out. Quite a battle developed, with Bray run down by a motor boat and Leeper knocked into the river with an oar. But the real hardball began afterwards—everyone's boat was held as "evidence" all summer long, together with the food they would have liked to have had for breakfast and lunch on the long trip to the Grand Junction jail. Leeper and Bray eventually did time in the slammer; probably making them the first kayakers to ever go to jail for the heinous crime of kayaking in a national park. The situation is not improving in Dinosaur or anywhere else.

A permit is required to run this river from: Dinosaur National Monument, P.O. Box 210, Dinosaur, Colorado 81610, phone (303) 374-2216.

Detailed applications on an approved NPS official form must be sent in between December 1 and January 15. Maximum group size is 25 total people (noncommercial) or 25 customers and 10 crew (commercial). About 70 percent of the people who run the river each year are on commercial float trips. Campsites are assigned and have picnic tables, fire pans, and outhouses. Carry out all trash and ashes. The majority of noncommercial applicants are turned away. All would-be commercial passengers can be accommodated, and nationwide advertising campaigns are trying to attract more of them.

Off-season permits (before May 10, after September 10) are first-come, first-served.

It is well worth applying for the permit, for should you succeed, you will be (grudgingly) permitted — on your own — to enter one of the most cherishable spots on earth.

The river is at the bottom of a 2,000+-foot-deep canyon which twists and turns in all directions. The rapids are pool/drop with large, but harmless, waves (although Warm Springs Rapid has a hole which flips many rafts). Numerous side canyons provide splendid hiking. Stately boxelder trees shade the camping.

Crystal-clear water comes down the side streams, etc., etc., etc. Here is surely paradise on earth.

This river was first run in 1909 by fur trapper Nat Galloway. It was "first run" for the second time by a *Denver Post*-sponsored expedition in rowing boats in 1928 — at great personal hazard. It was first kayaked (we believe) by Willy Schaefler, Larry Jump, Keith Anderson (father of author Anderson of this guide), and others in foldboats in 1953.

It is possible to end this trip at Echo Park (confluence of the Yampa and Green rivers reached by a paved and dirt road which leaves U.S. 40, 25 miles away at Dinosaur, Colorado), but your permit entitles you to run on through Whirlpool and Split Mountain canyons of the Green River to Split Mountain Campground — an additional 25 miles. Those runs are covered under Green River farther on in this guide.

YAMPA TRIBUTARIES

THE LITTLE SNAKE RIVER: Baggs, Wyoming to Deer Lodge Park (confluence)

Circa 65 River Miles, Class I+; drops circa 10' per mile. Suitable for kayaks and canoes.

The Little Snake River, at runoff, has an estimated flow of about 1,000–1,500 cfs. It meanders through a (relatively) lush bottomland in the dry rolling sagebrush hills.

Several small ranches are located in groves of trees along the river. A poor quality dirt road vaguely follows the general trend of the river throughout its length on the south side. There is a bridge about 26 miles below Baggs, and a second bridge on Colorado 318 about 26 miles farther on. Deer Lodge Park is another 12 miles. Here is an interesting little river for an open canoeist with a desire to do some exploring.

The "Savory–Pothook" Bureau of Reclamation Project was to severely affect this river, but it was not funded.

THE ELK RIVER: Box Canyon Campground to Clark, Colorado

10 Miles, Class III, IV; drops a very crudely estimated 60' per mile. Suitable for kayaks.

This run is a short drive from Steamboat Springs, Colorado, and is a popular afternoon excursion for local paddlers. A dirt road parallels the entire stretch, and it is advisable to do considerable, seemingly unnecessary, scouting because of the astounding number of logs which fall into this river. It is not unusual to find logs which extend bank to bank and must be portaged. Eddies are small and the current is very swift. Typical June flows appear to exceed 3,000 cfs. By late August, the flow can be less than 500 cfs. The farther upstream you drive, the steeper the gradient and the harder the paddling. Otherwise, the river is more or less one ongoing rapid with harder and easier segments. The very last few miles are only Class II difficulty.

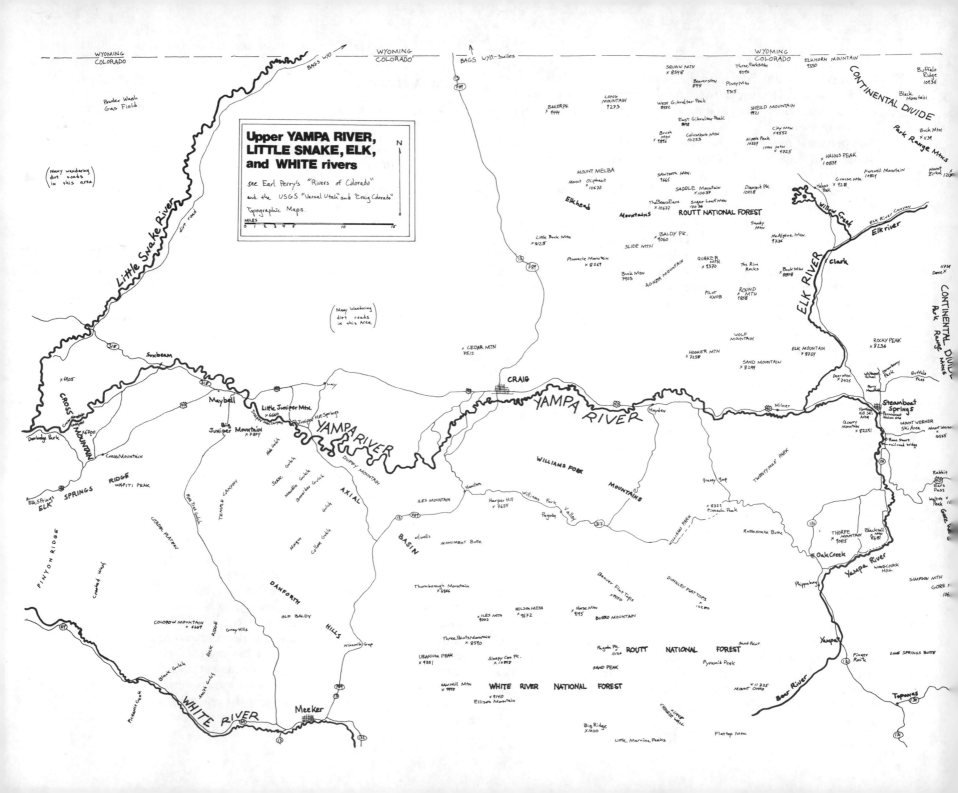

Upper YAMPA RIVER, LITTLE SNAKE, ELK, and WHITE rivers

see Earl Perry's "Rivers of Colorado"
and the USGS "Vernal Utah" and "Craig Colorado"
Topographic Maps.

N

MILES
0 1 2 3 4 5   10   15

THE ELK RIVER: Clark to Milner

Circa 20 River Miles, Class I, II; drops 15–20' (?) per mile. Suitable for kayaks, marginally suitable for rafts and canoes.

The road is parallel to, but not right next to, the river. The landowners are touchy and you *must* put-in off of the road right-of-way. *Do not* cross someone's fence to get over to the river. You can put-in from bridges at Clark, 7 miles farther down on a side road, 7 miles below there on another side road, and from U.S. 40 near Milner. The hostility that at least a couple of the Steamboat area ranchers feel toward tourists must be remembered. Nine out of ten ranchers are friendly. The tenth has his ranch on the Elk River. Don't attempt to figure out which of the many ranches is his, just respect the rights and property of all of them.

GREEN RIVER

General Description

Here was the largest and longest river of the Colorado drainage — surely the mainstream of the Rio Colorado of the West, whatever the claims of the government to the contrary. Here is the very model of a southwestern desert river: a big, muddy-brown (or if you have

Desolation Canyon, Green River (air view) (*NORS*)

the poetic vision of Ed Abbey, "Golden") river rumbling its way through deep and mysterious canyons remote from civilization and all its vices. The kind of place for which many of us must quietly profess curious and undefinable religious feelings of reverence.

Here is perhaps the only western river with a history of boating long enough to justify the term. Bear with us, therefore, through a few brief paragraphs, for it is in the context of these shadowy canyons that the soul of southwestern whitewater is revealed.

The earliest river running was at best an accident, for had the first river runners been aware of the rapids, they surely would not have entered the canyons. So, in 1825, did General William Henry Ashley find himself in the canyons of the Green River. Ashley was, for all appearances, a fur trapper; though one suspects that a general on temporary leave from the U.S. Army may have also been engaged in a bit of recognizance of what was then Hudson Bay Company territory. After a portage-filled passage from the Green River, Wyoming, vicinity through Split Mountain, Ashley and his men gladly left the river and headed overland.

Surely this great river, the Rio Colorado of the West, and the impenetrable Grand Canyon were related, yet great geographic mysteries remained. In 1869, John Wesley Powell and his party set out to solve them, reaching the Grand Wash Cliffs of Nevada many months later in poor condition without two of their boats and three of their companions. In 1871–1872, Powell knew more about whitewater and his second trip was a pleasant, though still adventurous cruise.

Powell's successes proved to trappers like Nathaniel Galloway of Vernal, Utah, and Bert Loper of Hite that the canyons were accessible. In the 1910s, they began rowing the river in search of beaver and otter.

Studying the newest U.S. geographic survey maps of the West in 1939, Alexander "Zee" Grant of the Appalachian Mountain Club came to an inspired conclusion: "Though other rivers are fully as exciting, and many have a more attractive climate and surrounding countryside, the Colorado and its tributaries are the ultimate goal of those who enjoy downhill boating." And so he boarded the train with his foldboat for Salt Lake City and the great unknown. That two men in tiny little fragile folding wood and canvas boats could succeed where great expeditions of steel-shod wooden mammoths of boats still frequently met disaster was heresy to the natives of Vernal, Utah (and still is!). Yet Grant was right and they were wrong.

The awesome Disaster Falls and Hell's Half Mile were child's play for these pioneer kayakers. More importantly, the lightly equipped campers left behind no trace of their passage and the whole expedition cost only $20. The message did not reach the high impact oarsmen, but it was there all the same.

Bus Hatch knew of the exploits of his neighbor Galloway and was drawn into the canyon in the 1940s by pure curiosity. Others, he reasoned, would be equally curious but would lack the techniques and equipment to run the river themselves. He was correct. Today, His sons, Ted and Don, run a multimillion-dollar rafting business spread over seven states.

In 1954, Keith Anderson came to the gates of Ladore and with him his six-year-old son Fletcher. "Just exactly what are you plannin' to do with them boats?" asked the first of many generations of hostile park rangers. Upon hearing the obvious reply, he began to grow hysterical. "Why that's suicide!" he cried. "Have you ever been there?" asked Keith Anderson. "No, but it's suicide!" Then appeared six-year-old Fletcher to interrupt the conversation with "Daddy, have you seen my life jacket?" "Do you intend to take him too?" The ranger's eyes were threatening to leave their sockets. "He has his own boat, but he will follow me closely in the rapids," replied the senior Anderson with studied calm. "Why that's murder!" screamed the ranger. "It's murder and suicide!" He began jabbing Keith in the chest with his index finger and screaming incoherently, "Murder and suicide!" (jab) "Murder and suicide!" (jab). It was neither murder nor suicide, but the Anderson families' bad rapport with the Park Service has continued to this day. Little Fletcher has been arrested by the Park Service three times for kayaking the monument and is defended in Federal Court by Keith Anderson, now retired from the rivers.

Suicidal though they may have been, the early foldboaters never had a serious accident and never left behind anything but footprints — a record rafters could envy. Today, the Park Service has banned foldboats from the river. Rafts are welcome.

THE UPPER GREEN RIVER:

From the Wind River Mountains to Green River, Wyoming, a clear little river slides gently through the miles of endless sagebrush. Fishermen float it in canoes and rafts, and their catches are said to be good (the river in Wyoming is outside the scope of this guide).

THE GREEN RIVER: Expedition Island to Flaming Gorge Dam

92 Miles (lost forever); 0 drop. Suitable for gumbahs.

For historical purposes, one might wish to launch from Expedition's Island in Green River, Wyoming — but why bother, for the reservoir is only 2 miles below. What spectacular visions inspired the name of this first canyon: the Flaming Gorge? We shall never know, for it is lost to us now. Here, in the reservoir, the river is actually green in color — but it is the sickly green of Gatorade and the name sticks in one's throat. Study well the lessons of Flaming Gorge and understand why we oppose the Cross Mountain–Juniper Project which intends the same fate for the Yampa.

THE GREEN RIVER: Flaming Gorge Dam to Ladore Ranger Station

36 Miles, Class I, II; drops 7½' per mile. Suitable for kayaks, rafts, and whitewater canoes.

This run is in the Belknap *Dinosaur River Guide.* It is administered by the Flaming Gorge National Recreation Area, the Ashley National Forest, the BLM, and the Brown's Park National Wildlife Refuge. Permits are not required, and there are some "improved" campsites marked in the Belknap Guide.

A road from the dam leads to a launching ramp at its base. Several little rapids occur in the first 7 miles of river in what is called "Red Canyon." A 5-mile road from Dutch John, Wyoming, leads to an access point at Little Hole (BLM) Campground 7 miles below the dam.

After an additional 7 miles of canyon, you reach the wide-open bottomland of Brown's Park. There is a take-out or put-in at the bridge (16 river miles below the dam). There is a short bit of canyon again, and then the BLM "Swallow Canyon" boat ramp (27 miles from the dam). Eleven miles farther on across the sandbars of Brown's Park is the Wildlife Refuge launch ramp. Eight miles below there is the Ladore Ranger Station boat ramp.

THE GREEN RIVER: Ladore Ranger Station to Echo Park Ranger Station (Ladore Canyon). In Dinosaur National Monument.

19 Miles, Class II, III; drops 14½' per mile. Suitable for kayaks and rafts; suitable for whitewater open canoes at low water.

This run, too, is detailed in the Belknap *Dinosaur River Guide.* Here you are again within the domains of the National Park Service—the land of rules, regulations, permits, assigned campgrounds, picnic tables, and red ants. A permit is required from: U.S. National Park Service, Dinosaur National Monument, P.O. Box 210, Dinosaur, Colorado 81610, phone (303) 374-2216.

The requirements for application are discussed under the Yampa River section of this guide. One permit entitles you to run either the Yampa or the Green, but not both. The number of permits are limited, and you probably can't get one. Guided trips are incredibly expensive, but you don't need a permit if you hire a tour guide and space is always available.

Andrew Hall, on the Powell Expedition in 1869, was reminded of the Robert Southey nursery rhyme:

> Its caverns and rocks among:
> Rising and leaping,
> Sinking and creeping,
> Swelling and sweeping,
> Flying and flinging,
> Writhing and wringing,
> Eddying and whisking,
> Spouting and frisking,
> Turning and twisting,
> Around and around
> With endless rebound!
> Smiting and fighting,
> A sight to delight in;
> Confounding, astounding,
> Dizzying and deafening the ear
> —with its sound.
> With a crash and a splash
> And a leap and a roar:
> Thus does the water come
> down at Ladore.

What more could one add?

Remember that the hikes up side canyons are every bit as enchanting as the river itself.

Modern-day river runners tend to scoff at the awesome name of Class II+, II—Hell's Half Mile Rapid. Remember that the 30-foot drop used to look more threatening with 15,000 cfs of water than it does today with a dam-controlled typical flow of about 1,000 cfs or less. Remember too, the rapid ratings made by federal agencies are intended to dissuade the unprepared, not inform the competent. Thus, their ridiculous Class IV, V rating made by and for relatively inexperienced river runners has a certain logic to it.

The sorrowfully low water releases do have their benefits: at peak season, the river is still too low for the giant tourist-filled pontoons, so relatively fewer people visit the canyon of Ladore than visit the Yampa. By October, November, or later, there will still be adequate water releases for warmly clad kayakers and canoeists and they will have the popular canyon almost all to themselves.

THE GREEN RIVER: Echo Park to Split Mountain Campground (Whirlpool and Split Mountain Canyon). In Dinosaur National Monument

25 Miles, Class I, II, II+; drops 11' per mile. Suitable for kayaks and rafts; suitable for open whitewater canoes at low water.

You are still within the domains of the National Park Service. The permit which got you here via the Yampa or Green rivers allows you to continue on. It is also possible to get a one-day trip permit to launch from Rainbow Park and run the last 8 miles of Split Mountain.

The river passes through three distinct personalities here. Whirlpool Canyon is a deep and dark canyon with no rapids above II difficulty, but plenty of surfing waves. The name derives from the myriad of boils and whirlpools which abound at high water. Midway through Whirlpool Canyon is Jone's Hole, which receives a recommendation and a word of caution. Jone's Hole Creek is a beautiful, warm, clear spring-fed stream with excellent swimming. Its tree-shaded little valley is in its own way the most beautiful site in the monument. There are pictographs to be examined and nearly tame deer to be observed, but all this has its price. There are five camping spaces at the Jone's Hole Campground. With any luck, the other four will all have commercial float trips of 40 or more people in them. This will be their last night free from the restraints of civilization and they will be frantically trying to make their last party the biggest one of their trip. You can join them, or you can attempt to sleep through the blare of their portable radios and tapedecks, and the shrieks and screams of their last big chance to really cut loose. Jone's Hole Campground is a wilderness slum. We strongly recommend that you not miss Jone's Hole, and we equally strongly recommend that you don't camp there during the tourist season.

Below Whirlpool Canyon lie the sandbars, glassy calm waters and wooded islands of Island Park. It is wide open here, you meander around islands and take in distant desert vistas.

Below Island Park, a huge rounded anticline attempts to block

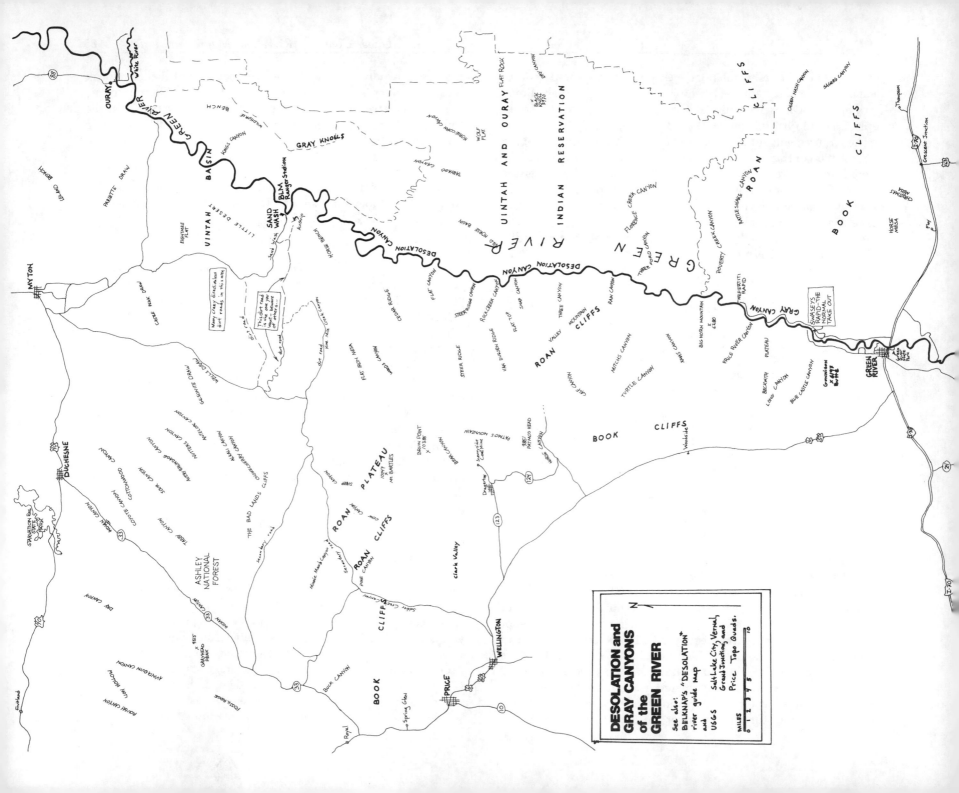

the river. The river has had to cut a 600-foot-deep, U-shaped notch through its very center. This is Split Mountain Canyon. Here are eight or nine wide-open easy Class II rapids with great big exhilarating rolling waves. The Park Service thoughtfully placed sign boards on the bank that said helpful things like "Warning: Moonshine Rapid—Class IV—portage trail," etc. These have recently been removed.

All too soon, and without warning, you round a blind corner and are at the take-out at Split Mountain Campground. Winnebagos! Signposts! Trashcans! Asphalt! Rangerettes! You hit the whole mess instantly. In the past, if the rangerette didn't like you, she would issue you some variety of $25 ticket. If you disputed it with her, she would issue you another. You could, as we did, go to court and win against these ridiculous charges. Then you would have spent literally hundreds of dollars and hours traveling to the courthouse. Remember boating safety rule number 1: Never hassle anyone with a badge or a gun. Thankfully, a change in park personnel has ended some of these practices, but not all—rangers with telescopes up on the canyon rim may still radio their counterparts at the take-out to intercept lifejacket violators!

Desolation Canyon, Green River (*NORS*)

THE GREEN RIVER: Split Mountain to Sand Wash BLM Ranger Station

Circa 85–95 Miles (river meanders widely), Class I; drops 4' per mile. Suitable for kayaks, canoes—slow current and sandbars impede rafts.

This rather long section of river has an intermediate access point at Jensen, Utah (circa 12 river miles from Split Mountain), and at Ouray, Utah (circa 35 winding miles from Jensen). All else being equal, the best run and the worst shuttle is probably Ouray to Sand Wash (35 river miles).

Here is a true, but not a government-designated, sort of wilderness. The low surrounding hills are covered by endless miles of sagebrush and desert. Here and there one encounters segments of little dirt roads which surely connect someplace not worth remembering with somewhere not worth getting to (usually a drill site). Occasional isolated ranches appear long abandoned, and rare cattle look long neglected. Clouds of mosquitoes hover along the riverbank waiting for a better meal to come paddling by. Somehow, this unlikely combination of factors can be strongly appealing and this section of river has devotees. Is it the antisocial joy of running a river others could not tolerate? Is it the peculiar mystique of the lover of deserts and desolation? Or is it merely the novelty of the thing? If any of these answers appeal to you, here is your river.

THE GREEN RIVER: Sand Wash to Green River, Utah (Desolation and Gray's canyons)

Circa 80 River Miles, Class II; drops less than 10' per mile. Suitable for kayaks, rafts; large waves are a hazard for open canoes.

This is a Bureau of Land Management river and you must obtain a permit from: River Manager, Desolation Canyon River Unit, Bureau of Land Management, P.O. Drawer AB, Price, Utah 84501, phone (801) 634-4584. Applications are accepted January 1 to March 1, maximum party size of 25 persons. Fire pans, porta-potties, and repair kits are required and the Belknap *Desolation River Guide* is recommended. The Ute Indians own most of the left side of the river and could possibly have the legal authority to issue permits as well. They licensed a commercial outfitter for the 1981 season. The shuttle is over 200 miles long—much of it on gravel roads. It is possible to shorten the trip by 4 or 5 miles by taking-out at the Gunnison Butte (Swaysey's Rapid) picnic ground, north of Green River on the east bank. Many people shuttle by leaving their cars in Green

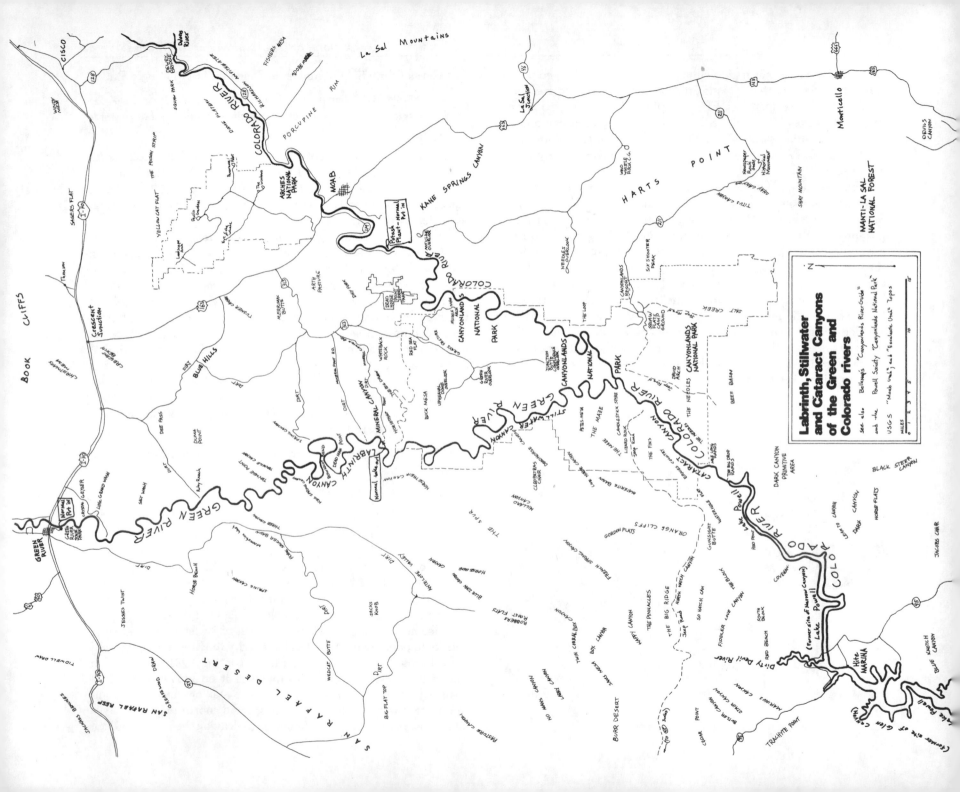

Labrinth, Stillwater and Cataract Canyons of the Green and Colorado rivers

See also Belknap's "Canyonlands River Guide"
and the Powell Society "Canyonlands National Park"
USGS "Moab Vals" and "Escalante Unit" Topos

MILES
0 1 2 3 4 5   10   15

River and getting flown in to a dirt airstrip at Sand Wash.

Flatwater and clouds of mosquitoes surround the Sand Wash Ranger Station, and it is wise to rig quickly and get at least 15 miles downstream before camping.

Although the numerous little Class II rapids are easy enough, many Class I boaters are getting their first experience with whitewater in this canyon, and this is an ideal training ground for them. A determined first-time kayaker could certainly run this canyon safely, though not without a few swims.

Commercial outfitters in the past could not sell very many "Desolation" river trips, so many of them now bill the same run as "The Green River Wilderness." Now they sell plenty of trips and their customers are none the wiser.

There is some crowding during the months of June and July, but not very much. The odds of obtaining a private permit are still pretty good. Your chances of finding a tour operator with space, are, as everywhere, 100 percent.

It is possible to drive another 5 miles or so upstream from the Gunnison Butte take-out to Nefertiti Rapid and make a day trip which includes the last few rapids.

THE GREEN RIVER: Green River, Utah, through first half of Labyrinth Canyon to Horsethief Bottom

70 (?) Miles, Class I; drops 7' (?) per mile. Suitable for kayaks, rafts, and canoes.

This river is managed by: Bureau of Land Management, San Rafael Resource Area, P.O. Drawer AB, Price, Utah 84501, phone (801) 637-4584.

There are no permits or special regulations. A four-wheel-drive road enters at Horsethief Bottom, 70 river miles below Green River. It is 27 dirt miles on this road to a point on U.S. 163, 6 miles north of the Arches National Park entrance. The road parallels the river for 5 miles upstream and 8 downstream.

The name Labyrinth derives from the canyon's intricately convoluted course. The water is glassy smooth throughout the entire length of the run and the river provides easy access for hiking the many side canyons. The country here is pure Utah desert and the lush river bottom is in sharp contrast with the surrounding barren sandstone cliffs. This is also more of the same topography which was responsible for the creation of Canyonlands National Park—a favorite haunt of backpackers and their nemesis, the four-wheelers. Labyrinth Canyon attracts both the "silent" self-propelled river runners and *their* nemesis, outboard motor-boaters. The Memorial Day weekend is particularly to be avoided, for over that three-day period over 500 motorboats will leave Green River en masse, descend under screaming two-stroke power to the confluence, and ascend the Colorado at full throttle to Moab. Forget about any sort of personal communion with nature on that weekend—go watch the Indianapolis 500 instead.

The river is sometimes subject to ice flows and freezing over in January and February. Otherwise it is boatable year round.

THE GREEN RIVER: Horsethief Bottom to confluence (Labyrinth and Stillwater canyons)

51 Miles, Class I; drops 7' (?) per mile. Suitable for kayaks, rafts, and canoes.

Everything said of the upper half of Labyrinth Canyon still holds true. The name Stillwater Canyon is applied to the last 31 miles of this canyon somewhat arbitrarily. However, once you pass Horsethief Bottom there is no other take-out until Lake Powell. To reach it, you must pass through Cataract Canyon of the Colorado River with its tremendous rapids and permit requirements. Off-road vehicle equipped backpackers might argue that you could jeep and hike out of Spanish Bottom on the Colorado. We don't recommend doing so. You could also hire a motorboat to drive you back upriver to Moab. Determined canoe paddlers Jerry Nyre and Bob Feraldi paddled upriver from the confluence to Moab in two eight-hour days.

Cataract Canyon is covered in the Lower Colorado portion of this guide.

GREEN RIVER TRIBUTARIES

THE WHITE RIVER

Here is a river only lately come into popularity and due to fade from it when the synfuel boys are finished raping the region, for it cuts its canyon right in the center of the oil shale formations. Open canoeists hold this to be one of the finest little rivers in the region. Kayakers and rafters hardly know it at all. It is indeed a *little* river and is possibly unboatable in drought years.

THE WHITE RIVER: Buford to Meeker

22 Miles, Class II; drops 20'+ (?) per mile. Suitable for kayaks.

A *very* tiny White River is marginally boatable in June as it leaves the Trapper's Peak region of the White River National Forest. Colorado Route 120 parallels the river.

THE WHITE RIVER: Meeker to Rangely

55 Miles, Class I, II; drops 16' per mile. Suitable for kayaks.

A fast-moving small river of continuous gradient flows along Colorado Route 64 in a shallow canyon edged with steep-sided buttes. The clean, clear water is severely threatened by oil shale development, due to the nature of the shale. The impervious shales contain a very limited amount of low-grade oil-like material and a lot of soluble alkaline salts. To free the oil, you must fracture and crush the shale—thus exposing the alkaline salts to leaching. The total amount of spent shale debris could annually exceed all other types of mine tailings in the region combined (including coal strip mines) by even the most conservative scenarios. Once contaminated by leachates, the water will be useless for irrigation or for any sort of livestock watering. Once the groundwater and river contamination starts, the process will be irreversible. Nearly all the water rights in the area are owned by oil companies. When they exercise those rights, agriculture will cease. When all the oil has been extracted 30 years later, they will leave behind a wasteland. Oil shale could (if developed to the maximum) supply less than 1 percent per annum of our nation's energy.

Midway through this run, the White River is joined by Piceance Creek (pronounced Pee-ance). The additional flows are enough to give this stretch a season of about four to six weeks around June. Piceance Creek could become the most polluted stream in western Colorado. At present, it is drinkable (but not recommended). The remaining ranchers pride themselves on their ability to pronounce Piceance. The transient energy trash call it "Piss Ant" Creek. Several of the oil shale tracts lie astride Piceance Creek and energy companies have quietly acquired the rights to its water.

THE WHITE RIVER: Rangely to the Green River near Ouray

60 (?) River Miles, Class I, II; drops 8' per mile. Suitable for kayaks, canoes; too small for some rafts.

Rangely is a formerly dying oil boomtown, temporarily revived by the threat of oil shale. Oil wells, pipelines, storage tanks, and a refinery surround Rangely. Not the sort of thing a great wilderness run is made of—but just below town the river enters (surprise!) a 600-foot-deep canyon. In a typical June, the peak flow is estimated to be still under 2,000 cfs. The season is short, but the flow is more than adequate for open canoeists.

About 25 river miles below Rangely, Utah Route 45 crosses the river. A dirt road parallels this first section on the south side of the stream.

Below Route 45, the river crosses a truly barren stretch of land with less than 5 inches of rainfall per year. This land isn't even fit for a dog, reasoned the Bureau of Indian Affairs, so they put Indians here instead. Thus the Ute Indians, whose home was once the cool, clear mountains east of Meeker, are now desert dwellers and making the best of it. The river makes this desert pleasant and intriguing rather than harsh and barren.

The dirt road between Bonanza and Ouray, Utah, is close to, but not right on, the last 10 miles of river. A dirt road south from Ouray reaches the confluence 2 miles below town. Ouray was one of the last chiefs of the Mountain Utes. But for him and his associate chief Colorow and others, the situation of the Utes would be far worse today than it actually is. Their names linger on throughout this region and the area south of the San Juan Mountains, where the other half of their divided nation lives.

The coal and oil shale formations lie, for the most part, just east of the reservation lands. Poisonous leachates from the energy development would flow down the little river at which the Utes water their livestock.

COLORADO RIVER IN CANYONLANDS NATIONAL PARK

General Description

This run is presented in two sections: above and below the confluence with the Green River. Above the confluence, there are no rapids, but below it are the very demanding rapids of Cataract Canyon. A permit is required for Cataract, but not for the flat water above. However, there is *no take-out* at the end of the flat water so you must either motor back upstream or run Cataract Canyon.

These combined runs are generally regarded as a sort of second-rate Grand Canyon. There is a certain logic to that idea, for the desert canyon here is smaller, and the rapids easier, than those of the Grand Canyon. The designation is an unfortunate one, for Canyonlands National Park is unique and possesses a character in many ways quite distinct from and in no way inferior to Grand Canyon.

John Wesley Powell, in his 1875 report, described Canyonlands as follows:

> A whole land of naked rock, with giant forms carved on it: cathedral-shaped buttes, towering hundreds or thousands of feet; cliffs that cannot be scaled, and canyon walls that shrink the river into insignificance, with vast, hollow domes, and tall pinnacles, and shafts set on the verge overhead, and all highly colored—buff, gray, red, brown, and chocolate; never lichened; never moss-covered; but bare and often polished.
>
> But a wilderness of rocks; deep gorges, where the rivers are lost below cliffs and towers and pinnacles; and ten thousand strangely carved forms in every direction; and beyond them mountains blending with the clouds.
>
> Cliffs where the soaring eagle is lost to view 'ere he reaches the summit.

Powell's language may seem excessively florid when viewed in the black and white print of a government publication; yet it appears almost subdued when read while staring into the true wonderment of the land he describes.

You can backpack into this region, struggling along from water hole to water hole in the 110° sun; you can defile the very concept of wilderness with an earth churning 4×4; you can blast down the river with the rasp of a screaming outboard motor echoing off the canyon walls; or you can slip in unobtrusively in comparative luxury in a tiny human-propelled boat. If you have come this far in the guidebook, you must surely realize our prejudices in favor of the last option.

COLORADO RIVER: Moab potash mines to Cataract Canyon

48 Miles, Class I; drops circa 1½' per mile. Recommended for rafts and kayaks.

The potash mines are on the right side of the river, 15 miles below Moab. Putting in there avoids the "industrialized" section of the canyon. A poor quality road reaches the river 2 miles farther down on the left side—we don't know how bad the drive is. This whole run is mapped in the Belknap *Canyonlands River Guide,* and we recommend you carry a copy to gauge your progress, if nothing else.

The water is indeed dead flat and barely moving, save for a tiny

stretch just above the confluence called "the slide." Annoying motor boats drone up and down. Don't just struggle through these flats—take your time and hike the side canyons into the rocks Powell described.

Cataract Canyon commences at the confluence of the Green and Colorado rivers.

COLORADO RIVER: Cataract Canyon (confluence to Lake Powell)

15 Miles, Class IV (?—see description); drops 11' per mile. Recommended for kayaks and rafts.

A permit is required to run this river from: Superintendent, Canyonlands National Park, Moab, Utah 84532, phone (801) 259-7165. Permits are issued first-come, first-served, for applications received after December 1. Maximum group size is 40 people. Fire pans, first aid, spare oars, etc., required. Carry out all human waste.

Cataract Canyon was once longer, but Lake Powell has flooded its lower reaches.

In this 15-mile stretch lie 25 large distinct pool/drop rapids. At high water, one rapid flows into the next and the number decreases. The individual drops were named by surveyor William Chenoweth in 1921, and his colorful names persist to this day. He called the

The long, calm-water approach to Cataract Canyon (*Judy Fox*)

drops #1, #2, #3, etc., through #28 (now flooded). However, drops #13 through #18 are collectively called "the mile-long rapid" and numbers #21 through #23 are "the big drop."

River flows during May and June can frequently exceed 55,000 cfs (and even exceed 10,000 cfs as late as August), and the result is a sort of rapid rarely encountered anywhere in the world except in the desert canyons of the Southwest. "The big drop" is often termed a Class V, but is frequently run successfully by kayakers of only Class III ability and is occasionally accidentally floated successfully by rafters with no experience or ability whatsoever.

In a word, the rapids are huge. Waves of over 7 feet high are not uncommon, and to a kayaker whose eye level is only 2½ feet above the water, 7 feet is a towering height indeed. But the waves are not hazards or obstacles: you brace into them and ride over the top like a roller coaster. Occasionally, one of these waves may flip a raft as easily as the wind scatters dry leaves and nothing the boatman does can prevent it. Normally, however, nothing the boatman does could induce a raft to flip, despite whatever gravity-defying angles of lean it may assume. There are awesome thundering holes in some of these rapids, but the routes to avoid them are maybe 50 yards wide and require absolutely no maneuvering. Kayakers with a wild streak sometimes deliberately paddle into these monsters. Their boats are tumbled like match sticks in a washing machine, and they emerge motion sick, but otherwise unharmed, their faces hidden behind ear to ear grins—for these holes are definitely "stoppers," but almost never "keepers." One or two incredibly violent recycles and you are free (usually anyway . . .).

So now after a thrilling 15 miles of rapids, you are dumped into the lake—which reaches the very tail waves of the big drop rapid. Hite Marina is the next possible take-out and it is 34 miles across the lake. What are you going to do now? Figure this out before you get here! Environmental purists in their kayaks often paddle out. Everyone else either brings an outboard motor with them or hires a boat from Hite to come up and give them a tow. For a truly first class trip, you can hire a houseboat to come and get you—a practice which has led Wyoming's wildest canoeist, Mike Crenshaw, to refer to the lake as "Cadillac Canyon."

This canyon was first run by the Powell expedition in 1869, and later by Stanton and other early explorers, all of whom resorted to numerous multi-day portages and told tales of real and imagined disaster.

Kayaker Harold Leich attempted to paddle the canyon in 1933—smashing his boat in Big Drop Rapid. He swam (!) the remaining 40 miles to Hite and walked out another 40 miles from there to Hanksville, Utah.

The first commercial trip was made in 1938 when two women—Lois Jotter and Elzada Clover—were rowed through.

In January of that same year (1938), kayakers Antoine de Seynes, Bernard de Colmont, and Madame de Colmont (all of the Paris Museum of Natural History) had paddled from Green River, Wyoming, to Phantom Ranch in the Grand Canyon (where they were stopped by river ice). They portaged the Big Drop in Cataract Canyon, but no other rapids. Historians have made much of Jotter and Clover as the first women to "conquer" the canyons—though they were merely passengers on a trip which made many portages. Of the intrepid Madame de Colmont—who actually *ran* all the rapids, save lower "Big Drop," herself in a fragile single-seat foldboat—history has little to say. Even her first name has been forgotten, for macho commercial river runners are unhappy with the idea of a mere woman in a canvas kayak preceding them into their most perilous rapids.

The legendary Walter Kirschbaum was the first kayaker to paddle all the rapids without portage (in 1959). The equally legendary

Judy Fox runs "The Big Drop" rapid, Cataract Canyon, Colorado River, Canyonlands National Park (*Will Perry*)

Georgie White was the first to raft them without portage (in 1947). In 1954, Georgie lashed three rafts together to form the first triple rig and began taking thousands of passengers for hire. The canyons have never been the same.

Editor's note for the kayak desperadoes: circa 1 mile long. A hiking trail leads from a jeep road at "the doll house" down to Spanish Bottom, 3 miles below the confluence and ½ mile above the first rapid. If you don't have a permit, you could sneak in here and (hopefully) no one will be the wiser. Now a ranger is permanently camped at Spanish Bottom waiting for you. If caught, you face a maximum penalty of $500 and/or six months in jail. Is it worth the risk? The 40 miles of lake at the end of this run make it less popular with noncommercial river runners, as they are generally not into the whole motorized recreation scene. Permits here are less difficult to obtain than elsewhere. That situation may change dramatically in a few years as the number of people rejected elsewhere grows.

Glen Canyon

Rest in Peace

Glen Canyon (Rest in Peace)

200 Miles, no class whatsoever; no drop.

From the end of Cataract to Lee's Ferry, Arizona, there used to stretch about 200 miles of canyon which is the subject of the Eliot Porter Sierra Club coffee-table book *The Place Which No One Knew*. The 2.8-foot-per-mile gradient precluded the formation of any rapids, and it was possible to row up the canyon, as well as down. John Wesley Powell wrote in 1869 "August 3, 1869: The features of this canyon are greatly diversified. We have a curious ensemble of carved walls, royal arches, glens, alcove gulches, mounds and monuments. From which of these shall we select a name? We decide to call it Glen Canyon."

Today, a stagnant green body of water fills the region, ironically named Lake Powell after the man who first described the beauties of the canyon it covers. Surely Powell must be rolling over in his grave. Lake Powell today is the home of the floating Winnebago style houseboat and water ski boat—but strangely seems to have no canoes, no sailboats, and no kayaks or rowboats.

It is fashionable today for Grand Canyon boatmen to raise their voices in outrage about the horrors of the Glen Canyon Dam—a project which was built too soon for many of them to oppose. Yet, where were those voices when we tried to stop the McPhee Dam on the Dolores in 1977, where are they now as we try to stop the Cache la Poudre dams, and where will they be when we fight the Cross Mountain–Juniper dams on the Yampa? Boatmen: here are opportunities to put your multimillions of tourist dollars where your mouth is. What is holding you back? The next time you begin spouting your "right on" Glen Canyon environmental rap, ask yourself where the same thing is happening today.

Colorado River: Glen Canyon Dam to Lee's Ferry (the last remnant of Glen Canyon)

15 Miles, Class I; drops 1.2' per mile. Recommended for kayaks, rafts, and canoes.

What was Glen Canyon actually like? This 15-mile stretch cannot really tell you, but it is a beautiful little piece of canyon. Seven small side canyons enter, the lowest three of which are within 3 upstream river miles of Lee's Ferry, and provide outstanding peaceful hiking. They are within but a brief half hour's paddle from the bus station atmosphere of the paved Lee's Ferry boat ramp.

The government maintains a boat launching ramp at the very foot of the Glen Canyon Dam, reached via a tunnel from the rim—but *you* cannot use it, as it is reserved for the exclusive use of float trip operators and their clients and is closed to the public. Fishermen leave Lee's Ferry in outboard motorboats headed upstream, and the unnaturally crystal clear, ice-cold water harbors a stocked population of rainbow trout.

Grand Canyon

Grand Canyon of the Colorado River

230 River Miles, 47 lake, Class (opinion varies) Deseret 10? Drops 8' per mile. Suitable for kayaks and rafts.

As is the summit of Mount Everest or as is the South Pole, the Grand Canyon is one of the definitive end points of the earth. Nowhere else is like it, it is surely the ultimate whitewater boating experience.

On September 7, 1867, Mormon settlers in Callville, Nevada, dragged a wasted and incoherent James White from a battered drift-

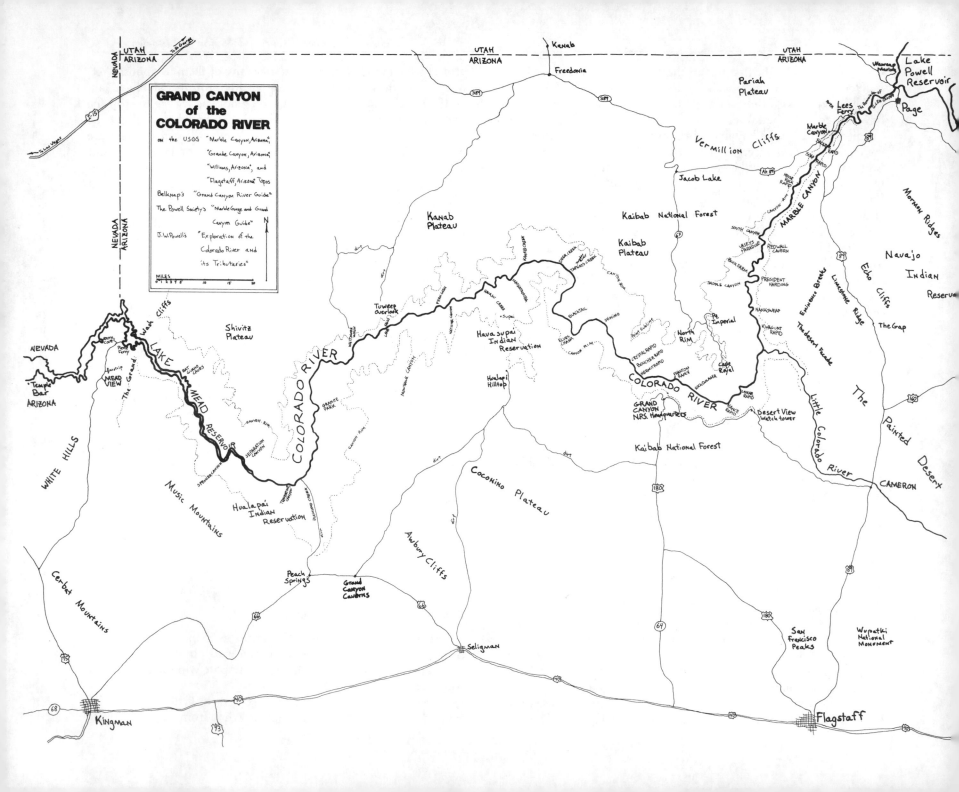

GRAND CANYON of the COLORADO RIVER

on the USGS "Marble Canyon, Arizona",
"Grand Canyon, Arizona",
"Williams, Arizona", and
"Flagstaff, Arizona" Topos

Belknap's "Grand Canyon River Guide"

The Powell Society's "Marble Gorge and Grand
Canyon Guide"

J.W. Powell's "Exploration of the
Colorado River and
its Tributaries"

MILES
0 1 2 3 4 5   10   15   20

N

wood raft. By his own account, his party had been attacked by Indians near the San Juan River three weeks previously. White and one other man had escaped by building a driftwood raft. The other man had drowned. White himself survived by gnawing two rawhide knife scabbards for 18 days. Given the time it took him to drift and the apparent locale of the Indian attack, White must have run the Grand Canyon. His description of calm water followed by various rapids agrees with the known geography of Glen Canyon and the Grand Canyon. Controversy still surrounds both his memory and his honesty. More likely he entered the river below Diamond Creek.

No such controversy surrounds the elaborate geographical and geological 1875 report of John Wesley Powell to the Smithsonian Institution. Powell and his companions made the first (1869) and the longest (1871 and 1872 with a hike in and out during the winter) runs of the canyon. The techniques of running whitewater were, at best, poorly understood in Powell's day, and his expedition was made with great hardship. Few people were anxious to duplicate his feat.

Eventually, a trickle of prospectors and surveyors followed. Prominent among these is the remarkable William Brewster Stanton, who was looking for a railroad route west to California. All of these earlier explorers portaged all major rapids.

Haldane "Buzz" Holstrom soloed the canyon in 1937 in a mammoth wooden cataract boat. He was the first to try this.

The first kayakers in the canyon were Madame and M. Bernard de Colmont and Antoine de Seynes, who ran in 1938. Ice forced them to take-out at Phantom Ranch in January.

The following summer, Norm Nevills took two women passengers down the canyon. Years later he began offering the first commercial trips.

Ed Hudson and "Doc" Otis Marston drove the inboard motor boat *Esmerelda II* down the canyon to a speed record of four and one half days in 1949. Elated by their success, they made a second attempt in 1950 in a racing Chriscraft — but they spent too much time making repairs to the boat's fragile bottom to beat their old record. They took a party of beautiful women for a little spin on Lake Mead before loading the boat on the trailer, and it nearly sank!

In 1951, record high water flowed through the canyon. Taking advantage of the fast current and washed-out rapids, Jim and Bob Rigg, of Flagstaff, rowed day and night through the canyon. They reached Lake Powell about 60 hours later, setting a speed record that was to stand until 1978.

In the 1950s, gigantic inflatable pontoon bridge components became available on the surplus market. Georgie White lashed together three pontoons from a bridge built to carry Sherman tanks to create a mammoth raft 36 feet long and 27 feet wide, powered by a snarling outboard motor. The old guiding business of pioneers like Norm Nevills was a romantic life, but a lousy business. Nevills was scarcely getting rich with his one or two customers per trip (and he worked damn hard for what money he got, portaging and lining his heavy wooden cataract boat around the worst rapids). Georgie White could carry 50 passengers on her monstrous "G-rig" with no portages and nary a dip of an oar for the entire run. Her leviathan rubber barge agreed with her customers' desires to enjoy nature while holding it at a comfortable distance. It was a goldmine. Inflatable craft of all shapes and sizes began flooding the rivers as fast as tourists could be lured into filling them. And so the days of the iron men setting forth into the depths of the canyon like Odysseus upon the wine dark sea were ended. In the blinking of an eye, the Great Unknown was about to become Disneyland.

The swan song of the hard men was at hand, yet they persisted. Several attempts at the speed record were made without success. Then, in 1958, Les Jones of Heber City, Utah (and scroll map fame), set out at very high water for a fast solo run — and bagged the new solo speed record of five days. The unquestioned river hard man of all time, Walter Kirschbaum, left Lee's Ferry in June of 1960 in his fragile canvas-decked kayak, becoming soon afterward the first kayaker to run the Grand Canyon without portage. Getting a Park Service permit to make the run, he observed, was more difficult than the river itself — sentiments certainly shared by modern kayakers. "This was certainly my greatest boating adventure," wrote Kirschbaum, "it was 'grand' and I will remain attracted by the 'Grand' for the rest of my days."

And in 1963 it was all over. The Glen Canyon Dam shut off the wild inexorable flow of churning, blood-warm, muddy water forever; replacing it with a predictable, ice-cold, crystal-clear stream of more manageable proportions. Two more dams were almost built in the canyon itself — would have been, save for vigorous opposition from the Sierra Club. Speed record attempts were surely over. "Wilderness experiences" were likely to be interrupted by the din of outboard motors and the shrieks of tourists riding the rubber roller coasters.

As of this writing, the Bureau of Reclamation has proposed

changes in the operation of Glen Canyon Dam which would do incredible environmental damage to the canyon. New electrical generating capacity would be added to the dam, and water would be released primarily to generate electricity during the hours of peak demand. Thus there would be a daily fluctuation of flow from 3,000 to 45,000 cfs and back again. At low flows, many rapids would be unraftable. At high flows, many camps would be completely inundated. If the water came up at night (as it often does), your camp could be flooded out with you in it (just as well, since some rapids would be unraftably shallow during daylight hours).

These are mere inconveniences compared to the environmental damage they would accompany: in three years of such operation, fully a third of all the beaches in the canyon would be washed away forever. Native vegetation could not stand the changes in water level and would be replaced by impenetrable tamarisk thickets.

Needless to say, with a third of the campsites gone, the Park Service would have to reduce the number of permits they issue each year. The waiting list is already over ten years long.

The Peaking Power Proposal is being fought by all the big environmental groups, by the outfitters' lobbies, and by N.O.R.S.

Yet, the canyon survives. The immensity of the place, save for the river itself and its destroyed littoral habitat, is scarcely affected by water flowing at less than its normal rate, and in the evening when the motors are shut down and the tourists cluster together at the dinner table, a curious calm settles into the depths of the canyon on the last fading rays of sunset. Strangely isolated puffs of glowing hot or icy cold air dart across the water. Deer slip down to drink at the river's edge. Black-painted Indians speak with featureless presences at the mouth of the Little Colorado. The canyon becomes not a place, but a living being, exerting a pull on some of those who hear its whispers which cannot be resisted. Boatmen privately wonder about the incontinuity of their gaudily-painted craft in the somber canyon as they sink slowly into sleep.

A few river runners of the old school persist. One must preface any mention of their activities with "allegedly," for the Park Service, in its wisdom, has declared them all illegals.

So (allegedly), in 1977 you could have seen a solo kayaker called "Fox" resupplying himself from hidden food caches as he slipped down the river.

That winter (not allegedly, for they were caught and arrested), you might have heard the tale of two Flagstaff kayakers who rode

Havasu Creek (*Ann Hopkinson*)

a muddy rain and snow flood down the Little Colorado into the canyon's bottom.

In 1978 (still allegedly), a solo kayaker named Fletcher pushed through in a fog of physical and mental exhaustion to a new speed record of 49 hours total elapsed time and a personal catharsis which turned around the impending crisis of a misdirected portion of his life.

Torn by the loss of a close friend in 1979, a solo kayaker (allegedly) called "Big Brian" entered the canyon carrying the last remains in a waterproof bag. His departed friend's ashes are scattered through the canyon now and his soul laid to rest.

This strangely religious river running is incompatible with motorized recreation and industrial tourism. A confrontation is brewing. In the meantime, thousands of people are putting their names on the now already 10-year-long waiting list, for there is more in the canyon and in themselves waiting for their discovery—and it is worth the wait. And in all the world, there is only one Grand Canyon.

Permits: The inequities and injustices of the Grand Canyon permit systems are as legendary as the river itself. A multimillion-dollar commercial recreation industry operates standardized river tours in the canyon, and they are able to exert considerable influence over river management policy. The principal goal of river management policy (albeit an unspoken one) is to create a favorable business climate for concessionaire operations. This is done in part by severely restricting noncommercial use so that the overwhelming majority of would-be, noncommercial river runners are forced to turn to commercial tour operators to purchase river access. It must be borne in mind that not all outfitters advocate this sort of policy, nor do all Park Service administrators. Those outfitters who *do* advocate such policies may even be in a minority, but their political clout is so overwhelming that they unquestionably have the final say in such matters.

Permit allocation history: As recently as the 1960s, river management policy for the Grand Canyon was simply not an issue. Noncommercial river runners were dissuaded by the length of the trip and by unfounded rumors of rapids too large for their tiny craft to run. Despite some fairly sophisticated advertising, the commercial recreation industry could not attract enough customers to create crowding.

All of that had changed dramatically by 1970. Ever-increasing numbers of fast, noisy, large motor balloon boats, combined with crowding and litter, were in serious conflict with growing public interest in wilderness preservation, natural resource protection, and noncommercial river use.

Outfitters were notified in advance that their use levels would be frozen at whatever maximum river use they could generate during 1972. Accordingly, they gave away numerous free river trips in order to inflate their use figures. The outfitters were so successful at fabricating demand that season that the Park Service later actually cut back their use below the 1972 levels. This was no hardship for the outfitters, as they still controlled 98 percent of the total number of people running the canyon.

Noncommercial river runners tried for the remaining available access in an annual lottery with odds that reached 9:1 against getting a permit. Dissatisfaction with this system was widespread and took

Olo Canyon (*Ann Hopkinson*)

the form of protest runs of the river, magazine exposés, two lawsuits, and an unending stream of angry mail to the Park Service.

Eight years later, in 1980, a new river management plan was put into effect which increased noncommercial use to about 19–20 percent of the total number of people running the river. That use was (and is still) allocated by a waiting list, now nearly 20 years long. The new plan was also designed to provide a token wilderness experience through a lengthy gradual phaseout of motorized recreation within the canyon. The wilderness concept was unacceptable to at least a few of the outfitters. By now, those outfitters were running multimillion-dollar operations with considerable political clout. The outfitters pulled a few strings in Washington to have the plan overruled by Congress. We are now back to where we began, trying to come up with a new plan. The Park Service recognizes the political clout of the outfitters and biases river management policy accordingly.

Permit application procedure: There is no need for you to wonder about whether or not you have the skills necessary to run the canyon—should you apply today, you will have many, many years to acquire those skills before you get your permit. If you have the money and don't want to wait up to 20 years, you can run the river now as a tour operator's customer. To do so, you must usually make a reservation as much as two months or more in advance of your launch date.

To obtain a list of outfitters, or to put your name on the noncommercial waiting list, write: River Manager, Grand Canyon National Park, P.O. Box 129, Grand Canyon, Arizona 86023, phone (602) 638-2411.

Regulations: The regulations are revised annually. Twenty years from now, when your name comes up on the waiting list, they may have changed dramatically. Today, the regulations can be summarized as follows:

1. Carry out all human waste.

2. No campfires in the summer season (unless you carry in your wood and carry out your ashes).

3. No camping at certain specified areas.

4. No hiking at some specified areas.

5. Hike only on improved trails in some areas.

6. Wear life jackets at all times.

7. Strain all dishwater.

8. No soap in side streams.

9. No nudity.

10. Self-supported kayak trips by special permit only.

11. Solo trips by special permit only.

12. Carry a first-aid kit.

13. Carry an aircraft signal mirror.

14. Carry aircraft signal panels.

15. Carry an approved map (we recommend Belknap's *Grand Canyon River Guide*, available through N.O.R.S.).

16. Attend an official pretrip briefing.

17. Carry an official identification (such as a driver's license) and present it to the check-in ranger.

18. Carry spare oars and paddles.

19. Finalize your passenger list way in advance.

20. Don't try to sleep near the put-in—drive to the campground 4 miles away.

21. Only 15 people per noncommercial trip; 30+ people per commercial.

22. Only one noncommercial launch per day of 15 people or less.

23. No more than 150 commercial passengers launched per day.

24. Etc., etc.

Surely we have forgotten some of the regulations. They fill a book which the Park Service will send you if you get a permit. The official pretrip briefing will remind you of them.

The majority of these regulations, however arbitrary they may seem, serve valid environmental purposes and we sincerely hope that they are obeyed. The fragile ecosystem of the desert requires a different and more cautious treatment than, say, the much wetter forests of Idaho. A few regulations serve primarily to harrass noncommercial boaters and/or to protect commercial businesses. This category of regulations is annoying, but if you violate any of them, you can expect big trouble with the law.

The nudity rules and life jacket (even in flatwater) rules are strictly observed by commercial trips and almost universally disregarded by noncommercials. The outfitters have been complaining about noncommercial nudity to the Park Service.

The requirement that the trip participant list be finalized one month in advance of the launch date causes a lot of difficulty for noncommercial trips (and is not required for commercial ones). This difficulty is usually overcome through the use of phony IDs. These are available from advertisers in the classifieds of *Rolling Stone* magazine. Alternately, it is possible to hike into the canyon and join a trip at Badger Creek Rapids, thereby avoiding the ID check. Kayakers without proper IDs sometimes launch before dawn and hide out in the bushes downstream to await the rest of their groups.

Assuming that you somehow manage to outwit, circumvent, or disregard the outrageous permit allocation system, what will you actually encounter in the canyon? *Scenic wonderment, breathtaking sights, astounding vistas, and more of the same old rocks.*

(More General Description):

If you didn't already know that stuff was down there, why did you want to go? The Grand Canyon is the subject of innumerable coffee-table picture books, all of which depict the most beautiful sights beheld anywhere in the world. None of these books does justice to the real thing. To describe the place merely as "beautiful" is degrading.

John Wesley Powell wrote as he entered Marble Canyon: "August 9, 1869 . . . We have cut through the sandstones and limestones met in the upper part of the canyon, and through one great bed of marble a thousand feet in thickness. In this, great numbers of caves are hollowed out, and carvings are seen which suggest architectural forms, though on a scale so grand that architectural terms belittle them." Powell's language tells us primarily that he found the experience overwhelming (there is no bed of marble 1,000 feet thick—it's really just limestone). You should be overwhelmed as well. If you blast through in a traveling 30-person suburban cocktail party, pushed by a 90-decibel outboard motor, you can't possibly experience any sort of personal communion with nature. A trip in the Grand Canyon—any trip—every trip—should be a once-in-a-lifetime experience. You owe it to yourself to occasionally get away from your group and spend a little time quietly alone in the canyon. At least 90 percent of the lure of the canyon is off the river. The whirlwind guided tour will never experience it. Worse, an excess of noisy, motorized, whirlwind tours can preempt other river users' experiences as well.

Running the river: Am I good enough to run it, everyone asks? How should we know—we've never boated with you. Remember that the river only drops 10 feet per mile. Thus, whatever the flow, 90 percent of the water in the Grand Canyon is flat. What actually goes on is that for several miles the river will drop at a rate more like 3–4 feet per mile. After 3 miles, it will have stored up a drop of nearly

View of Colorado River above Elve's Chasm
(*Fletcher Anderson*)

20 feet. Suddenly, the entire river will plunge over a blind lip into a series of waves up to 10 feet high. After a fairly short rapid, you find yourself once again in flatwater.

The rapids are caused by flash flooding from side canyons. The outwash dams the river, thus producing the rapid. Somewhere in each 100-yard-wide rapid there may be a hole or two. There is usually a 20-yard-wide clear path still open.

The rapids are most difficult at flows of about 25,000 cfs. At lower flows they lose push, and at higher flows they wash out slightly.

How much rafting ability is required to run the canyon? In 1977 a raft belonging to O.A.R.S. tours came untied at camp near Nankoweap (mile 53). Some days later it was recovered in an eddy above Havasu Creek (mile 156). It was still right side up and it still had all its gear aboard—including some life jackets which were not tied

Three-times world champion Roger Paris enters Lava Falls (*Eric Leeper*)

in. It had successfully run 40 major rapids of the inner granite gorge (including Hermit and Crystal) *without a boatman*. Perhaps that establishes the minimum ability required to raft the canyon. Nevertheless, even the giant 35-foot motor balloon boats do occasionally tip over, and it would seem that when the wrong combination of waves occurs, there is nothing a boatman can do to prevent a flip. If you are good enough to row the Arkansas, Dinosaur Monument, Glenwood Canyon, or, say, the Salmon River in Idaho, you are more than good enough to row the Grand Canyon. The most important talents of a rafter are his ability to read the water, to tie down gear and to catch the right eddy for lunch or camp.

The same cannot be said about kayaking. The maneuvers required to run the Grand Canyon rapids are trivial even for kayakers of very modest ability, but passing through breaking waves up to 10 feet high requires an ability to brace not called for on other western rivers. The technique for such bracing is not inherently different than that used in smaller water, but many kayakers of low-intermediate ability discover to their dismay that they don't really know how to brace very well. Even the best paddlers occasionally flip in Grand Canyon rapids. Rolling up in such turbulent water requires a certain presence of mind and calm disposition. Although the summer air temperature can exceed 100°F, the water is extremely cold (occasionally less than

50° at Lee's Ferry). Dress for immersion in the water, because, particularly in the inner gorge, it is very difficult for a swimmer to break the eddy line and swim to shore. Thus, a swim might last a long time in very cold water. The Grand Canyon is one of few places on earth were you can suffer from both hypothermia and heat prostration within the same 10-minute period. In summary, you need not be a super expert kayaker to paddle the Grand Canyon (many people have done so who are not), but your trip will be considerably more enjoyable if you have a very reliable roll and if experts are standing by to rescue swimmers. If you *are* an expert paddler with a love of big, powerful water, the Grand Canyon rapids are paradise. Every rapid offers surfing the likes of which is not to be found anywhere else on earth. Endo spots abound. Whirlpools beckon. Threatening though they may appear, the largest and most violent holes in the river are not keepers. The big holes in Crystal, in Lava Falls, and all the other rapids, have all been kayaked — right side up, on purpose, and many times over. And should anything go wrong, just hang on and ride it out — all the rapids are pool/drop. The late Walt Blackadar used to run Lava Falls entirely upside down from the entrance wave on, not even bothering to attempt a roll until he washed out the bottom.

Campsite selection: Water flow in the Grand Canyon is determined solely by releases from Glen Canyon Dam, which may someday range from 45,000 cfs to less than 1,000 cfs. Typical daily fluctuations range from 5,000 to over 20,000 cfs. Care must be taken in selecting a camp which will be above the night's high water mark. The sediment load of the river is trapped behind Glen Canyon Dam and existing beaches are being eroded away. The Bureau of Reclamation is trying to add new generators to Glen Canyon Dam and change the daily release patterns. The beaches would be gone in five years if they succeed.

The big motor rigs generally pull into camp rather early in the afternoon. In some parts of the canyon camping space is limited and they will motor on ahead of you and grab the best spots. If you talk to them beforehand, you can sometimes reach an agreement about camping space. Occasionally, when they know there is only one camp left, they will roar on ahead and grab it anyway, leaving you to continue on down the river in your tiny boat well after dark. Plan ahead — study your Belknap Guide Map and keep in mind more than one potential camping spot.

Problem areas: Once you pass Soap Rapid (mile 12), you will en-

Datura flower opens in the dark and closes in sunlight (*Fletcher Anderson*)

counter very few camps for the next 20 miles. There is one at House Rock Rapid (mile 17), one at North Canyon (mile 20.5), some in the 20-mile series of rapids, one at Shinumo Wash (mile 29), and one at South Canyon (mile 31.5). Missing a camp in this vicinity might also mean missing a number of side canyons you wanted to explore.

After Hance Rapid (mile 76.5), there is essentially only one more desirable camp before Phantom Ranch (mile 88). That camp is on the left near Grapevine Rapid (mile 82). A lot of commercial trips plan to exchange passengers at Phantom Ranch. They *must* camp beforehand and some of them will not hesitate to motor right over the top of a kayaker to occupy that camp. A small party could camp at Clear Creek (mile 84) or at a very tiny marginal beach on the left at about mile 86.75.

It is possible to hike from Tapeats Creek (mile 133.5) over the top of the plateau to Deer Creek (mile 136). A permit must be obtained to camp in the side canyon at Tapeats. Camping is prohibited at Deer Creek, but is allowed at Thunder River (by special permit), a 60-minute hike upstream from the mouth of Tapeats. The camping spot on the right, a mere 50 yards above the mouth of Tapeats Creek, is in great demand with parties intending to make the hike.

Olo Canyon, Matkatamiba, and Havasu Creek are obligatory side excursions for every trip in the canyon. Leaving Deer Creek Falls (mile 136), you pass only one preferred camp (Kanab Creek, mile 143.5) before Olo (mile 145). Camping is prohibited at Matkatamiba (mile 148). Between Matkatamiba and Havasu (mile 157) are only two cramped camps at miles 149.5 and 155.5. These are the ledges called "last chance" and "very last chance." Camping is prohibited at the mouth of Havasu Creek.

Between Diamond Creek (mile 226) and Separation Canyon (mile 239, already in Lake Mead) camping is limited, but not in demand because most trips end at Diamond Creek.

Put-ins and take-outs: The normal put-in is, of course, the Lee's Ferry launching ramp. Illegal trips sometimes prefer to launch from the picnic grounds at the mouth of the Pariah River, a mile downstream.

For all practical purposes, boats launched at Lee's Ferry must run the entire canyon. However, it is quite possible to exchange passengers at a number of locations. Trips as short as one day are thus feasible.

One could hike in or out in less than a day at the Little Colorado River (mile 61), at the Tanner Trail (mile 68), at Hance Trail (mile 77), at Phantom Ranch (mile 88), at Hermit Creek (mile 95), at Bass Trail (mile 108), at Tapeats Creek (mile 133), at Havasu Creek (mile 157), and at Whitmore Wash (mile 188). The hot sun means that some of these can be two-day hikes. Hiking permits must be obtained from the Park Service at South Rim Headquarters.

Commercial trips use burros to carry people in and out at Phantom Ranch and Whitmore Wash. They helicopter people in and out from the Little Colorado and Lava Falls. On peak days, Lava Falls may experience 10 or 15 helicopter flights a day. People objecting to this noisy intrusion into what they regard as a wilderness setting run up against the political power of the nonwilderness-oriented concessionaires. The helicopter flights continue.

Most river trips in the Grand Canyon end at the Diamond Creek Road (mile 226). This is probably the most reasonable place for a rowing raft trip to end, for only 9 more miles of river remains between there and the lake. There are 45 miles of lake to traverse before reaching Pierce Ferry (mile 280)—the first take-out in Lake Mead.

Unfortunately, the Hualapai Indians have discovered that controlling use of the U.S. government built and maintained Diamond Creek Road is a lucrative proposition.

Olo Canyon (*Fletcher Anderson*)

A loaded raft can row out in approximately 14 hours (of rowing).

One option is to eat dinner at Separation Canyon (mile 239), spread out sleeping bags on the raft, and drift off down the lake at night—a practice that can make crossing the otherwise hot and boring lake very pleasant indeed. There is no chance of drifting past Pierce Ferry, as the current in the lake ends completely at the Grand Wash Cliffs (about 3 miles short of Pierce Ferry). Usually, there will still be plenty of lake to deal with (i.e., 20–25 miles with head winds).

Shuttle: The Grand Canyon shuttle is a full day's drive one way. Local enquiries through the Fort Lee Company or the Marble Canyon Lodge (both in Marble Canyon, Arizona) can sometimes lead you to a shuttle driver. A good argument can be made that it is less expensive to have Lake Powell Air Service in Page, Arizona, fly you back from Pierce Ferry for a shuttle than it is to drive a shuttle car round trip.

When we last checked, it cost $25 per vehicle to use the road. Added to this were surcharges of $25 per raft, $10 per kayak, and $5 per person. Should you make the mistake of camping at Diamond Creek, you could be charged an additional $5 per person camping fee (unimproved camp) and at times there is a $2 per person charge for hiking up Diamond Peak. A typical kayak trip could easily end up spending over $400 for the privilege of taking out at Diamond Creek (above and beyond the tax money already spent to maintain the road). This expense is nothing for a commercial tour operator who has charged his 25 customers $1,000 each for the trip. It can be a major expense for a private party that otherwise would spend only $150 each for the entire trip. People negotiating a price over the phone sometimes discover at the riverbank that the crafty Hualapais have changed the rates. All of this argues in favor of running the remaining 9 miles of river and floating down the lake to Pierce Ferry.

The most reasonable way to cross the lake with a raft is to use an outboard motor. Alternately, arrangements can be made through Meadview, Arizona, to have a motor boat come and tow you out. We once managed to sail most of the way out with a rain fly. The big commercial tours usually have a jet boat come and take their passengers off before motoring out. A kayaker can easily paddle out.

Sandbar near Saddle Canyon (*Fletcher Anderson*)

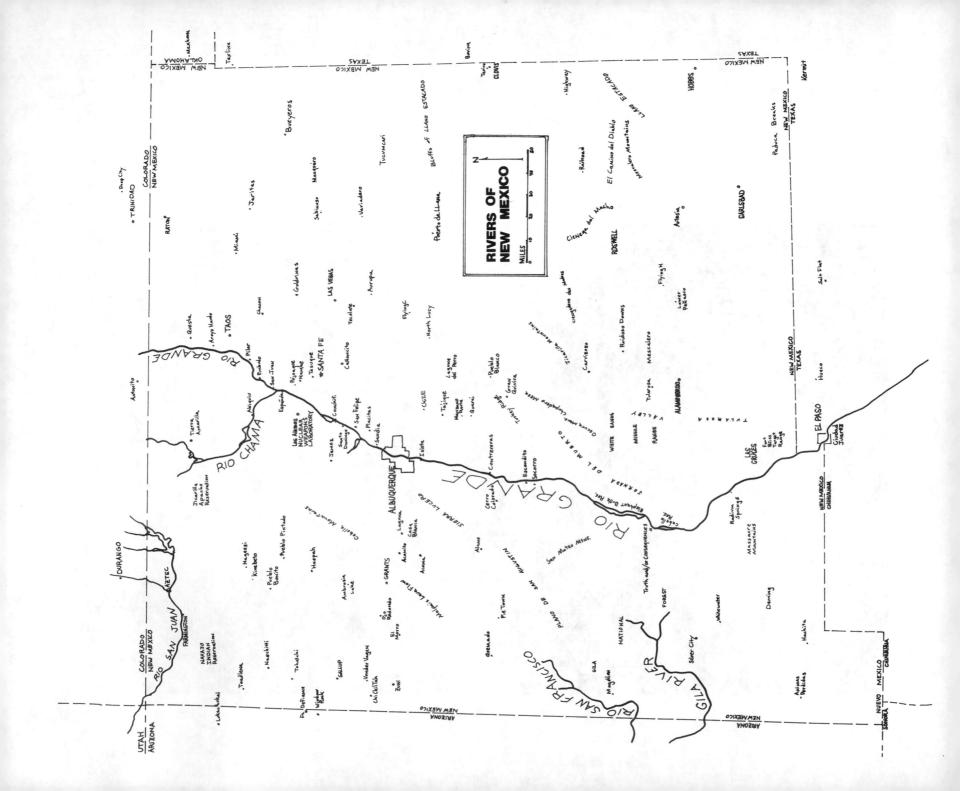

Chapter V

RIO GRANDE DRAINAGE

Chama River
Rio Grande

CHAMA RIVER
New Mexico

General Description

If you've never been to New Mexico, paddling the Chama is a superb way to get to know and love it. Or, if you are living in New Mexico, paddling the Chama is a good way to get to know and like it better. The El Vado to Abiquiu run is a delightful two or three day trip.

There is a special light and air in New Mexico (not counting Albuquerque). The air is so dry and clear that one almost sees the rays of sunlight streaming through it. Every bush, rock, and tree presents itself in unexcelled clarity and purity. Odors are sharp and dry, unencumbered by water molecules. Sunlight-enriched browns, whites, and varied earth tones are contrasted against a vivid blue sky.

The canyon of the Chama is steeply sloping, partially forested. It never becomes tight or cliff-lined. The water is clear and blue. The rapids are all visible and straightforward with minimal maneuvering required. The number of rapids increases toward the end of the trip. Campsites are ample. In the author's experience (one trip), the river was totally uncrowded.

CHAMA RIVER: El Vado Ranch to Abiquiu

28–33 Miles, Class I, II+; drops 20' per mile. Suitable for kayaks, small rafts, and possible for canoes.

Flows and Season: During a normal snow year, there is a boating season from mid- or late April through May, when the Chama overflows the El Vado Dam. The flows reach a high of 3,000–4,000 cfs.

In addition to the overflow period, one can boat during the dam releases made for irrigation. These provide flows of no more than 1,000 cfs and occur after the Rio Grande has gone down. There are usually some in June and then again in August.

Water flow information can be obtained by calling the BLM in Taos at (505) 758-8851. It is best to check with them to be sure you will have enough water.

Kayaking the Rio Grande *(Bob Weaver)*

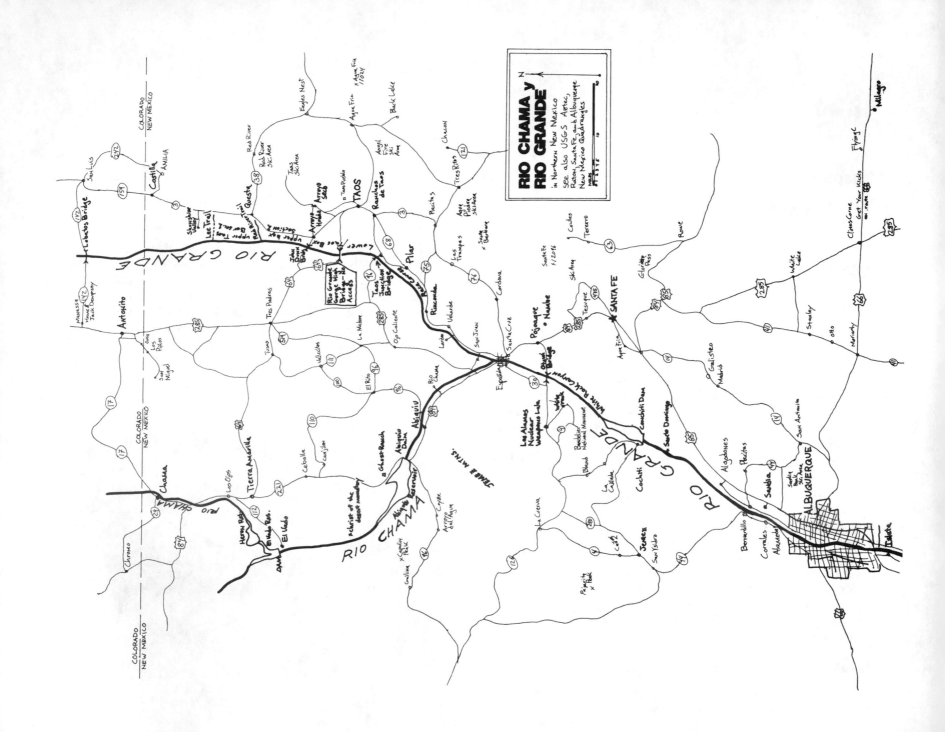

Access: To reach the put-in, take the El Vado Reservoir Road (Rt. 112) which heads southwest from Rt. 84 just south of Park View, New Mexico. Turn off at El Vado Ranch (there is a sign). Ask permission to put-in and park because the put-in is on private land. Be courteous, clean, etc.

The take-out can be performed anywhere along a 5-mile stretch above Abiquiu. The most often employed spot is reached via a short dirt road which leaves Highway 84 and 96, ½ mile north of the Ghost Ranch Museum and heads southwest toward the river.

CHAMA RIVER: Below Abiquiu

30 Miles to confluence, Class I. Suitable for kayaks and canoes.

Flat, meandering through ranchland, many irrigation diversions.

RIO GRANDE
Southern Colorado, New Mexico

General Description

The Rio Grande Valley is the route by which Spanish and Mexican colonists achieved their northernmost penetrations into the interior of what is now the territory of the United States, and one may define the extent of their settlement by observing the Spanish place names of towns throughout the area.

Here they encountered the towns of the various Pueblo Indian nations—whom they promptly attempted to enslave. This was the most remote outpost of the Mexican Empire, and the Mexican attitude toward it may be judged by the names given to geographic features. The Purgatoire River was "El Rio de Las Animas Perdidas en el Purgatorio"[4]—the river of souls lost in Purgatory; the nearby snow-covered peaks "El Sangre de Cristo"—the blood of Jesus. The way here from Mexico was the "Jounadad del Muerto."

The Rio Grande Valley in 1845, at least as seen from faraway Mexico City, was a sleepy little backwater of the empire, difficult to trade with and quiet enough not to require garrisoning with very many troops. This was a view which conveniently forgot the valley's own history (the Pueblo Indians had risen in 1680 and driven the Mexicans entirely out of New Mexico) and neglected the

[4]As was the name of the Animas River near Durango, Colorado.

westward expansion of the United States. Thus, in August 1845, Steven Kearney and a ragtag detachment of the United States Army, on their way to explore a route to California, detoured through Santa Fe at the urgings of the Bent brothers (fur traders who had established themselves in 1831 in a little adobe post on the lower Arkansas River near modern La Junta.). Kearney sized up the situation and annexed New Mexico on August 18 before heading west again. Despite an abortive and incredibly bloody revolt on January 14, 1847, by the Taos Pueblo Indians and Mexican allies which cost some members of the Bent family their lives in a hideously gruesome manner, and a second revolt in 1968 which brought National Guard tanks to Tierra Amarilla (near Chama); the state of New Mexico has been American territory ever since.

However inaccurate the "sleepy backwater" view of New Mexico may be, it has always appealed to many Americans. Thus, the state has survived successive invasions of artists in the 1940s, beatnicks in the 1950s, hippies in the 1960s, and retired persons in the 1970s. At the same time, it has also seemed a land of opportunity to hoards of Mexican immigrants in the 1920s and '30s, atomic bombers in the '40s, and carpet-bagging mineral developers and real-estate speculators up to the present day. All of these diverse groups appear to coexist well enough with each other, the native

Running the Rio Grande in a wooden box *(Bob Weaver)*

Indians, and the remaining descendants of the early Spanish settlers. All of this makes New Mexico something of a booming, sleepy little backwater on the go—accurately described in John Nichol's New Mexico trilogy.

UPPER RIO GRANDE: Rio Grande Reservoir to a point 12 miles up the road from Creede, Colorado

8 Miles, Class III, IV; drops 50' per mile. Suitable for kayaks.

This is the highest possible run on the Rio Grande. The river leaves behind the reservoir and the road to drop through a narrow defile over 1,000 feet deep before emerging on a broad flat floodplain above Creede. Flows are dependent on releases from Rio Rande Reservoir and are always minuscule, but for the narrow and constricted nature of the gorge. Beware of fallen trees, as well as constricted boulder gardens. This stretch is, at present, seldom run. There is only enough water to do so in late May or early June.

RIO GRANDE RIVER: Above Creede to Wagon Wheel Gap

Roughly 17 river miles, Class I; drops 18' per mile. Suitable for kayaks, some canoes, and small rafts. (This run is described in Earl Perry's Rivers of Colorado.)

The river is a sparkling trout stream winding its way across the bottom of a V-shaped valley. There is a gauge on the highway bridge 7 miles above Creede. Earl Perry suggests that 0 on the gauge is something like 140 cfs; 4 is something like 3,750 cfs. He suggests 0.5 as a minimum level for kayaks, 1.5 for rafts, and 1.5 as a level above which open canoes will be swamped. The flows crest at about 3 on the gauge in May or June. By mid-August they are below 1.

RIO GRANDE RIVER: Wagon Wheel Gap to South Fork

12 Miles, Class II; drops almost 25' per mile. Suitable for kayaks, small rafts, and some canoes. (This run is also in Perry's Rivers of Colorado.)

A more swiftly flowing river drops through several little Class II rapids as it works its way down a nearly 2,000-foot-deep, V-shaped valley. Highway 149 parallels the entire run, making scouting easy.

RIO GRANDE RIVER: South Fork to Colorado/New Mexico line (San Luis Valley)

90 Miles, Class I; drops initially at around 20' per mile, but in places less than 10' per mile. Suitable for kayaks, small rafts, and canoes.

The San Luis Valley is a broad, flat plain 100 miles long and 40 miles wide, lying at an elevation of about 7,500 feet between the 14,000-foot San Juan and Sangre de Cristo mountains. In the geologic past, it may have been the course of the ancestral Arkansas River. Now, the creeks flowing into its upper end fade away by mid-valley to be replaced by the Rio Grande (which also sometimes fades out when a combination of irrigation diversions and thirsty soils soak up *all* its water). Wind-carried sand cannot be lifted over the Sangre de Cristos and is left behind in a cluster of hundreds of feet high dunes at Great Sand Dunes National Monument. The valley has some of the best farmland in Colorado, but also some very marginal lands as well. The difference lies in water rights. There have been a number of real estate scams in the valley, based around the idea of reselling land in little 1, 2, and 5 acre parcels as recreational second home sites *without* their attendant water rights. When you see ads for Rocky Mountain homesites for reasonable prices in national magazines, this may be the land offered.

Migratory waterfowl flock to the valley, pausing in the Alamosa National Wildlife Refuge. Several dirt roads cross the river, the lowest of which (we think) is the road from Antonito and Lobatos to Mesita. The New Mexico state line is 5 miles downstream.

RIO GRANDE: Lobatos Bridge to Lee Trail

24 Miles, Class I, II. Suitable for kayaks, possible for small rafts and canoes. This section and Taos Box Canyon are part of the Wild and Scenic River System.

Leaving the San Luis Valley, the river begins cutting a deep gorge through the broad lava plain of northern New Mexico. Its severely depleted flow has been revived by several tributary creeks until it approaches its old proportions at the entrance to the valley (spring runoff 3,000–4,000 cfs). All this section has in common with that above is the name. The scenery, the climate, and even the very water itself is all new.

The next 24 miles contain a wild and beautiful run as the river

Local ambience, Rio Grande *(Fletcher Anderson)*

begins to form the upper part of the Taos Box Canyon. This section of the river is not unknown or unrun, but it is seldom visited. Here is a truly memorable little stretch of water for an overnight trip which you will have all to yourself.

Here is why: Almost no other boaters live near here, and anyone driving to this run must bypass several more popular and more accessible runs on the way. The put-in at Lobatos Bridge is (we think) the *only* reasonable put-in. The only take-out (unless you want to run the Class V Taos Box) is the 220-vertical-foot climb Lee Trail. The Lee Trail is accessible from a secondary road leaving the highway near Sunshine Valley, New Mexico.

Here, and everywhere else in New Mexico, it is an extremely bad idea to leave an unattended car on a back road. It will almost certainly be checked out by some of the locals who will not hesitate to break into it if they suspect it contains anything of value. Less frequently, it will be vandalized, and still less frequently stolen and taken for a joy ride. The same is true for unattended kayaks at put-ins and take-outs. Colorado kayak racers used to say (unfairly) that more kayaks and accessories were stolen at the Pilar, New Mexico, races than at all other races all over the United States and Canada, combined. Where all this loot went is a mystery, since no one ever seems to spot anyone using the stolen equipment.

"Unprotected" single women report that they are regarded as fair game and are often the victims of considerable (and sometimes violent) harassment by certain locals—particularly when camped alone at night. These harassments are not necessarily along racial lines, and the assailants are often Anglo red-necks.

On the balance, it should be pointed out that a great many other people you meet, particularly the local paddlers, will not hesitate to go way out of their way to make your visit more pleasant. Hitch-hiking is easy and drivers will frequently take you all the way to the river even when their own destination is somewhere altogether in another direction. If by chance you get a ride from a local paddler, you may have a hard time refusing an invitation to dinner and company for your next day's paddling.

RIO GRANDE: Upper Taos Box, Section I (Lee Trail to Red River confluence)

9 Miles, Class IV, V, some possible VI. Suitable for kayaks.

Here is one of the classic really difficult whitewater runs of the West. After only a few miles of easy paddling, you are deep within the vertical lava walls of the Taos Box Canyon. Large boulders have fallen from the walls to form a number of short, steeply-dropping boulder-choked rapids connected by stretches of more quiet water. Many of these rapids are of Class IV difficulty, a few are Class V, and at least one nasty little spot is a probable Class VI and is routinely portaged.

"Good" levels for the upper Taos Box are said to be when the gauge downstream at Embudo, New Mexico, reads above 2,000 cfs. (Phone 505-243-0702 for flow information.) These levels begin to occur in April when the southern Colorado snowmelt first hits and fade out in June when the remaining Colorado flows are being used for irrigation.

Rapids of the upper Taos Box increase considerably in difficulty with high water because of the added push. They do not increase substantially in complexity in low water, but the flat stretches are said to become extremely shallow and a couple of mandatory portages occur.

The way out of the first section of the upper box is via a long, steep hiking trail where the Red River joins the Rio Grande. This trail has an elevation gain of over 800 vertical feet. For this reason, few people like to carry up it and it is common practice to continue

Rafting the Rio Grande (*Fletcher Anderson*)

on and run the second half of the upper box. You can hike out here, camp with a car driven in from Questa, and hike back down to your boat in the morning.

RIO GRANDE: Upper Taos Box, Section 2 (Red River Trail to Dunn's Bridge)

12 Miles, Class III+ (IV at high). Suitable for kayaks. Is occasionally rafted.

Returning to the river via the Red River Trail, one finds, not surprisingly, more of the same sort of water as was encountered just above: pool/drop rapids connected by somewhat longer stretches of flats. The drop has moderated, the river channel proper is wider, and the river carries additional water from the Red River near Questa. If you have been drinking the river water above this point, definitely stop doing so now, because there is a molybdenum mine up the Red River which adds a variety of exotic pollutants to the flow. In contrast to the first section of the upper Taos Box Canyon, the drops on this section are more likely to be only Class III difficulty. Numerous hiking trails lead to the river in this vicinity, but they are too long and steep to provide reasonable access for someone carrying a boat (excellent for swimmers and fishermen, though).

As with the upper section of this canyon, difficult access provides a natural limiting force on river use. The run is pleasantly uncrowded. Dunn's Bridge is on a secondary road from the town of Arroyo Hondo. (Arroyo Hondo means either macabre or deep dry wash in English.)

RIO GRANDE: Lower Taos Box (Dunn's Bridge to Taos Junction)

12 Miles, Class III (IV at high water). Suitable for kayaks and rafts.

Access to this stretch of water is easy via bridges at the launch and take-out. The rapids are pretty straightforward (i.e., raftable) and there is a nearby tourist center (Taos). All of this combines to offer excellent business potential for commercial rafting, and the river has become crowded. Regulation is the inevitable result, and this run is regulated. You will need a permit from: Bureau of Land Management, Taos Resource Area, P.O. Box 1045, Taos, New Mexico 87571.

The "pioneer" kayakers who discovered this run in the early 1960s are about to find that once again industrial tourism is going to close another river to them. Perhaps the river managers here at least will not go for the unconscionable fixed-allotment scams of Utah and Arizona.

Barry Corbet runs the Rio Grande (Corbet rides in a wheelchair when off river) (*Fletcher Anderson*)

The season is from April to July. By late August, the river has all but dried up and is unuseable by rafts. Best levels for rafting are when the Embudo, New Mexico, gauge is above 2,000 cfs (phone 505-243-0702).

It is a deep and majestic canyon; the water itself is comparable in style and difficulty to Brown's Canyon on the Arkansas (p. 17), a real joy ride, when kicking, for those who can handle it. It is pool-drop in the 1,200–1,300 cfs range but has some tricky eddy lines and holes as does any large volume of water forced into a narrow rocky channel. At high levels (4,000–5,000 cfs) it is big water with big holes and weird currents. A dependable roll and strong brace are necessities for kayakers, as are a quality raft (with frame) and experience for rafters.

The last third of the run is extremely constricted. If you swim at the beginning of this stretch during high water, you probably won't get out for two miles. People (poorly equipped ones) have lost fingers and their desire to be rafters in that stretch.

Maps show a bridge over the middle of this run, but it is the very high Rio Grande Gorge Bridge which connects the rims of the canyon, with *no* river access. Taos Junction Bridge is the first real take-out.

Rio Grande: Taos Junction Bridge to Pilar, New Mexico Bridge

5 Miles, Class I. Suitable for rafts, kayaks, and canoes.

The canyon is over, the water flat, the scenery pleasant but unmemorable, and the boaters are few.

Rio Grande: Pilar, New Mexico Bridge to Rimconda, New Mexico Bridge

4½ Miles, Class II, III (III+ at high water). Suitable for kayaks, rafts, some canoes at low water.

This is the site of the annual Pilar, New Mexico, Whitewater Races. The abrupt pool/drop rapids of the box are replaced by longer, but easier, rapids. The race is held in early spring when mountain paddlers are glad to make the long drive for a little warm, sunny New Mexico weather.

Rio Grande: Rimconda to Otowi Bridge (New Mexico Route 4)

25 Miles, Class I. Suitable for kayaks, canoes, and rafts.

A Class I run with numerous access points, wire fences, and occasional irrigation diversion dams.

Rio Grande: Otowi Bridge to Cochiti Reservoir (White Canyon)

23 Miles, Class II (some possible III). Suitable for kayaks, canoes, and small rafts.

This is by far the most popular run in the state for open canoeists. The scenery is beautiful, and the rapids are nothing that a very determined novice couldn't survive. Rafters are usually dissuaded by the 4-mile paddle across the reservoir at the end of the run. The only reasonable access is via Otowi Bridge (put-in) and Cochiti Reservoir road (take-out).

Rio Grande: Cochiti Dam to Albuquerque and Beyond

50 Miles to Albuquerque, 300 Miles to El Paso, Texas, Class I. Sort of suitable for kayaks and canoes.

White Rock Canyon, Rio Grande (*Fletcher Anderson*)

Below Cochiti Dam, the river is continuously accessible from side roads off U.S. I-25. Irrigation diversions large and small withdraw its water mile-by-mile and its size decreases constantly. It is constantly crossed by barbed wire fences, and seldom boated, though often fished.

By the time it reaches El Paso, Texas, the river has, for the second time in its length, sometimes dried up completely.

Note # 1:

Considerably more detailed information on boating the Rio Grande is available from:

> Stretch Fretwell
> 758 47th Street
> Los Alamos, New Mexico 87544

Stretch is the recognized authority on paddling the Rio Grande and was one of that river's pioneer boaters. He also organizes the annual Pilar Races.

Note # 2:

The news that the Rio Grande ends at El Paso, Texas, comes as a shock to people who know of excellent whitewater canyons below

there in Big Bend National Park. Don't worry. At Presideo, Texas, the Rio Conchos enters the dry bed of the Rio Grande with a new batch of water. Any flows over 200 cfs are boatable—thus, the river is usually boatable year-round.

For the lower canyons, below Big Bend National Park, *any* flow at La Linda is boatable because springs along the way will add some 400 cfs.

Three hundred people launch on Thanksgiving, and still more do so around Easter. For the rest of the year, the canyon is empty save for illegal aliens and drug smugglers. Undoubtedly one or the other was the reason someone fired a rifle at author Anderson in February 1978.

Despite its relative isolation, this river has more garbage, litter, broken bottles, old tires, fire rings, and stray fishing gear than any other in the West. *Mariah/Outside* magazine, in a 1977 article, said they felt litter in so remote an area was reassuring. We feel otherwise.

Permits are required for boating in Big Bend from:

> U.S. National Park Service
> Big Bend National Park Headquarters
> Texas 79834

A comprehensive set of notes is available from:

> Bob Burlson
> 1st National Bank
> Temple, Texas 76501
> (817-778-1355)

The Texas Whitewater Association mailing address is:

> Texas Whitewater Association
> P.O. Drawer 5429
> Austin, Texas 78763
> (512-451-4966)

Kayaking the Rio Grande (*Bob Weaver*)

Riverside grass, Rio Grande *(Fletcher Anderson)*

Chapter VI

RIVERS OF THE GILA DRAINAGE

Doctor Strangelove Builds in the Desert (an interlude)
Rivers of Sothern Arizona
San Francisco River
Gila River
Salt River
Verde River

DOCTOR STRANGELOVE BUILDS IN THE DESERT
The Central Arizona Project

(An Interlude)

(The title is not ours, the Bureau of Reclamation named this monster the Central Arizona Project.)

Over most of southern Arizona scarcely 5 inches of rain falls on the ground every year. Summertime temperatures over 100° F are not uncommon. A unique faunal and floral assemblage has evolved to live in that seemingly intolerable climate, and the result is a curious ecosystem collectively called the Sonoran Desert. How exactly do the plants and animals adapt to such extremes of climate? What bizarre chemical compounds linger in them, and what is their pharmaceutical significance? The answers to these and other questions of unknown scientific import are not yet understood: the nature of the climate makes research difficult.

Yet, the Sonoran Desert is not all dry, for through it flow a small number of tiny streams which originate outside the desert, and along their banks is found a microclimate of oasis. Here are tall, leafy green trees: cottonwoods, willows, sycamores, and the ubi-

quitous invasive tamarisk. Here flock the wide ranging desert mammals and birds; here dwells the unique and endangered desert nesting southern bald eagle (there are believed to be six nesting pairs in the world: one in Colorado, five in Arizona habitats directly threatened by Central Arizona Project). Under the cool shade of these streamside trees, a man can escape the oppressive sun. Here he may graze a few animals and grow a few crops. He can divert the little streams to irrigate a little more land and increase the size of the oasis, and here he may build his home. So felt the region's various Indian nationalities who have made homes there for tens of thousands of years. So also felt the first white settlers who relocated the Indians slightly to one side. All of this was well and good (at least from the White point of view) and by the 1930s Phoenix, Tucson, and other Arizona communities were pleasant, if remote, little agricultural centers. The fledgling networks of canals had indeed made the desert bloom.

Phoenix burns and sinks back into the ashes: Shortly after World War II, it was apparent that the desert had already bloomed nearly as much as it ever could: more desert blooming would require more water and the available supplies were just about used up. It would appear that the growth of Phoenix, Tucson, etc., was about to come to an end and future growth would take place in wetter climates—like Arkansas or Louisiana.

Life never works like that. The cities sat atop natural aquifers which could be drilled for wells. Well water is a renewable resource, but only if water is drawn out at a lower rate than the aquifer is replenished. Clearly in the desert climate, the underground reservoirs were replenished extremely slowly. It was obvious to all that too many wells were extracting too much water: the water level in the wells dropped rapidly, and the very earth subsided (up to 25 feet in parts of Phoenix). Surely by now the limits of growth had been reached—indeed, had been exceeded. How much longer would the plainly exhaustable supply of water last? Ten years? Fifty years? Who cares, people argued, in 10 years the water will have made us rich. More and more wells keep getting drilled. The suburbs grow and the sprinkler systems struggle to keep the withered lawns of Kentucky blue grass green. (Why isn't all this growth taking place in Kentucky where the stuff grows wild?)

Paradise has been paved over, they put up parking lots. Most of the unique stream-side habitat has been dammed away. Life in Phoenix is a model of what life will be like on the moon: people shuttle in between hermetically sealed air-conditioned buildings in hermetically sealed air-conditioned cars. These air conditioners need electricity, some of which comes from the dam that destroyed Glen Canyon, and some of which comes from coal-burning power plants whose pollutants fall as acid rain on Colorado and New Mexico.

Now things are at a crisis stage. How much water actually does remain? The question is difficult to answer, and the answer is of life and death importance. How much more coal is there to run the plant that runs the air conditioners? This is it: Phoenix-Tucson (for they practically interconnect now) can definitely grow no larger.

Dr. Strangelove to the rescue: Now enters the mysterious mind of Dr. Strangelove. One hundred and fifty miles from Phoenix lies water in the stagnant artificial reservoir of Lake Havasu on the Colorado River—water enough, argues Strangelove, for another decade of suburb building. Unfortunately, that water is 2,000 vertical feet lower than Phoenix. Now you could build the suburbs down by the water (where everyone in them goes to spend their weekends) or you could pump the water uphill! Strangelove goes for the pumping option. Thus, over 300 miles of canal are under construction across desert and mountain. Massive pumping stations are to be supplied with electricity from huge coal-burning power plants between Grand Canyon National Park and Monument Valley. The sacred Black Mesa of the Navajos will be stripmined away from a people whose air quality will become worse than that of Los Angeles. The last remaining bits of the Sonoran stream-side habitat that brought the first settlers to Phoenix will be dammed or dried up.

Just how much water is Dr. Strangelove planning to pump, and where does he get it? Dr. Strangelove has claimed his share of the annual 16.5 million acre feet of appropriated Colorado River water. Nature, in its short sightedness, only sends 13.8 million acre feet down the river. Of this water, 4.55 million acre feet are used up in Colorado and Utah; 4.7 million acre feet go to California and Nevada; 1.5 million goes to Mexico, by treaty (in a pipe); 1.25 million is used in Arizona along the river; and 0.65 million acre feet evaporate off the reservoirs into the sky. Simple arithmetic leaves only 0.15 million acre feet for Dr. Strangelove and his fabulous piper, and this 0.15 million acre feet is actually being used now by someone else. Yet when the mad doctor throws the lever on his infernal pumps, he will suck 2 or 3 million acre feet out of the system. Somebody is going to come up dry and it will probably be farmers in California, for they are currently using 0.8 million acre feet of Bureau of Reclamation project's water in addition to their own.

The numbers still don't add up. What will happen when the Central Utah Project claims *its* 1.2 million acre feet of water? What will happen if the City of Denver diverts *its* unused water claims into the Two Forks Dam Project on the other side of the divide? What will happen when the McPhee Dam on the Dolores takes *its* water? What will happen if the Cross Mountain–Juniper, Fruitland Mesa, Savory Pothook, and Windy Gap dams are approved and take *their* water? The synfuel boys have the Colorado oil shale country up against the wall and are about to rape it. What if they, too, take *their* share of the water? What happens in another drought year like 1952, 1973, 1977, etc.? What happens when the Black Mesa coal deposit is mined out?

These are merely reactionary doomsday scenarios, Dr. Strangelove assures us. Admittedly, there *is not* enough water in the Colorado River, but there *is* enough water. Dr. Strangelove will ultimately pump the water from the Frazier River in British Columbia into the Columbia River in Oregon; then he will pump the Columbia River across the Nevada desert into the Colorado! It's always raining in British Columbia, so the Frazier will never run dry, but if it does, just pump the Yukon into the Frazier, and truck the polar ice cap into the Yukon! (Why not just build the suburbs in British Columbia, we wonder?) All of this pumping will require more energy than fossil fuels can provide—but don't worry, a whole generation of Navajos is already wasting their lives away in the uranium mines! Hazardous wastes bother you? We can just pump them into the ground under Phoenix where the water used to be! Dr. Strangelove has thought of everything! You can't fight progress!

Dr. Strangelove has dammed up most of the kayaking in central Arizona; but he has left untouched lots of prime whitewater in British Columbia. He's in the lumber business up there!

RIVERS OF SOUTHERN ARIZONA

General Description

Despite the machinations of Dr. Strangelove to satisfy the thirst of Phoenix, and despite the general absence of precipitation in any form in southern Arizona, there are some pleasant wilderness river runs in the Gila River drainage. The rivers are, by any standards, small. Despite the outstanding wilderness character of some of the areas the rivers run through, the runs would probably be of only local interest except for their seasons. High water season is generally from early March through late May. High water can also be encountered during any of the winter months following locally heavy rains. These runoff seasons occur at a time when the Rocky Mountains are locked in snow and the rivers which drain them are low.

River runners, hoping to escape the end of winter in the mountains, head for rivers of Arizona in the hope of catching a little sun. They frequently catch long periods of overcast weather and occasional rain and wind.

Summer touches the Sonoran Desert with severity and most of the rivers all but dry up entirely. You can run all of the rivers some of the time and you can run some of the rivers all of the time, but you cannot run all of the rivers all of the time.

Our information on these rivers is regrettably secondhand. Some of our informants have disagreed with others, and where such disagreement has occurred, it is noted. The various federal regulatory agencies listed will provide you with information, most of which is worthless. Typically, they inform you that the rivers are runnable, that they themselves know nothing of river running; and they don't explain exactly what portions of the rivers they are talking about.

With these caveats in mind, we present the rivers of southern Arizona.

SAN FRANCISCO RIVER

SAN FRANCISCO RIVER: (From the vicinity of) Alma, New Mexico to Clifton, Arizona

30 Miles, Class I, II. Suitable for kayaks, canoes, and small rafts —but presently closed to all.

There are three principal access routes to the river. These are at Frisco Hot Springs New Mexico, Dry Creek New Mexico, and Martinez Ranch Arizona. The first two locations would serve as put-ins, and the third as a take-out. The resulting river run would be about 30 miles. These locations, and the gravel roads which lead to them, are best comprehended on the Gila National Forest Map, which can be obtained for $1 from: U.S. Dept. of Agriculture, Forest Service, Glenwood Ranger District, Glenwood, New Mexico 88039.

The river is shallow and narrow, flowing through a lovely canyon filled with sycamore and cottonwood between steep rock cliffs. The canyon is the home of a wide variety of wildlife, including a large and healthy population of Rocky Mountain Bighorn Sheep. The canyon is a wilderness study area.

It is also a nesting ground for the Black Hawk and other sensitive nesting birds. *For this reason, the canyon is closed from March 15 through July 15 every year.* Unfortunately, for river runners, the closure dates encompass the entire time period during which there is enough water present to boat the river. Too bad, but presumably all of us understand the reasons for the closure and will abide by it.

GILA RIVER

UPPER GILA RIVER: Above Cliff, New Mexico

30 Miles, Class I, II; drops 24' per mile. Suitable for kayaks, whitewater canoes, and small rafts.

New Mexico Route 15 leads north 26 miles from Silver City, New Mexico, to a put-in. The take-out is at Cliff or Gila, New Mexico. The river flows through some of the most beautiful country in the Southwest. The Forest Service informs us that the river has been run in canoes and "kyaks" (*sic*) but for safety reasons, should be

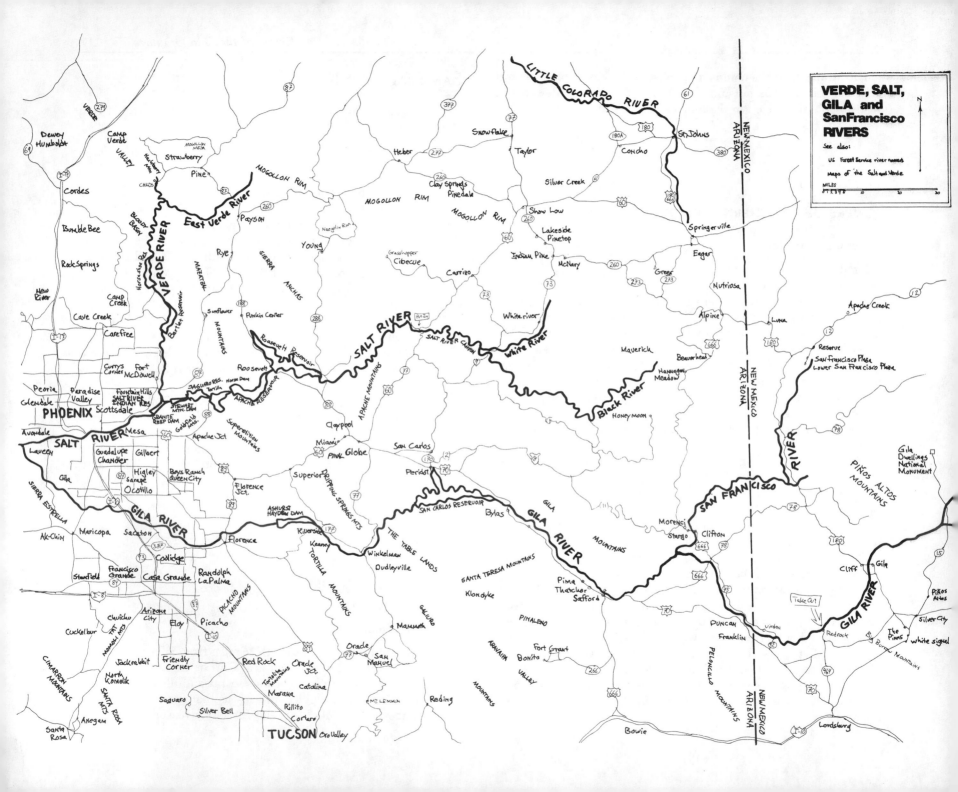

VERDE, SALT, GILA and SanFrancisco RIVERS

See also:

U.S. Forest Service river maps

Maps of the Salt and Verde

MILES
0 1 2 3 4 5   10   20   30

run in specialized whitewater rafts. Kayakers must realize that their choice of spelling and their views on the relative safety of various boats tells you a great deal about their knowledge of river running. Nevertheless, their information is accurate and helpful.

The Forest Service also provides some particularly useful information on river flows. Spring flows of 400 cfs to 750 cfs are typical and are the most satisfactory for running the river. The river can be run in small boats if it is flowing steadily at over 200 cfs. Some years, the river is too low to run at all.

Despite the apparently short length of the run, the Forest Service recommends allowing at least four days to make this run. In addition to rapids (which you may wish to scout) you will encounter numerous logjams and barbed wire fences which must be portaged.

A party of open canoeists from the River Recreation Association of Texas made this run during a period of unusually high water and found numerous Class III rapids and one possible Class IV. Logjams were particularly common, as were whirlpools. The rapids became "nonstop." They wrapped a canoe around a rock, and eventually emerged five days later feeling cold and miserable.

We suspect that the high water conditions which make open canoeing so difficult would be child's play for an expert kayaker. A canoe swamps, a kayak does not, but there would still be mandatory portages at the barbed wire fences and logjams.

A permit, flow information, and general information can be obtained from: U.S. Department of Agriculture, Forest Service, Gila City Ranger District, Route 8, Box 124-1, Silver City, New Mexico 88061.

MIDDLE BOX, GILA RIVER: Highway 180/Cliff, New Mexico, to Redrock, New Mexico

Approx. 15 Miles, Class II, III; drops 30' per mile. Suitable for kayaks; possible for some rafts and canoes.

The Middle Box of the Gila River is a unique Wild and Scenic river resource, though not yet protected as such. In addition to solitude and excellent whitewater, it is a heavily used nesting area for raptors and other birds. It is a strikingly beautiful narrow little canyon filled with cottonwood and sycamore trees

A 5–6-mile stretch with open gravel bar rapids, Class II, takes you to the start of the Box. The gorge itself is of metamorphic basement rock, a miniature Westwater Canyon (p. 53) with regular pool/drops,

fluted hard rock, and desert fauna. Although somewhat ominous looking, the gorge is a classic Class III, and continues for 6–7 miles. Most of the drops here are a bit narrow for rafts, although paddle rafters can squeak by. The gorge ends at a potential and imminent dam site. From there the river meanders through braided channel for 4 miles to the Redrock bridge take-out.

For most kayakers the run can be done in a day, even with the 2-hour shuttle (each way). Unfamiliarity with the stretch, or a desire not to see automobiles, or any number of other excuses, may warrant a longer trip.

A description of the river by employees of the BLM is available from: Bureau of Land Management, District Office, P.O. Box 1420, Las Cruces, New Mexico 88004.

The BLM employees ran the river in open canoes in March 1979 at a flow of about 800 to 1,000 cfs. Their first day on the river, they spent *18 hours* and traveled only 14 miles. One may surmise that they were fairly well exhausted by the time they made camp. On the second day, it took them *12 hours* to cover only 4 miles of river. By their account, the first 14 miles of river features numerous Class III rapids. In the next 4 miles, the canyon narrows and one encounters many Class IV rapids. Three of these rapids were portaged and two others were lined. Many other Class III and IV rapids required extensive scouting (hence only 4 miles in 12 hours). As the canyon grows tighter and tighter, scouting becomes more imperative, but requires considerable climbing. Two miles from the end of the canyon, scouting becomes impossible and one must run several more Class II rapids blind. Both canoes were swamped at various times.

Recommended flows: 500+ cfs minimum to 3000+.

Access: Take the road just south of where Highway 180 crosses the Gila. This road winds its way past two ranches and ends at Billings Vista Bird Refuge (public land, and the put-in). The take-out is at the Redrock bridge.

MIDDLE GILA RIVER: From Redrock, New Mexico, to Virden, New Mexico

About 15 Miles. Suitable (presumably) for kayaks, possibly for small rafts and canoes.

This stretch of river passes through a roadless area similar to that described for the run above. It, too, is administered by the BLM Las Cruces District Office. Presumably, this run is less difficult than the

Middle Box, but we have no information about it.

GILA RIVER: Virden, New Mexico, to Three Way, Arizona

Nearly 30 Miles. Suitable for kayaks? Possibly for canoes?

This nearly 30-mile stretch of the Gila River is closely paralleled by New Mexico Route 92 and U.S. 70. The river above and below this stretch offers excellent boating. Presumably, the river here is boatable as well. Access appears to be relatively easy, based on available maps, and there is no indication of anything which would cause major rapids. Nevertheless, we have no information about boating this part of the river.

LOWER GILA BOX

23 or 19 Miles, Class II, III. Suitable for kayaks, possible for canoes and small rafts. (Conflicting reports of difficulty.)

This river is under the management of the Bureau of Land Management, District Office, 425 East 4th Street, Safford, Arizona 85546.

The information available from this office of the BLM is less encouraging than the information from the neighboring BLM office upstream.

Their letter to us reads in part: "The policy of this office is not to encourage floating the Gila and San Francisco Rivers. Submerged debris, such as fence wire and trees, and fluctuating water levels (flooding) make floating these rivers very hazardous. However, floating does occur in a variety of water craft."

Their map of the area has printed on it in brilliant red ink: "WARNING– Due to extremely hazardous conditions this float trip is NOT RECOMMENDED for any boaters or innertubers, *regardless of experience.*"

However, in a catalogue of resources of the Safford BLM District,[5] one comes across the following description:

Gila River Box
As the Gila River enters the Safford district, it flows through an area steeped in the history of pioneer Arizona. The canyon tightens rapidly as the Gila nears its confluence with the San Francisco River.

This area is commonly known as the "Gila River Box." This is a spectacular gorge of unspoiled beauty, with sheer walls rising several hundred feet. The melodious calls of canyon wrens serenade the visitor and the beautiful rose-colored pyrrhuloxia add a sparkling touch of color to this primeval canyon.

During periods of high water, the Gila "Box" can be floated, with rubber rafts or aluminum canoes recommended. The route passes old settler cabins and still-standing wooden watermills.

The Gila Box extends approximately eleven miles. A good starting point is where the old Clifton-Safford road crosses the Gila. The trip is ideal for naturalists interested in studying desert birdlife and desert mountain flora. Back-packers should allow three or four days for the journey and wear canvas shoes or boots for frequent stream crossings.

What can we say? On the one hand, the BLM tells us the river is unrunnable, yet on the other hand they seem to be saying that it is sufficiently mild that it can be run in open canoes.

BLM wilderness coordinator Steve Knox frankly admits that he is not a boater and directs inquiries to: Thoran Lane, Chairman, Arizonans for Wild and Scenic Rivers, Box 87, Cortaro, Arizona 85130.

The put-in for this run is on the old Safford-Clifton road, as indicated in the BLM's advice. Drive upstream on a secondary road, northeast from Solomon, Arizona, 10 miles to the take-out.

The best information we have about the rapids is that they are Class II–III at worst, despite the BLM's doomsday warnings. A novice open canoeist could easily get into trouble in Class II water, and that may be the reason for this BLM district's generally negative view of river running.

GILA RIVER: Solomon, Arizona, to San Carlos Reservoir

35 Miles, Class I. Not recommended.

The Gila River flows through the Gila Valley near U.S. 70 under numerous barbed wire fences past many modern ranches. The barbed wire makes this run unpopular.

GILA RIVER: San Carlos Reservoir to Avondale (A Phoenix suburb)

About 130 Miles, Class I.

The river is close to numerous roads and the ever present barbed wire fences. San Carlos Reservoir and Coolidge Dam usually impound the water which would otherwise make this stretch boatable. Occasional dam releases are difficult to predict.

[5]Available from the Safford BLM office with a resource map of the area.

GILA RIVER: Phoenix area to confluence at Yuma

About 180 Miles, Class I.

The map shows a river running through the Sonoran Desert. Enough water is withdrawn from the river to render it almost always too shallow to paddle, usually absolutely dry. What little water does escape Phoenix is caught by Painted Rock Dam. Below that point, the riverbed is nearly always dry.

SALT RIVER

General Description

The upper Salt River is a beautiful little desert river leaving the White Mountains near the Arizona–New Mexico border, and descending rather quickly to Roosevelt Reservoir. While it lasts, it flows through a steep-walled, narrow little canyon. The canyon bottom is full of cottonwoods and sycamores and is a nesting area for numerous raptors and migrating birds.

This general description sounds a great deal like the Gila and the San Francisco — which is reasonable enough, as the rivers are quite similar. The river is generally felt to be somewhat more difficult to run than the Gila. An excellent and very detailed map and other information is available from: U.S. Department of Agriculture, Forest Service, Tonto National Forest, 102 South 28th Street, P.O. Box 29070, Phoenix, Arizona 85038.

The season could begin as early as February and extend through early May. Weather, at that time of year, is an important consideration for river runners, and is totally unpredictable. Occasional heavy, wet snowstorms can occur as late as April, though sunny weather is more common.

UPPER SALT RIVER: Arizona Route 9 to U.S. 60

25 Miles, Class II, III, IV. Suitable for kayaks.

Access: The put-in is on the Black River five miles above its confluence with the White to form the Salt.

Recommended flows: 500 cfs minimum to 2,500 cfs. The water gets seriously pushy above 2,500 cfs.

This section of the Salt is Class V-VI, for decked boats and experts only. Beyond it, Route 9 passes through the Fort Apache Indian

Salt River (*Eric Leeper*)

Reservation and access to the area is by permission only. If you can get permission from the tribe to put-in, there may be a charge.

For the first 15 miles or so, the river is scenic, Class II-III in difficulty. Below this the river begins cutting through limestone/diabase gorges and scouting becomes more necessary as one descends. At six miles above the Salt Canyon bridge, Highway 60, the river cuts dramatically into the metamorphic rock and portages are frequent. In here, depending on flows, the river encounters 15-foot vertical drops into Grand Canyon-sized holes, boulder seives and general havoc. Dugald Bremner ran it at flows over 3,000 cfs and reports that it took his group of experts around six hours to do these last six miles. Two to three miles up Highway 60 to the north a short but steep descent on foot via an old mining road allows scouting access to the last six miles of this stretch.

SALT RIVER: U.S. 60 to Route 288/Roosevelt Reservoir

Circa 60 Miles, Class III with portage; drops 24' per mile. Suitable for kayaks.

This is really one of the most enjoyable and spectacular desert runs in the Southwest, and to the dismay of those who knew its past solitude, it is now one of the most popular runs in the state. Saguaro cactus on the beaches and bald eagles in the sky contribute much to this river's character. Camps and good hiking are abundant as are archaeological sites. Up to this point in time the Salt remains both unregulated and undammed (above Roosevelt). It is hoped that all who run it will regulate themselves enough to keep it free from both regulation and impact, allowing it to retain these increasingly rare freedoms.

The Salt is bordered to the north by the Fort Apache Indian Reservation and to the south by the San Carlos Apaches for a few miles, subsequently by government land. The White Mountain Apaches charge $10 per day for camping rights.

This run is normally done in 4–5 days. Camping spots are frequent. The preferred spots are shown on the Forest Service map. This map also shows the location of numerous drownings. Drinking water is available from many side streams, but drinking from the main river is not recommended.

The run is serious Class III with some long and continuous sections. It passes through three successive gorges of Precambrian rock. At Quartzite Falls (Class V) the river drops over two 8-foot ledges and creates a powerful keeper at the bottom. This drop is portaged by a majority of the trips but has been the site of some terrible accidents. It has been run successfully at certain water levels.

Access: The put-in can be made at the Highway 60 bridge or 5 miles down a dirt road to the north of the bridge on the White Mountain Apache side. The river from the bridge to the lower put-in actually makes a great day run of 8 miles, Class II-III. The take-out is actually the most unanticipated danger of the whole trip, as the Salt drops over a 6-foot diversion dam into Roosevelt Reservoir, ½ mile below the Route 288 bridge. A short climb at the bridge itself provides a great take-out. With prior scouting, one can take out JUST above the dam on the right. Prudence is advised.

Recommended flows: 600+ cfs to 4,000+ cfs; 1,500 cfs minimum for rafts. Although flows are typically in the 1,000 cfs range, they can sometimes exceed 2,500 cfs. The river is no place for an open canoe at high water. Call the Salt River Project, (602) 267-9161, for flow information.

SALT RIVER: Below Roosevelt Reservoir

Not recommended.

Below Roosevelt Reservoir the river is almost back-to-back dams all the way to the Phoenix suburbs. The river through Phoenix is usually unboatable because no water is released. The river here is a popular motorcycling spot. Boaters living in the immediate vicinity sometimes play the out-wash eddies of the dam spillways for an hour or so in the afternoon when the dams are releasing.

VERDE RIVER

VERDE RIVER: Camp Verde to Childs

27 Miles, Class III. Suitable for rafts, kayaks, expert open canoeists.

Designated as a Wild and Scenic river stretch, this is a tremendously scenic canyon. The river passes through bald eagle nesting areas, and hosts of migratory birds are commonly seen. The stretch is Class III with lots of space betweeen the rapids, save one section that passes through a basalt gorge (beginning about 10 miles below Camp Verde). Verde Falls, portaged by many for the drop itself and/or the potential for a long swim in the following mile, will be encountered in this basalt section.

Salt River *(Eric Leeper)*

When runnable, the river is in flood; therefore, its brush and tree-covered gravel bars are underwater. A lack of good maneuverability skills combined with the length of the trip have made it troublesome for some beginners and inexperienced canoeists. There is a reward at the end: you can soak in a natural hot springs across from the take-out.

Access: Put-in at the lower bridge in Camp Verde or on a road west of the river beyond development site.

Recommended flows: 600 cfs to 6,000 cfs with a 1,500 cfs minimum for rafts.

VERDE RIVER: Childs, Arizona, to Horseshoe Reservoir

25 Miles (plus 2 miles of reservoir), Class I, II, III, IV. Suitable for kayaks, possible for canoes and small rafts. (Again, difficulty ratings are disputed.)

Our information on this run is secondhand. The Class IV rapids appear to have been rated by open canoeists. Out-of-state kayakers report substantially lower degrees of difficulty.

Excellent river runner maps of the upper Verde are available for 50¢ from: U.S. Department of Agriculture, Forest Service, Verde Ranger District, Star Route 1, Box 1100, Camp Verde, Arizona 86322, phone 567-4121.

The Verde River is generally paddleable by canoe or kayak in the early spring, but runoff varies greatly year to year, and it is not runnable every year. For that reason, it is advisable to phone the ranger and ask about local conditions before making the drive to the river. Although most of the river is narrow and fast moving, there are a few spots where it is wider and shallower and it is sometimes necessary to wade along, pushing your boat. This is particularly the case in the first couple of miles below Childs, before the confluence with the East Verde River. In a wet year, or during a rain flood, the river can crest at over 4,000 cfs. These flood conditions are somewhat dangerous because of overhanging branches near shore, barbed wire fences, and flood debris in the river.

The water is cold, and the Forest Service recommends wet suits. Weather in the early spring is unpredictable. Several days of miserable cold drizzle or even wet snow can be encountered with little warning as late as April or, on rare occasions, early May. Nevertheless, it is a beautiful little wilderness run and very enjoyable even in drizzle or sleet *if* you are sufficiently prepared for these conditions.

VERDE RIVER: Bartlett Reservoir to confluence

19 Miles, Class I, II. Suitable for kayaks and canoes.

Most of this stretch of river is paralleled by a dirt road leading north from Fort McDowell, Arizona. It is possible to use that road to make trips shorter than the full 19 miles. For that reason, this is a popular afternoon paddle for Phoenix area boaters *when it has enough water.*

Usually, Horseshoe and Bartlett reservoirs take the highs off of the high flows and release a paddleable minimum flow. Occasionally, when the upper Verde is in flood, they release very large flows to keep from overfilling. In a dry year, however, they might not be releasing enough water to float in. If you are unsure of releases, phone Verde District Ranger at 567-4121.

In midsummer, the air temperature in Phoenix can go over 110°. When that happens, the local radio stations often report releases from Bartlett Reservoir. At times when the other Phoenix area rivers are dry Bartlett Reservoir often releases enough water to float several thousand delighted innertubers.

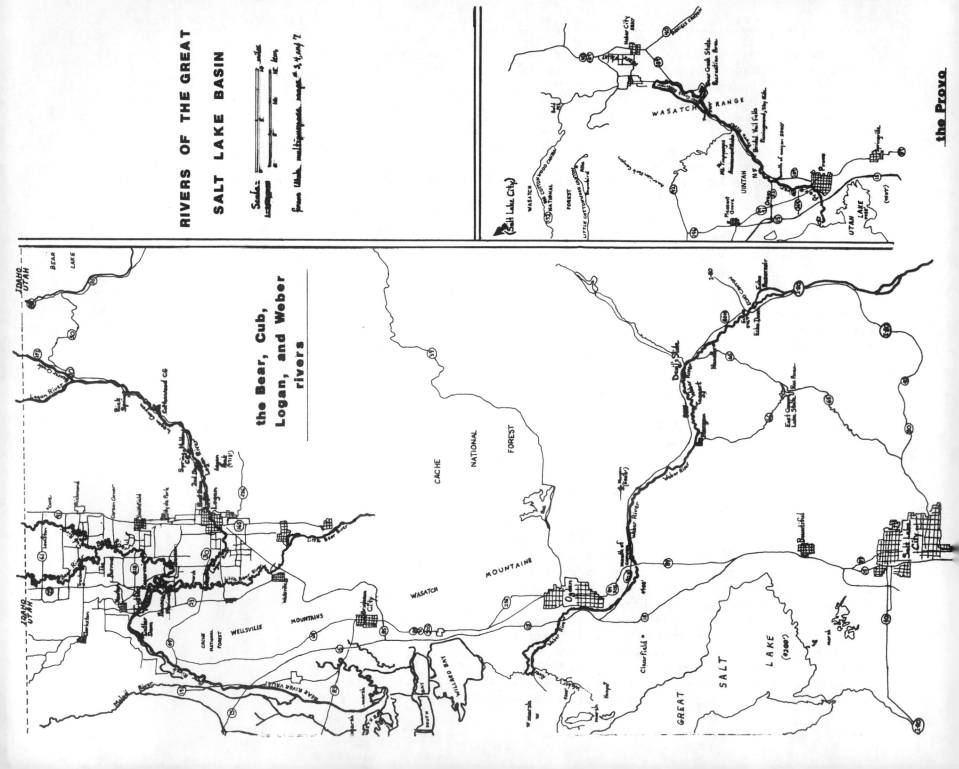

Chapter VII

RIVERS OF THE GREAT
SALT LAKE BASIN

the Bear, Cub,
Logan, and Weber
rivers

the Provo

RIVERS OF THE SALT LAKE VALLEY

Utah

Provo River

Weber River

Logan River

Bear River

Cub River

Big Empty Space (an interlude)

UTAH

The Salt Lake Valley

General Description

The rivers of the Salt Lake Valley all terminate in the flat desert environs of the Great Salt Lake. They are basically of two types: either small, rocky streams cascading from the mountains; or slow valley meanderers. The Wasatch Mountain Range flanks the valley on the east and captures a great deal of moisture. The Salt Lake Valley is as lush as it is due almost solely to the mountain runoff.

In early historical times, the valley was full of game attracted by thick grass and mild climes. Mountain men regarded the area as the promised land and many of them wintered there. Stories of this promised land eventually reached the long-persecuted Mormons, who made their massive migration to Utah in the 1850s and '60s. They settled, irrigated, and cultivated the valley, and they have made it the unique place that it is today.

There are several boatable rivers in the Salt Lake Valley, which locals take the trouble to travel to and paddle. None of these are recommended as ideal places to boat. They get the use that they do primarily because they are close to the population centers of Utah. All of our information on them is compiled from various Utah residents and we are indebted to them for their information. Wasatch Touring, Timberline Sports in Salt Lake City, and Trailhead Sports in Logan are local kayak dealers and are friendly about answering questions.

Several phone services provide river flow information for the area:

Salt Lake River Service: 524-5130
Weber River, call: 825-1677 — Layton, Utah
Provo River, call: 244-1935 — Provo, Utah

PROVO RIVER

General Description

The Provo River and its banks here are entirely government-owned, lying within the boundaries of Uinta National Forest and Deer Creek State Recreation Area. It is a clear mountain-type stream, flowing through an alpine ecozone. This is a very popular area, so do not expect to find solitude.

As you enter the mouth of Provo Canyon on the drive up, you may see the Provo streaming by at more than a thousand cubic feet per second. Do not be misled: you will not be boating on most of this water. It is diverted and carried away through a big green pipe and not returned until beyond the good boatable stretches.

In summer, the river undergoes daily fluctuations in water flow. It is usually highest around 4–5 P.M. One can check the flow by dialing: 244-1935 (in Provo, Utah). The flows generally range between 200 and 700 cfs.

PROVO RIVER: Deer Creek Reservoir Outlet to (above) diversion dam

6 Miles, Class I, II. Suitable for kayaks.

Provo Canyon here is semiscenic. The road is not visible from the water, although it parallels the river channel. This is a standard first-timer's run containing a slow current and rocks for practicing those shaky maneuvers.

The take-out is anywhere on the backed up water above the diversion dam, but normally people take-out just below the trailer park.

PROVO RIVER: (Just above) Bridal Veil Falls to next road crossing

1 Mile, continuous Class III, IV. Suitable for kayaks.

The river is still within a deep canyon and is narrow (about 15 yards wide), but now a road runs along it. This stretch is not as scenic as the upper one, but the water is more interesting. There are some private cottages along the river. Many have low bridges leading to them.

Bridal Veil Falls is the site of an annual slalom race. It, and the rapids below it, should be scouted, especially at high water (700 cfs). It is good to check with local boaters because there are low bridges at acute angles to the current, and the rapids worsen considerably at high water. The river is very tight and narrow. There are many jammed logs.

The put-in is just above the tram. The hardest stretch cannot be seen from the road. There is one continuous 50-yard stretch of Class IV which is only runnable at higher water.

Below the take-out, the river is too tight and obstructed by logs to be boatable.

WEBER RIVER

General Description

Season: June through the end of August, sometimes limited by low flows.

There is one good thing that Utah surely has, and that is good highways. No matter how remote and infrequently visited a place is, whether inhabited or not, it will have a smooth, unblemished ribbon of pavement leading to it. An extension of this rule is I-80 N in that it has 8 or 10 of these smooth, flawless lanes. One usually encounters occasional other cars when traveling on it. However, the ratio of car per lane which one finds on remote desert roads is preserved on 80 N. Every car normally can have an entire lane to itself when outside of the city. This massive 8-laner does not enrich one's boating experience on the Weber. I suppose the canyon was once fairly nice, but now its sole function appears to be to provide a smooth, fast ride straight on into what is sometimes referred to as "Scoopland." In short, we are forced to give this entire river a less than scenic rating, due to the proximity of the interstate.

More information on the Weber than is provided herein can be obtained from Timberline Sports in Salt Lake City, Utah. They run the race on the Weber as well as paddle there. We are indebted to them for much of the following information.

WEBER RIVER: Echo Dam to Devil's Slide

9 Miles, Class I, II (plus one Class III feature, easily portaged). Popular open canoe and kayak run.

This stretch is less than ideal for boating, due to assorted barbed wire fences (duckable) and small irrigation dams (runnable) with drops of about 12 inches. There is one dam which has a dangerous reversal at its base. It would be a bad place to flip since it is a keeper. It can be seen from the highway about halfway between the dam and Devil's Slide. Fortunately, it can be portaged easily.

WEBER RIVER: Henefer to Taggert

6 Miles, Class II (one Class III drop—Taggert Falls). Suitable for kayaks, possible for canoes.

The grade increases compared to the previous stretch, and several Class II rapids are encountered. The stream is quite rocky, the rapids are rock garden variety.

The downriver and slalom races are held in this section. Just beyond Devil's Slide comes Taggert Falls, a 6-foot drop which it is advisable to scout. It is usually run on the far left. The most difficult part of this stretch is negotiating all the highway bridge pylons.

This run can be lengthened by running from Devil's Slide to Morgan. The character of the stream remains Class II, rocky. There is a diversion dam in the town of Morgan which is not runnable. The take-out is above it.

WEBER RIVER: Morgan to mouth of Weber Canyon

17 Miles, Class IV+. Suitable for kayaks. Season: May through summer depends on level.

This is the "meanest water in Northern Utah" and "a real boat muncher" according to several reliable sources. The last 6 miles of the canyon are the most difficult. Whenever the river leaves sight of the road, its difficulty increases greatly; i.e., scouting is not possible from the road.

One of the "meanest" is called "Scrambled Eggs." There are a number of obvious access points via dirt roads. The lower 6-mile stretch is on Forest Service land.

LOGAN RIVER

LOGAN RIVER: Above the town of Logan

Class II–IV; drops 50' per mile. Suitable for kayaks. Optimal season: late June through late July.

The Logan River above the town of Logan, is a small, narrow (15–30-foot wide) river with flows ranging from 100–500 cfs. It has a steep gradient and a swift current of clear cold water. It winds through a picturesque alpine canyon. The streambed is often choked with fallen logs and piles of debris. Low bridges are a hazard at high water. Before the end of June, the Logan here is generally unrunnable because a boat cannot fit under the bridges. It is advisable to check with local boaters or with Trailhead Sports in Logan for current information on this and all the other northern Utah rivers.

Access: Route 89 follows the Logan River from the town of Logan all the way up to the Idaho border. Access points are numerous, as are picnic areas and campgrounds.

The standard runs are described below, but where one puts-in or takes-out can be flexible.

LOGAN RIVER: Rick Springs (a tourist pull-out) to Cottonwood Campground

6 Miles, Class III, IV. Suitable for kayaks.

The river is tight, narrow, and rocky with few eddies and lots of overhanging brush. Difficulty increases with higher water.

LOGAN RIVER: Cottonwood Campground to Spring Hollow Campground

6 Miles, Class II, III. Suitable for kayaks.

This is the most popular run on the Logan River. The hardest part of this stretch is found in the first 2 miles. There are many access points throughout the run, which is quite scenic, despite the presence of the road.

LOGAN RIVER: "2nd Dam" to 1st Dam (mouth of canyon)

3 Miles, Class IV. Suitable for kayaks.

The "2nd Dam" is 3 miles up from the mouth of the canyon (measured from the lowest bridge). A U.S.F.S. information trailer is parked here in the summer. The water is swift Class IV with low bridges and overhanging trees. Scout all bridges and/or check with local boaters or Trailhead Sports to make sure a boat will fit under the bridges. The take-out is at a dam at the mouth of the canyon. This stretch is the most difficult of the Logan River's runnable sections. Most of it can be scouted from the road, but some of the low bridges (to private homes) cannot be.

LOWER LOGAN RIVER

Below the town of Logan, the riverbed flattens out and meanders across the valley floor until it empties into Cutter Reservoir.

LOWER LOGAN RIVER: (Town of) Logan to Route 30

8 Miles, Class I, II; drops 20' per mile. Suitable for kayaks and canoes. Season: Early June through August.

This stretch of the Logan winds its way across the Cache Valley floor and provides boaters with a delightful three hour trip (on the average) through wooded areas, farmland, and marsh. The river is still narrow with overhanging branches in places. Ducks, geese, beaver, and deer are common sights with an occasional junked car thrown in for variety.

The trip starts on 6th West in Logan, where the river crosses the road. Access is easy and parking is ample. There is a boat ramp and public parking area where Route 30 (Valley View Highway) intersects the river 6 miles west of town.

The river continues to meander down to Cutter Reservoir for another 4 miles. It has several access points which are visible on the map.

Low water flows limit the boating season for this run. It is usually deep enough from June through August.

BEAR RIVER

BEAR RIVER: UTAH-IDAHO BORDER TO CUTLER RESERVOIR

20 Miles, Class I. Suitable for kayaks, canoes, and small rafts. Season: May through September.

This is a wide, slow, meandering, river which flows through dairy farmland. The Bear River is actually a river—as opposed to a stream like most of the aforementioned waterways of the Salt Lake Valley. It has flows of about 2,000 cfs. Wildlife and birdlife are abundant, making this a popular run with the Audubon Society. The water is warm and muddy and gives off a bovine aroma. The higher one goes, the cleaner and more kinetic the water becomes (i.e., up around Richmond).

Access is good; both paved and dirt roads cross the river at frequent intervals so that trips of any desired length can be arranged with ease.

A downriver race is held annually in early spring from the town of Benson to Benson Marina. One of the more popular runs begins at Highway 170 east of Clarkston and ends at the Highway 218 Bridge.

CUB RIVER

CUB RIVER: Richmond, Utah to confluence with Bear River

Class I, II. Suitable for kayaks and canoes. Season: June through September.

The Cub River flows through scenic and fertile bottomland with lots of birds, but without farms or houses. It is small and narrow with clear water.

The Cub River has no waves or rapids, but has a Class II rating because of some bridges set at acute angles to the current, and others in narrow places where the river bends sharply.

There are many points of access which can be gleaned from study of the map.

BIG EMPTY SPACE

A Close Encounter
of the Third Kind
at night in southern Utah

(An Interlude)

Despite modern energy developments and the attendant demand for nighttime sinning, most of southern Utah still closes down completely after sunset. Deep in the midst of an all-night shuttle drive with my gas gauge below empty and my mind long since shifted over to automatic pilot from lack of sleep, I saw an eerie green glow loom up out of the desert beyond my headlights. My consciousness struggled vaguely toward alertness, for over the next hill must lie one of the rarest of desert phenomenon: an open all-night gas station!

Only one pump was operating and someone else was using it—a peculiar and somehow melancholy man, yet vaguely familiar. His pants were a size too large at the waist and several inches too short at the ankle, despite an overly long pair of suspenders which held them rather lower on the hip than normal standards of decency would require. His shirt lacked several key buttons and both elbows—a fitting complement to the fenders of his car, through which the desert breeze passed scarcely affected by the remaining bits of rusted metal—and to his mouth, which lacked an upper tooth. Yet his hat was once a stylish sort of yachting cap (long since out of fashion) and, looking beyond it, I realized with a start that his car, like mine, carried a kayak—and what a kayak it was: its state of repair was in keeping with the rest of his person. The boat's aluminum bottom was dented and a rip in its canvas deck bore a poorly adhering mass of duct tape. His boat was a full two feet shorter than my own and its cockpit a good foot longer. There was something more peculiar still. My mind flickered in the gray realm between sleeping and awaking as I absentmindedly ran my hand over the mass of dead insects plastered on my boat and car. It couldn't be, but it was—here, several hot dry hours from the nearest river, his boat was still covered with a fine film of muddy water.

He directed an overtly hostile stare through strangely unparalleled eyes at my boat, a stare which relaxed to a mere unfriendly gaze when he determined that my boat, like his, was clearly homemade. Something in those unparalleled eyes touched a memory lost far back in my childhood.

"Why," I exclaimed, "aren't you old . . ."

"How the hell do you know who I am?" He spit out the words rather than speaking them.

"Don't you remember me? I'm Fletcher Anderson, one of Keith Anderson's boys. We kayaked the Yampa with you back in 1954."

"Hell, how could I recognize you? You was only six years old then."

It was him all right. Where had he been paddling in the desert in the middle of the night? Where had he gone when he faded away so quietly back in the early 1960s? His voice changed from overt hostility to mere gruffness as he began to explain.

"Well, when your Dad built that fiberglass boat back in '55, that was the beginning of the end. Now, it used to take some real skill to paddle them foldboats down your wilder rivers and most folks wouldn't do it, but hell any damn fool can get through with fiberglass. And then there's all them damned rafts! Why, it's like the canyons was invaded with a bunch of Winnebagos!

"They didn't even know what a kayak was in Utah, so I moved over to Salt Lake and paddled the Beaver and the Weber. Then I saw a kayak there too. Well, it just wasn't the same any more. I give it up for a while, but I guess you just can't walk away from the rivers.

"I paddled the Escalante and then for a while—no whitewater, of course, but I go for the solitude more than excitement, you know.

"Several years back I saw somebody else there. That was when I built this boat. She's short because there's a lot of tight turns on the little rivers I paddle. They're all too shallow to Eskimo roll in anyway, so I made the cockpit real big. I have to jump out a lot when I come to fences and fallen trees and all.

"Now the Sevier over by Panguitch. There's a nice little river. I run that once all the way down to the dry lake bed in Millard County. Let me tell you, that's one god awful hike out of there!

"The Price, the Strawberry, the San Rafael—course you catch hell from the BLM if they find out cause you end up in the Green. I mostly run those in the winter.

"The Dirty Devil below Hanksville's been one of my favorites. 'Course all these little creeks you got to catch them when they're up, which usually means you got to wait for a good rainstorm and paddle the flash flood. 'Course, you have to do a lot of portages and sometimes you wade along pushing your boat with your paddle. There's quite a few places big enough to float a boat in so long as she's empty. Pushing a boat along beats carrying a backpack.

"I thought a lot about running Kanab Creek, but hell, once I got to the bottom I'd be smack in the Grand Canyon."

"I thought you loved the Canyon," I said. (I felt I should say something just to prove I was listening.)

"I did and I still do, but I love it the way it was twenty-five years ago. You think I want to kayak a god-damned amusement park?

"I guess for that matter I might as well tell you I don't paddle any of the rivers I just mentioned anymore."

"Where do you go?" I asked.

There was something in my question that destroyed his confidence in me. He paused and looked suspiciously off into the darkness.

"Well, smaller streams I guess."

Finally, he admitted that one day driving past Moab after a thunderstorm he looked out in the middle of a field and saw a whole row of big standing waves. It opened up a new world. Now he paddles dry washes exclusively. He just waits out in the middle of the desert for a thunderstorm and catches the crest of the flash flood. When its over, he *drags* the boat back to his car. That's why it has an aluminum bottom. If the weather report is wrong, he sits out in the desert and does something else.

The way he sees it, all the rivers everyone else paddles now are about to be dammed up. When that happens, only his kind of whitewater will be left and he's not about to tell anybody where the really good dry washes are.

I awoke with a start, still at the wheel of my car. Better get some coffee before I run off the road.

I put on my brakes and turned off the highway toward the pumps. My gas gauge read empty. Was this the next gas station, one tankful farther down the road, or was this the same gas station? Had it all been a dream?

Overview of the goosenecks of the San Juan River (*Fletcher Anderson*)

Epilogue

(This is what happened to a river no one protected.)

The government sent Lt. Joseph C. Ives to determine the upper limits of steam navigability of the lower Colorado River and explore the surrounding country. We pick up his narrative on April 3, 1958:

> It was a cool lovely morning, and a favorable day for travel. After proceeding a mile or two, we issued from the hills and entered a region totally different from any that we had seen during the expedition. A broad table land, unbroken by the volcanic that had overspread the country since leaving Fort Yuma extended before us, rising in a gradual swell toward the north. The road became hard and smooth, and the plain was covered with excellent grass. Herds of antelope and deer were seen bounding over the slopes. Groves of cedar occurred, and with every mile became more frequent and of larger size. At the end of ten miles the ridge of the swell was attained, and a splendid panorama burst suddenly into view. In the foreground were low table-hills, intersected by numberless ravines; beyond these a lofty line of bluffs marked the edge of an immense cañon; a wide gap was directly ahead, and through it were beheld, to the extreme limit of vision, vast plateaus, towering one above the other thousands of feet in the air, the long horizontal bands broken at intervals by wide and profound abysses, and extending a hundred miles to the north, til the deep azure blue faded into a light cerulean tint that blended with the dome of the heavens.

The point where Ives stood (and the point of including this quote) is now covered by Lake Mead. Nearly the entire area covered by the Ives expedition from the sea to Diamond Creek is one long series of stagnant reservoirs evaporating away in the desert sun. The mighty river up which Ives traveled in his steamboat is gone. By the time the last of the reservoirs has withdrawn its share of diverted water and generated its last kilowatt of electricity there scarcely remains enough water to fulfill treaty obligations with Mexico. True enough, a flotilla of aluminum shingled houseboats grinds in stately procession beneath the transplanted stones of London Bridge on Lake Havasu, but the kind of boating that readers of this guide might do is ended. Do an eddy turn at the outwash wave from one of the power plants—that's about the extent of it.

The loss of boating is, of course, only an easily identifiable symbol of the lost environment. The remaining free-flowing rivers should serve to remind us of what we have already lost. Perhaps future generations will preserve their environment better than we have ours. There is always a risk in predicting the future: Joseph Ives thought that the lower Colorado would become the major transportation route to the center of the continent, but of the area south of the Grand Canyon near modern Peach Springs, Arizona, he wrote:

> This last region explored is, of course, altogether valueless. It can be approached only from the south, and after entering it there is nothing to do but to leave. Ours has been the first, and will doubtless be the last, party of whites to visit this profitless locality. It seems intended by nature that the Colorado river, along the greater portion of its lonely and majestic way, shall be forever unvisited and undisturbed.
>
> April 18, 1858

Deseret Class 6 water (*Bert Henderson*)

Appendix I

MULTI-DAY TRIPS:

Appendix II

HAIR RUNS (Class V runs) "Hair" rating only counts at high water:

*(*the four classic "hair" runs of the Southwest)*

Appendix III

EASY RUNS to which we would direct the attention of the novice river runner:

Solar Rooftop DIY

THE COUNTRYMAN PRESS

A division of W. W. Norton & Company

Independent Publishers Since 1923

Solar Rooftop DIY

MIKE
SULLIVAN

The Homeowner's Guide to
Installing Your Own Photovoltaic
Energy System

COUNTRYMAN KNOW HOW

Printed in the United States of America

For information about permission to reproduce selections from this book, write to Permissions, The Countryman Press, 500 Fifth Avenue, New York, NY 10110

For information about special discounts for bulk purchases, please contact W. W. Norton Special Sales at specialsales@wwnorton.com or 800-233-4830

THE COUNTRYMAN PRESS
www.countrymanpress.com

A division of W. W. Norton & Company
500 Fifth Avenue, New York, NY 10110
www.wwnorton.com

978-1-58157-398-5 (pbk.)

10 9 8 7 6 5 4 3 2 1

Photo Credits

Page 6: © EzumeImages/iStockphoto.com; 8: © HadelProductions/iStockphoto.com; 10: © schmidt-z/iStockphoto.com; 19: © almir1968/iStockphoto.com; 39: © shaunl/iStockphoto.com; 64: © manfredxy/iStockphoto.com; 84: © AndreyPopov/iStockphoto.com; 91: © querbeet/iStockphoto.com; 94: © Pgiam/iStockphoto.com, 103: © Imaginima/iStockphoto.com; 105: © Carlos Alvarez/iStockphoto.com; © BlackJack3D/iStockphoto.com; © Tran The Vuong/iStockphoto.com; 109: © Samuel Kessler/iStockphoto.com; baytunc/iStockphoto.com; 110: © travellinglight/iStockphoto.com; 111: © Peter Mukherjee/iStockphoto.com; 112: © zstockphotos/iStockphoto.com; © levkr/iStockphoto.com; 119: © tzahiV/iStockphoto.com; © 129: tomprout/iStockphoto.com;

Photographs on pages 13, 14, 25, 34, 36, 37, 38, 57, 83, and 160 courtesy of National Renewable Energy Laboratory. © 2016 by National Renewable Energy Laboratory.

All other photographs courtesy of the author.

DEDICATION

To my loving children and four beautiful grandchildren.

CONTENTS

Overview

This book is written for the benefit of homeowners all over the world, especially those who care about the environment and those who want to save money by permanently reducing their monthly electric bill. The book provides a useful step-by-step guide full of photos to help DIY enthusiasts and others understand the basics of installing a solar photovoltaic (PV) rooftop system.

The book is written in everyday language that is easy for readers to understand and doesn't bog them down in technical terms and diagrams or engineering concepts. Solar energy is a high-tech business, but this book simplifies and demystifies the technology for everyone interested in this amazing source of free energy.

Millions of homeowners around the world are already enjoying the benefits of clean solar energy and saving a lot of money in the process. You'll learn why and how within the chapters of this guide book. The book will explain the various options as well as the main features, components, advantages, and disadvantages of the different basic technologies available, and it will provide detailed installation planning tips. I'll answer all your questions and help you select the best system for your needs and your budget. I'll also show you how much you can expect to spend for any size and type of installation and how to calculate the substantial savings you can expect over the short and long term.

Go solar, go green, save money, and help the environment. It's a timely and unstoppable global trend.

Benefits of Photovoltaic (PV) Solar Systems

Most municipalities permit homeowners or do-it-yourself enthusiasts to install a PV rooftop solar system; often a simple inspection and approval by a qualified electrician or certified solar installer will be all you need.

They're fast to install. Usually an installation can be completed in a week—even by a DIYer—after all the required equipment and materials are on site. Energy independence is an advantage that has strong appeal for many homeowners, and PV solar systems can reduce vulnerability to power loss from grid blackouts or power outages. You should see immediate savings on your electric bills and begin recovering your investment right away.

PV solar systems are also flexible; you can start small and add more PV panels later on. With solar rooftop systems, everything is modular.

Leasing is available in most areas. If you have limited cash flow, this option can provide an easy way to get a PV solar system installed on your roof-top. It's also easy to obtain financing, if required; most US banks have ample experience financing solar PV rooftop systems. In addition, government cash rebates, tax exemptions, and other financial incentives are often available, and these can substantially reduce the cash investment you need to make. PV systems have a relatively short payback period that can be as short as six or seven years—or even less, with rebates and other government incentives.

Your solar panel system should have a long and useful life. A warranty of 25 years from module manufacturers is standard. Systems can be installed on both flat and sloped roofs, and even on vertical surfaces. They provide myriad long-term environmental benefits and require almost zero maintenance.

Lastly, they immediately increase the value of your home, often by more than the cost of the PV solar system itself.

This is a formidable list of advantages to installing a PV solar system in your home. The only "negative" factor is the substantial investment or capital cost of the PV system, but this is generally more than offset by the advantages, financial and otherwise. The guidelines in this book will make it easy for you to calculate the financial and economic aspects of whichever PV solar system you choose for your home. I'll also help you perform a simple cost-benefit analysis of your project or proposed PV system. Reading this book will put you in control.

THE THREE BASIC TYPES OF TECHNOLOGY FOR PV SOLAR PANELS OR MODULES:

- Monocrystalline silicon panels
- Polycrystalline silicon panels
- Thin-film technology (in panels or other formats)

The best-known and most common of these is the polycrystalline silicon panel, and the third type, "thin film," has up to four different versions, meaning that there are actually up to six kinds of PV technology to choose from. This might seem confusing at first, but this book will make it easy for you to determine which PV technology type is best for your particular needs.

Here are a few more photographs that illus-trate the versatility of solar panel applications and installations.

This book will help you understand the various PV solar technologies and enable you to choose the most advantageous system for your home and budget. It will also give you valuable tips on how to choose a contractor, if this is the route you decide to take. It will show you how to calculate the electric power you can produce using any given system and how much money your chosen system can save on your monthly electric bills.

In Chapter 1, I will outline the main features, advantages, and disadvantages of each available technology type so that you can choose from the diverse range of options and components.

In Chapter 2, I will discuss and illustrate three different options for connecting or not connecting to the electric utility grid: "grid-tied," "off-grid," and "hybrid."

In Chapter 3, I will illustrate and summarize all the major components of a PV solar rooftop system.

In Chapter 4, I will show you how to determine the optimum size of your proposed PV solar rooftop system.

In Chapter 5, I will explain how to calculate the annual energy output of any given PV solar rooftop system, and I'll give you two simple ways to calculate the optimum number of solar panels needed to produce the amount of energy you will require under your particular set of circumstances and in your specific location. Chapter 5 will also show you an easy way to calculate how much money your PV

Top: In this photo, we can see the solar PV system is being installed at the same time as the installation of a new roof. Left: Here, we can see a do-it-yourself crew of three installing mono panels on the aluminum rails of an array that aligns very close to the edge of the roof just above the eaves trough. Right: A close-up shot of the corner of a mono panel at the end of an array.

Here we see the installer tightening a mid-bracket between two poly panels and securing them to the railings of the support framework.

The installer is securing this thin film array onto a very steep roof flush with the roof surface.

Numerous solar arrays with over 50 panels mounted on a flat condo rooftop with a tilt of about 20 degrees indicating that this installation is in a location with a latitude of about 20 degrees.

A low-level rancher with an array of 11 panels mounted flush to the roof surface.

solar system can save you compared to your existing monthly utility bills over a 12-month period.

In Chapters 4 and 5, you will also learn to calculate how long it will take to recover your initial investment—normally only six or seven years, depending on the amount of solar irradiance available throughout the year at your location, and depending on government subsidies, rebates, and other incentives you may qualify for, as explained in Chapter 6.

In Chapter 7, I will summarize the environmental benefits of residential and commercial PV solar systems and show you how to calculate the annual amount of CO_2 emissions that can be prevented from entering the atmosphere with any solar PV system.

In Chapter 8, you will learn many useful and effective measures and complementary mini-projects that will maximize the benefits to be gained with a solar PV project for your home. These measures should not only save you money in the long run, they will also reduce the required size and cost of the solar PV system needed to power 100 percent of your home's requirements. Lots of good ideas here!

In Chapter 9, I will show you how to find a qualified and registered solar installer in your area—or even a DIY coach, who can help you to save money by doing the installation yourself.

In Chapter 10, I will include a detailed, step-by-step photographic procedure on how to install a complete PV solar rooftop system.

In Chapter 11, I will summarize the main conclu-sions from previous chapters and, using this book as a guide, provide you with some helpful basic recommendations on how you might best proceed with plans to execute your PV solar project.

Solar Rooftop Systems: An Introduction

This is your handbook to planning your own PV solar rooftop system. I'll help you develop a customized action plan for a successful project that will benefit you and your family for decades to come. Photovoltaics, or PV technology, continue to be used in different ways and in new devices all the time: for powering parking-lot and highway lighting; for schools in remote villages with no access to the utility grid; for residential, commercial, and industrial applications; for electric vehicle charging stations; for remote microwave transmission stations; and even for boats, small power tools, and other devices.

Predictions of a solar revolution become more common with every passing year, and in some countries it's already becoming a reality. In Germany, for example, PV solar–installed capacity in 2012 increased by 7.6 Gigawatts to a total of over 35 Gigawatts by late 2013. This represents approximately 3.5 percent of the nation's electricity production. Some market analysts believe this figure could reach 25 percent by 2050. But the government has even higher goals than those predicted by market analysts. Germany announced an official goal of producing 35 percent of electricity from renewable sources by 2020—and 100 percent by 2050! These are formidable national goals, and some would say they are overly optimistic. But the trend is definitely upward around the world.

This phenomenon has been created in large part due to feed-in tariff (or FiT) schemes. These government financial incentive programs—in Germany and in other countries worldwide—have for decades provided subsidies to homeowners in order to encourage and stimulate the growth of the PV solar energy infrastructure.

Other countries that have been following Germany's lead in developing PV solar energy as an important renewable power source include England, the USA, India, Spain, Italy, Australia, France, Canada, Japan, and numerous countries in Southeast Asia. The expansion of the PV solar energy industry has short- and long-term environmental benefits, but there are more powerful economic and political factors behind the growing universal government support for solar energy. The political element usually involves developing solar power in order to decrease future dependency on carbon-based fuel imports, such as diesel and liquefied natural gas (LNG), and to reduce national expenditures on these imports. The goal is to achieve independence from foreign control over energy supplies.

Two important long-term economic trends have also provided incentives for more solar. These trends include, on the one hand, the year-by-year reduction in manufacturing costs and the market price index for PV solar panels, and on the other hand, the increasing annual cost of electricity produced by the national-grid utility companies that use carbon-based fuels, a finite natural resource. Crude-oil prices on the world market go up or down in any given year, but the five-year average trend has generally been upward over the long term. Between 2015 and '16, it is well known that there was a huge drop in crude oil prices on the world market and this was reflected, to some degree, by decreases in gasoline and fuel oil prices in most countries. However, this did not affect in any major way the cost of electricity to homeowners because the utility's electricity rates to the public are not so directly tied to global crude oil prices, being that the amortized annual cost of the capital equipment used in oil burning generating stations is proportionately so much greater than the cost of the crude oil consumed in these gigantic plants. In any case, the utilities are reluctant or very slow to pass on any savings to a significant degree. Utility rates may decrease slightly for a while but they can be expected to continue to increase over the long term. The net result is that global crude oil prices are of limited consequence to the solar PV residential market.

These two trends will eventually lead to what is known as "grid parity," the point at which the cost of PV solar power to the consumer or end user is equal to the cost of electricity from the national electric grid, usually measured in terms of a cost figure per kilo-watt hour, i.e.: "$/kWh" in North America or

An array of nine large mono panels installed parallel to a rooftop has a very minor slant of about 15 degrees, indicating that this location is likely near 15 degrees latitude, probably in the southern United States.

Two DIY installers start to install a large number of poly panels on a low-tilt roof of white asphalt tiles. You will notice that the aluminum rails of the solar system support structure have already been completed without any additional tilt.

Four arrays of five poly modules, each installed with two arrays on the main house and two equal-size arrays on the garage. We can see that the roof has a tilt of about 30 degrees and the arrays are mounted with an additional tilt of about 15 degrees for a total tilt of about 45 degrees, indicating that this house is likely located near the 45th degree of latitude to face the sun at 90 degrees for maximum energy output. This is explained in detail in Chapter 5.

Three arrays of 12 poly modules, each that are ground-mounted on three terraces in steep terrain. When your rooftop space is insufficient for your solar power requirements, this type of ground-mounted supplementary PV installation may be a good solution if the extra space is available somewhere behind your house.

"€/kWh" in Europe. Grid power in Europe has traditionally been much more expensive than in North America.

In many countries, grid parity has already become a reality and the trends leading to grid parity are generally considered to be irreversible. In countries where conventional electric energy from carbon-based power plants is still relatively cheap, the incentive to install solar is usually less than in countries closer to grid parity, but these trends are present worldwide.

These political and economic factors are further reinforced by the environmental benefits of using PV solar. Photovoltaics are a totally clean source of electric energy, a stark contrast to conventional energy sources that burn highly toxic carbon-based fuels (diesel oil, coal, or liquid natural gas) to power large electric generators in big buildings characterized by tall, wide-diameter chimneys. During combustion, these conventional carbon-based fuels emit large amounts of carbon dioxide—or CO_2—that are released into the atmosphere and contribute directly to the greenhouse effect that causes global warming. These CO_2 gas emissions are quantified in terms of tons of CO_2. In Chapter 7, I'll show you how to calculate the savings in CO_2 emissions you can achieve with any PV solar rooftop system for any given time period.

Accurate statistics are available that show how much conventional carbon-based fuel is consumed in the production of a given amount of electricity, measured in kWh. Statistics are easily calculated as to how many tons of CO_2 are emitted by carbon-based fuels while generating electricity, i.e.: for every MWh (1,000 kWh) of power. Therefore, if we know the amount of power produced by a PV solar system in kilowatt hours or megawatt hours, we can calculate exactly how many tons of CO_2 gas emissions are prevented from entering the atmosphere by virtue of using renewable photovoltaic energy instead of conventional carbon-based fuels.

Of all electricity-producing plants, coal-fired generators produce the highest level of CO_2 emissions. Solar PV farms and rooftop PV solar systems produce zero CO_2. The ability to precisely measure CO_2 emissions enables regulatory bodies such as the United Nations (UN) to establish international treaties and national limits for CO_2 emissions. This has led to an international system of carbon credits, which enables us to determine how much CO_2 (in tons) a given PV system prevents from entering the atmosphere.

CHAPTER 1

Basic Types of Solar Panels: Monocrystalline, Polycrystalline, and Thin-Film

There are many factors you'll want to take into account when choosing a solar (PV) system for your home. In this chapter, I will provide the basic information about the different types of solar panels for home use (monocrystalline, polycrystalline, and thin-film).

PV cells are fabricated using semiconductors as light-absorbing layers that convert the energy of photons into electricity without causing any noise or air pollution. When photons enter the cell through a transparent contact, they're absorbed by the semiconductor, thus creating electron-hole pairs. A special layer called a "junction" in the body of the device provides the electric field that separates and gathers the generated electrically charged carriers, which are then collected by wires attached to the solar cell.

Multiple cells are strung together in a protective package to form a PV module. Then many modules are interconnected to form an array. Balance of System (BOS) components are the final element of a working PV system.

To help you better understand what kind of solar panels make sense for your proposed system, there's a simple recommendation you can keep in mind that will save time and help you make the best decisions for your home. It can be summarized as follows: If the homeowner wants to obtain the maximum power from his or her available rooftop space, then monocrystalline or polycrystalline solar modules will be the best choice. Which of these alternatives you choose will depend on several factors, as explained later in this chapter. Only under special circumstances and for certain special applications would I recommend that you consider thin-film solar cells.

Once you have a pretty good idea about the space issue and other specific conditions at your location, then the above criterion will determine which sections of the book you'll want to focus on.

Let's start with the most common types of solar panels on the market and list their benefits and disadvantages. Then we'll look at a few typical scenarios in which certain types of PV solar modules would be better than others.

Crystalline Silicon (c-Si) (Includes all monocrystalline and polycrystalline PV cells)

Between 85 and 90 percent of the world's photovoltaics are based on some variation of silicon. In recent years, about 95 percent of all PV solar system shipments by US manufacturers to the residential sector were crystalline silicon solar panels.

The silicon used in PV solar cells takes many forms. The main difference between monocrystalline silicon cells and polycrystalline silicon cells is in the purity of the silicon, and this depends on the

manufacturing process. But what does silicon purity really mean? The more perfectly aligned the silicon molecules are, the more efficient the solar cell will be at converting solar energy (sunlight) into electricity (the photoelectric effect).

The efficiency of solar panels goes hand-in-hand with the level of silicon purity in the cells that make up the panels, or modules. But the processes used to enhance the purity of silicon are complex and expensive. However, the energy conversion efficiency rating of the PV solar panel shouldn't be your primary concern. As you'll soon discover, cost and space efficiency are the key factors for most people in selecting the optimum PV solar system, as well as the number of panels or modules and the power or number of watts per panel.

What's important to remember right now is that the total number of panels used for a PV rooftop installation, multiplied by the power rating in watts peak (Wp) of each panel, divided by 1,000, will give you the total power of the entire system in kWp. The significance of the term "peak" will be explained later.

Crystalline vs. Thin-Film

The thin-film type of PV panel is often the most cost-effective choice for tropical applications or for hot, desert-like climates. Thin-film panels can produce up to 30 percent more energy per year in hot climates as compared to crystalline panels.

Many consumers tend to analyze the different types of photovoltaic panels and make their decision based on the estimated kilowatt hours produced annually by the system, not on the watts peak (Wp) value. But you'll see later in this chapter that there are other factors you'll need to take into account besides the potential annual kWh produced.

Let's take a moment to clarify what the Wp value really means. The watts peak figure, given for any photovoltaic panel, is not the output from that panel. The actual output depends on the surface temperature of the panel, the intensity of light reaching the panel (the Insolation Index), the average daily "sun hours" at the site location, and the angle (tilt to the horizontal plane) and east-west orientation (azimuth angle) of the array to the sun, as well as the type and model of panel being considered. Watts peak (Wp) is a figure obtained under controlled laboratory conditions that do not occur in real life. It's the maximum output of the panel, under perfect conditions. It's important to point out that these laboratory "Wp" conditions apply only to crystalline panels, not to thin-film panels.

The website energyinformative.org/solar-panel-comparison is one of the most comprehensive and up-to-date solar panel comparison resources on the Internet. The solar cell comparison table below provides a quick overview that will also be helpful. This chart lists the most commonly used solar cell technologies today, with their basic characteristics and summary specifications.

A compact array of six mono panels installed flush with the roof surface—a very typical mounting.

Thin-film solar cells include four sub-categories, defined as follows:

1. Amorphous silicon (A-Si)

2. Cadmium telluride (CdTe)

3. Copper indium gallium selenide (CIS/CIGS)

4. Organic (or polymer) solar cells (in early stages of research and development)

Before proceeding with your purchase, be aware that whichever PV solar technology you select, you must be diligent and careful to analyze the reputa-

Solar Cell Comparison Chart by Technology Type: Monocrystalline, Polycrystalline, and Thin-Film

DESCRIPTION	MONOCRYSTALLINE	POLYCRYSTALLINE	AMORPHOUS SILICON	CDTE	CIS/CIGS
Typical module efficiency	16–18 percent	14–16 percent	7–8.1 percent	13–14 percent	14–15 percent
Best research cell efficiency	25 percent	21 percent	13.4 percent	19 percent	20.4 percent
Area in meters squared (M2) required for 1 kWp or equivalent (Space efficiency)	6–9 M2	8–9 M2	13–20 M2	11–13 M2	9–11 M2
Typical length of warranty (see warning note below)	25 years	25 years	10–15 years	10–15 years	10–15 years
Lowest price (subject to change)	0.75 $/W	0.62 $/W	0.69 $/W	0.57 $/W	n/a
Temperature resistance	Performance drops 10–15 percent at high temperatures.	Slightly less temperature resistant than monocrystalline or thin film.	Tolerates high ambient temperature.	Relatively low impact on performance.	
Additional details	Oldest cell technology and widely used.	Less silicon waste in the production process. Well-proven technology. Widely used.	Tend to degrade over time faster than crystalline-based solar panels. Durability and stability issues. The cadmium in CdTe is highly toxic.		
			Low availability in the market in many regions. A-Si proven successful for small electronic devices like portable calculators.		

Note: Thin-film systems include the three columns on the right side of this table.

The data above is obtained from the website of the National Renewable Energy Laboratory at www.nrel.gov.

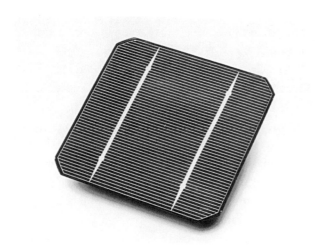

A close-up shot of a mono cell, the basic building block of a monocrystalline PV panel.

tion of the available module manufacturers as well as their standard warranty terms. It really pays to read the fine print. You should look beyond efficiency ratings to the financial health and long-term prospects of the companies issuing these warranties. We'll explore this issue in more detail below.

Monocrystalline Silicon Solar Cells

Invented in 1955, monocrystalline, meaning single crystal, is the original PV technology. Commercially, monocrystalline entered the market in the late 1970s and is well known for its durability. The useful life of monocrystalline solar modules is about 35 years.

They're consistent in performance and reliability. Single-crystal modules are composed of cells also called "wafers" cut from a cylindrical block of continuous crystal. Monocrystalline cells may be fully round, or they may be trimmed into other shapes. Because each cell is cut from a single crystal, it has a uniform color that's dark blue or dark gray with a hint of blue.

Solar cells made of monocrystalline silicon (mono-Si), also called single-crystalline silicon cells (single-crystal-Si), are quite easily recognizable by their even coloring and uniform look, indicating high-purity silicon.

Monocrystalline and polycrystalline solar panels are easy to differentiate. Polycrystalline solar cells are perfectly rectangular, with no rounded edges. They typically have a speckled bright blue color.

Since they're made out of the highest-grade silicon, monocrystalline solar panels have the highest efficiency rates, running from 16 to 18 percent, typically, over the last decade. In recent years, SunPower has produced the highest-efficiency solar panels on the US market to date. Their E20 series provides panel conversion efficiencies of up to 20.1 percent. SunPower more recently released their X-series, with an impressive efficiency rating of 21.5 percent.

In addition, monocrystalline silicon solar panels are the most space efficient. Since these solar panels yield the highest power outputs, they also require the least amount of space compared to any other type of solar panel. They produce up to four times the amount of electricity compared to most thin-film solar panels for the same panel surface area. This is good to remember if your available rooftop space is somewhat insufficient.

Furthermore, monocrystalline solar panels last the longest. Most solar panel manufacturers put a 25-year warranty on their monocrystalline solar panels. The monocrystalline silicon modules manufactured in the early 1980s are still functioning, according to many accounts.

Lastly, these particular solar panels tend to perform better than similarly rated polycrystalline solar panels under low-light conditions. For many climates, this also is an important consideration.

However, monocrystalline solar panels also have some disadvantages. They're the most expensive of all photovoltaic solar module types. From a financial standpoint, a solar panel made of polycrystalline silicon might be a better choice for some homeowners, depending on the desired power output and available rooftop space.

Another downside is that if the solar panel is partially covered with shade, dirt, or snow, the entire array circuit can break down. Consider getting micro-inverters instead of the old standard conventional central inverters if you think shading or other obstructions such as snow might be a problem. Micro-inverters will make sure that the entire solar array isn't affected by shade hitting only one or two of the panels in the array. The critically important topic of whether to choose micro-inverters or central or string inverters is discussed in more detail in Chapter 3.

The Czochralski process used to produce monocrystalline silicon is technically complex and requires very expensive equipment. This process creates large cylindrical ingots. Four sides are cut out of the ingots, and the four corners are rounded to make silicon wafers. Therefore, a significant amount of the original silicon ends up as waste. This is another factor that contributes to the higher cost of monocrystalline panels.

Finally, be aware that monocrystalline solar panels tend to be more efficient than the alternatives in hotter climates. The performance of all solar panel types, including monocrystalline, will suffer where average temperatures are much higher, but this is truer for polycrystalline solar panels. However, for most American homeowners, temperature won't be a major concern.

Polycrystalline Silicon Solar Cells

Polycrystalline cells are made from a similar silicon material as that of monocrystalline cells, except that instead of being grown into a large single crystal, the raw material of polycrystalline cells is melted and poured into a mold. This mold forms the silicon into a square block that is then cut into square wafers, which waste less space and material than the round-cornered single-crystal mono-wafers. As the material cools, it crystallizes in an imperfect manner, forming random crystal boundaries and irregular color textures.

The efficiency of energy conversion for polycrystalline is slightly lower than monocrystalline cells of equal surface area. This means that the surface area per watt of energy produced by a polycrystalline module is greater than that of a monocrystalline or single-crystal module. The poly cells look different from the mono- or single-crystal cells, as their surface has a jumbled or speckled look with many variations of bright blue colors. In fact, they're often quite beautiful.

Some companies have developed alternatives to the traditional molds, such as ribbon growth and growth of crystalline film on glass. Most crystalline silicon technologies yield similar results with high durability. Twenty-five-year warranties are common for crystalline silicon modules.

The silicon used to produce crystalline modules is derived from silicon sand. It's the second most common element on earth, so why is it so expensive? Well, in order to produce the photovoltaic effect, the silicon must be purified to an extremely high degree. Such pure semiconductor grade silicon is very expensive to produce. It's also in high demand in the electronics industry because it's the base material for computer chips and many other devices. Crystalline solar cells are about as thick as a fingernail; therefore, an entire solar PV module uses a relatively large amount of silicon.

Regardless of the technique used in growing

Two poly arrays on two different slopes of the same roof.

A small array of seven poly modules.

the crystals, the construction of finished modules from crystalline silicon cells is generally the same. The most common construction method involves laminating the cells between a tempered glass front and a plastic backing, and then applying a clear adhesive similar to that used in automotive safety glass between the layers. The sheets are rectangular and all have approximately the same dimensions, usually about 1 meter wide by 1.8 meters long. The laminated sheets are then framed around the four edges with a sturdy aluminum "U" channel. The finished panel is about five to six centimeters thick and weighs approximately 30 kilos, which can be easily handled by one installer. That being said, the mounting of a module onto its rooftop support framework is usually handled by two installers, as shown in many of the photographs in Chapter 10.

The first solar panels based on polycrystalline silicon, also known as polysilicon (p-Si) or multi-crystalline silicon (mc-Si), were introduced to the market in the 1980s. Unlike monocrystalline-based solar panels, polycrystalline solar panels do not require the Czochralski process.

Ultimately, the process used to make polycrystalline silicon cells and modules is simpler and costs less compared to monocrystalline. In addition, the amount of waste silicon in the manufacturing process of polycrystalline cells is much less compared to monocrystalline. This reduces the production costs of polycrystalline cells.

Polycrystalline solar panels tend to have slightly lower heat tolerance than monocrystalline. In practical terms, this means that they perform at a slightly lower level compared to monocrystalline solar panels in high ambient temperatures, for example over 40 degrees C (104 degrees F). Very high ambient temperatures can slightly shorten the panels' useful lifespan. However, this effect is minor, and most homeowners don't need to take it into account unless they live in a very dry, hot desert.

As compared to monocrystalline, the efficiency rating of polycrystalline-based solar panels is typically 14 to 16 percent, which is due to lower silicon purity. Its space efficiency is lower as well. You generally need to cover a nominally larger surface to generate the same amount of electrical power as you would generate with a solar panel made of monocrystalline silicon.

Another drawback to polycrystalline panels is their aesthetic appeal. Monocrystalline and thin-film solar panels can sometimes be more aesthetically pleasing since they have a more uniform look as compared to the irregular, speckled blue colors of polycrystalline silicon, as shown in the photograph below.

However, this doesn't mean that every monocrystalline solar panel performs better than polycrystalline silicon panels. You must take into account your unique situation and its needs when comparing the two.

Thin-Film Technologies

Imagine if a PV cell was made with a microscopically thin deposit of silicon instead of a thick wafer. It would use very little of the precious material. Now, imagine if it was deposited on a sheet of film or thin metal or glass, without the time-consuming and costly work of slicing wafers from ingots with special equipment. Imagine the individual cells deposited next to each other, instead of being mechanically assembled. That's the idea behind thin-film technology. It is also called amorphous, meaning "not crystalline." The active material may be silicon, or it may be a more exotic material such as cadmium telluride.

These thin-film panels can be made flexible and lightweight by using plastic glazing. Some flexible panels can tolerate a bullet hole without failing. Some perform slightly better than crystalline modules under low-light conditions, such as when the sky is slightly overcast with a thin layer of clouds. Many websites still claim that thin-film PV panels are less susceptible to losing power on the entire

PV Panel Characteristics Comparison: Crystalline vs. Thin-Film

CRYSTALLINE
Very low shadow tolerance.
100-watts peak crystalline panel is 25 percent smaller but produces 35 percent less power per year during the hot summer or in tropical climates.
Crystalline panels suffer a slightly higher voltage drop when heated by the sun in very hot climates, though modern crystalline panels now have three sub-strings, which has reduced output losses.   Crystalline panels that are 16–17 percent efficient at 70–80°F will be only 10–12 percent efficient with a surface temperature of over 190°F.
Crystalline panels suffer from an average deterioration of 1.0 percent to 1.4 percent per year from the stated watts peak value in tropical climates.   The original rated output is given as the output before any deterioration. Crystalline panels are much more efficient than thin-film, and they're considered more stable and reliable long-term. This is one of the reasons why crystalline panels have generally had longer warranty periods, compared to thin-film.
Crystalline cells are a bit more expensive than thin-film, unless you also consider space efficiency.
Crystalline panels are very expensive to make in smaller sizes, and this increase in cost prevents them from taking advantage of the smaller modular formats available with thin-film.
Conclusion: Crystalline silicon PV panels have advantages that outweigh thin-film technology. In almost all cases, for homeowners in the US looking for a solar PV rooftop system, either monocrystalline silicon or polycrystalline silicon is recommended.

array when only one or two modules are shaded. However, these early claims of superior shade tolerance seem to have been exaggerated.

The major disadvantages of thin-film technology are lower efficiency and uncertain durability. Depending on the technology, thin-film module prototypes have reached efficiencies between 7 and 12 percent, and production modules typically operate at about 9 to 10 percent. Some predict that future module efficiencies will climb to between 11 and 13 percent. Lower efficiency means that more roof space and mounting hardware are required compared to monocrystalline or polycrystalline modules to produce the same power output. Thin-film materials also

THIN-FILM
Slightly better shadow tolerance, though not as good as has been claimed by manufacturers. Even in recent years, this was generally considered one of thin-film's biggest advantages, but in practice the performance of thin-film under slightly shady conditions is not noticeably better than crystalline silicon.
One-hundred-watts peak thin-film panel is 25 percent bigger but produces 10 percent to 15 percent more energy per year in hot climates. In these situations, thin-film gives slightly more energy for the same surface area.
Thin-film panels perform at a slightly higher voltage output under direct heat and can still produce over 20 volts at 150°F or higher surface temperature. This would not apply in Canada, Europe, or most parts of the United States.
Over the long term, thin-film panels suffer from an average yearly deterioration of slightly less than 1 percent per year from the stated watts peak value.   The thin-film panel rated output is given as the output after the initial 30 percent initial deterioration during the first 3 or 4 months. A thin-film panel will then have only slightly less deterioration than crystalline.
Thin-film cells are slightly less costly for a specified PV system output in kWh.
The advantages of using small modular format solar voltaic thin-film panels include lower wind resistance, fewer system failures (if a small module is broken, it makes little difference to the total output), and fewer repair costs (replacing a small module is much cheaper than replacing a large broken panel).
Conclusion: Only in rare cases and special circumstances should you consider thin-film.

tend to be less stable than those used in crystalline panels, and thin-film can suffer relatively more efficiency degradation during the initial months of operation and beyond. However, thin-film technology is the subject of constant research. We will likely see many new thin-film products introduced in the coming years with higher efficiencies and longer warranties.

The market for thin-film PV grew appreciably starting in 2002. In recent years, about 5 percent of US photovoltaic module shipments to the residential sector have been based on thin-film technology. It continues to have a sizeable market for small electronic devices and special applications, including building-integrated photovoltaics (BIPV). Thin-film

Two DIY installers holding a long, amorphous silicon thin-film panel that can easily adapt to a curved substrate or surface.

A fairly common ground-mounted thin-film PV solar farm.

technology has also been popular for very large solar farms in deserts, where the land cost is very low and the solar insulation index is very high.

TYPES OF THIN-FILM SOLAR CELLS

Thin-film solar cells are manufactured by depositing one or several very thin layers of photovoltaic material onto a substrate. They're also known as "thin-film photovoltaic cells" (TFPV). The different types of thin-film solar cells are generally categorized by the kind of photovoltaic material that is deposited onto the substrate. Commercial production of thin-film solar cells is currently based on three basic types: amorphous silicon (A-Si), cadmium telluride (CdTe), and copper indium gallium selenide (CIGS). Very recently, a fourth type has been developed, namely organic solar cells. Solar panels based on amorphous silicon, cadmium telluride, and copper indium gallium selenide are currently the only thin-film technologies commercially available on the market. Organic or polymer solar cells may be available for some applications by 2020.

An organic solar cell or plastic solar cell is a

type of photovoltaic that uses organic electronics, a branch of electronics that deals with conductive organic polymers. An example of an organic photovoltaic is the polymer solar cell. As of late 2015, polymer solar cells were reported in research projects to have reached efficiencies of up to 10 percent. However, figures for production models will not be available for several years. These PV cells have low production costs and may be cost-effective for some photovoltaic applications. The main disadvantages associated with organic photovoltaic cells are low efficiency, low stability, and low strength compared to crystalline silicon solar cells. This type of organic solar cell is not yet considered commercially competitive, and the technology is still in the early stages of research and development. Therefore, the homeowner looking for a solar PV rooftop system should not seriously consider it.

Because their electrical power output is low, solar cells based on amorphous silicon have traditionally only been used for small-scale applications such as in-pocket or portable calculators. However, recent innovations have made them more attractive for larger scale applications. With a manufacturing technique called "stacking," several layers of amorphous silicon solar cells can be combined, resulting in higher efficiency rates (in the 6 to 8 percent range). Only about 2 percent of the silicon used in crystalline silicon solar cells is required in the manufacture of amorphous silicon solar cells. This makes a-Si cells extremely cost competitive per watt

if you ignore the cost and availability of the space required. On the other hand, stacking is a relatively expensive process.

Cadmium Telluride (CdTe) Solar Cells

Cadmium telluride (CdTe) photovoltaics make use of a photovoltaic technology that is based on the use of cadmium telluride thin-film, a semiconductor layer designed to absorb and convert sunlight into electricity. Cadmium telluride is the only thin-film solar panel technology that, in some cases, has surpassed the cost-efficiency of crystalline silicon solar panels for multi-megawatt systems. The average efficiency of solar panels made with cadmium telluride is generally considered to be in the range of 10 to 12 percent.

First Solar has installed over five gigawatts (GW) of cadmium telluride thin-film solar panels worldwide. First Solar holds the world record for CdTe PV module efficiency at 14.4 percent.

Flexible thin-film solar cells that can be produced by roll-to-roll manufacturing are a highly promising route to cheaper solar electricity. Scientists from Empa, the Swiss Federal Laboratories for Materials Science and Technology, have made significant progress in paving the way for the industrialization of flexible, lightweight, and low-cost cadmium telluride (CdTe) solar cells on metal foils. They also succeeded in increasing the efficiency rating of

A ground-mounted cadmium telerium PV solar array used for research. Cadmium telerium is often referred to as "CdTe."

the cells from below 8 percent up to 11.5 percent by "doping" the cells with copper.

After crystalline silicon, CdTe solar cells are the next most abundant photovoltaic product in the world, currently representing about 4 percent of the world market. CdTe thin-film solar cells can be manufactured quickly and inexpensively, providing a lower-cost alternative to conventional silicon-based technologies. The record efficiency for a laboratory CdTe solar cell is 18.7 percent, which is well above the efficiency of current commercial CdTe modules that run between 10 percent and 13 percent.

Polyimide film is a new material currently in development for use as a flexible superstrate for cadmium telluride (CdTe) thin-film photovoltaic modules. Because Kapton film is over 100 times thinner and 200 times lighter than the glass typically used for PV panels, there are inherent advantages in transitioning to flexible, film-based CdTe systems. High-speed and low-cost roll-to-roll adhesion technologies can be applied for high-throughput manufacturing of flexible solar cells on polymer film. The new polyimide film potentially enables significantly thinner and lighter-weight flexible modules that are easier to handle and less expensive to install, which would make them a candidate for many applications, including building-integrated photovoltaics.

However, due to low efficiencies and other limitations, as well as the premature stage of development of polyimide film PV technology, this type is not recommend to the homeowner looking for a PV solar rooftop system.

As it provides a solution to key issues like climate change and water scarcity, CdTe PV is considered the most eco-friendly technology among the available types, and it may provide some element of energy security. It's also considered the most eco-efficient PV technology when comparing a range of applications, including installation on commercial rooftops or large-scale ground-mounted PV systems. Some claim that CdTe PV has the smallest carbon footprint, lowest water use, and fastest energy payback time of all solar technologies.

CIGS component elements are used to make thin-film solar cells (TFSC). Compared to the other thin-film technologies summarized above, CIGS solar cells have demonstrated the most potential in terms of efficiency. These solar cells contain lower amounts of the toxic material cadmium than is found in CdTe solar cells. Commercial production of flexible CIGS solar panels was initiated in Germany in 2011. The efficiency ratings for CIGS solar panels are in the range of 10 to 13 percent, but this may increase over time.

CIGS features much higher absorption than silicon, so a layer of CIGS can absorb more light than a silicon layer of the same thickness. With thin-film, some of the light-gathering efficiency is given up in exchange for the advantages of thinness. But with the highly absorptive CIGS, the efficiency trade-off is less severe than with silicon PV cells. The record efficiencies for thin-film CIGS cells are slightly lower than that of CIGS used in lab-scale, top-performance cells, which are rated at 19.9 percent efficiency. Compared

A ground-mounted solar array.

with those achieved by other thin-film technologies such as cadmium telluride or amorphous silicon, this is the highest efficiency rating reported.

CIGS solar cells are not as efficient as crystalline silicon solar cells, for which the record efficiency is over 25 percent. However, many companies argue that CIGS is substantially cheaper due to lower fabrication costs and significantly lower material costs. A direct band gap material, CIGS has very strong light absorption. Two micrometers of CIGS is enough to absorb most of the sunlight that strikes it; a much greater thickness of crystalline silicon is required for the same amount of absorption.

The active layer of CIGS can be deposited directly onto molybdenum-coated glass sheets or steel bands. This takes less energy than growing large crystals, which is a necessary step in the manufacture of crystalline silicon solar cells. Also, unlike crystalline silicon, these substrates can be flexible, a notable advantage when it comes to design and fitting solar cells to curved surfaces, as demonstrated in the photos below.

Many thin-film solar cell types are still early stages of research and testing. Some seem to offer promising potential, and we can expect to see more of them in the future. Indeed, the initial attraction of CIGS was its promise of lower-cost manufacturing, both in terms of the materials required and in its streamlined, roll-to-roll manufacturing process. However, crystalline silicon market prices have decreased so much in recent years that this former advantage of CIGS has been erased.

Three CIGS arrays of four panels, each suspended by rope or cable demonstrate their flexibility.

An attractive example of BIPV with the PV solar system installed on this very steep, two-roof house in Colorado where there is often big snowfalls in winter.

C-Si (crystalline silicon) manufacturing has become much more streamlined and standardized, while CIGS remains a customized technology. And CIGS's conversion efficiencies haven't kept pace with c-Si. As of recently, Miasole was the current CIGS module record-holder, at 15.7 percent efficiency.

Building-Integrated Photovoltaics (BIPV)

Lastly, I'll briefly touch on the subject of building-integrated photovoltaics. Rather than being an individual type of solar cell technology, building-integrated photovoltaics have different methods of integration. BIPV can be developed with either crystalline or thin-film solar cells. They can be incorporated into facades, roofs, skylights, windows, walls, and other building surfaces that can be manufactured with one of the basic photovoltaic cell materials listed above. Smaller surfaces like covered walkways and solariums can also be designed and built as mini-BIPV projects.

If you have the extra money and want to seamlessly integrate photovoltaics with the rest of your home or condominium project, you might consider building-integrated photovoltaics, especially if your home is still in the design stage. These panels are extremely versatile and can be used to replace conventional building materials for practically any part of the building's exterior. BIPV is increasingly being incorporated into the construction of new buildings

as a principal or back-up source of electrical power, although existing buildings may also be retrofitted with similar technology. The advantage of building-integrated photovoltaics over more common nonintegrated systems is that the initial capital cost can be substantially offset by reducing the amount spent on building materials and labor that would normally be used to construct the roof or the other part of the building that the BIPV modules replace. These advantages make BIPV one of the fastest-growing segments of the photovoltaic industry for residential, commercial, and industrial applications.

How to Choose the Best Solar Panel Type for Your Home

After you've done some basic research by reading this book, and after you have a pretty good outline of your PV solar rooftop project, it's a good idea to have your project evaluated by an expert. This will help you determine what type and quantity of solar panels would be best for your home.

One aspect to consider is space limitations. The majority of homeowners don't have enough space for thin-film solar panels. In this case, crystalline silicon–based solar panels are usually your best choice. Regardless of space issues, though, you'll likely want to choose between monocrystalline and polycrystalline PV modules. Furthermore, in many areas there are no residential solar installers who offer a thin-film solar panel option.

Summary of Advantages and Disadvantages of Basic Thin-Film Technologies

TECHNOLOGY	MAXIMUM DEMONSTRATED EFFICIENCY	ADVANTAGES	DISADVANTAGES
Amorphous Silicon (a-Si)	12.2 percent	Mature manufacturing technology	Low efficiency; High equipment costs to manufacture
Cadmium Telluride (CdTe)	16.5 percent	Low-cost manufacturing	Medium efficiency; Rigid glass substrate
Copper Indium Gallium Selenide (CIGS)	19.9 percent	High efficiency; Glass or flexible substrates	Film uniformity is a challenge on large substrates
Organic Solar Cells or Polymer Solar Cells	10 percent	Low manufacturing cost; Wide variety of possible substrates; Very light weight	Instability problems; Efficiency problems; Still in early stages of R&D as of 2016

You'll likely have a choice of different solar panel sizes. The 180, 200, and 220-watt rated solar panels (and even higher wattages) are usually the same physical size. They're manufactured in exactly the same way but perform differently when tested, and hence they fall into different categories for power output. If available area is very limited, you'll logically select the highest-rated power output for a particular physical size of module, and that will be monocrystalline.

Both monocrystalline and polycrystalline solar panels are good choices and offer similar advantages. Even though polycrystalline solar panels tend to be less space efficient and monocrystalline solar panels tend to produce more electrical power, this is not always the case. It would be nearly impossible to recommend one or the other without examining the alternative solar panels available, as well as your specific location and its physical conditions.

Monocrystalline solar panels are slightly more expensive but also slightly more space efficient. If you had one polycrystalline and one monocrystalline solar panel, both rated 220-watt, they would generate the same amount of electricity. But the one made of monocrystalline silicon would take up slightly less space, and this can be an important factor in deciding which type of PV module to use.

Two large arrays of poly panels mounted on the sloping roof of a low-rise commercial building.

In addition to the different PV technology descriptions and comparisons, there are numerous other factors and considerations you should take into account before making a final decision about which solar panel to buy.

For homes and buildings with ample roof space,

a panel's peak efficiency shouldn't be the primary consideration. It's more important to consider the system as a whole, balancing price with quality. Where space is really limited, efficiency considerations may outweigh the desired output of the solar system. These, of course, will carry a higher price

A small array of mono panels mounted flush to the surface of a wooden shingle roof. Wood roof shingles are normally made of cedar that has a natural attractive finish and they have a long useful life to match the expected useful life of PV panels.

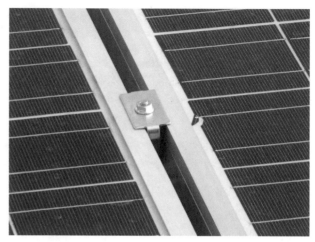

A close-up shot of the mid-bracket securing two poly panels to the support railing below (not visible here).

tag. But for the budget-conscious homeowner, the number to look at will be dollars-per-watt for the entire PV system.

In the end, the cost and performance of your system will depend not only on the panels you use, but also on the inverter you choose. If you hire a contractor, his or her installation costs will also come into play. Performance will also be affected by the east-west orientation (azimuth) of your roof and the tilt angle of your panels, which are commonly installed at an angle parallel to the roof.

It's also important to look beyond module-efficiency ratings. As a prospective solar system owner, you'll need to consider the company behind the product you're buying. Although quality technology is important in the selection of solar panels, you must remember that both monocrystalline and polycrystalline silicon solar cells are proven technologies, and one should not automatically be considered better than the other.

Manufacturing equipment for silicon wafers is more readily available than ever. The market for PV solar panels is relatively easy for large companies to enter. A critical difference between quality manufacturers and others is whether the company in question invests seriously in research and development. R&D investment by a manufacturer is indicative of the company's commitment to creating innovative

A small array of six poly panels on a small steep roof.

and high-quality products. It also shows that the company is planning to be active in the market for a long time.

For most households, balancing affordability with reliability is important. Solar-power systems are expected to work for 30 years or more, and warranties are usually valid for 25 years. But warranties are only useful if the manufacturer remains a solvent company. Though it's impossible to know what will happen to a company 15 or 25 years from now, it's still wise to form an idea whether the manufacturer is financially sound and likely to be around for at least as long as the warranty period. If panels need repairing or replacing, the cost could become substantial if the warranty is of no use. Most of the PV module manufacturers are public

A DIY installer inspecting his mono panels up on an aluminum ladder. This kind of ladder is not recommended for use when wiring the PV rooftop system as it can conduct electric current. I always insist that DIY PV system installers use only wooden ladders.

companies. This makes it easy for you to ascertain if they're financially solid and if they are seriously investing in R&D. These criteria will determine if the warranty is of real value.

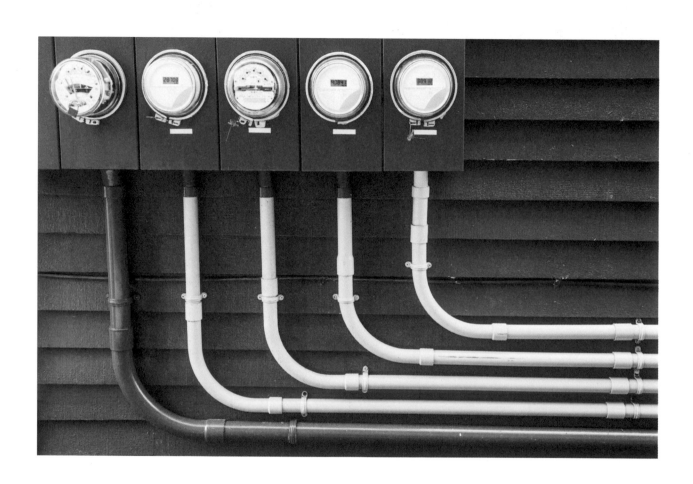

CHAPTER 2

Types of PV System Connections

Once you have a general understanding of how the solar-energy system functions, choosing the right parts will be easier. It's not complicated. I'll now describe the parts of a standard grid tie, or "on-grid PV system." We'll also look briefly at what is known as an "off-grid PV system," and I'll explain the differences between the on-grid and off-grid systems and the normal conditions and criteria for selecting a system.

First, let's look at the components of the grid-tied or on-grid system so that you know what you need to buy and what to plan for. Then I'll review some of the options available for the various component parts. I'll show you how to determine the size of the system you want and the positioning and layout of the panels, as well as the factors you'll want to consider for the mounting framework that will attach the panels to your roof. We'll also discuss some installation details that will complement the step-by-step photographic installation procedures illustrated and explained in Chapter 10. Lastly, I'll review some financial assistance possibilities that may be available to you.

Basically, an on-grid PV system involves staying connected to the power grid. This means you'll still receive power from the utility company when you need it, and in many areas you'll be able to sell your excess power back to the utility under a simple registered agreement. Selling the excess power back will involve the installation of a net metering system that tracks and records how much credit you receive for the excess power your system feeds back into the grid.

An off-grid PV system is a solar electric generating system that is usually relatively small and is not connected to the utility grid. There can be many reasons for installing an off-grid PV system. It might be that the location of the system is not anywhere close to the nearest grid connection. The off-grid system might be used for a remote cabin, a small ranch, a hunting lodge, or for a remote research station or microwave station. Usually an off-grid PV system will include a battery storage subsystem, as there will be no power available from the grid for energy requirements after dark or in bad weather.

What are the benefits of grid-connected solar panels versus living off the grid? Deciding whether or not to grid-tie your solar array is usually pretty straightforward. The clear-cut benefits of being grid-tied appeal to most homeowners. There are, however, some who choose to live off-grid.

Let's take a closer look at the benefits and downsides of grid-tied, off-grid, and hybrid connection solar systems.

Grid-Tied Solar Systems

Grid-tied, on-grid, utility-interactive, grid inter-tie, and grid back-feeding are all terms used to describe the same concept: a solar PV system that is connected to the utility power grid.

One advantage of grid-tying is that compared to the other two basic connection types, a grid connection will allow you to save more money with your

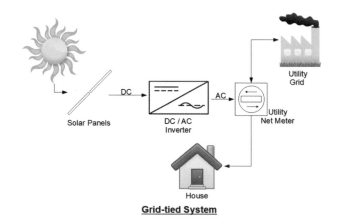

A schematic of a "grid-tied" solar system.

solar PV array through lower rates granted by the utility company, net metering, and lower equipment and installation costs. For a fully functional off-grid solar system, batteries and other stand-alone equipment are required, and these will add to both the initial cost of the system as well as maintenance costs down the road. Grid-tied solar systems are therefore generally cheaper and simpler to install, as long as the grid is reasonably close to your home.

On bright days, your solar panels will usually generate more electricity than you will consume during the daylight hours. With net metering, homeowners can put this excess electricity onto the utility grid rather than store it themselves in a battery-bank storage system, which would involve a considerably larger initial investment.

Net metering (called a "feed-in tariff" scheme in many countries) has played a very important role in how solar power has been supported by governments to incentivize new buyers. Without it, residential solar systems are much less financially feasible. With net metering, most utility companies are required to buy electricity from homeowners at the same rate as they sell it themselves. In this way, the utility grid acts as a huge virtual battery system.

Let me explain this battery concept. Electricity has to be spent in real time. However, it can be temporarily stored as other forms of energy (e.g. chemical energy in batteries), though storage involves significant losses. The electric power grid also works like a battery, but without the need for maintenance or replacements and with much higher efficiency. In other words, more electricity and more money goes to waste with conventional battery systems compared to grid-tied systems.

Annual US electricity transmission and distribution losses average about 7 percent of the electricity transmitted, according to the Energy Information Administration (EIA) data. Lead-acid batteries, which are commonly used with solar panels, are only about 80-85 percent efficient at storing energy, and their performance degrades over time depending on factors like rate of discharge and the degree of discharge, or "DOD." The DOD is the minimum charge level at which point your PV system stops draining the battery and starts the recharge cycle again. The battery "charge controller" manages this DOD cut-off level. This DOD control system is used to protect the battery or battery

bank because if you drain the batteries too much it will reduce their useful life.

Additional perks of being grid-tied include access to backup power from the utility grid in case your solar system stops generating electricity for one reason or another. At the same time, you'll also help to mitigate the utility company's peak load. As a result, the overall efficiency of the electrical grid system is improved.

EQUIPMENT COMPONENTS OF A GRID-TIED SOLAR SYSTEM

There are a few key differences between the equipment needed for grid-tied, off-grid, and hybrid PV solar systems. In addition to the PV panels, mounting support system hardware, and other standard items like DC and AC disconnect switches, grid-tied solar systems rely on grid-tie inverters (GTI) or micro-inverters, and power meters (net metering type).

GRID-TIED INVERTERS (GTI)

What's the job of PV solar system inverters? They regulate the voltage and convert the direct current (DC) received from your solar panels. The direct current generated by your solar panel array is converted by a central inverter or by many micro-inverters into alternating current (AC), which is the type of current utilized by the electrical appliances in your home. It might be noted here that it's now possible in some areas to purchase DC appliances. In addition, grid-tied inverters, also known as grid-interactive or synchronous inverters, synchronize the phase and frequency of the current to fit the utility grid, nominally 60Hz. The output voltage is also adjusted slightly higher than the grid voltage, in order for excess electricity to flow outwards to the grid.

POWER METERS (NET METERING TYPE)

Most homeowners will need to replace their current power meter with one designed for net metering. This device, often called a net meter or a two-way meter, is capable of measuring power going in both directions, from the grid to your house and vice versa. You should consult with your local utility company and see what net metering options you have. In some places, the utility company will issue a power meter for free, and they'll pay full price for the electricity you generate and deliver to the grid (the same price $/kWh as they charge you). However, this is not always the case.

Off-Grid Solar Systems

An off-grid solar system is the obvious alternative to a grid-tied system. For homeowners with access to the grid, off-grid solar systems are usually not preferred because in order to ensure access to electricity at all times, off-grid solar systems require battery storage and a backup generator. On top of this, a battery bank typically needs to be replaced after ten years. Batteries are complex, they involve a high initial cost with respect to the overall system, and they also slightly decrease overall system efficiency.

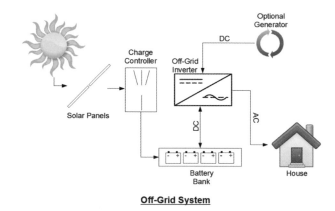

A schematic of an "off-grid" solar system.

However, an off-grid system can provide a viable solution in the case that you have no access (or very difficult access) to the utility grid. This type of system can be cheaper than extending power lines in most remote areas, so you might consider an off-grid system if your location is more than 200 yards from the grid. The cost for new overhead transmission lines start at around $174,000 per mile ($108,000 per Km) for rural construction, and they can run into the millions of dollars per mile for urban construction.

Off-grid systems also provide a solution for those who want to be energy independent. To many, the idea of living off the grid and being self-sufficient just feels good. For some people, this feeling is worth more than saving money. Energy self-sufficiency is also a form of security. Local or regional power failures in the utility grid do not affect off-grid PV solar systems. On the other hand, batteries can only store a limited amount of energy, and during cloudy times, sometimes security actually lies in being connected to the grid. To manage this risk, you might be wise to consider installing a backup diesel-fuel electric generator to be prepared for extended periods of rainy and cloudy weather.

Typical off-grid solar systems require the following extra components in addition to the PV solar modules and mounting support framework hardware:

- Solar Charge Controller
- Battery Bank
- DC and AC Disconnect Switches
- Off-Grid Central Inverter or Micro-Inverters
- Backup Generator (optional but recommended)

Solar charge controllers are also known as charge regulators or battery regulators. The last term is probably the best for describing what this device actually does: Solar battery charger controllers limit the rate of current being delivered to the battery storage bank and protect the batteries from overcharging. Good charge controllers are crucial for keeping batteries healthy and ensuring that the lifetime of a battery bank is maximized. If you have a battery-based inverter, chances are the charge controller is integrated into the inverter.

A "battery bank" of 10 batteries.

BATTERY BANKS

Without a battery bank or a backup generator, an off-grid system will mean "lights out" at sunset. A battery bank is essentially a group of batteries wired together, connected to the inverter with a DC disconnect switch, and then connected to selected wire circuits to provide power after dark to certain lights, as well as to selected electrical outlets for appliances like a television, computer, or refrigerator. LED lights will help extend the power provided before the battery bank runs out of energy.

The above photos illustrate the diversity and flexibility of PV solar battery bank systems:

A DC disconnect switch, a meter, and an AC disconnect switch.

A different DC disconnect switch.

The inside view of a DC disconnect switch.

The beauty of solar battery banks is they're completely modular, which enables the homeowner to expand the energy storage system whenever desired. Depending on proper maintenance, frequency of use, and "depth of discharge," the solar batteries will be serviceable for up to ten years before they'll need to be replaced. We go into more details about battery systems and back-up generators in Chapter 3.

DC DISCONNECT SWITCH

AC and DC safety disconnects are required for all solar systems. For off-grid solar systems, one additional DC disconnect is installed between the battery bank and the off-grid inverter. It's used to switch off the current flowing between these com-

ponents. This is important for maintenance, troubleshooting, and protection against electrical fires.

OFF-GRID INVERTERS

There's no need for an inverter if you're only setting up solar panels for your boat or your RV, or for electric loads that use only direct current. However, you'll need an inverter to convert DC to AC for all other standard electrical appliances in your home. Off-grid inverters do not have to match phase with the utility sine wave as opposed to grid-tied inverters. Therefore, you can expect a given manufacturer's off-grid converter to be technically simpler and slightly more economical than its grid-tied counterpart. Electrical current flows from the solar panels

A metering device with a DC disconnect switch.

petroleum (diesel), or gasoline. Backup generators typically produce an AC output, which can be sent through the inverter for direct use or can be converted into DC for battery storage.

Hybrid Solar Systems

Hybrid solar systems combine the best elements from both grid-tied and off-grid solar systems. These systems can either be described as off-grid solar with utility backup power, or grid-tied solar with backup battery storage. If you own a grid-tied solar system and drive a vehicle that runs on electricity, you already have something similar to a hybrid system. In essence, electric vehicles are battery systems on four wheels.

A hybrid solar system is a grid-tied system with

through the solar charge controller and the battery bank before it's finally converted into AC by the off-grid inverter.

It takes a lot of money and big batteries to prepare for several consecutive days without the sun shining or access to the grid. This is where backup diesel generators can play a key role. In most cases, installing a backup generator that runs on diesel is a better choice than investing in an oversized battery bank that seldom gets to operate at full potential. Backup generators will normally run on propane,

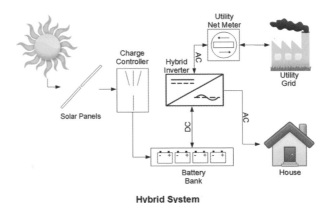

Hybrid System

A typical hybrid connection solar system often simply referred to as a "hybrid solar system."

backup energy storage that incorporates a battery bank. Hybrid solar systems are less expensive than off-grid solar systems. Often you don't really need a backup generator, and the capacity of your battery bank can be downsized. Off-peak electricity from the utility company is cheaper than using a backup diesel generator. Also, the noise of a generator motor may be an issue to consider.

Hybrid solar systems utilize battery-based grid-tie inverters. Combining these devices can draw electrical power to and from battery banks, as well as synchronize with the utility grid. The new inverters let homeowners take advantage of changes in the utility electricity rates throughout the day. Solar panels usually output the most electrical power around noon, just before the time when the price of electricity peaks. Your home can be programmed to consume power during off-peak hours by appropriately programming your rooftop PV solar system. Consequently, you can temporarily store excess electricity from your PV solar panels in your battery storage system, and then automatically feed it into the utility grid at a time when you will be paid the most for every kWh.

Smart solar holds a lot of promise, as the introduction of hybrid solar systems has opened up opportunities for many interesting innovations. The concept will become increasingly important as we transition towards the so-called "smart grid" in the coming years.

But for now, the vast majority of homeowners who have a solar energy system find that tapping the utility grid for electricity while also using the grid for energy storage is significantly cheaper and more practical than using hybrid systems with battery banks and backup generators. Complete independence from the grid system may be attractive to many on principle, but it increases the cost of the initial investment substantially. Therefore, this option is usually discarded in favor of a simple grid-tied solar system.

Of course, where the home or weekend cottage is in a remote location without access to the grid or where the cost of installing a line is prohibitive, owners might gladly pay for the extra cost of a battery storage system, and maybe also a generator.

CHAPTER 3

Major Components of a Solar PV Rooftop System

When choosing a solar energy system for your home, there are three major components that you'll need to be concerned about: solar modules, solar racking or support frames, and inverters. The components you choose will determine the reliability and output of your solar array for the duration of the system's time on your home.

Solar PV Modules and Mounting Support Hardware

In a grid-tied system, electricity is initially generated by several to many PV solar modules. Chapter 2 provided a detailed description and analysis of the various types of solar modules available. Once the type and size of the system are chosen, a simple rooftop mounting frame, to which the modules can be attached, will be installed. See example in the photo on the following page.

There are some good options for solar mounting equipment. Solar tracking devices are now more economical and easier to install than earlier systems, with new products coming to market all the time.

Of course, the mounting frame is installed on the side of the roof that provides maximum sunlight exposure. In the northern hemisphere, this would logically be on the south-facing part of the roof, which is slanted toward the equator. The more perpendicular to the equator the mounting frame supports are, the better, but this line does not need

A top view of three rows of support rails mounted on the roof with micro-inverters already attached and waiting to be connected to the PV modules.

to be exactly 90 degrees for the PV solar system to function well.

The type of mounting system you'll need depends on where you plan to install the modules of your PV solar energy system. With crystalline panels, you have three options for location: mounting the panels on your roof, on the ground, or on a pivoting stand.

Most people think a roof mount is the most convenient and aesthetically pleasing, but there are many reasons that people choose other options. For example, if your roof is small, unstable, in the shade, or if you aren't able to face the panel towards the equator (facing south in the northern hemisphere or facing north in the southern hemisphere), you may consider mounting your system elsewhere. You may find that you like the simplicity of a ground mount if you have extra land available.

Pivoting stands are an attractive alternative because they're able to follow the sun throughout the day, so they can be far more efficient. But they're also more expensive. If you have enough open space and your roof has major disadvantages, then a ground mount may be the best choice. With any of these mounting options, you should make sure there are no local ordinances or homeowners association rules against them.

There are viable solar panel racks and mounting hardware for every solar panel installation style; your solar array depends on your property. If you're not sure about the different choices, any qualified solar contractor can help you make the right decision.

Two rows of support rails installed and waiting for installation of the PV panels and, if applicable, the micro-inverters first go on the rails before being connected to the PV panels.

Flush support frames are the most popular choice. They provide an inexpensive and simple option that is suitable for most roof-mounted solar panel installations. They're generally not adjustable and are usually designed to position the solar panels at a consistent height above the surface of the roof on which they are mounted. There are suitable leak-proof anchor bolts or fasteners for any kind of roof. Tilted mounts, which improve the angle of the PV panels for roof installations, are also available. These are definitely recommended for flat roofs.

Ground-mounted support frames can provide an excellent alternative—space permitting, and assuming there are no serious shading problems—that will allow you to install your solar panels at ground level anywhere on your property. Ground mounts are usually designed with a fixed-tilt angle. But they're often adjustable, allowing you to tilt your solar modules to the appropriate level for optimal solar collection, depending on your latitude.

There are also fully automated, adjustable-tilt tracking mechanisms that can substantially increase the solar efficiency of your system. Generally speaking, the lower the latitude, the less tilt your mount will require. Four-way tilt-control tracking systems can maintain the panels in a perpendicular position to the sun's rays from east to west, following the arc of the sun.

For those requiring a non-roof installation, pole mounts are another solution. These mounts come in one of three alternative types that are distinguished from one another by how they're positioned on the pole: top of pole, side of pole, and pole with tracking device.

Regardless of the type of mounting you and your solar contractor decide on, your support frame or pole-mount system will provide safety and security for your solar investment.

While most people might want to focus on panels and inverters, it's important to remember that the solar panel mounting frames can also be critical to the success of your overall system. Besides the orientation and shading issues we discussed above, you also need to find out the wind category for your area, and also check the conditions of the ground if you plan to install a good ground-mount system.

Even with off-the-shelf parts, many permit offices will not give you a permit if the proposed ground-mount system doesn't have a civil engineer's stamp of approval. You should be able to hire an engineer for $500 or even less, depending on your location.

DC AND AC DISCONNECT SWITCHES

Now let's look at another component of a PV system: disconnect switches. A shutoff switch, more commonly known as a "disconnect switch," separates the panels from the rest of the system so that you'll be safe if you ever need to make any repairs or changes to the system, such as adding additional panels. The first disconnect switch is the DC disconnect switch.

The DC disconnect switch is relatively small and can be easily installed anywhere convenient along the chosen routing for the PV cables that connect the rooftop modules to the inverter. Usually, you would choose your routing for the PV cables in the least conspicuous layout, taking advantage of any chimney, rooftop sun windows, attic bedroom

A DC disconnect switch, central inverter, AC disconnect switch, and metering device.

An off-grid disconnect switch.

roof protrusions, or eave troughs. You will want to pick a color for your PV cables that will tend to blend in with the existing rooftop colors, most often dark brown. Here are a few photographs of standard disconnect switches.

A solar PV system typically has two safety disconnects. The first is the PV disconnect (or Array DC Disconnect). The PV disconnect allows the direct current coming from the modules to be interrupted before reaching the inverter for service and safety reasons.

The second disconnect is the AC disconnect. The AC disconnect is used to separate the inverter from the house's main distribution panel and also

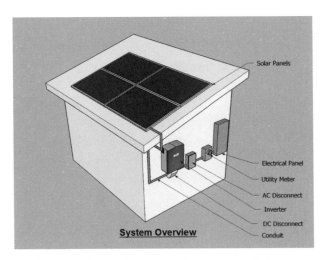

Solar Panels

Electrical Panel

Utility Meter

AC Disconnect

Inverter

DC Disconnect

Conduit

System Overview

A schematic of a simple, small PV system installed on a garage.

from the electrical grid. In a solar PV system, the AC disconnect is usually mounted to the wall between the inverter and utility meter. The AC disconnect may be a breaker on a service panel, or it may be a stand-alone switch. This disconnect is sized based on the output current of the inverter or micro-inverters.

SOLAR PV SYSTEM GRID-TIED INVERTERS

Having chosen your solar modules, you'll need to decide on a solar inverter. Solar inverters are a critical component to your PV solar energy system. Inverters change the direct current coming from the panels into the alternating current that your appliances and light fixtures use. There are several considerations here. First, you need an inverter that can handle what your panels generate, so make sure the wattage of the inverter is at least as strong as the wattage of your array. Second, you can consider solar micro-inverters, which are smaller inverters that connect to each panel instead of a central inverter that converts the DC of the entire system as a whole.

Below is a photograph of a typical inverter unit. There are several well-known manufacturers of inverters, including SMA and InfluxGreen. They all make quality equipment that has been tested and approved by national and international electric standards authorities.

A typical central inverter.

Grid-connected inverters must supply AC electricity in a "sinusoidal" form that is synchronized to the grid frequency. These inverters limit feed-in voltage to no higher than the grid voltage and disconnect from the grid if the grid voltage is turned off. Islanding inverters need only produce regulated voltages and frequencies in a sinusoidal wave shape, as no synchronization or coordination with grid supplies is required.

A solar inverter is usually connected to an array of solar panels. For safety reasons, a circuit breaker or disconnect switch is provided both on the DC and the AC side of the central inverter to enable maintenance. The AC output is connected through an electricity meter into the public grid and into the home's main panel. In some installations, a solar micro-inverter is connected to each solar panel. We'll discuss the subject of micro-inverters in more detail a little later.

OFF-GRID INVERTERS

Single phase off-grid PV inverters such as those made by InfluxGreen (Models IGSCI-0.5kVA to 7.0kVA) are an integrated system comprising a solar charger, AC charger, inverter, AC bypass switch, and transformer—all with battery control options. This inverter is versatile and can be used with a grid-tied system or with an off-grid system where the grid is not readily available. The IGSCI solution provides a cost-effective, reliable, and efficient stand-alone system with battery backup to meet specific user needs.

Solar installations typically have a central inverter that takes the direct current generated by a group of PV panels and converts it into AC for the home and/or for the electrical grid. Micro-inverters function essentially the same way but are installed on the back of each solar panel. They have some distinct advantages over central inverters. Micro-inverters make a rooftop PV system or large commercial PV installation more efficient. They also make it easier to monitor power generation of each panel and quickly pinpoint a failure in the system. This can

A standard Enphase M215 micro-inverter—industry leader for many years.

A side view of the same three rows of support rails mounted on the roof with micro-inverters already attached.

save a lot of time and money. The idea is basically that the added expense of using micro-inverters is more than offset by the savings created by increased efficiency and lower maintenance costs. Hanwha SolarOne is one of several manufacturers that incorporate a micro-inverter into every solar module.

When using a central inverter, economies of scale can certainly decrease the cost-per-kilowatt-hour of your solar PV system as you increase the size of the array. Many DC/AC central inverters are sized for systems up to five kilowatts. However, if your PV array is smaller (three or four kilowatts, for example), you might still be wise to buy the same 5 kW inverter. This is because the difference in the cost of the inverters is minimal. But this will facilitate adding more PV panels later on and will end up saving you money.

Until recently, central inverters dominated the

solar industry. The introduction of micro-inverters marks one of the biggest technology shifts in the PV industry to date. Manufacturers of micro-inverters claim at least a 15 percent increase in power output over central inverters, which in the long run can result in substantial savings for the homeowners who choose micro-inverters for their PV rooftop system.

Micro-inverters have been available since 1993. In 2007, Enphase Energy was the first company to build a commercially successful micro-inverter. More than one million units of the Enphase Micro-

Nine poly PV modules mounted after having the micro-inverters connected from the support rails and then to the modules.

The conduit wiring from the micro-inverters across the roof and down to the electrical control equipment.

Inverter Model M175 have been sold since its release in 2008. Several other solar companies have since followed suit and launched their own micro-inverters, validating their potential and reliability.

Micro-inverters are quite small and are installed on the back of each solar panel in the upper right-hand corner. Alternatively, the micro-inverters may come separately and installed directly onto the support rails before being connected to the PV modules. Each micro-inverter is protected by the aluminum edge of the PV modules. In this way, the inverter doesn't interfere with stacking the panels when they're laid flat on top of one another for shipping and storage.

There has been a lot of debate on whether micro-inverters are better than central (string) inverters, but for most PV rooftop systems micro-inverters have distinct advantages.

Additionally, homeowners who are subject to shading issues should definitely consider micro-inverters for their system, as they'll likely perform better compared to installing a central inverter. An analysis of the comparative advantages and disadvantages of the two systems will usually come out in favor of micro-inverters. For example, one central inverter would normally cover the requirements of an entire residential PV rooftop solar system (assuming that the central inverter has enough capacity for your entire array). Micro-inverters, on the other hand, sit on the back of every solar panel and offer several important benefits over central inverters.

For each individual PV system, the homeowner will want to determine whether the benefits of using micro-inverters outweigh the extra costs. Earlier it was stated that for those installations where shading is an issue, micro-inverters are preferred over a central inverter. This is because with even a small shading problem, a central inverter will negatively affect all of the PV modules in the array, whereas with micro-inverters only the shaded modules are affected.

Ultimately, micro-inverters make the PV system more modular and easier to expand. To subsequently increase the size of your solar electric system, you can simply add one or more panels with a micro-inverter for each new panel. Also, these new additional panels can be of different wattages and even from different manufacturers, two more significant advantages.

With the latest technological advancements, the new micro-inverters being developed may be able to harvest up to 20 percent more energy than central inverters over their lifetime. That's a lot of energy! Therefore, even though they cost more initially, it appears likely that they'll recoup the difference in a relatively short time. This also means more income from feed-in tariffs for the PV system owners who have a grid-tied or hybrid system.

Micro-inverters make a rooftop PV system or a large commercial installation more efficient. They also make it easier to monitor the power generation of each panel and enable a service technician to quickly pinpoint a failure in the system.

Micro-inverters are gaining acceptance in the solar energy market, particularly in residential applications. The market leader for many years has been Enphase, but there are a number of companies who claim to be at various stages of developing better and cheaper micro-inverters. Two relatively new companies building micro-inverters are Enecsys and SolarBridge. These two companies appear determined to be competitive; they both initially offered longer warranties than Enphase. In response, Enphase has extended their warranty period.

GreenRay, another new micro-inverter manufacturer, recently developed an interesting innovation. They have fully integrated a micro-inverter into the

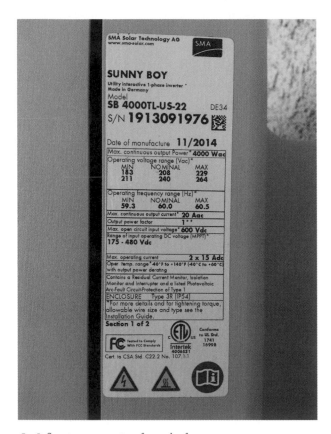

An Influx inverter—view from the front.

An Influx inverter—view from the back.

solar panel. Another new competitor is InfluxGreen. Their IGSM series of grid-tied PV micro-inverters (single phase 200W to 270W) appear to be cost-competitive, and the manufacturer states they can achieve a peak efficiency of up to 95 percent.

Although the market is rapidly expanding, it's not likely to be large enough to support all of the existing and proposed micro-inverter competitors.

The market is becoming overly competitive, and some of the smaller companies will likely drop out of the race at some point. However, this need not worry the homeowner, because different makes of micro-inverters can operate together in the same array of PV panels without any compatibility problems.

Micro-inverters optimize output for each solar panel—not for the entire system, as a central inverter would. This enables every solar panel to perform at its maximum potential. In other words, one solar panel alone cannot drag down the performance of the entire solar array, whereas a central inverter can only optimize output according to the weakest link. For example, shading of as little as 9 percent of a solar system connected to a central inverter can lead to a system-wide decline in power output by as much as 50 percent. If one solar panel in a string had abnormally high resistance due to a manufacturing defect, the performance of every solar panel connected to that same central inverter would suffer.

One of the tricky things about solar cells is that the voltage needs to be adjusted to the right level for maximum output of power. In other words, the performance of a solar panel is dependent on the voltage load that's applied to the inverter. Maximum power point tracking, or MPPT, is a technique used to find the right voltage, or the "maximum power point." With micro-inverters, MPPT is applied to each individual panel as opposed to the solar system as a whole; performance will naturally increase.

Unlike central inverters, micro-inverters are not exposed to high power voltages or to high heat loads. Therefore, they tend to last significantly longer. Nowadays, micro-inverters typically come with a warranty of 25 years, averaging ten years longer than central inverters. The 25-year warranty for micro-inverters conveniently matches the warranty period of the solar modules, particularly if the micro-inverters are installed into the PV solar modules at the panel manufacturer's plant.

Central inverters come in limited sizes, and you might end up having to pay for an inverter bigger than what you actually need.

I recommend that you purchase or ask your solar contractor to install a monitoring system to follow the energy output of your entire PV array. But remember, with a central inverter you cannot see the output at the individual panel level. With micro-inverters, you can connect each panel to a computer

The main electrical panel for the house. In this case, there is a grid-connection via a back-fed breaker in the panel. While this does serve as a disconnecting means for the panel, utilities generally require a separate, accessible, dedicated AC disconnect switch such as those illustrated earlier in this chapter under the heading "DC and AC Disconnect Switches."

monitoring system so you can easily pinpoint which panel is experiencing lower efficiency rates. This is helpful in discovering faulty panels or equipment. With micro-inverters, web-based monitoring on a panel-by-panel basis is usually available for both the homeowner and the installer. The DIY installer should invest the small extra amount required for a monitoring system. Continually analyzing the health of your PV solar rooftop system can pave the way for additional performance improvements. There are even mobile applications that enable you to monitor your PV system when you're travelling.

Solar panels are connected in a series before they're fed into a central inverter, typically with an effective nominal rating of 300-600 VDC (volts of direct current); the larger central inverters can reach up to 1,000 volts DC. This current is potentially life threatening if safety precautions are ignored—for instance, if the DC disconnect switch is left in the "ON" position while maintenance is being done on the system. You should always refer to the safety data sheets for the module and the inverter and follow all safety instructions. However, micro-inverters eliminate the need for high-voltage DC wiring, which improves safety for solar installers and system owners—an important consideration, especially for DIY installers. Once again, we recommend reading the safety data sheet of whatever type of inverter you plan to install.

Micro-inverters also generate significantly less heat than central inverters do, and as a result there's no need for active cooling. This enables micro-

inverters to operate without any appreciable noise, another advantage over central inverters.

Regarding the higher initial cost, it must be said that for any given PV system, micro-inverters are a more expensive option than using a central inverter. But micro-inverters are definitely worthy of consideration due to the superior long-term benefits. In recent years, central inverters had an average cost of about $0.40/Wp (watts–peak), while the average cost of micro-inverters has been about 30 percent higher: $0.52/Wp. If the micro-inverters are already incorporated into the PV modules, then you'll simply compare the combined cost of the modules and micro-inverters versus the cost of the central inverter plus the cost of the PV modules.

Finally, installing solar panels with micro-inverters is simpler and less time consuming, which typically cuts about 10 percent off the installation costs.

DUAL MICRO-INVERTERS

A few years ago, dual micro-inverters were introduced to the market. They essentially do the same thing as regular micro-inverters, but they convert the DC of two solar panels instead of one. This lowers the initial system cost slightly, but at the price of performance, so there may be very little net benefit. A homeowner will often ask the contractor, "Are micro-inverters, or dual micro-inverters, or a central string inverter the best choice in my situation?" It depends on the site conditions, the homeowner's budget, and other factors. However in most situations, regular micro-inverters should be given serious consideration.

However, it's only fair that we touch on the characteristics of central inverters before you make your final decision. First, central (or string) inverters are less expensive initially and have fewer moving parts when comparing the two systems overall. But in the long run, micro-inverters are usually more economical.

Still, the original single central inverter is very popular among homeowners and investors alike. The main reasons are familiarity and trust: Central inverters have simply been on the market longer, and they're believed to be efficient since they have a history of proven results. A typical central inverter has a maximum efficiency rate of 95 percent, and if there are no shading issues, they perform well. Because of this, they hold great promise for large industrial- and utility-sized projects, because solar systems designed for those projects usually don't confront shading challenges. For these larger installations, central inverters are significantly less expensive than micro-inverters.

Central inverters have only one point of failure. An analogy might be a ceiling with ten track lights versus a ceiling with a single lamp. Over the past year or so, there have been many claims about the reliability or unreliability of one technology over the other, but more time is needed to determine conclusively whether central inverters or micro-inverters are more reliable. You can easily guess which special interest group is making which claim. In any case, each instal-lation should be analyzed separately. Both inverter systems have a valid role to play, depending on the site conditions, the size of the PV system, financial considerations, and desired system flexibility.

Though both central inverters and micro-inverters have a place in the market, micro-inverters are gaining ground and have become the inverter of choice for many residential PV solar installation companies throughout the US and overseas. We can evaluate the benefits of micro-inverters versus central inverters by looking at two numbers:

· Lifetime costs ($)
· Lifetime energy production (kWh)

These two figures, calculated for both types of inverters, are essential numbers. Divide costs by energy production and you can determine how much money you'll pay for every kWh your solar system will produce. Every situation is different. There are several variables to take into account in order to find these two numbers.

Enecsys, one of the leading micro-inverter manufacturers, sums it up like this: "A total cost-of-ownership analysis of a PV solar system can only be carried out after detailed examination of capital and maintenance costs, and an understand-ing of how much energy will be harvested over the life of the system."

However, if your solar contractor recommends using a standard central inverter for your installa-tion, and some good reasons are provided, this is fine. The central inverter is a readily available and well-proven system.

Your central or string inverter unit is not much bigger than a typical disconnect switch, and they can be installed side-by-side for convenience and an aesthetically pleasing appearance. Both the disconnect switch and the inverter can be installed close to your main breaker panel or breaker box. Between the local grid line transformer and the main breaker panel, your electrician will install a "smart meter," which will measure in real time the electric power provided by the PV solar system to your residence. If you have selected an in-grid system, the smart meter will also be connected to the external power grid, probably near the existing conventional electric meter.

Below are three schematic diagrams of the different available metering systems, "FiT," "PPA," and "Net Metering":

The smart meter will measure and record the power in kilowatt hours consumed by your home, as well as the excess amount of power fed back into the external grid of your utility company. Thus, the term "net metering" is used to describe the net amount of power consumed. As mentioned before, most utility companies will pay you in the form of credit for any excess daily power generated from your PV system. For domestic consumers, there's usually an upper limit to these credits that is equal to the charges for power consumed. So, theoretically, you could have some months with a net metering month-end bill of zero. To qualify for net metering, your PV system

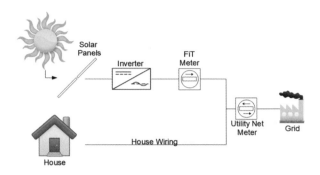

A schematic of a FiT meter connection.

must be less than a specified maximum generating capacity, which is regulated by your electric utility. In the US, the most common maximum size cap is 10 kW for residential systems.

The location of your existing breaker panel box may be where you install the PV solar DC disconnect switch, inverter, and smart meter. The breaker panel is usually installed on a wall in a garage, or in a hallway near the back door, or on a wall outside of the house.

Power moves from the DC/AC inverter to your home breaker panel box and is distributed to the rest of the household. A power meter with net metering capability is a little different from the standard meter you have now. It's capable of measuring power going into the grid or being pulled from the grid at the end of the line, and it will measure the amount of electricity that is either consumed or being sold back to the utility company.

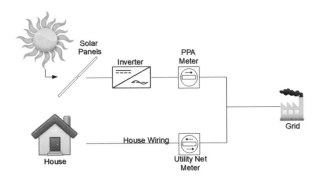

A schematic of a PPA meter connection.

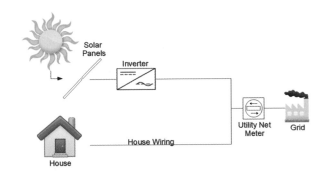

A schematic of a net metering connection.

With net metering, safety is an issue as well. The utility has to make sure that if there's a power outage in your immediate area or neighborhood, your PV system won't continue to feed electricity into power lines that a lineman might think are dead. This is a dangerous situation called "islanding," but it can be avoided with an anti-islanding inverter. Most inverters incorporate the anti-islanding protection feature.

The thought of living at the whim of the weatherman probably doesn't thrill most people, but three main options can ensure you still have power even if the sun isn't cooperating. If you want to live completely off the grid but don't trust your PV panels to supply all the electricity you'll need in a pinch, you can use a backup portable diesel generator when sunlight is low or if you wish to have power after dark or during a blackout in your area.

The second stand-alone system involves energy storage in the form of batteries. Several batteries connected together form what is commonly called a "battery bank." Unfortunately, batteries can add a lot of cost and maintenance to a PV solar rooftop system. But installing a battery bank is a necessity if you want to be completely independent of the electric utility company grid. However, if you find that the cost of a battery bank and backup generator large enough for your requirements is excessive, then the alternative is to connect your PV solar system to the utility grid, assuming it's available, buying power when you need it, and selling it back to the utility when your PV system produces more power than you use. A more detailed description and several images of battery banks are provided in Chapter 2.

If you decide to use batteries instead, keep in mind that they'll have to be maintained, and they must be replaced after a certain number of years. Most solar panels tend to last at least 30 years—and improved longevity continues as a main research goal—but batteries just don't have that kind of useful life. Depending on various factors, solar batteries might last up to 10 or 11 years before they must be replaced. Also, be aware that PV battery bank systems can be potentially dangerous because of the energy they store and the acidic electrolytes they contain, so you'll need a well-ventilated space and a nonmetallic enclosure or rack where they can operate safely.

Although several different kinds of batteries are commonly used for PV systems, make sure they're deep-cycle batteries. Unlike your car battery, which is a shallow-cycle battery, deep-cycle batteries can discharge more of their stored energy while still maintaining long life. Car batteries discharge a large current for a very short time to start the car engine, and then the alternator immediately recharges them as you drive. PV solar batteries generally have to discharge a smaller current for a much longer period of time, such as at night or during a power outage, while being charged during the sunny parts of the day. The most commonly used deep-cycle batteries are lead-acid batteries (both sealed and vented) and nickel-cadmium batteries, both of which have various pros and cons. Refer to Chapter 2 for more information, and, as recommended above for inverters, be sure to read the safety data sheet, or SDS, that comes with every important piece of electrical equipment. Any distributor or contractor can provide you with the SDS for any piece of equipment they sell or install.

Other Components Needed for Your PV Solar Rooftop System

CHARGE CONTROLLER

The use of batteries requires the installation of another component called a "charge controller." Batteries last a lot longer if they aren't overcharged or drained too much. That is one of the functions of a charge controller. Once the batteries are fully charged, the charge controller doesn't let current from the PV modules continue to flow into them. Similarly, once the batteries have been drained to a certain predetermined level of voltage, the charge controller won't allow more current to be drained from the batteries until they have been recharged. The use of a charge controller is essential for long battery life.

The other challenge, besides your energy storage system, is that the electric current generated by your solar panels—or extracted from your batteries, if you choose to use them—is not in the form that is supplied by the utility, namely AC, which is also the form of current required by the electrical appliances in your home. A solar system generates DC, so you need an inverter to convert it into alternating current. As discussed earlier, apart from switching DC to AC, most inverters are also designed to protect against islanding if your system is hooked up to the power grid.

Most large inverters will allow you to automatically control how your system works. Some PV modules, called AC modules, actually have a small inverter already built into each module, eliminating the need for a central inverter and simplifying wiring issues; refer to the comparison of inverters and micro-inverters above.

In addition to your PV array of panels and mounting support hardware, the wiring, conduits, junction boxes, grounding equipment, over-current protection, DC and AC disconnect switches, net metering equipment, and other accessories identified above will round out the essential components of a PV solar system. Of course, both DIY installers and solar contractors must follow regulations governed by electrical codes; there is a section in the National Electrical Code just for PV solar systems. There may also be state regulations or municipal regulations that apply to the installation of your PV solar rooftop system.

I recommend that you contact a licensed electrician who has experience with PV solar systems to connect the electric control equipment and measuring devices during your installation. In Chapter 9, I provide links to websites that supply contact information for experienced solar contractors and PV electricians, information that will help you contact experienced solar contractors in your hometown or nearby. Generally speaking, solar contractors are willing to let DIY enthusiasts handle much of the PV solar rooftop installation process, including mounting the support system, the PV modules, and the conduits.

Once installed, a PV solar rooftop system requires very little maintenance, especially if no batteries are used, and will provide electricity cleanly and quietly for 25 to 30 years.

CHAPTER 4

How to Determine the Optimal Size of Your System

You need to need to know a few basic things before you can proceed to design the layout for your solar energy system. First of all, you need to determine how much energy you want your proposed rooftop PV solar system to produce. If you're going to install a PV solar system on the rooftop of your existing home, and you aren't contemplating building any additional rooms, then it's an easy task to determine your electric consumption by analyzing your monthly utility bills. You can simply record and add up the kilowatt hours (kWh) during the previous 12 months and calculate an average. For most single-family dwellings, this will be in the range of 7,000 to 9,000 kWh per month. This number can vary a lot, depending on the size of the house, number and ages of the children, consumption habits of all family members, and weather conditions.

If you're building a new home, you won't have any electric bills to indicate a monthly consumption level. In this case, you'll need to do some calculations to determine your future electric consumption by adding up the estimated consumption of all the appliances, lights, etc., and estimating the number of hours per 24-hour day each item will be in use on average. Approximations or rough estimates will suffice.

Step 1: Determine Your Power Consumption Requirements

Make a list of the appliances and other electrical devices you are planning to power from your PV system. Using the table here as a guide, find out how much power each electrical item in the house consumes when it's operating or turned on. Most appliances and other electric or electronic devices have a label on the back that lists the wattage. Specification sheets, local appliance dealers, and product manufacturers are other sources of information. For your convenience, the chart here lists typical power consumption levels or wattage ratings of common household appliances and devices. With the wattage ratings for each electric appliance and other power consuming devices, you will be ready to fill out a "load-sizing worksheet" (example provided on page 77).

Typical Power Consumption of Household Appliances and Other Domestic Electric Devices

APPLIANCE OR ELECTRIC DEVICE	WATTS
Blender	300
Blow Dryer	1000
CB Radio	5
CD Player	35
Ceiling Fan	10–50
Clock Radio	1
Clothes Dryer (electric)	400
Clothes Dryer (gas heated)	300–400
Coffee Pot	200
Coffeemaker	800
Compact Fluorescent Incandescent (40 watt equivalent)	11
Compact Fluorescent Incandescent (60 watt equivalent)	16
Compact Fluorescent Incandescent (75 watt equivalent)	20
Compact Fluorescent Incandescent (100 watt equivalent)	30

APPLIANCE OR ELECTRIC DEVICE	WATTS
Computer Laptop	20–50
Computer PC	80–150
Computer Printer	100
Electric Blanket	200
Electric Clock	3
Freezer, 14cf (15 hours)	440
Freezer, 14cf (14 hours)	350
Freezer, 19cf (10 hours)	112
Hot Plate	1200
Iron	1000
Light Bulb (100W Incandescent)	100
Light Bulb (25W Compact Fluorescent)	28
Light Bulb (50W DC Incandescent)	50
Light Bulb (40W DC Halogen)	40
Light Bulb (20W Compact Fluorescent)	22
Microwave	600–1500
Refrigerator/Freezer, 20 cf 1.8 kwh per day (15 hours)	540

APPLIANCE OR ELECTRIC DEVICE	WATTS
Refrigerator/Freezer, 16 cf 1.6 kwh per day (13 hours)	475
Refrigerator, 16cf DC (7 hours)	112
Refrigerator, 12cf DC (7 hours)	70
Satellite Dish	30
Sewing Machine	100
Shaver	15
Stereo System	10–30
Table Fan	10–25
Toaster	800–1500
TV (25")	150
TV (19")	70
Vacuum Cleaner (upright)	200–700
Vacuum Cleaner (hand)	100
VCR	40
Washing Machine (automatic)	500
Washing Machine (manual)	300
Water Pump	250–500

Step 2: Load-Sizing Procedure

First, list all of the electrical appliances to be powered by your PV system. Then separate AC and DC devices, if applicable, and enter them in the table. Then insert a column for the number of items (more columns, if you have two or more of the same appliance). Next, you can record the operating wattage of each item. Then you need to specify the approximate number of hours per day each item will be used. Next, you multiply the three numerical columns to determine average daily watt-hour usage per line item. Then you need to insert another column and enter the number of days per week you'll be using each item to determine the total watt-hours per week each appliance will require. Most appliances have a label on the back that lists the wattage. Local appliance dealers and product manufacturers are other sources of information.

Finally, add all the numbers in column E and insert that number into the bottom right-hand cell. Excel can add these numbers for you automatically: Highlight all the cells to be added horizontally (including the last cell on the bottom row), then simply click the cursor on the "sum" function key in the top menu of the Excel spreadsheet. The sum total will immediately appear in the bottom right hand cell.

If you have any DC appliances or devices, you can do a separate small spreadsheet. Or you can include them in the same table. What you want is the "total watts per week" (column E), regardless of whether the items are AC or DC. In any case, most homeowners will not have any DC appliances.

You can easily adapt the columns and rows to your specific situation.

Step 3: Size Your Battery Storage System

Many homeowners will elect to go with a grid-tied PV system and net metering, relying on grid power to supply all electricity that can't be supplied by the solar panels, including at night and during the day when it's raining or heavy cloud conditions prevail. These homeowners are satisfied to use their solar PV system as much as sunlight hours will allow and to rely on the utility grid to make up the difference.

These homeowners will normally decide not to install a battery storage system because of the substantial increase it would represent to the total cost of the system. In addition, batteries require more maintenance than PV panels and batteries have a shorter life. After eight or ten years, they must be replaced with new batteries at substantial cost.

Nonetheless, there are a number of homeowners who want a battery storage system, either because their home does not have access to the utility grid, or because their goal is to be totally independent of grid power.

If, for whatever reason, you're definitely interested in a battery storage system, you should feel

Load-Sizing Worksheet (Part 1)					
	A	B	C	D = A × B × C	E = D × 7
APPLIANCE OR DEVICE	WATTS	QUANTITY	AVG HRS/ DAY	= WH/DAY	= WH/WK
1)					
2)					
3)					
4)					
5)					
Continue the list until complete					
TOTAL	n/a	n/a	n/a	n/a	

(The easiest way to do this is using a simple Excel worksheet.)

comfortable choosing an appropriate deep-cycle battery to use as a backup energy storage system. After reading this chapter, you'll be ready to fill out a battery sizing worksheet (example provided on page 80).

The first decision you'll need to make is how much energy storage (average daily power consumption multiplied by the reserve power time in days) you would like your battery bank to provide. This means how many consecutive days you want your PV system to power your home without using the utility grid power, or how many consecutive cloudy or rainy days do you want to operate on your battery system. Often, this is expressed as "days of autonomy," because it's based on the number of days you expect your system to provide power without receiving an input charge from the solar array. In addition to days of autonomy, you should also consider your usage or consumption patterns and any significant differences in your consumption needs for different seasons.

If you're installing a system for a weekend home, you might want to consider a larger battery bank, because your system will have all week to charge and store energy. Alternatively, if you're adding a PV array as a supplement to a generator-based system, your battery bank can be slightly smaller, since the generator can be operated if needed during the recharging cycles.

Batteries are sensitive to temperature extremes, and you cannot take as much energy out of a cold battery as a warm one. However, you can use the chart provided to factor in temperature adjustments. Although you can get more than rated capacity from a hot battery, operation at very hot temperatures will shorten battery life slightly. Try to keep your batteries near room temperature. Charge controllers can be purchased with a temperature compensation option to optimize the charging cycle at various temperatures and lengthen your battery life.

Under "Grid-Tied Solar Systems" (see page 40), I stated that the depth of discharge, "DOD," is defined as the minimum charge level at which point your PV system stops draining the battery and starts the recharge cycle again. The DOD can also be referred to as the percentage of the rated battery capacity (ampere-hours) that can safely be extracted from the battery before a recharge cycle is needed. The capability of a battery to withstand discharge depends on its construction. The terms

"shallow-cycle" and "deep-cycle" are commonly used to describe the two main types of batteries. Shallow-cycle batteries are lighter, less expensive, and have a short lifetime. For this reason, deep-cycle batteries should always be used for stand-alone PV systems. These units have thicker plates and most will withstand daily discharges of up to 80 percent of their rated capacity, although most battery manufacturers recommend a maximum discharge of 50 percent. Most deep-cycle batteries are referred to as "flooded electrolyte." This means that the plates are covered with the electrolyte solution, so the level of fluid must be monitored and distilled water must periodically be added to keep the plates fully covered. If this doesn't appeal to you, go with sealed lead-acid batteries, which don't require liquid refills. For special applications there are other types of deep-cycle batteries, such as nickel cadmium, as discussed in Chapter 2.

The depth of discharge value used for sizing should be the worst case scenario, or the maximum expected discharge that the battery will experience—for example 50 percent, 55 percent, or 60 percent. The system control unit, or charge controller, should be set to prevent discharge beyond whichever specified level you choose.

The ampere-hour (Ah) capacity of a battery is usually specified as well, together with a standard-hour reference such as 10 or 20 hours. For example, suppose the battery is rated at 100 ampere-hours and a 20-hour discharge time is specified. When the battery is fully charged, it can deliver a discharge current of 5 amperes for 20 hours (5A × 20 hrs = 100 ampere-hours). If you're ever confused or have doubts about your understanding of the relationship between the capacity of a battery and the load current, information is always provided in the literature that comes with every battery and on the website of the battery manufacturer.

Because it is dependent on factors such as charge rate, discharge rate, depth of discharge, number of cycles, frequency of use, and operating-temperature extremes, the precise lifetime of any battery is difficult to predict. It would be quite unusual for a lead-acid battery to last longer than 11 or 12 years in a PV system, but some may last longer, depending on how often they're used and how they are maintained.

Batteries require periodic maintenance. Even a sealed battery should be checked to make sure connections are tight and there is no indication of overcharging. For flooded batteries, the electrolyte level should be maintained above the plates and the voltage of the battery kept at the proper charge level. The specific gravity of each cell should also be checked to ensure consistent values between cells. Wide variations between the cell readings would probably indicate problems. The specific gravity of the cells should be checked with a hydrometer and recorded, particularly before the onset of winter in temperate climates.

In very cold environments, the electrolyte in lead-acid batteries may freeze. The freezing temperature is a function of the battery's state of charge.

When a battery is completely discharged, the electrolyte essentially becomes water, and the battery may be subject to freezing. If you live in a climate with very cold winter months, try to keep your battery bank in a room that doesn't get too cold.

Now you're ready to calculate how many batteries you'll need for your system, based on your own particular criteria. Just fill in the blanks. It'll be easy with the information, tables, and formulas discussed above.

If a battery bank of this size is too costly, or if it requires more space than you have available, you might want to consider reducing the size of your battery bank by reducing the daily amp-hour requirement (line 1, above). This is logically more feasible for a hybrid system. And since battery storage systems are modular, it's relatively simple to increase the size of your battery bank later, if you want.

How to Use Your Local Insolation (or Solar Irradiance) Index and Power Consumption Requirements to Determine the Optimal Size of a PV Array for Your Home

You'll need to determine how many solar panels can fit on your roof, how much solar radiation you receive at your location, your average monthly power consumption requirements, and how big a system you can afford or wish to buy. An array can

Worksheet for Calculating the Number of Batteries You Require

ITEM	FORMULA OR DESCRIPTION	ANSWER/UNIT
1	Enter here the daily power consumption or amp-hour requirement. (Obtain this number from the Load Sizing Worksheet above, line 5).	_____ Ah/day
2	Enter here the number of days you want your system to provide power autonomously, without your PV panels receiving any charge (that is, the number of continuous days of rain or overcast weather).	_____ days
3	Multiply the amp-hour requirement (line 1) by the number of days of autonomy desired (line 2). This is the amount of amp-hours your battery system will need to store.	_____ Ah
4	Enter the depth of discharge for the battery you have chosen. This is a safety measure used to avoid excess discharge of the battery bank. (Example: If the DOD you chose is 50 percent, use 0.5 here. Your DOD should not be more than 0.8).	_____ (e.g. 0.5 to 0.8)
5	Divide the amp-hours needed (line 3) by the DOD (line 4). This is the number of Ah required if the ambient temperature is above 80°F / 26.7°C.	_____ Ah
6	Enter the "temperature factor multiplier." Use the estimated lowest ambient winter temperature of the room or space where your battery bank is to be located. Consult the list of temperature factor multipliers below and use the entry that corresponds with your estimated lowest ambient winter temperature.	_____ [temperature factor multiplier]
7	Multiply line 5 by line 6. This will be the total energy storage capacity required by your battery bank.	_____ = _____ Ah (Total)
8	Enter the amp-hour rating of your individual batteries. You can find this on the spec sheet that comes in each battery box. Use the 20-hour rating provided on the spec sheet.	_____ batteries
9	Divide the total energy storage capacity (line 7) by the amp-hour rating for 20 hours of usage. Round up to the next whole number. This will be the number of batteries needed to be wired in parallel.	_____ batteries
10	Divide the nominal system voltage (12V, 24V, or 48V) by the individual battery voltage. This will be the number of batteries to be wired in the series. Round up to the nearest whole number.	_____ batteries
11	Multiply line 9 by line 10. This will give you the total number of batteries you need for your chosen battery bank.	_____ batteries

Use the Temperature Factor Multiplier for line 6. Pick the lowest winter temperature where your batteries will be installed. A simple estimate will suffice.

Temperature Factor Multiplier	
LOWEST AMBIENT WINTER TEMPERATURE	**MULTIPLIER**
80°F 26.7°C	1.00
70°F 21.2°C	1.04
60°F 15.6°C	1.11
50°F 10.0°C	1.19
40°F 4.4°C	1.30
30°F -1.1°C	1.40
20°F -6.7°C	1.59

Once you know what your target monthly output is in kilowatt hours (kWh), simple math will let you calculate how big an array you need. Then you can focus on choosing the type of solar panels you want, where to install them (the layout or configuration), and how many panels you'll need.

When looking at your utility bills, don't forget that your electricity consumption changes with the seasons, especially in temperate climates and countries that are subject to cold winters and hot summers. Most homes in the northern US and in most of continental Europe use 700–900 kWh each month, but this consumption level can differ substantially according to the country, the season, the type and size of home, family size, energy efficiency of appliances and lighting fixtures, and the family's energy consumption habits.

You can divide your expected monthly consumption level in kWh by the peak sun hours you receive each day to determine the size of your system. Peak sun hours are the number of hours each day when the insolation (or solar irradiance) equals 1000 watts/square meter. Information on peak sun hours in nearly every town and city in the world is readily available on the Internet. In the United States, for example, you can find out how much sunlight you receive per day on the National Renewable Energy Laboratory website under the "US Solar Resource Map" for photovoltaics, at www.nrel.gov/gis/solar.html.

For a clearer picture, let's take the example of 900 kWh/month, which is 30 kWh/day. If you use

be planned depending on any or all of these considerations, but taking all of these factors into account will be the wisest approach.

Knowing how much power you currently consume on average is the best starting place if you already own your own home; this information is readily available from your monthly electric bills. With this information, you can estimate the array size that will produce the same amount of energy on a monthly basis, how much energy can be produced in the space available, or how much energy you can produce on the budget you have allowed for the project.

A typical installation of poly modules that I estimate will have an installed capacity of 900 kWh/month, depending on the location of where it is installed.

30 kW daily, and you receive an average of four hours of sunlight per day, and if the PV panels you selected have a rated capacity of 250 Wp (watts peak), you'll need to make an adjustment because the panels' capacity is measured in direct current whereas the electricity we use in our homes and offices is always alternating current, and the DC produced by the PV panels is converted into AC power by an inverter. This process by which AC is converted to DC involves the loss of a certain amount of power. This loss is calculated by multiplying the Wp in DC by a number we call the "derate factor" to get

the equivalent power output in AC. The derate factor may vary a little, depending on the system and the inverter used, but a safe average derate factor we can use for calculating our system is 0.82. This means that your PV panel rated at 250 Wp DC will actually deliver 250 × 0.82 = 205 watts AC. So in our example, this home is consuming 30 kW daily = 30,000 Wh/day (AC).

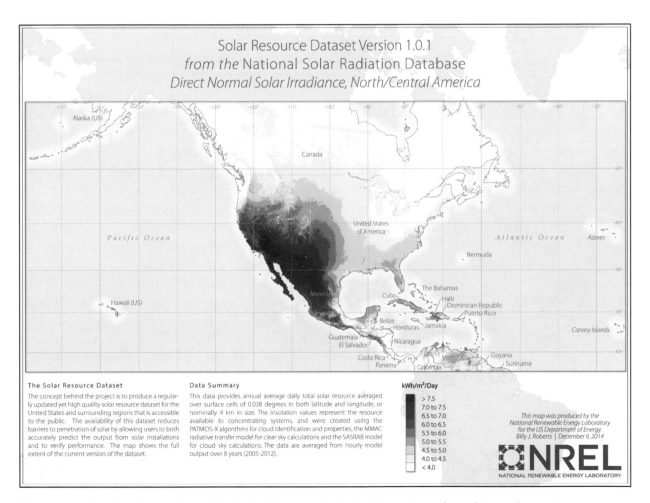

This map provides the solar irradiance levels for all areas in the United States, Canada, and Central America.

Therefore, divide 30,000 Wh/d by the average hours of sunlight available at your location, otherwise known as the local insolation index. For simplicity, many people will use 4 hours per day. But we want to be more precise, so you'll need to use the exact insolation index number for your location, as given in the table below (for Europe and other areas, we refer to other tables on the Internet). Let us use the example of Los Angeles, California, which has an insolation idex of 5.62 (yearly average). So we divide 30,000 Wh/d by 5.62 h/d, which gives us 5,338 W. Then this number is divided by the adjusted PV panel power delivery rating of 205 W/panel (AC). Thus, the calculation is 5,338 ÷ 205 = 26.0 panels. This means that the array will require 26 panels to produce power equivalent to the home's daily average consumption of 30 kW/d, using the PV modules specified above and rated at 250 Wp (DC).

Step 4: Determine the Average Sun Hours Available Per Day

Several factors, including seasonal usage, typical local weather conditions, fixed mountings versus trackers, and location and angle of the PV array, influence how much solar power your modules will be exposed to.

The following table provides the number of hours of full sunlight available to generate electricity. Your solar array power generation capacity is dependent on the angle of the sun's rays as they hit the modules.

Peak power occurs when the sun's rays are at right angles, or perpendicular, to the modules. As the angle deviates from perpendicular, more and more of the energy is reflected rather than absorbed by the modules. Depending on your application and your budget, sun-tracking mounts can be used to enhance your power output by automatically adjusting the position of the panels to track or follow the sun while maintaining a 90-degree angle.

The solar insolation table below (also known as the solar irradiance) tells us the amount of sunlight available during spring, summer, autumn, and winter, measured in peak sun hours or simply "sun hours." It's more difficult to produce energy during the winter because of shorter days, increased cloudiness, and the sun's lower position in the sky. This table lists the sun-hour ratings for over 75 cities in North America for three categories: summer, winter, and yearly average.

If you use your system primarily in the summer, use the summer value. If you're using your system year-round, especially for a critical application, use the winter value. And finally, if you're using the system most of the year (spring, summer, and fall) or the application is not critical, use the average value.

Wherever you live in North America or overseas, you should be able to determine a reasonable estimate of the sun's availability (peak hours) in your area by using the map above and the table below. The map provides color coding matched with index numbers that indicate the general solar insolation index number for anywhere on the globe.

Solar Insolation or Solar Irradience Levels (Peak Sun Hours) for Cities in the USA and Canada

USA BY STATE, CITY	SUMMER AVG.	WINTER AVG.	YEAR AVG.
AL, Montgomery	4.69	3.37	4.23
AK, Bethel	6.29	2.37	3.81
AK, Fairbanks	5.87	2.12	3.99
AK, Mantanuska—Susitna Borough	5.24	1.74	3.55
AZ, Page	7.3	5.65	6.36
AZ, Phoenix	7.13	5.78	6.58
AZ, Tucson	7.42	6.01	6.57
AR, Little Rock	5.29	3.88	4.69
CA, Davis	6.09	3.31	5.1
CA, Fresno	6.19	3.42	5.38
CA, Inyokern	8.7	6.97	7.66
CA, La Jolla	5.24	4.29	4.77
CA, Los Angeles	6.14	5.03	5.62
CA, Riverside	6.35	5.35	5.87
CA, Santa Maria	6.52	5.42	5.94
CA, Soda Springs	6.47	4.4	5.6
CO, Boulder	5.72	4.44	4.87
CO, Granby	7.47	5.15	5.69
CO, Grand Junction	6.34	5.23	5.86
CO, Grand Lake	5.86	3.56	5.08
DC, Washington	4.69	3.37	4.23
FL, Apalachicola	5.98	4.92	5.49
FL, Belle Island	5.31	4.58	4.99

continues

USA BY STATE, CITY	SUMMER AVG.	WINTER AVG.	YEAR AVG.
FL, Gainesville	5.81	4.71	5.27
FL, Miami	6.26	5.05	5.62
FL, Tampa	6.16	5.26	5.67
GA, Atlanta	5.16	4.09	4.74
GA, Griffin	5.41	4.26	4.99
HI, Honolulu	6.71	5.59	6.02
IA, Ames	4.8	3.73	4.4
ID, Twin Falls	5.42	3.41	4.7
ID, Boise	5.83	3.33	4.92
IL, Chicago	4.08	1.47	3.14
IN, Indianapolis	5.02	2.55	4.21
KS, Dodge City	4.14	5.28	5.79
KS, Manhattan	5.08	3.62	4.57
KY, Lexington	5.97	3.6	4.94
LA, Lake Charles	5.73	4.29	4.93
LA, New Orleans	5.71	3.63	4.92
LA, Shreveport	4.99	3.87	4.63
ME, Blue Hill	4.38	3.33	4.05
MA, Boston	4.27	2.99	3.84
MA, E. Wareham	4.48	3.06	3.99
MA, Lynn	4.6	2.33	3.79
MA, Natick	4.62	3.09	4.1
MD, Silver Hill	4.71	3.84	4.47
ME, Caribou	5.62	2.57	4.19

USA BY STATE, CITY	SUMMER AVG.	WINTER AVG.	YEAR AVG.
ME, Portland	5.2	3.56	4.51
MI, E. Lansing	4.71	2.7	4.0
MI, Sault Ste. Marie	4.83	2.33	4.2
MN, St. Cloud	5.43	3.53	4.53
MO, Columbia	5.5	3.97	4.73
MO, St. Louis	4.87	3.24	3.78
MS, Meridian	4.86	3.64	4.44
MT, Glasgow	5.97	4.09	5.15
MT, Great Falls	5.7	3.66	4.93
NC, Cape Hatteras	5.81	4.69	5.31
NC, Greensboro	5.05	4.0	4.71
ND, Bismarck	5.48	3.97	5.01
NE, Lincoln	5.4	4.38	4.79
NE, North Omaha	5.28	4.26	4.9
NJ, Seabrook	4.76	3.2	4.21
NM, Albuquerque	7.16	6.21	6.77
NV, Ely	6.48	5.49	5.98
NV, Las Vegas	7.13	5.83	6.41
NY, Bridgehampton	3.93	1.62	3.16
NY, Ithaca	4.57	2.29	3.79
NY, New York	4.97	3.03	4.08
NY, Rochester	4.22	1.58	3.31
NY, Schenectady	3.92	2.53	3.55
OH, Cleveland	4.79	2.69	3.94

continues

USA BY STATE, CITY	SUMMER AVG.	WINTER AVG.	YEAR AVG.
OH, Columbus	5.26	2.66	4.15
OK, Oklahoma City	6.26	4.98	5.59
OK, Stillwater	5.52	4.22	4.99
OR, Astoria	4.76	1.99	3.72
OR, Corvallis	5.71	1.9	4.03
OR, Medford	5.84	2.02	4.51
PA, Pittsburgh	4.19	1.45	3.28
PA, State College	4.44	2.78	3.91
RI, Newport	4.69	3.58	4.23
SC, Charleston	5.72	4.23	5.06
SD, Rapid City	5.91	4.56	5.23
TN, Nashville	5.2	3.14	4.45
TN, Oak Ridge	5.06	3.22	4.37
TX, Brownsville	5.49	4.42	4.92
TX, El Paso	7.42	5.87	6.72
TX, Fort Worth	6.0	4.8	5.83
TX, Midland	6.33	5.23	5.83
TX, San Antonio	5.88	4.65	5.3
UT, Flaming Gorge	6.63	5.48	5.83
UT, Salt Lake City	6.09	3.78	5.26
VA, Richmond	4.5	3.37	4.13
WA, Prosser	6.21	3.06	5.03
WA, Pullman	6.07	2.9	4.73
WA, Richland	6.13	2.01	4.43
WA, Seattle	4.83	1.6	3.57

USA BY STATE, CITY	SUMMER AVG.	WINTER AVG.	YEAR AVG.
WA, Spokane	5.53	1.16	4.48
WV, Charleston	4.12	2.47	3.65
WI, Madison	4.85	3.28	4.29
WY, Lander	6.81	5.5	6.06
CANADA BY PROVINCE, CITY			
Alberta, Edmonton	4.95	2.13	3.75
Alberta, Suffield	5.19	2.75	4.1
British Columbia, Kamloops	4.48	1.46	3.29
British Columbia, Prince George	4.13	1.33	3.14
British Columbia, Vancouver	4.23	1.33	3.14
Manitoba, The Pas	5.02	2.02	3.56
Manitoba, Winnipeg	5.23	2.77	4.02
New Brunswick, Fredericton	4.23	2.54	3.56
Newfoundland, Goose Bay	4.65	2.02	3.33
Newfoundland, St. Johns	3.89	1.83	3.15
Northwest Territory, Fort Smith	5.16	0.88	3.29
Northwest Territory, Norman Wells	5.04	0.06	2.89
Nova Scotia, Halifax	4.02	2.16	3.38
Ontario, Ottawa	4.63	2.35	3.7
Ontario, Toronto	3.98	2.13	3.44
Prince Edward Isl., Charlottetown	4.31	2.29	3.56
Quebec, Montreal	4.21	2.29	3.5
Quebec, Sept-Isles	4.29	2.33	3.5
Saskatchewan, Swift Current	5.25	2.77	4.23
Yukon, Whitehorse	4.81	0.69	3.1

Step 5: Size the Optimal PV System for Your Home

With the information calculated above, we now have enough data to calculate the optimal size for your personally specified solar PV array, as follows:

Worksheet to Calculate the Size (Total Capacity) of Your PV Solar System (Number of PV Panels and Total System Power in Watts)	
1. Enter your daily amp-hour requirement (from line 5 of the "load sizing worksheet").	_____ Ah/day
2. Enter the sun-hours per day (solar irradiation index number) for your area. Refer to chart in Step 4.	_____ h/day
3. Divide line 1 by line 2. This is the total amperage required from your solar array.	_____ amps
4. Enter the peak amperage (DC) rating of the solar module you have selected.	_____ amps
5. Divide line 3 by line 4. This is the number of solar modules needed in parallel.	_____ panels (in parallel)
6. Select the required modules in series from the following chart. **BATTERY BANK VOLTAGE** / **NUMBER OF MODULES IN SERIES** 12V — 1 24V — 2 48V — 4	_____ panels (in series)
7. Multiply line 5 by line 6 to find the total number of modules needed in your array.	Total: _____ panels
8. Enter the adjusted nominal power rating (in watts) of the module you have chosen. This is the Wp rating multiplied by the "derate factor."	_____ watts
9. Multiply line 7 by line 8. This is the nominal power output of your personally specified PV solar rooftop system.	_____ watts

How Much Money Can We Save with PV Solar?

Instead of evaluating a solar system by its capacity in kilowatts (kW), you might want to estimate how many kilowatt-hours (kWh) any solar system can be expected to generate over its estimated lifetime. If we divide this number into the overall cost of the system and then divide the result by the number of years of useful life expected from the system (use the warranty period of 25 years), we obtain the average annual cost of the electricity produced by your proposed PV system in $/kWh/year. In this way, we can also compare equivalent annual cost figures for different PV solar systems. You're now left with how much you are paying for every kWh of electricity the solar panels produce ($/kWh). Divide again by 100 to get cents/kWh.

Electricity prices in the United States typically range from 8 to 17 cents/kWh, depending on the state or region. Therefore, you can easily calculate the annual savings produced by your PV system by taking the standard utility rate for electricity in your area (in cents/kWh) and subtracting the number you calculated above for the average cost of the electricity (also in cents/kWh) generated by your proposed PV solar system. Then, take the difference of these two figures and multiply that number by the sum of your actual 12 months of consumption (in kWh). You can extract this number from the previous 12 months of your utility bills. This will give you the average annual savings provided by your PV solar system.

If you're just comparing two different solar panels, and the length of their warranties is the same, doing a similar analysis for the first year (as opposed to their lifetime) will be sufficient. When making this comparison, it's helpful to know that nowadays, solar panels typically have a warranty period of 25 years. The performance of solar panels degrades very slowly over time, usually less than 1 percent per year. For this reason, solar panel manufacturers usually guarantee that the power output of their solar panels will stay above 75 to 80 percent until the warranty expires.

Solar System 2 is superior from a financial standpoint ($38,000 vs. $42,000), and most homeowners would choose it for this reason. System 1 is a better option for homeowners who lack roof space (375 ft^2 vs. 485 ft^2). The slightly more expensive solar system will save space at a moderately higher system cost per kWh. Generally speaking, the less efficient and cheaper solar panels tend to produce slightly more electricity in a year for the same amount of money compared to more expensive, high-efficiency solar panels.

Case Study: Polycrystalline Modules

DESCRIPTION	SOLAR SYSTEM 1	SOLAR SYSTEM 2
Manufacturer	SunPower	Canadian Solar
Model	SPR-210-WHT-U	CS6P-250P
Efficiency	16.9 percent	16.1 percent
Number of Solar Panels	28	28
Output (Year 1)	8,930 kWh	9,066 kWh
Total System Cost	$42,000	$38,000
Area	375 ft^2 (34.8 m^2)	485 ft^2 (45.1 m^2)
Cost per kWh	$4.70/kWh	$4.19/kWh

Note: The total system costs used above will vary considerably from region to region and may change substantially over time. Thus, the reader should not use these figures to compare with any local quotations.

CHAPTER 5

How to Calculate the Annual Output of a System and the Optimal Number of Panels

The conventional formula used to estimate the electricity generated in annual output of a photovoltaic system is: Energy (kWh) = A × r × H × PR

Where:

A = Total solar panel Area (m²)

r = Solar panel yield (percent)

H = Annual average solar radiation on tilted panels (zero shading)

PR = Performance Ratio: provides a coefficient for energy losses (see details below)

In the above equation, r is the yield of the solar panel, given in terms of the ratio of electrical power (in kWp) of one solar panel to the glass surface area (in m²) of the panel or module covering the solar cells. For example, the solar panel yield r of a PV module of 250 Wp with an area of 1.6 m² is 0.250 / 1.6 = 15.6 percent.

This nominal ratio is given for standard test conditions (STC): solar radiation equal to 1000 W/m², a cell temperature of 25°C, and a wind speed of 1 m/s. The nominal power of a photovoltaic panel under these standard test conditions is referred to as "watts peak" (Wp). All PV solar panels are rated in this way. For example, a Wp rating of 250 indicates the theoretical, rather than the actual, amount of power that will be produced by a given PV panel, because Wp does not account for the losses that can occur. See "Performance Ratio" below.

H refers to the solar radiation or insolation value. You do not need to calculate this value yourself. You can find the solar radiation value for any location worldwide free of charge on several web sites, or from the above table for North America. For more extensive coverage of many other locations and countries, you can visit: www.photovoltaic-software.com/solar-radiation-database.php.

You'll have to find the global annual radiation incident on your PV panels, which is determined by your specific location (see tables above). Sometimes this needs to be modified with respect to your specific installation data, including the inclination (slope or tilt) and orientation or compass alignment (azimuth) of your panels. However, most of the major solar radiation websites will provide the solar radiation values for any given location, already taking into account the optimal inclination (number of degrees from the equator), and optimal orientation (i.e. due south).

PR (performance ratio): Knowing the PR is an important part of evaluating the quality of a photovoltaic installation, because it indicates how well the installation will perform independent of its orientation or inclination. It includes all losses. Factors that could cause energy losses that would affect the PR value include: the site; the PV technology; the type of inverter to be used; the sizing of the system; and the weather conditions determined by geographical location, as summarized below:

The following analysis of solar module performance factors will help explain the conversion from the solar module power rating (watts peak DC STC) to the energy (kilowatt-hours AC) produced by the PV solar system you propose to install at your home.

The "Performance Factors" for PV solar modules are summarized and quantified as follows:

MODULE POWER RATING

Modules are rated in DC watts at STC by all manufacturers. For example: manufacturer rating 100 watts STC DC. All solar module manufacturers test the power of their solar modules under specific standard test conditions in the factory. The test results are used to rate the modules according to the tested power output. For example, a factory-test module that produces 100W of DC power would be rated and labeled as a 100W STC DC solar module.

MODULE TEMPERATURE FACTOR

The operating temperature of PV modules increases when the modules come in contact with the rays of the sun. As the operating temperature increases, the power output decreases slightly due to the properties of the solar cell conversion materials. This applies to all solar modules. The PV USA Test Condition (PTC) ratings, which are based primarily on the specific module temperature characteristics, take this into consideration. The PTC ratings are different for each module and can vary from approximately 87 percent to 92 percent of the STC rating. A typical decrease in power output is approximately 12 percent for crystalline-based solar modules. This decrease would result, for example, in a STC rated 100-watt DC solar module being PTC rated at approximately 88 watts DC.

PARTICULATE BUILD-UP FACTOR

When a PV solar module is mounted on a rooftop, airborne particulates such as dust settle and accumulate over time on the glass surface of the module, just as dust settles on the glass windshield of your car wherever it may be parked. These particulates prevent a certain amount of light from reaching the module and therefore reduce the power produced by the module. As you know by now, modules produce more power when exposed to more light. Depending on local conditions and on the maintenance provided by the homeowner, the reduction in power from particulate build-up can be anywhere from 2 percent to 14 percent. A typical value for this factor can be estimated at 7 percent, giving a particulate loss multiplier of 93 percent. A module installed in a wet weather climate would have less "soiling" than a module installed in a drier climate, due to rainwater rinsing off the module's glass surface. Particulate build-up results in the power decreasing from 88 watts to approximately 82 watts (88W × 0.93 = 82W).

SYSTEM WIRING AND MODULE OUTPUT DIFFERENCE FACTOR

Typical solar electric systems require that modules be connected to one another. The wires used to connect the modules create a slight resistance in the electrical flow, decreasing the total power output of the system, a phenomenon similar to what happens when low-pressure water flows through a long hose. In addition, slight differences in power output from module to module reduce the maximum power output available from each module. The system AC and DC wiring losses and individual module power output differences could reduce the total system-rated energy output by 3 percent to 7 percent. A typical

value for these losses is 5 percent. This results in the estimated power output decreasing from 82 watts DC to 78 watts DC (82 W × 0.95 = 78W).

INVERTER CONVERSION LOSSES FACTOR

In order for the DC power from the solar modules to be converted to standard utility AC power, a power inverter (DC to AC) is installed along with the PV solar system. The conversion from DC power to AC power results in an energy loss of between approximately 6 percent and 8 percent. This is mainly due to energy losses in the form of heat, but this can vary between different inverters. A typical value used for these losses is 6 percent. This gives a loss multiplier of 0.94. This results in the estimated power output decreasing from 78 watts DC to 73 watts AC (78 W DC × 0.94 = 73 W AC). Now we have the power in alternating current after the inverter.

MODULE TILT ANGLE FACTOR

First of all, not every roof has the optimal orientation or "angle of inclination" to take full advantage of the sun's energy. Non-tracking PV systems in the northern hemisphere should ideally point toward true south, although orientations that face in more easterly or westerly directions can work too, albeit by sacrificing varying amounts of efficiency.

Solar panels should also be inclined at an angle as close to the area's latitude as possible to absorb the maximum amount of energy year-round. A different orientation and/or inclination could be used if you want to maximize energy production for the morning or afternoon, and/or the summer or winter. Of course, the modules should never be shaded by nearby trees or buildings, no matter the time of day or the time of year. In a PV module, if even just one of its cells is shaded, power production can be significantly reduced (slightly more for central inverters or somewhat less if micro-inverters are used).

The module installation angle in relation to the sun affects the module energy output. The module produces more power (watts) and, as a result, energy (watt-hours), when the light source is perpendicular to the surface of the module. For this reason, solar module installations are often tilted towards the sun to maximize the amount and intensity of light exposure.

As the sun angle changes throughout the year (higher in the sky during summer and lower in the sky during winter), the amount of light falling directly on the module changes, as does the energy output. In southern California, a typical optimum tilt angle for average module power production over the course of a year in a fixed-tilt system is approximately 30 degrees. The typical southern California residential roof is tilted approximately 15 degrees. The reduction in the average annual energy output for a module, which is mounted at a south-facing, 15-degree tilt, is approximately 3 percent when compared to the optimal tilt angle of approximately 30 degrees.

This 3 percent reduction gives us a loss multiplier of 0.97 and results in a power reduction from 73 watts AC down to 71 watts AC (97 percent x 73 = 71).

For flat-mounted systems (zero tilt), the reduction in average annual energy output for a module is approximately 11 percent when compared to the optimal tilt of approximately 30 degrees.

MODULE COMPASS DIRECTION/ AZIMUTH FACTOR

The amount of sunlight shining on the module is partially dependent on the direction the PV system array is facing relative to the equator. As the sun moves across the sky throughout the day, from the east in the morning to the west in the afternoon, the compass direction (south, southwest, east, etc.) of the module affects the cumulative energy output. Assuming you're in the Northern Hemisphere, it's best to install a south-facing module in order to obtain the maximum amount of direct sunlight exposure on your PV modules. If the module is facing east or west, it will be exposed to less direct sunlight as the sun moves across the sky.

There is no loss factor for south-facing modules, so the estimated energy output (from one hour of exposure) for this particular example will remain at 71 watt hours AC.

If the module was not facing south, the estimated energy output would have been reduced. For example, the estimated energy output for a southwest-facing module would be reduced by approximately 3 percent.

SOLAR IRRADIATION INDEX FACTOR

The amount of sunshine on your modules is determined to a great degree by the extent of the sun's year-round intensity at your particular location, known as the solar irradiation index or solar insolation index.

Refer to the Solar Irradiance Map in Chapter 4, which illustrates and explains the different solar irradiance levels measured in average peak sun hours/day for any location in North America. The map accompanies the long table showing the "Sun Hours" for approximately 100 cities in the United States and Canada.

Every location on earth has a different amount of sunlight exposure throughout the year, referred to as solar irradiation, which is measured in kWh/M2 expressed as "sun hours." For example, a coastal California city like Malibu or San Francisco will have a lower average amount of yearly sun hours compared with desert cities like Palm Springs or Phoenix because of fog and moisture in the air in coastal locations. Since solar modules produce power and energy when exposed to sunlight, the more sun hours a location receives, the more energy will be produced from a PV solar module installed at that location.

"One sun" refers to the peak noon sunlight power intensity in the middle of summer. "One sun hour" is the energy produced by the peak noon sunlight intensity in the middle of summer, over one hour. Because the sun's energy is converted by a solar module, recorded sun hour data for particular locations is used to help approximate the energy produced by a solar PV module.

The amount of sun hours for a particular loca-

SUN HOURS

(Southern California = 5.5 daily sun hours), 391 watt hours AC per Day (71 watt hours AC × 5.5 h/day), equivalent to 142 kWh/year (391 Wh/day × 365 days divided by 1,000 W/kW).

tion differs from day to day. There are multiple sun hour data sources, which differ slightly from one another. The US Department of Energy and NASA have calculated average daily sun hour data for most locations for over 20 years, which helps predict yearly energy output. This recorded data shows an approximate daily sun hour average of 5.5 hours throughout the year for many southern California locations.

A table in Chapter 4 specifies the average yearly sun hours available for more than 120 cities in the United States and Canada. This table also provides the average summer and winter sun hours, or irradiation index, for each city. In southern California, for example, there are approximately 7.1 sun hours per day during the summer and approximately 3.9 sun hours per day during the winter. These seasonal averages result in a yearly average of approximately 5.5 sun hours per day ((7.1 + 3.9) / 2 = 5.5).

Final Calculations of Solar Energy Output

In order to estimate the yearly energy production of a solar module, simply multiply the estimated module energy output (from exposure to one sun hour, 1000W/m2 over one hour), 71 watt hours AC (remember we used a PV panel of 100Wp adjusted by all the power-loss factors), by the number of sun hours for the particular location: 5.5 per day, in our example. This produces approximately 71W × 5.5h/day = 391 watt hours AC per day. Expressed in kilowatts, this is 0.391 kWh/day per panel. When estimating yearly energy production, the estimated daily energy production, .391 kWh AC, is multiplied by 365, the total number of days in a year. This results in approximately 142 kWh/yr AC energy production. Therefore, one 100-watt (100 Wp) DC module will produce approximately 142 kilowatt hours/year AC of electric energy under the specified conditions in this example.

If the module rating were higher than 100 Wp DC—for example, many polycrystalline modules have a rating of 250 Wp DC—you would simply multiply 142 by the ratio 250/100 (142 x 2.5) = 355 kWh/yr of AC power for one PV panel rated at 250 Wp.

The key figure to remember in all of this is the estimated module energy output, which is 0.71 watt hours AC for every 1.0 Wp DC of rated module power. This is equivalent to 29 percent total energy losses.

Once you make the commitment to go solar, the next step is to determine how big your solar PV system must be to meet the electricity needs of your home and to see if the total net cost is within your budget, taking into account any government financial incentives and subsidies, and then adjusting the size of your proposed system if necessary.

Start by reviewing your electricity bills over the past year to get an idea of your typical electricity usage measured in kilowatt hours. For example, in recent years the average American household used about 11,000 kilowatt hours of electricity per year, according to the US Energy Information Administration (EIA). Using the calculations above, to obtain 11,000 kWh of power over the course of one year in an average California city, we would need 31 modules rated at 250 Wp DC. The calculation is: 11,000 kWh/yr divided by 355 kWh/yr/panel = 30.9 panels (for PV panels rated at 250 Wp DC).

Of course, the above calculations were based on the solar irradiation index of an imaginary California city, and you will want to recalculate using the irradiation index in your particular location, which you can obtain from the table and map in Chapter 4.

Many utility companies also offer complimentary energy audits, and this can provide greater insight into your family's energy use habits and the basic requirements for your proposed PV solar system.

Some arid regions of the US Southwest can receive more than six hours of peak sun, while in the northeastern states it would be only about four hours.

The process of comparing your power needs to your sunlight availability is known as your load calculation, and this simple calculation is critically important for planning the size of your PV solar system.

Let's take another, simpler example to understand how you may calculate the required size of your solar array. Let's use the typical North American family's monthly consumption figure of 900 kWh. To arrive at a daily consumption figure we divide the monthly figure by 30, the average number of days in one month. 900 kWh/month divided by 30 days/month = 30 kWh/day AC.

Now we want to calculate the size at which a solar array will produce 30kWh/day. We know this depends on peak sun hours available, and we'll use for this example five peak sun hours. Depending on your location, 30 kWh/day divided by five peak sun hours = 6 kW/day AC.

We need to remember to convert this back to DC power because all PV panels are rated in Wp DC. As detailed above, we learned the DC/AC conversion factor, allowing for all normal losses in 1.0 Wp DC = 0.71 W AC. Therefore, 6 kW/day AC divided by 0.71 = 8.45 kW/day DC.

Number of PV Panels of Different Ratings Required to Produce Specified Levels of Daily Power Consumption

DAILY CONSUMPTION AC	EQUIVALENT DC POWER	NUMBER OF PANELS REQUIRED USING 200WP PANELS	NUMBER OF PANELS REQUIRED USING 240WP PANELS	NUMBER OF PANELS REQUIRED USING 285WP PANELS
4,000 W/d AC	5,634 W/d DC	28	24	20
5,000 W/d AC	7,042 W/d DC	35	29	25
6,000 W/d AC	8,450 W/d DC	42	35	30
7,000 W/d AC	9,859 W/d DC	49	41	35
8,000 W/d AC	11,267 W/d DC	56	47	40

Note: The number of panels is rounded off to the nearest whole number.

Therefore, for a 6,000 W/d AC (8,450 W/d DC), you would need forty-two 200Wp panels (8,450 / 200 = 42), or thirty-five 240Wp panels (8,450 / 240 = 35), or thirty 285Wp panels (8,450 / 285 = 30). This calculation is included in the table below.

Those of you with three- or four-bedroom homes who are putting in solar PV systems will want to off-set most of your electrical requirements with a PV solar array that is between 4kW/d and 8kW/d (daily consumption AC). Using this simple formula provided above, we can calculate the number of panels for different power levels as described below

If your monthly average consumption figure varies much from the 900 kWh/month example, or if you receive fewer than five peak sun hours on average, then it's simple math to calculate your own daily consumption figure and the number of panels in accordance with their rated capacity. The basic formula is as follows:

Monthly consumption _____ kWh/month, divided by (30 d/m × 1,000 W/kW) = _____ W/d, divided by number of peak sun hours _____ h/d, divided by the capacity of each solar panel _____ Wp DC = _____ , the total number of panels required for your system. (Note: To be practical, we round up or down to the nearest whole number.)

Links to Online Energy Output and System Size Calculators for PV Grid-Connected Systems

The National Renewable Energy Laboratory (NREL) developed the world's most widely used computer model to estimate the energy production and energy cost of grid-connected photovoltaic solar energy systems. It can be used for existing or proposed PV solar systems anywhere in the world. This service, and specifically their PVWatts calculator, enables homeowners, small building owners, installers, and others to quickly develop estimates of performance for potential PV solar installations. The calculator can be accessed here: http://pvwatts.nrel.gov

In the UK, Scotland, and Wales, there's a quality solar energy calculator that estimates the income and savings the homeowner can receive from the domestic feed-in tariff scheme, which is available for eligible PV installations of up to 4kWp. The calculator uses the latest tariff rates and is available here: www.energysavingtrust.org.uk/domestic /solar-energy-calculator.

A site for an easy-to-use online solar energy calculator for US and Canadian PV solar customers that computes how many tons of CO_2 emissions any proposed PV solar rooftop system will avoid can be reached through this web address: www.solarenergy .org/solar-calculator.

The following website is for the USA-Canada market, and it provides some useful programs that can calculate the size of the PV solar rooftop you need, as well as system costs. It also helps you determine the government financial incentives you may qualify for.

Here is a link to the calculator in reference:

www.solar-estimate.org/?page=solar-calculator

The following links to solar calculators each enable you to build your own customized calculator to match your particular desired conditions or energy consumption level:

www.findsolar.com/Content/SolarCalculator.aspx (USA–Canada)

www.energymatters.com.au/climate-data (Australia)

www.affordable-solar.com/residential-solar-home/ Residential-Calculator (USA)

The last website above also provides a national map of peak sun hours summarized by state.

Chapter 10 contains information about numerous websites that provide reputable cost savings calculators, which can automatically compute the annual cost savings of your proposed PV solar rooftop system as compared to your future yearly electricity bills if you don't install a solar system.

Finally, it's important to note that the figures generated by online solar calculators should only be used as a rough estimate. Some calculators may not include data on federal, state, or local solar incentives and rebates. Site-specific factors may also influence designs and output that an online calculator would not factor into the computations. A solar contractor will usually be able to provide you with a more accurate estimate.

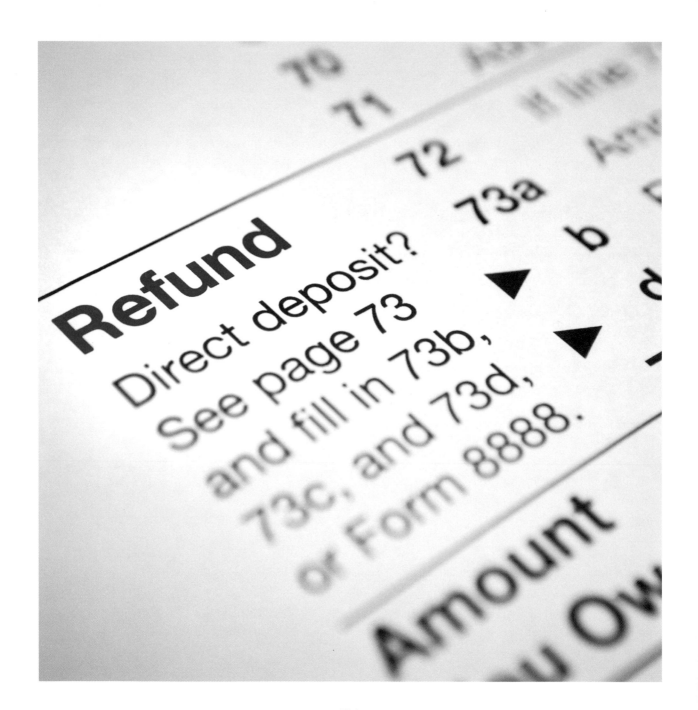

Government Incentives, Rebates, Subsidies, Grants, Tax Credits, and Private Leasing Programs

Government economic incentives will lighten the financial burden. Now that your system is planned, you only need to figure out the financing alternatives and sources for your solar power system. There are also some standard legal issues, mainly to do with permits.

If you live in the United States, we recommend you visit a government organization known as the Database of State Incentives for Renewables & Efficiency (DSIRE) at www.dsireusa.org. This website has an up-to-date database of energy efficiency financial incentives. The United States government currently provides a 30 percent tax credit for eligible costs of your solar array, and you can find more grants, loans, and tax credits by consulting your state or local government. DSIRE also has information on utilities that will buy electricity back from you.

While you're reviewing this material, keep in mind that some incentive programs are exclusive to PV solar systems installed by a certified installer. These aren't available to DIYers who install their system themselves, so be clear on the eligibility requirements of these programs.

Now all you need to do is select a good solar energy installer. Even if you're a handyman type, make sure to hire a licensed electrician for a safety inspection and for helping with wiring challenges. Electricians are licensed and can pull permits with

A very typical PV solar rooftop installation of (2 rows x 6 panels) = 12 poly panels that would qualify for optimal government incentives in most states of the United States.

your local building office. In principle, you can install your system all the way into your breaker box, but it will need inspection. In many jurisdictions, you aren't allowed to install a solar energy system without obtaining the permits required by your local government authority. Local laws may require safety measures, including building permits and compliance with national electrical codes, so be sure these requirements are met before you begin to install your PV system.

Quite often, the greatest challenge is the inability of homeowners to obtain financing for the often-hefty down payment on equipment and installation. In an effort to encourage the adoption of renewable energy systems and support the growth of the solar industry, federal, state, and many municipal governments, as well as some utility companies, offer cash rebates and/or other economic incentives to subsidize the cost of PV solar system installations.

The various incentives can be confusing at the beginning. In general, the most valuable economic incentives are federal tax credits and state and local rebates. I'll summarize each of these programs below, and we'll also discuss lesser-known incentives that may be valuable, especially as more states look for alternatives to up-front rebates.

Many states, municipalities, and utilities offer rebate programs or cash incentives. These rebates usually take the form of a per-watt cash rebate ranging from $1.50/watt to $5.00/watt. For example, a rebate for a 5kW system under a program offering $3/watt would equal $15,000. These cash rebates can offset the cost of a solar installation by as much as 45 percent. Most cash rebate programs have an upper limit to the refund, often set at 5kW, and PV systems bigger than that can only claim a rebate up to the specified limit.

In most locations, as the state's renewable-energy targets are achieved, the available per-watt rebate ceiling may be reduced. That means a state may offer a $4/watt rebate today, but only a $2.50/watt rebate down the road, once a certain number of solar installations have been achieved statewide.

Normally, a finite amount of money is allocated for rebate programs. Due to high demand, the funds are often quickly exhausted. However, once the funds are gone, many programs offer waitlists until the next round of funds is made available. In addition to rebates, tax credits may also be available. At both the federal and state level, laws have been put in place to credit a percentage of the purchase price of a PV solar power system against a solar energy system owner's annual tax bill. A tax credit is more valuable to the taxpayer than an equivalent tax deduction. That's because a credit reduces your taxes dollar-for-dollar, while a deduction only lowers your taxable income before applying the corresponding tax rate that gives your "tax payable" amount.

At the federal level, the Federal Investment Tax Credit entitles owners of both commercial and residential renewable-energy systems to a credit of 30 percent of the net system cost, with no set limit, for all systems placed in service before December 31, 2016. The credit can be carried forward 15 years or back three years. It's unknown if this deadline for federal solar investment tax credits will be extended. A number of states are also offering tax credits equaling a percentage of the installed cost of any PV solar energy system. The percentage varies from state-to-state.

I should note that if a customer receives a rebate, any tax credit is computed on the remaining balance, not the pre-credit total. For example, if the total solar energy system cost is $35,000, and a customer receives a $15,000 rebate, the credit of 30 percent is calculated only on the remaining system cost balance of $20,000, for a total credit of $6,000.

Most states and some municipalities can also provide some sort of property tax exemption for individuals and businesses that install PV solar energy systems. Even though a solar installation will normally increase your property value by tens of thousands of dollars, states that offer a property tax exemption do not increase your tax liability to match your property's new value. This is a nice plus for the homeowner.

Some states offer a 100 percent exemption for the entire value of the system, while others offer a partial exemption (typically 75 percent or some other percentage of the total system's value). Depending on the state, the exemption may apply for one of the following options: 1) the first year of a system's installation; 2) a pre-set term that typically ranges from 10 to 20 years; or 3) for the lifetime of the solar energy system (no time limit). Usually, one of the last two options will apply.

Other states provide an exemption only for the added value of the renewable energy system above the value of a conventional energy system. For example, if a solar energy system costs $25,000 to install and a conventional system costs $14,000, the property tax will be assessed on an increased value of only $11,000.

When filing taxes, a customer may only be able to take full advantage of the exemption if the system was installed and operative throughout the 12-month period preceding December 31st of the tax year. If the system was operative for only some portion of the 12-month period, the exemption will likely be reduced proportionally.

Along with property tax exemption, many states don't collect state sales tax on the cost of renewable energy equipment, which can significantly reduce the upfront costs of a solar installation.

Renewable Energy Credits, or RECs, are certificates issued by the state for the amount of clean solar energy that a grid-tied solar system produces. In some markets, RECs may also be called SRECs (Solar Renewable Energy Credits/Certificates) or Green Tags. Utility companies may purchase RECs from clean power generators as one way to meet the Renewable Portfolio Standards (RPSs) that have been put in place by state legislatures to mandate that utility companies obtain a percentage of their power from renewable sources. In addition, a company such as a manufacturer or coal plant may also buy RECs on the open market as a way to offset the greenhouse gases they emit. The value of a REC on the local market varies by state, and it fluctuates based on supply and demand. The means by which RECs can be sold also vary by state.

As you now know, net metering is the process some utility companies use to keep track of any extra power that a grid-tied solar system produces as well as the amount of power that is fed back into the grid. During the summer months, or during daylight hours, a household or business uses more electricity than during winter or at night. On a hot summer day, therefore, a household PV solar system will likely produce more energy than is required by the home, and on a cold winter night it's likely to use less. In a net metering arrangement, the utility keeps track of energy usage and stores any extra power your solar system generates. During those times when a solar energy system generates more power than is being used, the extra electricity makes the electric meter spin backwards. At the end of the month or the year (depending on the utility company), the customer receives a bill that reflects the net result of what the solar panels produced against the amount of electricity the household or business consumed. With net metering, the annual electricity bill could be, for some installations, as little as $100. In some states, a utility company will not pay the customer if the solar energy system generates more power than is used during the course of a year. In this case, the annual bill will be $0, but all excess power will be donated to the utility company. In other states, utilities will pay for the extra production at various rates. To optimally take advantage of net metering, a solar system

should be sized to meet your home's power requirements in periods or hours of maximum demand.

Having jumpstarted the solar industry in countries like Germany and Spain, feed-in tariff (FiT) schemes were introduced in the US, with states like Vermont and California leading the way. A FiT is an incentive system in which the utility company compensates a person who is generating clean power. Typically the FiT agreement covers a time period of up to 20 years. Under some FiT schemes, a residence or business that installs a grid-tied PV solar system essentially becomes a mini-utility that generates power both for the home and for the grid. Some months the utility company may send the system owner a check that may even be higher than the equivalent amount of the electric bill for that month, or the utility may credit the account each month under the net metering system up to a maximum of the total year's power consumption of the PV system. Some state FiT programs are more short-term and serve as a quick way to increase solar installations and solar power generation. FiT programs in some jurisdictions may be reserved for large-scale installations, and they may exclude residential installations.

For homeowners who haven't saved quite enough money to get started, taking out a loan might be a viable option. Several states and utility companies are leading the way with innovative programs that provide low-interest loans to homeowners and businesses for PV solar installations. In New Jersey, for example, utility company PSE&G recently committed to provide more than $100 million toward the financing of solar system installations over a two-year period. New Jersey and many other states are firmly committed to financially assisting homeowners who wish to invest in a PV solar rooftop system for their home. In California, cities and counties are making loans available to consumers who are then able to repay the loans as part of their property taxes (this scheme is often referred to as the "Berkeley Model" after the city that introduced it: Berkeley, California). Loan balances are transferred to whoever owns the property if it's sold during the course of the loan repayment period.

Before you make the commitment towards a loan, a grant may be available in your area to help fund your project. Unlike loans, grants do not have to be repaid. Some states offer grant funding for residential and commercial properties for the installation of PV solar systems. Typically, grants are awarded on an agreed-upon dollar value per watt up to a maximum, e.g., $1.25/watt up to $10,000.

With so many different types of incentives available and so much variation state-to-state, it's essential for anyone contemplating a solar installation to do his or her homework to ensure that all possible benefits are realized.

Under various schemes, including the California Solar Initiative, individuals and companies can receive cash rebates for electricity provided to the grid from PV systems that are owned outright.

In the case of leased systems, residents of buildings with rooftop PV installed pay a third party leasing company to provide and install the system. The leasing company is also responsible for maintenance. The appeal for a householder of leasing a rooftop PV system is the simplicity of becoming involved in solar power generation and saving money on energy bills without facing the immediate capital outlay associated with installing and running a system by themselves. The benefits to a lease company include receiving the 30 percent tax credit (as long as the program stays in force) as well as receiving renewable energy credits against the amount of electricity generated and carbon dioxide offset of the leased PV solar system.

According to a recent CPI (Climate Policy Initiative) study, the number of leased rooftop PV installations in California compared to the number of total new solar installations grew from 10 percent of all new installations in 2007 to 56 percent of all new installations in 2011, jumping to 75 percent of all new installations in 2012. At present, leasing is allowed in most, but not all, states. In 2015, the state legislatures of Georgia and of South Carolina approved legislation allowing third-party ownership of PV solar systems. Florida and North Carolina are expected to approve similar legislation in late 2016 or 2017.

The solar leasing market in the United States received another positive boost recently with the announcement that global solar panel manufacturer SunPower and Bank of America Merrill Lynch have joined to provide the rooftop PV solar sector with $220 million in financing, which will assist

US homeowners in financing solar power systems through solar leases provided by SunPower. An estimated 50,000 US households have already signed lease agreements under this program, which offers low monthly payments and includes one of the few direct-from-manufacturer performance guarantees for installers.

SolarCity, SunPower, Sungevity, and Solar3D are only a few of the major US PV solar system manufacturers and suppliers of rooftop systems offering leasing packages to homeowners. Of these companies, SolarCity is considered to be the most aggressive group in the PV solar system leasing sector, but SunPower is also very competitive, and the others are expanding their solar system leasing businesses.

In Europe, leasing PV solar rooftop systems has not yet been established because they do not have net metering systems. However, there are a few companies in Germany (including DZ-4) that are developing different business models for PV solar leasing, and many of these companies have initiated pilot projects. Likewise, several large German banks are studying leasing models for PV solar residential systems. These systems in Germany will normally incorporate a PV battery bank storage system. Feed-in tariff programs, on the other hand, have had amazing success in helping solar customers to invest in PV solar systems in Germany and throughout Europe.

CHAPTER 7

Environmental Benefits of PV Solar Systems

Many prospective buyers of a rooftop PV solar system ask: How much harmful CO_2 will we avoid when we go solar? Reliable statistics are available that show how much conventional carbon-based fuel is consumed in the production of a given amount of electricity, measured in kWh. Also, we know how many tons of CO_2 are emitted by the consumption of carbon-based fuels to generate a given amount of electricity, i.e. for every 1 kWh or 1,000 kWh (1 MWh) of power. Therefore, if we know the amount of power consumed by a PV solar system in kilowatt hours or megawatt hours, we can calculate exactly how many tons of CO_2 gas emissions are prevented from entering the atmosphere by virtue of using photovoltaics renewable energy.

To produce 1,000 kWh of electricity, a conventional power plant using carbon-based fuels will produce 0.706 metric tons of CO_2, on average. A photovoltaic solar system will produce the same 1,000 kWh of electricity with zero CO_2 emissions. Therefore, if we know the average daily or monthly electric consumption of a residential PV rooftop system, we can calculate the equivalent of CO_2 emissions that are prevented from entering the atmosphere over a month, a year, 20 years, or a period of any length.

A photovoltaic residential rooftop system of average size may have an installed capacity of 7 kW/h. If this system receives an average of five hours of sunlight per day, this would produce approximately 7kW/h × 5 h/day = 35 kWh/day × 365 days/year = 12,775 kWh/year. Using the above figure of 0.706 metric tons of CO_2 per 1,000 kWh and multiplying that times 12.775 kWh/year would be equivalent to 9.02 metric tons of CO_2 emissions that were prevented from entering the atmosphere over the course of 12 months.

If we take the useful life of the PV system as 25 years, then this system would save the equivalent of between 225 and 270 metric tons of CO_2. When we multiply this by the millions of systems installed globally, it represents a significant contribution to the reduction of global warming.

To contribute this much to saving the environment while at the same time saving money with every monthly electric utility bill is very meaningful to most homeowners. It's a true win-win situation.

CHAPTER 8

Maximize the Benefits from Your PV Solar Energy Rooftop Installation

There can be huge benefits and savings if you install energy-efficient lights and appliances throughout your home before installing solar energy. By doing this you will save money and benefit in two distinct ways.

First, if you're seriously looking at using solar energy in your home, you should know that by replacing existing energy-inefficient systems and appliances with newer, more efficient ones, and by being more conscientious with your electric consumption habits, you can substantially reduce your monthly electricity bills—often by as much as 40 percent. This, in turn, can reduce the size and overall capital cost of any PV solar energy system to be installed in the home by a similar percentage. Conservation will also make the investment in solar energy more effective and reduce your payback period.

You can draw up a useful electrical energy efficiency checklist, as follows:

Refrigerators

Most homes have at least one or two refrigerators. If your model has a manufacture date (found on the name plate on the back of the unit) prior to 2002, chances are it's one of the older, inefficient models, probably consuming about 500 to 750 watts per hour. These units should be traded in for a newer, quieter, more energy efficient model with a rating of 350 watts.

Newer models have additional advantages and new convenience features, such as automatic ice cube makers, auto defrost, useful interior designs, and attractive exterior designs with longer-lasting, more user-friendly door handles. Eventually, the

monthly savings from the electric bills will pay for the cost of the new refrigerator.

Air Conditioners

In many parts of North America and Europe, and in all tropical countries, homes use unsightly window units. These are often older, noisy, and energy inefficient. If not maintained and cleaned properly, some older units will leak water inside the house—a truly annoying situation. By universal convention and industry standards, the power and electric consumption of air conditioners is indicated by the BTU (British Thermal Units) rating. A very small home may use a unit as small as 1,200 BTUs. In larger homes with large rooms, there may be several units as large as 36,000 BTUs. The earlier models—dating from eight to twelve years ago—tend to be inefficient and consume a lot of electricity.

If these older units are recycled and replaced with modern, high-efficiency ceiling units, the resultant savings to the monthly electric bills can be substantial. In addition, large open cracks or spaces around outside windows and doors can result in a lot of unnecessary losses and are easy to fix with rubber or foam-based door- and window-sealer strips.

Turning off the air conditioner when you leave the room can also reduce consumption. Even more savings can be achieved by switching from the

air conditioner to a floor or wall fan at night, when the outside ambient air temperature goes down. Combining these recommendations can make for big reductions to the monthly electric bills, and the savings can be seen within a month or two of making the changes. If you're designing a new home or doing a major renovation, and if the size of your home is large enough, then a modern, high-efficiency central air conditioning unit can be considered. These offer benefits including low electric consumption, even temperature control, less maintenance, and improved aesthetics.

Electric Water Heaters, Electric Clothes Dryers, and Portable Electric Space Heaters

The older models of these appliances are generally not efficient, and their combined electricity consumption often comprises a sizeable portion of the monthly electric bill. Typical power consumption ratings are usually in the following ranges:

Electric Water Heaters: 4,000 to 5,000 watts
Electric Clothes Dryers: 3,000 to 4,000 watts
Electric Space Heaters: 2,000 to 2,500 watts

Adopting the formula for energy consumption calculation on the previous page, and using the lower end of the range for each appliance and a reasonable average household usage time, we get the following energy consumption levels:

Electric Water Heaters: 4,000 W × 3 / 1000 = 12 kWh/day = 4,380 kWh/yr
Electric Clothes Dryers: 3,000 W × 2.5 / 1000 = 7.5 kWh/day = 2,737.5 kWh/yr
Electric Space Heaters: 2,000 W × 8 / 1000 = 16 kWh/day = 5,840 kWh/yr
Total = 12,957.5 kWh/yr

If you pay $0.12/kWh for your electricity, this represents an annual cost of $1,555 per year.

Substantial savings can be achieved by recycling these electric appliances and converting to natural-gas appliances or, where natural gas lines are not available, using large residential propane tanks with small diameter copper tubing.

It is highly recommended to study the advantages of installing a solar rooftop water heating sys-tem instead of using traditional water heaters. Solar thermal water heating systems are the most efficient of all renewable energy systems. Their energy-conversion efficiency (sunlight to heat for hot water) is approximately 75 percent. Compare this to PV solar panels (converting sunlight into electricity) that typically have efficiency factors in the range of 18 percent to 21 percent. As a result, a solar thermal rooftop water-heating system has a very short payback period and will substantially reduce the size of the PV solar system needed for the same residence. The two systems are very compatible, assuming sufficient space is available for both. Usually only three or four hot water collector panels are sufficient for the average home.

Home Lighting Fixtures

Incandescent lighting uses those standard old-fashioned round light bulbs that burn your fingers and have to be replaced frequently. Incandescent lighting is still in widespread use around the world and is an extremely inefficient technology. These fixtures typically convert up to 86 percent to 92 percent of the electric input into heat (a huge loss) and only 8 percent to 14 percent into light. This is very wasteful and easy to remedy by replacing these incandescent fixtures with compact fluorescent lamps, commonly referred to as "CFLs," or—even better—with "Light Emitting Diodes" (LED lighting).

Left: Incandescent; Middle: Compact Fluorescent; Right: LED.

The following chart illustrates the striking differences between the old and the new lighting technologies.

As the table indicates, LED lighting uses far less power (watts) per unit of light generated (lumens). Traditional incandescent bulbs use nine to twelve times more power than LED lights for the same light intensity or lumens rating. LED lighting also substantially lowers electric bills. But there are two other economic advantages. One advantage is that LED lights have an immensely longer useful life than incandescent bulbs and will need replacing far less often, saving the homeowner money and a lot of bother buying new bulbs and changing burnt-out ones. A final advantage: By converting to LED lighting, homeowners who want to install a PV solar rooftop system will need fewer solar panels to power the home's lighting.

When you add up the power savings by using LED lighting and follow the other energy saving recommendations above, you'll not only save money every month by consuming less electricity, you'll also reduce the size of the required PV solar rooftop installation, once again saving a lot of money. And you'll get to enjoy those stylish, attractive new appliances!

There is one other significant advantage to LEDs that is mainly environmental but also has long-term economic benefits for society and the planet as a whole. When you multiply the LED reductions in kWh/year by hundreds of thousands of homes, you'll see that LED lighting can help to

Lighting: Energy Efficiency Cost Comparison Chart

ENERGY EFFICIENCY AND ENERGY COSTS	LIGHT EMITTING DIODES (LEDS)	INCANDESCENT LIGHT BULBS	COMPACT FLUORESCENTS (CFLS)
Life Span (average) Note: Incandescent bulbs have terribly inconsistent quality and can often burn out in 800 hours or less.	50,000 hours	1,200 hours	8,000 hours
Watts of electricity used (LED and CFL equivalent to a 60-watt incandescent bulb).	6-8 watts	60 watts	13-15 watts
Kilowatts of electricity used (30 incandescent bulbs per year or equivalent)	329 kWh/year	3285 kWh/year	767 kWh/year
ANNUAL OPERATING COSTS FOR 30 INCANDESCENT BULBS PER YEAR OR EQUIVALENT			
USA (US$0.12/kWh)	$39.48/year	$394.20/year	$92.04/year
France (US$0.19/kWh)	$62.51/Yr	$624.15/Yr	$145.73/year
UK (US$0.20/kWh)	$65.80/Yr	$657.00/Yr	$153.40/year
Japan (US$0.26/kWh)	$85.54/Yr	$854.10/Yr	$199.42/year
Australia (US$0.29/kWh)	$95.41/Yr	$952.65/Yr	$222.43/year
Spain (US$0.30/kWh)	$98.70/Yr	$985.50/Yr	$230.10/year
Germany (US$0.35/kWh)	$115.15/Yr	$1,149.75/Yr	$268.45/year
Denmark (US$0.41/kWh)	$134.89/Yr	$1,346.85/Yr	$314.47/year

ENERGY EFFICIENCY AND ENERGY COSTS	LIGHT EMITTING DIODES (LEDS)	INCANDESCENT LIGHT BULBS	COMPACT FLUORESCENTS (CFLS)
ENVIRONMENTAL IMPACT			
Contains toxic mercury	No	No	Yes — mercury is very toxic to human health and the environment
Compliant with International Electric Codes and Standards	Yes	Yes	No — contains 1mg-5mg of mercury and is a major risk to the environment
Carbon dioxide emissions (30 bulbs per year)	451 pounds/year (205 kgs)	4500 pounds/year (2,045 kgs)	1051 pounds/year (477.7 kgs)
OTHER IMPORTANT CHARACTERISTICS			
Sensitive to high and low temperatures	No	Somewhat	Yes — may not work under negative 10 degrees Fahrenheit or over 120 degrees Fahrenheit
Sensitive to humidity	No	Somewhat	Yes
Effects of on/off cycling (Switching a CFL on/off quickly, in a closet for instance, may decrease the lifespan of the bulb.)	None	Some	Can reduce lifespan significantly
Light turns on instantly	Yes	Yes	No — takes time to warm up
Durability	Very durable. LEDs can handle jarring and bumping.	Short durability. The glass bulb or the filament can break easily.	Not very durable. Glass can break easily.
Heat emitted	3.4 BTUs/hour	85 BTUs/hour	30 BTUs/hour
Failure modes	Not typical	Some	Yes — may catch on fire, smoke, or omit an odor

continues

ENERGY EFFICIENCY AND ENERGY COSTS	LIGHT EMITTING DIODES (LEDS)	INCANDESCENT LIGHT BULBS	COMPACT FLUORESCENTS (CFLS)
LIGHT OUTPUT			
Lumens	Watts	Watts	Watts
450	4-5	40	9-13
800	6-8	60	13-15
1,100	9-13	75	18-25
1,600	16-20	100	23-30
2,600	25-28	150	30-55

reduce greenhouse gas emissions from power plants due to a corresponding decrease in the carbon-based fossil fuels needed to power the residences that convert from incandescent lighting to LED lighting.

In the case of the United States, where electricity costs average about $0.12/kWh, the conversion of 60 incandescent 60W bulbs (or 36 100W bulbs) to LED lighting alone could save the residents of a single home about $722 per year plus the savings in purchases of replacements for burnt-out bulbs—let's say $150/year—for an overall per-home savings of $872/year. If we multiply this by the minimum life of a PV solar rooftop system—25 years—this would be a total savings of $21,800 and this is only for the lighting!

T-12 fluorescent lamps (the old 1 1/2-inch diameter tubes)

This is really old technology—from the 1940s and '50s—but there are still lots of these lighting fixtures around. They should be replaced by the newer generation of T-8 (1-inch diameter) and T-5 (5/8-inch diameter) fluorescent fixtures, which use a more efficient ballast design and have a higher operating fre-

in two variations: ultrasonic sensors and passive infrared sensors. Occupancy sensor lights receive a signal whenever a person moves into the predetermined conical space, set at a convenient diameter where the light strikes the floor. As long as there is someone moving in this space, the light will remain on. When there is no motion, the occupancy sensor light will turn off the light following a predetermined time interval that can be preset by the customer, usually with four time interval options. These controllers are suitable in kitchens, laundry

quency. They're more energy efficient, less obtrusive, and more modern looking, and they give off better light by using an improved coating on the inside of the tube. Care must be taken to recycle or dispose properly of the old fixtures and T-12 lamps.

Automatic Light Controllers and Dimmers

As lights are so easily left on when not in use, it's wise to install timer switches or occupancy sensors to overcome the "forget-to-switch-off" syndrome. After a light is switched on, a timer switch will automatically turn off the light after a set time interval. The best applications are for areas where the light is needed for a short time only, such as in closets, hallways, stairwells, and garages.

Occupancy sensor light controllers are available

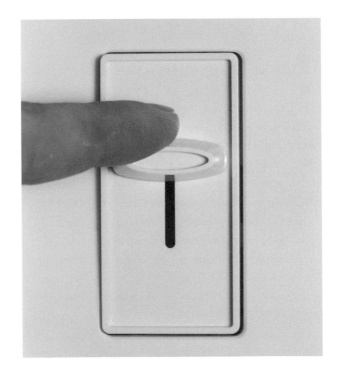

areas, garages, workshops, and porches. They aren't recommended where there's a lot of movement by pets. Also, they aren't convenient where a person might be immobile for relatively long periods, as the inactivity will cause the sensor to turn off the light. Ultrasonic or dual-sensor type controllers are often used in bathrooms and bedrooms.

The original generation of CFLs could generally not be used in conjunction with dimmers, but the new generation of CFLs has overcome this limitation. Dimmers can save electricity as well as creating a calm atmosphere or romantic mood, when desired.

Double-Pane Windows

If you're designing a new home or doing major renovations to an older one, you'll want to consider installing double-pane windows throughout the house. For both heating and cooling, the extra insulation provided by these windows is a good investment and can produce substantial energy savings, which will positively affect your monthly electric bills while providing more even heat control and more effective and comfortable cooling.

Insulation

Many homes are built with improper or insufficient insulation, especially older homes. By having an insulation contractor inject granular insulation in the spaces between the inside and outside walls, you can substantially reduce your heating and cooling costs. These spaces are easily accessible to the contractor through the attic. The attic itself should also be inspected, to ensure that it's properly insulated with fiberglass packs that fit between the joists of the ceilings.

Weather Stripping

Installing weather stripping is an overlooked but simple way to prevent or reduce heat and cooling losses that might be costing you a lot more than you would guess. Oftentimes, the weather stripping on the bottom of a door gets damaged or torn off and not replaced.

Location and Use of Windows for Optimal Natural Ventilation

If you're building or planning to build a house, study the location of all the windows—maybe in consultation with your architect or building contractor—to see if you can relocate any windows to achieve better natural ventilation in the summer months.

Some other easy energy saving recommendations to consider include installing a low-flow showerhead and taking shorter showers to conserve both electricity and water. You can also lower the temperature setting of your water heater while waiting to replace it with a solar thermal water heating system and insulate all your exposed hot water pipes to reduce heat losses. Motivate your family to commit to being conscientious about turning off lights, appliances, and electronics when they're not in use. After you and your family put these commitments to practice, look over your monthly electric bills

together to see the positive results you've all been working toward.

By incorporating these recommendations, you'll benefit in the short-term by reducing the size of the PV solar rooftop system you install as well as the capital investment needed to install it. You'll also benefit in the long-term through savings on monthly electric bills and winter heating bills.

CHAPTER 9

Where to Find Professionally Certified Solar Installers in Your Area

If you're planning to install a PV solar rooftop system for your home, you'll want to know what your options are. If you've already decided to hire a solar systems installer-contractor, or even just a "solar system coach," then you can go online and visit the NABCEP website (details below).

First and foremost, double-check that the prospective solar PV installer has received training and a professional certification to prove their knowledge and competence. Many states require solar contractors to meet some type of licensing requirements. If your state isn't one of those, you'll need to confirm your contractor's credentials yourself to ensure a job well done. The most acceptable seal of approval comes from the North American Board of Certified Energy Professionals (NABCEP), which now certifies solar PV installers across the USA.

You can use the NABCEP website (www.nabcep .org/certified-installer-locator) to find profession-

als in your area who have received their certification. Many states now require that you use an NABCEP-certified installer in order to participate in any incentive programs. Here's the website of the NABCEP, where you can locate solar installers in most cities in the USA: www.nabcep.org /certification/pv-installer-certification.

If you're not able to find an installer with an NABCEP certification, you can look for other certifications to guarantee the professional installation of your solar electric system. Many states require that a licensed electrician be on your installation team. Not all licensed electricians are familiar with PV systems, so ask if they have received solar-specific training and/or possess experience installing solar systems. Any good professional installer or electrician should be happy to provide you with references from a couple previous customers. While you're at it, you might ask whether the potential installer has received formal training installing the particular brand of solar equipment you plan to buy. Many manufacturers offer continuing education to solar installers to ensure that they're familiar with all the features and intricacies of their unique systems and updates to their technology. Here are some guiding questions you can ask when contacting the provided references:

- How long did it take to complete the installation, from initial site visit through to the completion of the project?
- Were there any challenges involved in the installation of the solar system? If so, how did the installer cope with these challenges?
- How has the system performed since it was installed? Has it met expectations for efficiency and good service?
- How have any requests for maintenance been handled by the installer? Did it take long for the installer to respond and was the maintenance service satisfactory?

Solar Power World is one of the solar industry's leading sources of information for solar technology, developments, and installation news. This organization recently published a list of the leading 250 solar contractors in the USA. The list ranks companies according to the volume of PV systems they have installed in the residential and commercial solar energy markets. Residential installations are listed separately. This resource may provide you with some useful contacts: www.solarpowerworldonline.com /top-250-solar-contractors.

Your state will have a contractor's licensing board, through which you can verify the credentials of the potential solar PV installer. I strongly recommend you contact them before signing any contracts, as the board should be able to alert you to any serious complaints received against a specific installer. Finally, be sure to verify the presence of sufficient liability insurance by asking to see your contractor's insurance papers.

Having an installer who is up-to-date on all of the latest advances in the ever-evolving world of solar photovoltaics is a major plus. The PV solar industry sees new technologies for improving efficiencies and boosting performance on almost a monthly basis. The more current your installer's knowledge is, the more likely he'll be able to provide the highest-efficiency system for your unique situation, while averting any potential problems.

In many cases, experience will be just as important as formal training. Since structured certification and training programs are just now becoming conventional, there are many installers who have been apprenticed into their current positions, and their experience can be highly valuable. Here are some of

the queries you should consider to see whether your prospective installer's company is well-seasoned:

- Does the company have experience with both grid-tied and off-grid systems?
- How long has the company been in business, and how many solar energy installations have they completed? Installers who have completed a large number of installations over many years will have ample experience to ensure you get good results.
- Determine whether the company has both commercial and residential experience.
- Ask the installer to describe their last installation. Was it recent or some time ago?
- What types of add-on technologies have the company installed to improve monitoring and system efficiency?

Long-term customer service is of paramount importance when choosing a solar installer. Your final query for any solar installer should have to do with how they will treat you over the long term. In all likelihood, you should consider choosing an installer with warranties and service agreements that will make your solar installation a hassle-free investment over the life of the system.

If your solar products don't come with their own warranties from the manufacturer, you should ask whether the installer will warranty the equipment. Whether the warranty comes from the manufacturer or the installer, you should try to obtain coverage for the greatest number of conditions over the longest possible time to make sure you're not left with any bills for repairs to a non-functioning or defective system.

Figuring out what exactly is included in the service agreement offered by a solar installer can be tricky, especially if the agreement is full of legal terminology and technical information. Here are a few contractual questions to ask your proposed solar contractor:

- For how many years will service be provided after the installation?
- Are the installers certified to provide maintenance to a PV solar rooftop system?
- Will you receive any training from the installer on how to maintain your solar system for maximum energy production?
- Will a yearly check-up be performed on your system to determine whether it's performing as expected?
- Are web-based monitoring systems available to track the system's performance?
- What types of repairs and replacements does the service agreement cover?
- Does the service agreement state a guaranteed maximum length of time between a service request and the service call?
- What happens when the equipment doesn't perform as efficiently as promised? Are adjustments to improve efficiency included in the service agreement?

- Once the service agreement expires, how much will the installer charge you for repairs or service? Is it based on the cost of the new parts used plus an hourly rate?

As with all other inquiries during your evaluation of potential installers, the answers you receive from any major equipment vendors (for PV modules, inverters, etc.) will also give you a clear idea of how you'll be treated as a customer over the long-term. Once you've asked all of your questions and determined that you've found the right installer, get the installer's commitments in writing so you receive exactly the service you've been promised.

Lastly, if a relatively large photovoltaic system will be installed on your roof, you might want to hire a licensed roofer to calculate the stress the proposed new system will place on your home's structure. It's important to determine whether the load will be within safety tolerances. The size and type of your home PV system will determine the weight of the installation and will play a significant role in determining how to safely and securely fasten the equipment and support hardware to the roof surface.

Photographic Step-by-Step Guide on How to Install a Complete PV Solar Rooftop System

Now we are ready to commence our picture guide detailed in a step-by-step tour of a PV solar rooftop system installation. For the reader's convenience, the entire illustrated process is divided into four general "Photo Groups" and each "Group" is divided into several "Steps." Each "Step" is further divided into several photos, all in chronological order of the installation process.

Site Evaluations

STEP 1. EVALUATING THE ELECTRIC SERVICE LOCATION

1. In the photo, we can see the installer has located the main service panel and in this instance we can see that he is in the process of installing a combination PV meter/main service panel.

2. This photo shows the inside of the main service panel being installed and integrated with the utility meter. The installer is about to install as many internal circuit breakers as the home may require. Most will be 120V breakers but a few will be 220 to 240V breakers for certain appliances, such as the electric water heater.

3. This photo shows the large label that contains all the specifications of the main panel. You will find this label affixed inside the main service panel door.

4. This photo is a close-up of the main breaker inside the main service panel. Notice that the switch is labeled with the overall amperage of the panel—in this case, 200 amps. In terms of electrical infrastructure, this is a fairly large home.

5. This photo shows the site evaluator removing the face plate of the main service panel. Since this is a new installation, he is in the process of inspecting the main panel to see that all connections are secured and tight.

STEP 2: EVALUATE THE STRUCTURAL CAPACITY

6. In the photo, the installer is measuring the sub-roof structural beams. We can see by the tape measure that the width of these beams is a standard 9 inches, which is sometimes quoted as 10 inches.

7. In this photo, the installer is measuring the spacing between structural members. In this case it is a standard 16 inches between centers. With these two measurements we can easily find the load bearing capacity of this roof per square foot. To determine the load limits for specified open areas, we also need the length of the open beams between vertical supports. Standard load bearing tables will give us the answers. The lumber supply depot supplies tables with this load bearing information.

8. The information in this photo, namely the data printed on the side of the main beam, provides us with the basic truss identification and the manufacturer or the supplier/distributor can supply the load bearing tables.

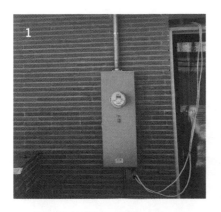

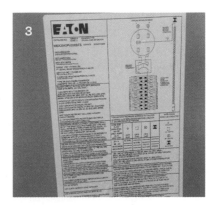

STEP 3: EVALUATE THE SHADING

9. In the photo to the right, we can see the site evaluator is taking solmetric readings to determine the level of solar access. This is the key number for calculating the average seasonal solar production that can be expected from each PV module and from the total array.

   You do not have to possess a solmetric measuring device. As explained in detail in subsection 5.6, you can obtain the insolation or irradiation index number for your precise location from the table provided, and also from the website identified in the same subsection. We explain how to use this irradiation index number, which gives you the average number of "sun hours" (summer average, winter average, and yearly average) for practically any location in North America.

STEP 4: MEASURE ROOF SURFACES

10. In the photo to the right, we see the DIY installer is taking accurate measurements of the roof surface to calculate a simple plan for a potential layout for the PV array.

11. In the photo to the right, we see the DIY installer is taking and recording careful measurements from the edge of the roof to all the built-in roof obstructions. These measurements will enable the installer to prepare a drawing with an optimal and accurate layout for the panel array.

Prepare the Roof for Mounting the Solar Panels

STEP 1: CHOOSE A GENERAL LAYOUT FOR THE SELECTED NUMBER OF PANELS

The objective here is to avoid shading onto the PV panels from nearby trees or other rooftop structures (chimneys, satellite dishes, etc.).

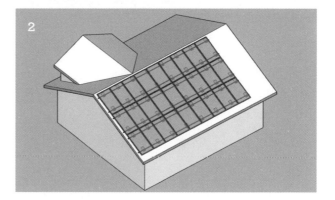

1. This is a frame taken from a simple 3-D modeling software that enables the homeowner to evaluate the effects from possible shading on the roof surfaces at different times of the year caused by nearby trees, other buildings, chimneys, satellite dishes, and other roof structures. This can be very useful for choosing a general layout and configuration for how you will eventually mount your solar array.

2. The image here is a 3-D rendering of the solar array as it is proposed to be mounted of the south slope of the roof. It is prepared on a user-friendly software that allows the homeowner to get a bird's eye view of what a 27 module array would look like in different configurations on the rooftop before deciding on a final layout configuration. Spacing can easily be adjusted to allow for a chimney or other obstruction as may be required.

3. In the image on the next page, our DIY solar coach has prepared an interactive graphic that enables the homeowner to experiment with alternative layouts for the array. In this example, there are a total of 27 modules divided into two strings, or groups, one string of 13 modules at the lower section of the roof and the other string of 14 modules fits into the space immediately above the lower 13 PV panels. The model indicates the positioning of the rail supports under the array of modules. It also displays the location of the junction box (lower right) and conduit that will contain the DC wiring of the modules ("homeruns") and channel

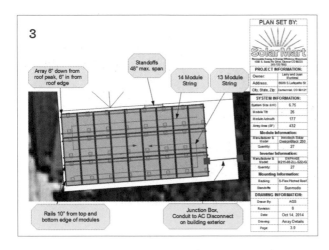

the wiring safely from above the roof and down through the roof to the AC disconnect switch located below on the side of the house under the eaves trough.

STEP 2: SELECTING A SUITABLE ANGLE AGAINST THE HORIZONTAL FOR THE PANEL MOUNTING SUPPORT FRAMES

4. In the photo, we see the DIY installer is in the process of choosing the best angle against the horizontal to enable the solar modules to optimize energy production. He does this by adjusting the height of the 3 vertical supports (that are each fixed at the bottom end of each support) to a fixed steel flashing bolted into one of the roof joists with lag bolts (see close-up photos below) and the flashing is fitted topside, above the shingles, with a mounting bracket that attaches to the vertical support. The same vertical support at the top end is attached to a long horizontal support tube and this tube is attached to the upper section of the 4 PV panels. Your solar contractor or installer will supply all of the specified items of the support hardware required by your PV panel supplier, if you are using one.

The small array above of 4 modules may be additional to modules installed on the other side of the roof to increase total system production, or, on the other hand, the main array might be mounted on this side to avoid a shading problem on the other side.

5. In this photo, the installer has mounted the PV panels in an array on a plane parallel to (or flush with) the surface of the roof. Even if the flush mount does not give the optimum tilt angle, it is often used for ease of installation and aesthetic reasons. Lowering the tilt angle below the optimum angle will result in very minor energy losses. (See details in Chapter 5.) In the lower right-hand corner of the photo we can see the location where the homeowner decided to install the central inverter, disconnect switches, main distribution panel, metering device, etc. This is apparently at the back of the house beside the living room windows. If you look closely you will also see the sky is partially overcast with sunshine at the top of the hill behind the house but with shade on the PV panels. So at this particular moment, we can assume that the PV solar rooftop system is not generating any power.

STEP 3: CHOOSE THE BEST AVAILABLE AZIMUTH EAST–WEST ANGLE FOR MOUNTING THE PV PANELS

6. In this photo, the DIY installer has just laid out the parallel markings (red lines) for the panel support mountings. The yellow 90-degree markings indicate the corners of a two-module group. The yellow circles indicate the drill points where the lag screws will attach the steel flashing mounts to the roof joists just below the shingles. The exact location of the joists is revealed to

the installer with the use of a quality electronic handheld stud-finder with the depth reading adjustment button set at maximum depth. This instrument is not expensive and it is accurate and reliable. The DIY installer will definitely want to buy one if he doesn't already own one.

7. In the photo, the installer is drilling a pilot hole for the flashing. The procedure to determine the exact locations for the drill holes and lag bolts is explained in detail in the subsection of the previous photo. For this job, if you are a DIY installer, you will need a good quality 1/2 HP portable electric drill with a spare rechargeable battery and a good set of drill bits if you don't already own these items.

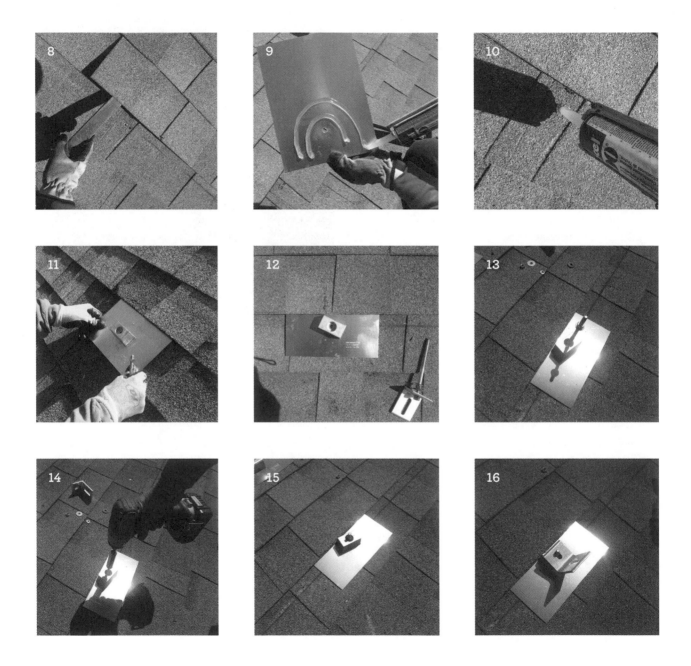

STEP 4: PREPARING THE LAYOUT FOR THE PANEL SUPPORT FRAMEWORK

8. In the photo, the installer is prying up a shingle where the steel flashing will be inserted between shingles and secured with a lag bolt to a roof joist below the shingles to hold the mounting framework.

9. In the photo, we see the installer applying a clear silicon sealant in a double semicircle fashion to the back of the steel flashing. The sealant semicircles will be pointed downward when the flashing is in final position and this way water leakage through the roof at the point of the lag bolt is prevented.

STEP 5: HOW MOUNTING SUPPORT HARDWARE SECURES THE PANEL FRAMEWORK TO THE ROOF

10. In the photo, the installer is applying the sealant to the pilot hole. This is a backup precaution in addition to the sealant applied to the underside of the steel flashing to prevent rainwater from getting into the hole. The hole in the center of the flashing will then be lined up with the pilot hole as shown in the following photo.

11. In the photo, we can see the DIY installer is fitting the steel flashing with a mounting bracket between the shingles as indicated by the red markings.

12. In the photo, we can see the installer has inserted the steel flashing into position between the shingles.

13. In the photo, we see the installer has positioned the lag screw ready to be screwed into the roof support framework joists immediately below the shingles. Drill holes are positioned with the use of a good quality "stud finder." The details of this procedure are discussed in the subsection of the photo above.

14. In the photo, our DIY installer is in the process of installing a lag screw into the roof support beam below the shingle. The lag screw will provide strength to the support framework rails that will be attached to one or several solar modules. (See additional photos below.)

15. In the photo, we can see one of the flashings that has just been installed.

16. In the photo, the installer has just prepared the steel support bracket for drilling through the flashing to the roof joist below. The joists below the shingles can be precisely located with a good quality large depth stud-finder.

17. In this photo, we can see the DIY installer is midway through installing one of the steel support brackets. Vertical supports will then be attached to a horizontal support railing. In this way, all the vertical supports will connect the horizontal railing to all the support brackets as illustrated in the photos below.

18. In the photo, we see the installer has just finished installing the steel support bracket on top of the steel flashing in line with the same red marking that lines up with the support brackets on either side of this one. This is how the vertical supports will align properly with the horizontal railings. Each PV solar module is attached with fittings called end-clamps or mid-clamps (see close-up photos below) to 2 horizontal railings, one about 20 centimeters from the top of the module and the other also at 20 centimeters from the bottom of the module. This means that each module or panel is attached firmly at 4 points around the outside of the panel to hold the panel tightly and securely, even in high wind conditions.

STEP 6: HOW THE PANEL MOUNTING FRAMEWORK ATTACHES TO THE SOLAR PANELS

19. In this photo, our DIY installer has just attached the support hardware (90 degree steel bracket) to the roof on top of the steel flashing with a steel spacer and he bolted the bracket onto the lower horizontal railing of the mounting frame support. The 2 horizontal railings (upper and lower) will provide the mounting support framework for the solar panels.

20. End-Clamp
A close-up photo of an "end-clamp." Two end-clamps attach the outside edge of one of the PV modules to the support railing. Usually there are 2 or sometimes 3 rows of modules in an array, so this means there would normally be 4 or 6 end-clamps on the same railing on the left and the same number of end-clamps on the right where the array ends.

21. Mid-Clamp
The other fitting shows a close-up photo of a "mid-clamp." There are usually 2 mid-clamps on the left and right of every module except for modules that are on the outside of the array, since the outside edge will be secured to the support railings logically with end-clamps, not mid-clamps.
    We recommend that the DIYer purchase a few extra end-clamps and mid-clamps because a worker might accidentally kick one or two clamps

lying on the roof into the garden and they won't be easily found. A little precaution here may save a lot of time not having to stop work to go to the suppliers shop to buy more clamps.

22. In the photo, the installer and his assistant are installing 2 end-clamps on the horizontal support railings, getting ready to secure an outside PV module.

23. In the photo on the next page, our DIY installer is using an open-end wrench to tighten up one of the 2 end-clamps (upper and lower), which will

attach the PV panel outer frame to the horizontal support railing.

Also, in the photo, we can see that this PV installation is using monocrystalline silicon PV modules as opposed to polycrystalline silicon modules. The differences in appearance and performance and the various pros and cons of these two types of modules are discussed and illustrated in Chapter 1.

24. In the photo on the next page, the DIY installer has captured a good close-up shot of exactly how an end-clamp is attached to the support

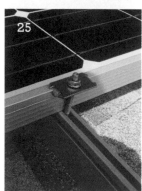

railing below and how the clamp secures the solar panel above to the support railing.

25. In the photo, we can see that the DIYer has installed one of 2 mid-clamps, getting ready to install the next panel parallel to the panel already installed.

26. In the photo, the installer is using a standard open-end wrench to tighten 2 mid-clamps holding in place 2 modules in perfect parallel position to one another.

STEP 7: WIRING THE ARRAY THROUGH THE ROOF TO THE ELECTRICAL COMPONENTS

27. In the photo, the installer has just connected the wires (homeruns) from the PV panels together and he is feeding them down through the shingles of the roof through a waterproof steel and rubber fixture called a "weather-head."

    The homeruns are then connected to a DC disconnect switch and then to the DC/AC inverter installed on the outside of the house in the electrical equipment area. More details are provided in photo groups 3 and 4.

Mounting the Solar Panels

STEP 1: HOW TO GET THE PV PANELS SAFELY UP ON THE ROOF

1. In the photo, the DIY homeowner and his assistant are manually uploading a solar panel from the man on the ladder (there is another helper at the bottom of the ladder). In this manner, each PV module can be safely and manually transferred from the ground level or the driveway up to the roof.

2. In the photo, the DIY installer's assistants are helping the delivery truck and crane to unload the solar PV modules and rails at the job site. These workers should be wearing construction hard hats and for safety should avoid standing directly under the load.

3. In the photo, we see the DIY installer and his crew guiding the crane driver and unloading the PV module packages onto the roof from the truck below. Notice that the horizontal support railings have already been installed and provide a bracing to prevent the module packages from sliding down or falling to the ground. A precautionary note: Be careful not to unload your module bundles in an unsafe position or on a dangerous slope of the roof where they might slide down and get damaged.

   This is a fairly large installation but for

smaller systems, the installer and his crew will often manually raise the PV modules up to the roof one by one using a ladder.

STEP 2: SAFETY PRECAUTIONS

4. In the photo, we see one of the installer crew using the recommended safety harness with a safety rope firmly attached at the peak of the roof. When handling fragile, heavy loads, you must always think "safety first." Not only for the safety of the PV glass and aluminum modules, but also for the safety of yourself (if you are a DIY installer) and for the whole installation crew.

5. In the photo, we can see that the DIYer is using an insulated fiberglass ladder that provides another measure of safety. Standard aluminum ladders are not recommended since they can act as electrical conductors. Once again, think "safety first!"

6. The photo demonstrates the kind of steel-toed standard safety boot recommended to be worn at the job site by all members of the installation crew.

STEP 3: INSTALLING PV PANELS TO SUPPORT THE FRAME

7. In the photo, the DIY installer and his assistant are in the process of installing the first PV module after they have installed the horizontal support rails. You will observe that the installer is not wearing his safety harness, a common lazy habit we recommend you avoid. "Safety first" should always be the number one rule for crews working on rooftops.

8. In the photo, we can see the DIY installation crew is in the process of installing the first PV module of the array on the bottom right hand corner of the roof. An observant reader may notice that the horizontal support railings are installed parallel with the bottom edge of the roof and that they are also secured equidistant from both the top and bottom edge of the module. When firmly installed, this mounting arrangement gives optimum strength for the modules to resist high wind conditions without damage.

9. In the photo, the DIY installer has selected the approximate position for installing the end module at the opposite end of the bottom row of the array.

10. In the photo, we can see that the install crew is getting ready to attach a "tension string marker" for the purpose of aligning the bottom

row of modules. This process is continued in the next photo.

11. Here, in the photo, we can see the installer has tightened the alignment string marker the entire length of the bottom row, which will facilitate aligning all the panels in the bottom row to be parallel with the edge of the roof and parallel with each other.

12. In the photo, we can see that the install crew has progressed and is now lining up and installing module (approximately) number 9, working from right to left. By taking extra care in the proper alignment of the bottom row of PV modules, the DIY installer is ensuring that the second and third rows will also be perfectly aligned and this will give an attractive finish to the final array that would make any home-owner proud of his PV solar system.

STEP 4: CONNECTING THE PV PANELS (MODULES)

13. The photo is a close-up shot of a female connector used to interconnect the modules together. These are used with quick-connect male connectors (as shown in the following two photos).

14. In the photo, we can see that the install crew has just mounted an upper railing to which

they are attaching the PV DC conductor wires or homeruns between the modules. These wires are secured to the railing with plastic tensor strips to resist high winds and will not be visible after the modules are installed, but the male–female connections will remain accessible for service if needed.

15. This close-up photo shows a male and female connection that have been attached to one another and this line is labeled as part of "string 1" that includes the 13 modules of the bottom row shown in the photos above.

16. The photo shows how the cables or leads arrive from the manufacturer, carefully taped to the back of the panel so they're easy to free up when the installer is ready to interconnect

the modules into a "string." It appears that our DIY installer is about to install and connect this PV panel.

STEP 5: HOW SOLAR PANELS ARE WIRED TOGETHER

17. The photo shows the DIY homeowner or his helper in the midst of wiring the first 3 PV modules of the bottom row of the array.

18. As shown here, it can be a bit of a tight fit to make the final connection between the leads of adjacent PV modules but the mounting support frames are engineered to allow a normal size person or worker to reach under the modules and complete the task of wiring the system.

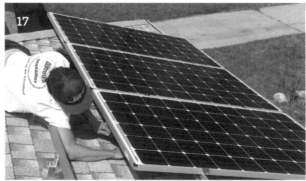

Installing the Electrical Components and Controls

STEP 1: INSTALLING THE CONDUIT FROM THE ARRAY

1. This is a close-up photo showing how the installer has just attached a junction box at the end of a string of PV modules (the array). The junction box simply unites several PV production wires or homeruns from the modules and combines them to run through the Electrical Metal Tubing (EMT) commonly referred to as the conduit, which then passes through a waterproof fitting from above the roof to below the roof where the wires will be connected to the electrical controls in the equipment area.

2. The photo is taken from the other side of the junction box and it shows how the DIY installer can use the conduit and a 90-degree conduit fitting to penetrate the roof. Notice the use of silicon to weatherproof the holes. The alternative is to feed the homeruns directly through a weather-head.

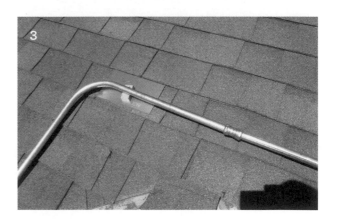

3. The photo shows how the DIY-install crew makes a 90-degree bend in the conduit tubing without the need to connect or disconnect interior wires. This part of the conduit is held in place by a steel flashing, clamp, and lag bolt.

4. In the photo, we can see the DIY-install crew is attaching the conduit to a flashing with a lag bolt, spacer, and clamp.

STEP 2: INSTALL DC DISCONNECT SWITCH BEFORE THE CENTRAL INVERTER

5. The photo shows a DC disconnect switch installed after the PV panels and just before the central inverter. When activated, this switch will isolate the solar modules when the inverter needs inspection or servicing, or for adding additional modules or other modifications to the system.

6. The photo shows the inside of the DC disconnect switch box. This switch is ready to be installed between the array modules and the central inverter.

7. In the photo, the DIY installer has just connected and wired a DC disconnect switch under the "Sunny Boy" central inverter.

8. In the photo, we see that the installer has removed the cover plate from the DC disconnect switch and we can see all of the wiring including the 4 (black) leads from the conduit coming from the module string. At the top of the switch box, we can see the red wires leading into the central inverter.

9. The photo is a good close-up of the 4 black wire homeruns entering through the conduit into the box and attached to the 4 green terminals of the DC disconnect switch. A standard good quality straight-blade small screwdriver is used to supply sufficient torque to fasten the homeruns.

STEP 3: INSTALL THE CENTRAL INVERTER

10. In the photo, the installer has just attached an inverter attachment fixture to the wall with an easy disconnect bracket in order to detach the central inverter for service.

11. In the photo, the inverter is hung on the wall attachment bracket but has not yet been wired.

STEP 4: INSTALL MICRO-INVERTERS (ALTERNATIVE TO A CENTRAL INVERTER)

Micro-inverters are an excellent alternative to central inverters. The basic differences as well as the advantages and disadvantages of each type of inverter are explained in detail in Chapter 4.

12. This is a close-up photo of a standard Enphase 215 watt micro-inverter being attached to the upper railing before installing the correspond-

ing PV module. This system is being installed with micro-inverters instead of a central inverter. Micro-inverters have been experiencing considerable success since their introduction into the market a few years ago. They have significant technological advantage (among other advantages) over central inverters and these advantages are explained in considerable detail in Chapter 4.

13. The photo shows a small micro-inverter with its 2 leads ready for connection. When micro-inverters are incorporated into each PV panels, you can find them installed on the backside of each module along the upper edge right-hand corner and they are not visible after installation from the side or from above.

STEP 5: INSTALL AC COMBINER PANEL AND AC DISCONNECT SWITCH

14. In the photo, several electrical devices are being connected in series, including: (L to R) the main service panel, the AC disconnect switch (this is separate from the DC disconnect switch), the photovoltaic system production meter, and the AC combiner panel.

15. The photo shows a close-up shot of the inside of the AC combiner panel with the wiring coming from the PV production meter (through the conduit at the bottom left side of the photo) and, after being combined in the box, the wiring carrying the current exits through the other conduit on the lower right side.

16. This photo shows the AC combiner panel all wired up with its face plate attached.

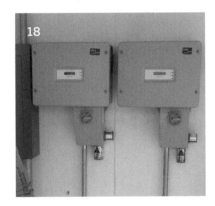

17. The photo shows an AC disconnect switch in the process of being installed.

STEP 6: INSTALL ELECTRICAL GUTTER BOX

18. The photo shows how the DIY installer crew has just installed an electrical gutter box that combines the output AC lines from the 2 inverters above.

STEP 7: INSTALL UTILITY NET METER

19. The photo shows the next step of the installation, which is the utility net meter. This meter charges the house account with the electricity consumed as received from the utility but it also credits the same account with any excess electricity generated from the PV system that is not used by the home; rather, it is fed back into the grid. The sum

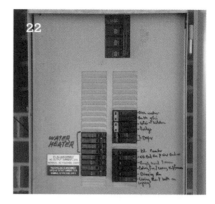

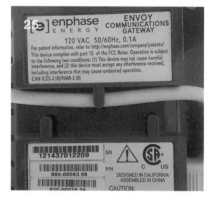

of these credits during the month can reduce your net electric utility bill significantly.

STEP 8: INSTALL THE UTILITY NET METER AND THE PV PRODUCTION METER IN A SEPARATE BOX

20. The above photo shows a large panel combining a utility meter with the main service panel. They can be together in the same panel but are often installed separately. The PV production meter (a separate meter) is then connected to the main service panel.

21. The above photo shows a close-up shot of a house waiting to be fitted with a photovoltaic production meter.

STEP 9: INSTALL HOME MAIN SERVICE PANEL AND PV BREAKER SWITCHES

22. The above photo shows that the DIY installer is beginning to install the main service panel and we can see he has started to label some breakers for easy identification of circuits when anyone is inspecting or servicing the main panel. The hand-written labeling identifies which breakers control which circuits or appliances.

23. The above photo shows how the installer has used two different breakers to connect to two separate PV circuits. For example, and for conve-nience, one breaker might control the lighting of a certain area of the house and the other breaker might protect specific appliances that need elec-tric backup in the event of a grid blackout.

STEP 10: INSTALL SURGE PROTECTOR

24. This is a close-up photo of a panel that has just had a surge protector installed.

STEP 11: INSTALL MONITORING DEVICE (OPTIONAL BUT RECOMMENDED)

25. In the above photo, we see the DIY-install crew has installed a final optional device known as a "monitoring gateway." This device will per-mit the homeowner and any service personnel to monitor the production performance of all the individual PV modules in the system and can help locate any defects that might need attention.

STEP 12: HOW IT ALL FITS TOGETHER

26. The above photo shows a relatively simple sys-tem where we can see the equipment area with the PV system equipment items installed. From left to right, the DIY-install crew has installed in series the DC disconnect switch that is con-nected directly into the bottom left of a cen-tral inverter; the inverter is then connected to the AC disconnect switch and then to the PV

production meter and then it is connected to a combined utility net meter and the main service panel. Note that the PV production meter housing is installed with conduits and wires but the PV meter has not yet been installed.

27. The photo shows a second system that is slightly larger than the system shown in the previous photo because it has two central inverters instead of one.

28. The photo shows the setup of the equipment area of a third, relatively simple PV solar system. Most of the same equipment items in the previous two systems are repeated here with only a few exceptions, but in this installation the current will flow from right to left.

CHAPTER 11

Conclusions and Suggestions

I trust that this book has helped demystify some of the vague unknowns and confusing propaganda about PV solar energy systems, and that it has shown you the basics of planning and properly installing an efficient PV solar rooftop system.

You've seen the layout of a system from the rooftop panels to the grid, and now you understand what components you'll need to buy and how to make intelligent decisions about choosing the optimal type and number of PV modules, selecting the best type of inverter for your system, and deciding on the type of mounting support system and how to determine the best layout of the PV panels for your particular roof.

Whether your goal is to save a lot of money on your electric bills, to generate your own clean energy, to increase the appraised value of your home, or all of the above, then investing in a PV solar rooftop electric system is a wise decision. Even a relatively small solar electric system can produce reliable, economical, pollution-free energy for your home.

A PV solar system that can provide 100 percent of your total consumption requirements might seem appealing, but it may not be financially feasible for your budget. Or it may not be practical due to space limitations on your rooftop. As a general rule, about 100 square feet (equivalent to five solar panels) will generate roughly one kilowatt per hour (kW/h) of electricity, but only when the sun is high and perpendicular to the panels. Most residential solar electric systems require at least 100 to 200 square feet (for small "starter" systems), and up to 1,000 square feet for 40 to 50 modules. Of course, commercial and industrial PV rooftop systems require much more surface area than this. Regardless of the PV system size, residential or commercial, the basic contents of this book will still apply.

The total installed cost of a PV solar system is

a considerable investment, but the overall cost is getting cheaper by the year, and in many countries the cost of PV power for the homeowner has already reached the goal of "grid parity." Grid parity is when the cost of producing electricity by PV solar is equal to the cost of conventional electricity produced by large generators that burn carbon-based fuels. PV solar-generated power becomes more attractive and more competitive as the electric utility billing rates go up. Moreover, since the investment payback period is usually only five or six years with government financial incentives, and since the electricity cost savings continue for another 20 years after payback (electricity essentially becomes free after the payback period), PV solar makes eminently good business sense, both for the homeowner and the banks that finance PV rooftop systems.

Some people have a flawed concept of solar energy. While it's true that sunlight is free, the electricity generated by PV systems is not. There are many factors involved in determining whether installing a PV system would be an economical alternative for any given home. There's the question of geographical location, installation cost, and true personal long-term benefits relating to your unique lifestyle and needs.

However, the demand for PV solar continues to grow as equipment prices fall, to the point where PV solar systems produce power at competitive levels (grid parity) with conventional power from the utility company. The demand for PV solar is also

stimulated as the world becomes increasingly aware of the environmental concerns associated with conventional power sources, which depend on burning carbon-based fuels. Considering all these growing trends worldwide, there's little doubt that photovoltaics have a bright future and will continue to grow.

Millions of homeowners worldwide have decided to go solar. They can't all be wrong!

Online Energy and Cost Savings Calculators

You can estimate energy and cost savings for energy-efficient products using the interactive calculators and Excel spreadsheets provided at the website of the US Department of Energy's Office of Energy Efficiency and Renewable Energy. Here's the website: energy.gov/eere/femp/energy-and-cost-savings-calculators-energy-efficient-products.

Energy Star–qualified appliances and products are normally of better quality and use less energy than standard products of the same type. Since they use less energy, Energy Star–qualified products save you money on your utility bills while helping to protect the environment by causing fewer harmful greenhouse gas emissions. The website cited below provides access to calculators that can estimate the annual dollar and energy savings you can expect if you install an Energy Star appliance in your home. Here's the link to this useful website: www.sba.gov/content/energy-saving-calculators-energy-star.

Heating and cooling can account for more than half of your home's total utility bill. When looking for ways to cut your energy costs, be sure to think about high-efficiency systems. High-efficiency systems are easily identified by checking the yellow and black energy guide label found on the back of the equipment. At this site, you'll find a useful cost-saving calculator provided by a reputable manufacturer:

www.lennox.com/resources/energycalculator.asp.

A very up-to-date energy cost savings calculator was recently created by the Lawrence Berkeley National Laboratory of the Environmental Energy Technologies Division of the US Department of Energy. The website's testimonials report that this service has saved homeowners thousands of dollars a year. It also provides updated information on "Energy Efficiency Tax Credits": www.homeenergysaver.lbl.gov/consumer/.

Of course, there are no guarantees, but I'm confident that the time you spend analyzing the advantages of converting to energy-efficient appliances and converting from incandescent to LED lighting, as well as the time you spend calculating the huge savings that should result from installing a PV solar rooftop system, will be very beneficial to you.

Online Links to Sources
for Determining Solar Radiation Values
for Any Location Worldwide

In addition to the solar radiation database table provided for most cities in the USA and Canada in Chapter 4, there is data available for global use available at: eosweb.larc.nasa.gov/sse/.

This site will lead you to numerous other websites, maintained by the National Aeronautics & Space Administration (NASA), that provide extensive data and maps dealing with solar radiation. PV solar energy system contractors and developers all over the world use NASA solar radiation data widely. Users will need to create a login for the NASA website. Then you'll be able to connect to the following URL: eosweb.larc.nasa.gov/cgi-bin/sse/register.cgi.

In the United States, a major program was undertaken by the National Renewable Energy Laboratory to correlate solar radiation data that can be used to estimate solar radiation for 239 sites in the US with extensive weather records. The data for the 239 sites is available in an excellent 250-page publication called *Solar Radiation Data Manual for Flat-Plate and Concentrating Collectors*. The data is available in HTML and PDF format from the following website: rredc.nrel.gov/solar/pubs/redbook.

Individual PDF files are available for the main body of the manual and for each of the 50 states, the Pacific Islands (Guam), and Puerto Rico. Compressed files containing the individual PDFs for the manual and the site data tables can be downloaded in three compression formats: PC, Macintosh, and Unix. Extensive maps from the data represented in the tables are also available for viewing.

Another valuable source for solar radiation data is provided by Solar Data Warehouse, whose URL is as follows: www.solardatawarehouse.com/Data.aspx. This group provides regularly updated solar data from 5,000 US ground stations and over 3,500 overseas ground stations. The site includes good coverage for most of Europe, South America, Asia, and Africa. Solar Data Warehouse claims that their solar data contains less than half of the errors typically found in satellite and "modeled data," and they offer proof of this impressive assertion.

Another excellent source for solar data in the US is provided by an organization called Solar Pathfinder here: www.solarpathfinder.com /solar_radiation.

One of the principal sources for European solar radiation databases is provided by the group Satel Light at this URL: www.satel-light.com/ indexes.htm.

Another good source of surface solar radiation satellite data for Europe, Africa, the Atlantic Ocean, and much of South America is provided at: climate dataguide.ucar.edu/climate-data/surface-solar -radiation-europe-africa-and-atlantic.

Ratings of PV Solar Panels by Independent Sources

If you want the lowest costs per rated power or, in other words, to pay as little as possible for a certain amount of electricity, you should investigate whether thin-film solar panels could in fact be a better choice than monocrystalline or polycrystalline solar panels. This is assuming you have ample space available to use thin-film panels.

Most homeowners don't really need the best performing solar panels on the market (unless their roof space is very limited). It's useful to compare solar panels by the price per watt to determine the best value, notwithstanding any space constraints.

Solar panel prices are sometimes listed as cost per watt ($/watt). This is not a sufficient criterion for determining the true value of a solar system.

You shouldn't judge solar modules on the simple price per watt. Rather you should base your buying decision on quality (reputation of the module manufacturer), warranty, available space, climate, availability of modules, and recommenda-tions from your chosen solar contractor. Price per watt does not address the issue of quality, and it may be wise to remember the old adage "you get what you pay for."

Also, you should review independent test reports about different solar modules published by solar magazines, not paid advertising. Inter-net forums, where users can report their personal experiences with specific makes of solar panels, can also be useful. Blogs can also be of interest. Due to the importance of these sources of infor-mation for the reader, I'm providing three lists of links to websites (magazines, discussion forums, and blogs). The following online links to rep-utable solar magazines and journals can provide the reader with objective analyses, ratings, test reports, and other comparisons of photo-voltaic modules, inverters, and other PV-related subjects.

Links to Free Online Magazines and Journals Dealing with Solar Energy

———————

SolarPro

www.solarprofessional.com

SolarPro magazine is a technical trade publication
   distributed to more than 25,000 professionals
   working in the North American solar market.

Solar Industry

www.solarindustrymag.com

Solar Industry magazine is a reputable industry
   publication.

Home Power

www.homepower.com

This is a hands-on journal of homemade power,
   with articles about living off-grid, plus how-to
   resources on solar, wind, and other renewable
   technologies. It focuses on renewable energy and
   efficiency.

Solar Power World

www.solarpowerworldonline.com

The reader can receive a free subscription
   to *Solar Power World* magazine.

Solar Today

www.solartoday.org

Bimonthly magazine of solar and renewable energy
   news. It covers all renewable energy technologies,
   including photovoltaics, passive solar, and other
   climate-responsive buildings and wind energy
   systems.

Solar International magazine

www.solar-international.net

Solar International is a magazine that provides
   up-to-date news, features, analysis, and awards
   across the entire photovoltaic value chain.

PV Resources

www.pvresources.com

Photovoltaic magazines with company profiles, all
within the fields of solar thermal, photovoltaics,
wind energy, and biomass.

PV Magazine

www.pv-magazine.com

PV Magazine debunks the myths
surrounding solar photovoltaics.

Renewable Energy World

www.renewableenergyworld.com

A magazine that provides the latest news in renewable technologies, including solar PV and wind
electric generators.

Solar Builder

www.solarbuildermag.com

Solar Builder magazine publishes current solar power contractor news and tips for solar
projects. Their online news is updated daily.

Online Solar Energy Discussion Forums

You may also be interested in reading about independent reports and personal experiences from solar PV discussion forums. Some of the following sites provide useful information and contacts. When you find a report that seems significant, you can discuss it with the originator and/or with your solar contractor.

Solar Discussion Forum
www.forum.solar-electric.com/forum.php
This forum offers a free online solar forum with basic and advanced solar Q&As.

Solar Forum
www.solarpaneltalk.com
This is a discussion forum where people can get their solar energy questions answered by professionals in the solar industry.

Solar Electric Power Discussion Forum
forum.solar-electric.com/forum.php
This is a forum with the latest news for off-grid solar panel systems, with updates about solar forums and websites. For non-technical discussion of all types of renewable energy.

My Solar Power
mysolarpowered.wordpress.com
Presents discussions about renewable, solar energy, solar power, solar power discussion boards, and solar power forums.

Renewable and Solar Energy Discussion Forum
www.builditsolar.com/References/Forums.htm
Presents the latest news and info on building solar PV systems.

Solar Projects to Save You Money
forums.moneysavingexpert.com
Presents discussions about how solar energy systems can save you money.

Solar Energy in Australia
www.esaa.com.au
Presents discussions and papers about solar research and policy issues in Australia.

Solar: The Contrarian Investor Discussion Board
forum.thecontrarianinvestor.com
Discussion of solar stocks and the impact the solar revolution will have.

Blogs Dealing with Solar Energy

Some readers will want to check out a few relevant blog sites. Here are numerous sites to choose from:

Solar Energy Featured Blogs:
    Renewable Energy World
    www.renewableenergyworld.com

Solar City Blog
    blog.solarcity.com
REC Solar Blog
    blog.recsolar.com
Mosaic Blog: The Bright Side of Solar
    https://joinmosaic.com/blog
The Solarblogger
    www.solarblogger.net
Blogs: Solar Power Portal
    www.solarpowerportal.co.uk/blogs/list
Redefining Power: The SolarEdge Blog
    www.solaredge.com/groups/blog
Solar Blog: PURE Energies Home Solar
    pureenergies.com/us/blog
Stellar Solar Blog
    stellarsolar.net/blog
Blog: WE CARE Solar
    wecaresolar.org/blog
Solar news
    www.re-volv.org

Websites and References for Additional Information

National Center for Photovoltaic Research web site. The National Renewable Energy Laboratory. Accessed January 21, 2010. www.nrel.gov/pv/ncpv.html.

Noufi, Rommel and Zweibel, Ken. "High-Efficiency CdTe and CIGS Thin-Film Solar Cells: Highlights and Challenges." National Renewable Energy Laboratory. May 2006. http://www.nrel.gov/docs/fy06osti/39894.pdf.

"Own Your Own Power! A Consumer Guide to Solar Electricity for the Home." The National Renewable Energy Laboratory. January 2009. http://www.nrel.gov/docs/fy09osti/43844.pdf.

"Solar Cell." *Encyclopedia Britannica*. Accessed January 21, 2010. http://www.britannica.com/EBchecked/topic/552875/solar-cell.

SolarPanelInfo.com web site. Accessed January 21, 2010. http://www.solarpanelinfo.com/.

"Solar Photovoltaic Technology." The National Renewable Energy Lab. September 29, 2009. http://www.nrel.gov/learning/re_photovoltaics.html.

Glossary of Terms

Ampere: Unit used in measuring intensity of flow of electricity. Its symbol is "I."

Alternating Current (AC): Electric current that reverses its direction of flow at regular intervals. For example, a current in a 60-cycle system would alternate 60 times every second. This type of current is commonly found in homes, apartment buildings, and businesses.

Bare Conductor: Wire or cable with no insulation or covering.

Current: Flow of electricity through a circuit; either AC or DC.

Circuit: Flow of electricity through two or more wires from the supply source to one or more outlets and back to the source.

Circuit Breaker: Safety device used to break the flow of electricity by opening the circuit automatically in the event of overloading; also used to open or close it manually.

Conductor: Any substance capable of conveying an electric current. In the home, copper wire is usually used.

Covered Conductor: Wire or cable covered with one or more layers of insulation.

Conductor Gauge: Numerical system used to label electric conductor sizes, stated as American Wire Gauge (AWG), with wire measured in square millimeters diameter.

Cable: Conductors insulated from one another.

Direct Current (DC): Electric current flowing in one direction. This type of current is commonly found in manufacturing industries. It's also the type of current produced by solar panels, which is then converted by an inverter into usable alternating current.

Electricity: Energy used to run household appliances and industrial machinery; can produce light, sound, heat, and has many other uses.

Frequency: The number of periods per unit time stated in cycles per seconds, or Hertz. For alternating current power lines, the most widely used frequencies are 60 and 50 Hertz.

Fuse: Safety device that cuts off the flow of electricity when the current flowing through exceeds the fuse's rated capacity.

Ground: To connect with the earth, as in grounding an electric wire directly to the earth or indirectly through a water pipe or some other conductor. Usually, a green-colored wire is used for grounding the whole electrical system to the earth. A white wire is usually used to ground individual electrical components.

Impedance: A measure of the complex resistive and reactive attributes of a component in an alternating current circuit.

Insulator: Material that will not permit the passage of electricity.

Inverter: An electric devise that converts direct current (DC) into alternating current (AC).

Neutral Wire: The third wire in a three wire distribution circuit. It's usually white or light gray and is connected indirectly to the ground.

Resistance: Restricts the flow of current; the unit of resistance is called an "Ohm." The more the resistance in Ohms, the less the current will flow.

Service: Conductor plus the equipment needed to deliver energy from the electricity supply system to the wiring system of the home or premises.

Service Drop: Overhead service connectors from the last pole connecting to the service conductors at the building or other electricity consumption destination.

Service Panel: Main panel or cabinet through which electricity is brought into a house or building and distributed. It contains the main disconnect switch and fuses or circuit breakers.

Short Circuit: Break in the flow of electricity due to excessive current, resulting from a fault or negligible impedance between live conductors having a difference in potential under normal operating conditions.

Voltage Drop: Voltage loss when wires carry current. The longer the cable or chord, the greater the voltage drop.

Volt: Unit for measuring electrical pressure or force, known as electromotive force. The symbol for volt is "E" or "V."

Wires: Conductors carrying the electric current or power to the load; usually black or red.

Watts: Unit of electric power, calculated by multiplying volts by amperes.

For the past several years, Mike Sullivan has been working in Southeast Asia in the field of solar energy with the Siam Pacific Engineering Group as project manager. He authored business plans for solar energy farms, and supervised rooftop solar photovoltaic projects for electricity generation and for solar water-heating systems. He has participated in many trade shows and conventions, researching and promoting renewable energy. He resides in Thailand.

Mr. Sullivan earned an MBA from the University of Phoenix. Before that, he managed a high-voltage electrical engineering company and won several international contracts in South America. His undergraduate studies in engineering were completed at the Central University of Mexico.

Over the course of his research in the field of solar energy, Mr. Sullivan realized there was a need for a simple, up-to-date, non-technical DIY guidebook that would use clear terms and a holistic approach to explain photovoltaic solar energy to homeowners and prospective homeowners. The book would provide detailed instructions for DIY enthusiasts on how to plan their own solar project and how to install their own system.

The book he envisioned would provide advice on how to incorporate energy-efficient electrical products and other home improvements that would help reduce monthly utility bills and multiply the savings generated by a solar energy PV system.

For credibility and for professional accuracy, Mr. Sullivan was fortunate to have the guidance of Dr. Thomas Bickl, PhD, an internationally recognized authority on solar energy who provided invaluable input for the manuscript.

ACKNOWLEDGMENTS

The author hereby expresses his profound gratitude to Mr. Barry Sullivan, M.Arch (Environmental), for his constant encouragement and support, without which this book would not have been written.

Sincere appreciation is also accorded to Dr. Thomas Bickl, PhD, for his encouragement, his constructive input, and his guidance for the revision and editing of portions of the technology chapters of the book. The author is also indebted to Dr. Supot Tejavibulya, PhD, for his constant encouragement and suggestions during the research and preparation of the manuscript.

The author also wishes to thank Dan Crissman for his superb guidance during the editing process and for his excellent suggestions as to the content and structure of the book.

The author also expresses his gratitude to Steven Harris (literary agent) for his astute guidance and support during the development of the manuscript and the selection of an excellent publisher.

Last but not least, the author hereby expresses his sincere appreciation to Alex Stutt for his invaluable and knowledgeable assistance in taking most of the photographs used in this book and for his preparation of color schematics and drawings to complement the manuscript.

INDEX

Italicized numbers indicate illustrations.

A

AC (alternating current), 47

AC disconnect switch, *50*, 57–58, *65*, 154, *155, 156*

AC modules, 70

air conditioners, 117

alternating current (AC), 47

America Merrill Lynch, 110

amorphous silicon (A-Si), 23, 32–33; and CIGS, 36; and comparison chart, *24*; definition of, 29; and thin-film technologies chart, 40

ampere-hour (Ah), 78–79

"angle of inclination," 97

annual output, calculation of, 95

appliances, and energy efficiency, 115

array, 21

Array DC Disconnect, 57

azimuth, 23; and global annual radiation incident, 96; and panel installation, 98, 139; and system performance, 42

B

Balance of System (BOS), 21

batteries: and AC current, 70; and ampere-hour, 78–79; and battery banks, 49–52; and battery number chart, *80*; and battery storage system, sizing of, 76–78; concept of, 47; danger of, 70; and deep-cycle, 78; and deep-cycle batteries, 70; and DOD, 47; flooded electrolyte, 78; lead-acid, 47; longevity of, 69–70; maintenance of, 79; and off-grid PV system, 46, 48–49; and regulators, 49; and shallow-cycle, 78; and temperature factor multiplier chart, *81*

battery bank, 49–52, *49*

battery-based grid-tie inverters, 52

battery-based inverter, 49

"Berkeley Model," 110

BTU, 117

building-integrated photovoltaics (BIPV), 31, 35, *38*, 39

bulbs, *119*

C

cadmium telluride (CdTe), 23, 29, 32; and solar cells, 33–37, *34, 36*

calculators, portable, 33

California Solar Initiative, 110

carbon credits, 20

carbon dioxide, 19–20, 113

CdTe. *See* cadmium telluride

charge controller, 47, 49, 70, 78

charge regulators, 49

Climate Policy Initiative (CPI), 110

clothes dryers, 117–18

combiner panel, installation of, 154, *155*

compact fluorescent lights (CFLs), 118, *119*

compass direction/azimuth factor, 98

connections, and PV systems, 45

consumption, daily, calculation of, 102

copper indium gallium selenide (CIS/CIGS), 23, 32, 35, *37*; and comparison chart, 24; and crystalline silicon, 36; manufacturing of, 39; and thin-film technologies chart, 40

crystalline panels, 55–56, 96. *See also* monocrystalline *and* polycrystalline

crystalline silicon (c-Si), 22, 39

Czochralski process, 26, 29

D

Database of State Incentives for Renewables & Efficiency (DSIRE), 105

"days of autonomy," 77

DC, 47

DC disconnect switch, 50, *50*, *51*, 56–57, 57; and breaker panel box, 68; and central inverters, 66; and homeruns, 144; installation of, 152–53, *152*, *153*, *156*; and wiring from above, 138

degree of discharge (DOD), 47, 78

derate factor, 82

diesel, 16

dimmers, 124

direct current, 47

disconnect switches, 56–58, *57*, 59. *See also* DC disconnect *and* AC disconnect

DOD, 47, 78

"doping," 35

DZ-4, 111

E

eco-friendly, and CdTe PV, 35

Electrical Metal Tubing (EMT), 151

electrical panel, 65, *65*

electricity, usage of, 100, 102

electron-hole pairs, 21

Empa, 33

end-clamps, 142

Enecsys, 63, 67

energy consumption calculation, 117

energy conversion efficiency, 22, 27, 118

Energy Information Administration (EIA), 47

energy, and online calculators, 161–62

energy output, calculations of, 100, 102–3

Enphase Energy, 61–62, 63

Enphase micro-inverter, *59*, *153*, *154*

Excel, 76

F

feed-in tariff (FiT), 16, 46, 63, 68, 109. *See also* net metering

First Solar, 33

fluorescent lighting, 118–22

G

generators, backup, 51

global annual radiation incident, 96

Green Tags, 108

greenhouse effect, 19

GreenRay, 63

grid back-feeding. *See* grid-tied solar systems

grid-interactive inverters, 47

grid inter-tie. *See* grid-tied solar systems

grid parity, 16, 160

grid-tied solar systems, 45, 46–48, 53–56

maximum power point tracking (MPPT), 65

meter, production, installation of, 154, *155*

metering device, *51*

Miasole, 39

mid-bracket, *42*

mid-clamps, 142

molybdenum coating, 36

"monitoring gateway," 157

monitoring system, and energy output, 65–66

monocrystalline (mono-Si) 12, 21–29, 40

mounting: and angle of, 138; and azimuth, 139; and electrical components and controls, installation of, 151; framework and panel attachment, 142; and layout, 137; and panels, alignment of, 147–49; and panels, connecting, 149; and panels, lifting onto roof, 145; and panels, wiring together of, 150; and support framework, 141; support hardware for, 53–56; and wiring, 144

multi-crystalline silicon (mc-Si). *See* polycrystalline silicon

N

National Electrical Code, 71

National Renewable Energy Laboratory (NREL), 81, 102

net metering, 45, 46–47, 68–69, *69*, 109, 155, 157, *155, 157*

North American Board of Certified Energy Professionals (NABCEP), 127

O

off-grid solar systems, 45, 46, 48–51

"one sun," 99

on-grid system. *See* grid-tied solar systems

optimal orientation, 97

organic electronics, 32

organic solar cells, 23, 32–33, 40

output, total, 22, 23

output difference factor, and system wiring, 97

P

panels, 40, 43, *101*

panels, and mounting: alignment of, 147–49; and angle of, 138; and attachment to mounting framework, 142; and azimuth, 139; connection of, 149; and layout, 137; lifting onto roof, 145; and safety precautions, 147; and support framework, 141; wiring of, 144, 150

particulate build-up factor, 96

peak power, 84

peak sun hours, 81

performance ratio (PR), 96

photons, 21

polycrystalline panels, 12, 25, 27, 40. *See also* polycrystalline silicon solar cells

polycrystalline silicon solar cells, 22, 26–29

polyimide film, 35

polymer solar cell, 23, 33

polysilicon (p-Si). *See* polycrystalline silicon

power consumption chart, *74–75*

power meter, 47, 48, 68

power rating, 96

PPA, 68, *69*

production meter, installation of, 157

PSE&G, 109